THE AMERICAN THOMISTIC REVIVAL IN THE PHILOSOPHICAL PAPERS OF R. J. HENLE, S.J.

THE AMERICAN THOMISTIC REVIVAL IN THE PHILOSOPHICAL PAPERS OF R. J. HENLE, S.J.

From the writing of

R. J. Henle, S.J.
Professor Emeritus of
Saint Louis University

St. Louis: Saint Louis University Press

Library of Congress Cataloging-in-Publication Data

Henle, R.J. (Robert John), 1909-
    The American Thomistic revival in the philosophical papers of R.J. Henle,
S.J.: from the writings of R.J. Henle.
      p. cm.
    Includes bibliographical references and index.
    ISBN 0-9652929-2-4
    1. Neo-Scholasticism. I. Title.

  B839 .H46 1999
  149'.91'0973–dc21

                                   99-046799

Distribution:

Saint Louis University
3663 Lindell Blvd.
St. Louis MO 63108-3342
314-977-3943

To:

I wish to dedicate this work to my family, to all the Henles, Konigsachers, Millers, Grosjeans and all the rest who have given me so much encouragement and loving support through all my life. I know too that their prayers have brought me many graces. It is impossible to express adequately my gratitude to them. So this dedication is a very small recognition of my personal debt to them. I also include as family all the very good friends who over the years have become as close to me as my natural family.

CONTENTS

FOREWORD

One concludes a confession by expressing sorrow not only for the offenses mentioned but also "for all the sins of my past life." Not having any sins to confess, Father Henle has brought together some of the high points of his career as a philosopher, and they are high points indeed. The reader will find in the following essays fundamental studies in epistemology and metaphysics as well as brief *jeux d'esprit* and elegant *aperçus*. Aristotle said that wisdom comes, if at all, with age. Father Henle has outlived Aristotle, but he proved the rule long ago by being an exception to it. Like his mentor Aquinas, Father Henle became wise when young. That wisdom has only ripened as he advanced into the golden years. These contributions represent different stages of his long and distinguished career.

The story of the Thomistic revival in North America awaits its historian. When that story is written, Saint Louis University will be seen as one of the powerhouses of that revival. Collins, Klubertanz, Bourke, and Father Henle himself will loom large. It will be seen that disciples of Saint Thomas were often at odds with one another and that several emphases vied for dominance. Father Henle can be most easily placed in terms of the quarrel between Transcendental Thomism and Thomistic Realism.

The task for Thomists was twofold. First, to grasp the thought of their master. This entailed careful historical and textual work, and Father Henle was schooled well in this at the Pontifical Institute of Mediaeval Studies at the University of Toronto. The second task was to bring the thought of Thomas to bear on the times in which we live. There were those who felt that the critical turn taken by Kant had forever altered the philosophical terrain and that consequently Thomism had to be rethought in more or less Kantian terms if it were to be at all relevant to contemporary thinking. Father Henle's critical assessment of Transcendental Thomism in Chapter XX is, I think, unanswerable. For his more positive view, and an account of Thomas's theory of knowledge, see Chapters IV through X, and XV through XVII.

Transcendental Thomism, with its turning away from Aristotle, led scholars (not all of them Transcendental Thomists) to examine the role of Plato in Thomas's intellectual life. Hitherto it had been assumed that when Thomas developed Aristotle's critique of Plato, he was speaking in his own name as well. But Aristotle had dismissed participation as an empty metaphor. Yet the most cursory glance at Thomas showed that participation was a key concept of the Thomistic synthesis. From this, some concluded that Thomas's Platonism had been overlooked and that when it was given the weight it deserved, his allegiance to Aristotle was called into question. Thomas, it was suggested, had moved from an uncritical to a critical attitude toward Aristotle and from a critical to a sympathetic attitude toward Plato. One of Father Henle's important contributions was to call into question these alleged asymmetrical shifts in Thomas's thought. In Chapters XI and XII, and then notably in his definitive work, *Saint Thomas and Platonism*, Father Henle dismantled the supposed textual basis for Thomas's turn to Plato.

One of the most delightful of the pieces brought together here is Chapter XIII, "The Three Philosophical Languages of Hume." This chapter as well as Chapter VII are indicative of Henle's lively interest in what some are pleased to think of as the philosophical mainstream. Hume provides Henle with a choice example of the way in which philosophers depart from common sense and common language and end with positions they would have instinctively rejected in their more clearheaded pre-philosophical days. It is fair enough that an exponent of a philosophical approach that is still accused of employing Scholastic jargon should draw attention to the radical unintelligibility of the language of a great Modern philosopher.

A few years ago, Father Henle published a translation and commentary on Thomas Aquinas's Treatise on Law. This was only fitting, since when Father Henle completed his stint as president of Georgetown University and returned to Saint Louis, he was named to a chair of justice. Chapters XVIII and XIX convey something of that dimension of Henle's thought.

The Thomistic Revival began when Leo XIII issued the encyclical *Aeterni Patris* in 1879. The first phase of the revival saw the establishment of institutes, societies, associations, journals, universities, international congresses, series of learned studies, to say nothing of the critical edition of the works of Thomas Aquinas, still in progress now more than a century later. The second phase was that of the great

Thomists, many of them laymen, and the emergence of the diverse trends which would agitate the movement up to the opening of Vatican II in 1962. We might say that the three main contenders for hegemony were Transcendental Thomism, Existential Thomism, and Aristotelian Thomism. Father Henle must be placed emphatically with the last.

With the Council, something happened that was unintended by the Fathers but perhaps devoutly wished by many *periti*, and that was the eclipse of Thomism. Pluralism was to reign. Other Aristotles were to be found by other Aquinases and new syntheses developed, more relevant to the modern mind. More than a quarter of a century has passed since Thomism was supposedly buried and a thousand intellectual flowers meant to bloom. It has not happened. We find ourselves standing in a fallow field. The great Catholic universities seem to have lost their way. Catholic thinkers are largely indistinguishable from non-Catholic thinkers. *Aggiornamento* was not meant to be the blowing away of the Catholic mind by the *zeitgeist*. But in that field a few flowers blow. Thomists, outnumbered, scattered, in diaspora, hard at work in obscurity for a quarter of a century, exhibit a new vitality. All around a new interest is shown in Thomas by thinkers who know they have reached the end of their tether. Monographs and studies of Thomas never stopped, of course. A faithful remnant continued the work that had been begun. The moment for the next phase of the Thomistic revival is here. It is no accident; rather it is manifest providence, that the Church has so consistently, in season and out of season, recommended Thomas Aquinas as our mentor in both philosophy and theology. The rightness of this advice was once learned by following it. Lately it has been learned negatively, by seeking to avoid it. As before, Thomists will make a motley crew, an honest race that does not speak well of one another, having in common only a love of truth and grounded confidence in Thomas Aquinas.

The text of Thomas will of course be the main source of inspiration. But the young now look back to the pre-conciliar giants, to Maritain and Gilson, and to R.J. Henle, S.J. Dante in the lower world remarked that he had not thought death had undone so many. But so it has. There are few who were part of the pre-conciliar Thomism who have survived to provide inspiration for this new phase. Father Henle has survived, and in many senses. He is, thank God, still among us, still at work, still marked by a tireless pursuit of truth. Long may he live. But long after he has gone to his reward, his writings will cast light for students of Saint Thomas and for philosophers generally. And this collection will be one of the means of the continuation of his influence.

Ralph McInerny
The Michael P. Grace
Professor of Medieval Studies
University of Notre Dame

Preface

Reviewing the many lectures, articles, and other publications of my past life I decided that a good number of them were still currently relevant and of some importance and value. I therefore decided to make a selection of some of the better articles and publish them in a single volume so that they would be more accessible than they are now, scattered as they are through many journals, proceedings, and so forth. I have done this and I also wrote a new introduction to each article which would locate it both thematically and historically and added a new comment which might revise it, supplement, illuminate, or defend it.

This volume is a fair summary of my contribution to neo-Thomism as well as to Philosophy in general. It might therefore also have historical value since I was a very active member of the Neo-Thomistic movement.

ACKNOWLEDGMENTS

The following publishers have generously given permission to reprint the following works of Rev. Robert J. Henle, S.J.

American Catholic Philosophical Association, Washington D.C. 20064: "The Basis of Philosophical Realism Re-examined," *The New Scholasticism*, 56, no.1 (winter 1982): 1–29; "Reflections on Current Reductionism," *The New Scholasticism*, 59, no. 2 (spring 1985): 131–55; "Existentialism and the Judgment," *Proceedings* of the ACPA, 21 (1946): 40–52. "Prudence and Insight," *Proceedings* of the ACPA, 56 (1982): 26–30.

American Maritain Association, Mishawaka, Indiana 46545: "Maritain's Metaphysics: A Summary Presentation," *Jacques Maritain's The Degrees of Knowledge,* eds. R. J. Henle, Marion Cordes and Jeanne Vatterott, (1981), 32–54.

Catholic Health Association of the United States, St. Louis MO, 63134–3797: "The Intellectual Development," *Hospital Progress* (May 1959): 86–91. Copyright by the Catholic Health Association. Reproduced from *Health Progress* with permission.

Catholic University of America Press, Washington, D.C. 20064: "A Philosopher's Interpretation of Anthropology's Contribution to the Understanding of Man," *Anthropological Quarterly* 32, no. 1 (January 1959): 22–40.

Catholic University of America, School of Philosophy, Washington, D.C. 20064: "Schopenhauer and Direct Realism," *Review of Metaphysics* 46, no. 1 (September 1992): 125–140.

Fordham University Press, New York, N.Y. 10458–5172: "Science and the Humanities," *Thought* 35, no. 139 (winter 1960): 513–536.

Editrice Pontificia Università Gregoriana, Roma, Italia: "St. Thomas' Methodology in the Treatment of Positiones with Particular Reference to 'Positiones Plationes Platonicae,'" *Gregorianum* 36, no. 3 (1955): 391–409.

Marquette University Press, Milwaukee, WI. 53201–1881: "An Experiential [Phenomenological] Approach to Realism," *An Etienne Gilson Tribute*, (1959), 68–85; "Man's Knowledges of Physical Reality," *Essays on Knowledge and Methodology*, Edward D. Simmons, ed., (1965) 73–86; "Method in Metaphysics," *The Aquinas Lecture* of 1950 published in 1951.

Saint Louis University, St. Louis, MO: "A Note on Certain Testual Evidence in Fabro's *La Nozione Metafisica de Partecipazione*," *The Modern Schoolman*, 34, no. 4 (May, 1957): 265–282; "St. Thomas and the Definition of Intelligence," *The Modern Schoolman* 53, no. 4 (May 1976): 335–346.

Pace University, Pleasantville, NY 10570–2799: "Levels of Natural Law," *Vera Lex*, 11, no. 2 (1991): 1–5.

Ohio State University, Columbus, OH 43210–1172: "Meditation About Knowing," *Boyd Memorial Lecture Series* (1964).

Loras College, Department of Philosophy, DuBuque, IA 52001: "The Three Philosophical Languages of Hume," *Eighteenth Annual Meeting of the Semiotic Society of America*, October 21–24 (1993).

Spring Hill College, Mobile, AL 36608–1791: "A Thomistic Explanation of the Relations Between Science and Philosophy," *Bulletin of Albertus Magnus Guild*, 3, no. 4 (October 1956): 4–6.

University of St. Thomas, Houston, TX 77006–4696: "Transcendental Thomism, A Critical Assessment," *One Hundred Years of Thomism: Aterni Patris and Afterwards*, Fr. Victor Brezik, C.S.B. ed. (1981), 90–116.

I

SCIENCE AND THE HUMANITIES

New Introduction: When this article was written in 1960 there was a very serious discussion going on with regard to the relationship of two of the basic subcultures in our general culture. That is to say, between the scientific culture and the humanistic culture. I was concerned about that discussion because of the tendency to give exclusive truth value to science and to the scientific method. I was also concerned with the effect on liberal education. It was because of this concern that the following first article was written.[1] I am placing this article at the beginning of these selections since it deals with the most fundamental problems of our modern intellectual culture, problems which arise from the multiplicity of disciplines, the necessity of specialization, and particularly the intellectual methodological imperialism of modern science. The problems outlined in this article from 1955 are, if anything, more acute today than they were when I wrote this piece. Subsequent developments have, in some cases, exacerbated the problems as some of the later articles in these selections will indicate. This article is fundamental, however, because it elaborates at some length the problems and my conviction which I still maintain that only an elaborate epistomological analysis can point the way to necessary solutions.

* * *

THE PROBLEM

The problem which I am about to discuss has been described as the

---

[1]This article is a revised version of an address delivered before the national meeting of the Catholic Commission on Intellectual Affairs at the Villanova University on May 14, 1960. First published in *Thought* 35, no. 139 (winter 1960): 513–536.

dichotomy, in our modern culture, between "the sciences" and "the humanities" with the resulting split of Western intellectual life into two polar groups, having little mutual understanding and less communication. [2]

Obviously this is an intricate and complicated problem. There are some elements or aspects which I would like to eliminate and with which I will not here be concerned. There may be too few scientists or engineers in our society. We are perhaps neglecting "pure" or "basic" research, too much taken up with "hardware" and not enough concerned with scientific theory. Perhaps there is a serious imbalance in the distribution of financial support among the disciplines. I am here going to ignore all these and similar questions.

I shall understand the problem to be one of the interrelationships between "science" and the "humanities" in our total culture. But again I would limit this. I do not think we should be immediately concerned with the outlook and attitudes or the education of each individual in our society. We might, for example, argue that the average college student simply does not know enough science or that more or a different kind of mathematics should be taught in high school. This sort of question is not at the heart of the problem. Rather the problem immediately concerns the outlook and views of the intellectual leaders, of scholars, researchers, writers, thinkers, educators, and, by derivation and consequently, the structure and content of education and the ideas current throughout the society. Fundamentally, we are dealing with the basic ideas, the values, the general views, the understanding and knowledge possessed and held by the intellectuals and scholars; held and possessed not only individually, which of course must be so, but also in mutual understanding, in communication, in conscious agreement—that is, socially—so that we can speak of a "common" culture.

For is not our attention here directed to an assertion that in current Western society such a "common" culture does not exist, has not been achieved or, having been achieved on some older basis, is now being destroyed and that the cause lies somewhere in the results of the

---

[2]Cf. C.P. Snow, *The Two Cultures and the Scientific Revolution*, the Rede Lecture 1959 (Cambridge: Cambridge University Press, 1959); Frederick Burkhardt, *Science and the Humanities*, Antioch College Founders Day Lecture (Yellow Springs: The Antioch Press, 1959); Gerald Holton, "Modern Science and the Intellectual Tradition," *Science* 131 (22 April 1960): 1187–1192.

"scientific revolution," usually dated as of the seventeenth century and in the indeterminate position of "science" itself in our culture?[3]

This new science which came into being within a previously existing and, in a very fundamental sense, unified culture, has not transformed our culture by being properly assimilated within the total culture. No one, I think, will deny that modern Western culture—and more recently all the world cultures—has been radically and eruptively affected by the scientific revolution, but many are saying that science still lies within our culture too, much like an undeveloped pearl in an oyster, a foreign body, an irritant, even though it be a stimulant to action.

HISTORICAL PARALLELS

For the sake of perspective I should like to remark that this is not the first time this sort of problem has been faced in Western culture. Our culture has been successively disrupted by intellectual and spiritual revolutions, by the incursion of strange gods and of foreign ideas. We can think of the inrush of Greek culture into Rome; of the clash between the wisdom of the Gospel and the wisdom of the World, of the invasion of the Gothic—of Norman and Teuton—into Europe, of the confrontation of Aristotle, Averroes and Augustine in thirteenth century Paris, of Scholasticism and the New Learning, and so on. In all these cases there was a period of struggle between extreme positions. Cato wished to expel the Greek rhetoricians and exile them from Rome forever. "What," cried Tertullian, "has Christ to do with Aristotle or Jerusalem with Athens?" This was his rhetorical rejection of Aristotle and Athens, but his pagan contemporaries would have echoed it as a rejection of Christ and Jerusalem. Yet in this confrontation, the active assimilation was so complete that Christianity itself seemed to become simply Roman and Greek.

In the three great cultural crises of Christian thought prior to the sixteenth century—classical culture versus Revelation, early mediaeval culture versus the Aristotelian-Arabian invasion, later mediaeval culture versus the New Learning of the Humanists—the oppositions were

---

[3] Historians of science usually speak of the scientific revolution of the seventeenth or of the sixteenth and seventeenth century; Snow speaks of the "scientific revolution" which is *currently going on*. Both uses are quite legitimate.

overcome and the opposing factors brought to a richer cultural synthesis by an active, intelligent and discriminating effort on the part of Christian intellectuals.[4]

A similar labor lies ahead of Christian intellectuals today—for we have not yet carried out this discriminating assimilation of the results of the scientific revolution; we have not done so, specifically, in Christian culture or in Western culture generally.

Let me just refer here to a neat case example. The second article of St. Thomas' *Summa Theologiae* asks "whether sacred doctrine is a science": (*Utrum Sacra Doctrina sit scientia*). This is a question which would not and could not have been asked in tenth century Christian culture. In this question, the Aristotelian theory of scientific knowledge is confronted with the tradition of Christian doctrine—a sort of pinpoint epitome of the Aristotelian crisis of the thirteenth century.

St. Thomas does not reject Aristotle's theory or deny its applicability in the matter of sacred doctrine. He treats both with the most careful respect and, by a sharp analysis, produces a genial solution, which, at the same time, transforms both *Sacra Doctrina* and the Aristotelian Epistemology.

APPROACHES TO A SOLUTION

Concern over the nonassimilation of "science" has been displayed in many different intellectual quarters and has been variously interpreted.

For some the proper reconstruction of a common culture will be achieved only when it is recognized that science, while not the whole of culture, is the most important part and should determine and give meaning to all the rest.[5]

This interpretation rests on an assumption that the "scientific method" is "the only reliable method for discovering something, or anything, that can be called 'truth.'" In this view, "Scientific research

---

[4]An interesting illustration of what has amounted almost to an identification of classical and Christian education is afforded by the Gaume controversy. Abbé Gaume attacked the use of the pagan classics in the lower years of seminary education; he was opposed vigorously by the distinguished Bishop of Orléans, Monsignor Dupanloup, who, finally, was supported by direct instructions from Rome.

[5]See Bentley Glass, *Science and Liberal Education* (Baton Rouge: Louisiana State University Press, 1960).

is directed at the whole of nature, at its most minute events and its farthermost galaxies. There is no special 'scientific field'; no aspect of the atom, no aspect of life, no aspect of time or space, can be conceived as lying outside its purview. Science would cease to be science and its victories over the unknown would decrease were it to fail to explore the whole of nature for exploration's sake. But no interpretation of the atom or of life or of time or of space can be accepted as other than mere speculation until it has been verified by acceptable scientific method."[6]

Thus, in its crudest form, this position denies any independent knowledge value to philosophy or the humanities and, of course, to Revelation and theology.

Philosophy may be allowed to be of some indirect value. As imaginative speculation, it suggests solutions, stimulates investigation, arouses the critical mind. It was all right and even useful for the philosophers of sixth century Greece to put forth their guesses about the celestial situation. How to explain the pinpoints of light that could be seen in the heavens on any Grecian night? Perhaps a black envelope, irregularly punctured, was between us and ever-burning fires; perhaps they were reflections from lights we could not see. This was all very well until the scientific astronomers found out the facts. Thus when the fifth century scientists proved that the moon shone with reflected light there was no longer room or need for philosophical speculation. Philosophy is finished as soon as we *know* the facts.

We can allow too that the humanities are useful, even necessary, but not in order to know or understand. Poetry may refine the emotions, stimulate feeling, like music, soothe the savage breast; but we do not *know* anything through it.

For this position the matter has already been settled *in principle*; it remains to reconstruct our culture. Some of the proponents of this view think we have failed to do so because of the powerful opposition of "organized" religion.[7] In any case, culture should be reconstructed on a scientific base.

There are various mitigated forms of this position, and I would

---

[6]Homer W. Smith, "Objectives and Objectivity in Science," *The Yale Scientific Magazine* 23, no. 5 (February 1949): 2.

[7]Oscar Riddle, *The Unleashing of Evolutionary Thought* (New York: Vantage Press, 1954).

incline to place John Dewey here, which really makes use of two meanings of "scientific method" not in any clear-cut way but in a sort of double-talk. "Scientific method" is simply the natural method of intelligent inquiry, and so on, and so may apply in any discipline in which intelligent inquiry is carried on, but ultimately it turns out that "intelligent inquiry" is really only a generalization of the basic pattern of specialized natural science not of human knowing taken in its full generality.

The program of these people is then to put science, taken in a fairly narrow sense, at the center of culture and to derive from it or at least check by it all the fundamental ideas and principles of culture—particularly of ethics. Science would, in this new culture, play all the knowledge roles played by philosophy, theology and the humanities in prescientific culture.

Burkhardt reports, without specific references, an opinion in which science is pretty well relegated "to furnishing services and material goods."[8] While one does not find this position put forth in a theoretically developed fashion, it does translate what seems to be the attitude of some humanists. Science is only the theoretical side of technology and has about as much to do with general intellectual culture as a theory of army logistics or a system for winning on the races.

There are others, especially among those concerned with education, who seem to take a sort of "quantified" view of the problem. Individuals in our culture do not possess enough knowledge of science or, on the other hand, of the humanities. What then we have to do is provide a sufficient number of courses from each discipline in our general education.

Others, likewise mostly among the educators, think we will solve the problem by "humanizing" the sciences, by teaching them in a "liberal" way and so really getting rid of the division by making science much the same sort of thing as the other humanities. On this side it is pointed out that when we speak of the "liberal arts and sciences," the phrase should mean the "liberal arts and the liberal sciences." Scientists often object to this as being a subterfuge which substitutes the history of science or some vague talk about science for genuine scientific training.

---

[8]Burkhardt, *Science and the Humanities*, 26.

HISTORY OF CULTURE AND
THE PROBLEM OF SPECIALIZATION

Here I should like to digress for a moment into the history of culture. This history can be and has been read in many different fashions. There is Comte's reading which fits it into the three stages, theological, philosophical, positivistic. One can see it as a long upward struggle against "the dogmatic, other-worldly, super-naturalistic, tender-minded, rationalistic, parochial . . ." toward "the critical, worldly, naturalistic, fact-minded, empirical, experimental, and universally applicable ways of thinking."[9] In general, this is the pattern adopted by Logical Positivists.[10] A very similar reading is used by the Deweyites; in fact, the Deweyite history of culture can be written in a series of stereotypes. Whenever anyone is discovered in previous history who seems to espouse the empirical scientific method or a "democratic" view, he is seen as opposed to his own culture, daringly challenging ancient superstitions and tyrannies, as ahead of his time, a forerunner and a prophet. This stereotype, in some cases, almost reduces itself to a set verbal formula:

Though a devout Franciscan monk living in the thirteenth century, he wrote "of the three ways in which men think they acquire knowledge of things, authority, reason and *experience, only the last is effective . . .*"[11]

. . . it is significant that within only two centuries Christopher Columbus had *dared to contradict* the teaching of traditional philosophy and theology *with evidence derived from the senses.*[12]

These *a priori* readings of history and the imposition of their

---

[9] Herbert Feigl, "Aims of Education for Our Age of Science: Reflections of a Logical Empiricist" in *Modern Philosophies and Education*, Fifty-fourth Yearbook (Chicago: The University of Chicago Press, 1955).

[10] See also the interpretation of the history of philosophy presented in Part One of Hans Reichenbach's *The Rise of Scientific Philosophy* (Berkeley and Los Angeles: University of California Press, 1951).

[11] I.N. Thut, *The Story of Education* (New York: McGraw-Hill, 1957), 208 (italics added).

[12] *Ibid.*, 210 (italics added).

stereotypes on historical data produce distortion of fact, often both incredible and amusing,[13] no less than did the imposition of the Hegelian pattern on the history of philosophy. Yet there are no doubt various legitimate ways of reading the history of culture—individually inadequate but mutually supplementary.

I should like to suggest that the history of Western culture can quite properly be read as a development and deployment of an increasing number of disciplines through the discovery and elaboration of different modes or ways of knowing.

Historians of philosophy have asked whether Thales' implicit question "What's it all made of?" or "What's basic in everything?" was a philosophical or physical or chemical question. When Thales spoke of "water" or "liquid" was he proposing a metaphysical principle, an ultimate entative stuff, or a state of matter (liquid as opposed to solid or gaseous), or a chemical substance something like H_2O. This topic is always an excellent discussion piece for the classroom. I think, however, that the truth of the matter is that Thales' question is all of these at once and yet none of them. We might argue in a plain-man sort of way that we are asking a simple straightforward question to which we want a straightforward answer. But the simplest questions turn out to be indeterminate. We find that we really cannot define a question until we have given an answer; that the answers we arrive at often define or redefine our question. Progress becomes possible only when it is seen that there is no single total answer to such a question; that it must be broken down not simply into partial questions but into different levels of questions.

So we can thus derive a rather simple paradigm for the advance-

---

[13] As an example which I find both incredible and hilarious, I quote the following from John Dewey's *How We Think* (New York: Heath, 1910, 5–6):

"Men *thought* the world was flat until Columbus *thought* it to be round. The earlier thought was a belief held because men had not the energy or the courage to question what those about them accepted and taught, especially as it suggested and seemingly confirmed by obvious sensible facts. The thought of Columbus was a *reasoned conclusion*. It marked the close of study into facts, of scrutiny and revision of evidence, of working out the implications of various hypotheses, and of comparing these theoretical results with one another and with known facts. Because Columbus did not accept unhesitatingly the current traditional theory, because he doubted and inquired, he arrived at his thought. Skeptical of what, from long habit, seemed most certain, and credulous of what seemed impossible, he went on thinking until he could produce evidence for both his confidence and his disbelief."

ment of knowledge: question—method—of solution or discovery—answer, in which all three parts are homogeneous and mutually determining. If it is asked, "What is it made of?" and the answer given is $C_9H_8O_3$, we know at once that the question was understood to be a chemical question and, by the same token, we know that the answer could be found only by a chemical method. In this history of culture questions are constantly being turned into multiple questions by the discovery of new methods, of new answers and even of suspicions of new answers. Intellectual progress has been possible only because of an increasing multiplicity of methodologies and disciplines.

Established methods and theories act, to a greater or lesser extent, as a prison to the mind and a drag on the imagination.[14] The emergence of a new method, or a new idea of organization in knowledge, generally brings in a period of confusion and readjustment as well as a new surge forward in discovery and understanding. The development of a geometrical mode of thinking in early Greece led to all the Pythagorean confusions between mathematical and physical analyses of real objects. The introduction of the full Aristotelian logic into western Europe set the pattern of University teaching for almost three centuries. The successful application of mathematics to problems of motions set off a wildly enthusiastic effort to apply mathematics everywhere. One Anglican divine attempted to parallel Newton's *Philosophiae Naturalis Principia Mathematica* with a *Theologiae Christianae Principia Mathematica* in which, it is said, he tried to work out mathematical formulae for the degrees of heavenly glory.

Gradually the new methods came to be understood and the new disciplines more clearly marked out. The question-method-answer formula is sharply defined and typical problems identified. Meanwhile, the resulting expansion of discovery, of knowledge and understanding, goes on apace.

Two relevant considerations can now be drawn from this historical digression.

First, we must point out that in a period of creative intellectual development, not merely of material extension of well-established disciplines, we cannot hope to arrive at a truly clear and well-defined pattern of disciplines within a common culture. We are in such a period

---

[14] See my "The Health Organization Research Program," in *Conference; Techniques of Research* (Saint Louis: Saint Louis University, 1960).

now and, specifically, with reference to science. I agree with Snow that what is now going on in science deserves to be called a new "revolution," not merely a continuation of the "revolution" of the seventeenth century. If we seek, then, a neat formula to solve our present problem, we will not find one, and the reason why we will not lies in the progressive and creative differentiation through which Western culture continues to go.

Secondly, the formal diversification of knowledge has been one of the essential factors in the vast expansion of knowledge. This formal diversification and this material accumulation of knowledge have now reached the point where the present level of culture and its continuing expansion are possible only through extreme specialization.

It may once have been possible for intelligent scholars to encompass many fields of learning, but it is no longer possible. For example, in the seventeenth century how much mathematics was there to know? I would guess that an intelligent person could have mastered it in a matter of months. One moved to the frontiers of disciplines very quickly, when Boyle's law was a discovery and not simply one of many items in an elementary textbook, when Torricelli's experiment was eagerly studied by the best men of the time rather than simply repeated endlessly in high school classrooms. Things are vastly different now. We need not overwhelm ourselves with statistics, yet they do stroke out the problem boldly. There are now some 50,000 scientific and technical journals publishing something like 1,200,000 articles annually. Annually there appear some 60,000 new science books and about 100,000 research reports. [15]

The problem of cultural dichotomy with which we are dealing is often thought of as resulting from specialization or, at least, from overspecialization. It is now clear, I think, that we cannot eliminate specialization from the world of scholarship. At the upper levels of all disciplines we continue to need specialists, who will make themselves continually more and more specialized with a kind of intense intellectual asceticism.

We cannot think of producing any significant number of first-rate scholars who, at the level of scholarship, will be in any true sense generalists or universal scholars. Moreover, even if we could do so, we

---

[15] Holten, "Modern Science," 1187; cf. Conway Zirkle, "Our Splintered Learning and the Status of Scientists," *Science*, 121, no. 3146 (15 April 1955): 513–519.

would not solve our problem, for to locate two disciplines within a single mind is not to establish their interrelation or their value. Indeed, if the question of principle is not solved, such a situation would result either in an inner intellectual dichotomy with insulated intellectual compartments, as sometimes is seen in religious scientists, or in a far worse confusion. The solution cannot lie either in eliminating or in mixing specialization at the highest level of scholarship.

A PROBLEM OF KNOWLEDGE

Now every conception of the role science should play in our intellectual culture and of the way it should be assimilated into our common culture rests upon an evaluation of the sort of knowledge science is. We cannot determine whether science should supersede philosophy or whether it should be entirely subordinated to the humanities without deciding, at least implicitly, what sorts of knowledge we have in these disciplines. I propose to approach the general problem through this question which I believe is the primary and commanding question in the entire discussion, "What sorts of knowledge do we human beings have?" Moreover, if the reading of cultural history which I have suggested is at all sound, the solution to this knowledge question will likewise illumine the historical situation to which we have come.

If now we reflect on the proposed question, it appears to be a very special type of question. We would, for example, have to ask, "What sort of knowledge is chemistry?" Yet this is not a chemical question which can be studied by chemical methods and answered in chemical terms. We cannot ask a chemist, *qua* chemist, to determine the nature of chemical knowledge. We are asking a question that is outside chemistry, that looks at the totality of chemistry; the chemist as such is within chemistry. Moreover, the very problem is to define a chemist as a knower. By the same token and even more clearly, the question as to the value and place of chemical knowledge in the totality of culture is not a chemical question.

What sort of questions then are these? These questions have traditionally been called philosophical and are still so considered especially in Catholic philosophical circles. I accept this as a philosophical task and therefore as the responsibility of the philosopher, in particular, of the epistemologist. But one is immediately faced with difficulties which cannot be ignored and, which cannot, either, be permitted to block us. For this decision forces us to take a stand about the nature of philosophy and the validity of its claims to judge all knowledge, even its own, according to its nature as knowledge. This claim to some sort of intellectual jurisdiction over other and indeed autonomous disciplines arouses understandable resentment. Yet, in all honesty, the issue cannot be avoided; the problem is philosophical and must be so handled.

Moreover, the task makes an almost impossible demand upon the philosopher himself. He must, of course, be trained and experienced in philosophical method and philosophical thinking. But he cannot answer these "knowledge" questions out of some pure philosophical theory of his own. There is no *a priori* answer. The task demands a philosophical examination, not dictation, of what the scientist, the humanist and even the theologian do as knowers. There is no neat pattern that lays all this out in advance. We cannot find some precious formula in St. Thomas and by it instruct the sociologist how he should go about the business of sociological thinking. The philosopher is dependent upon the actual existence of disciplines for the development of his theory. Hence, the work of the epistemologist is never done; he must be careful to maintain an open theory, ready to develop with the appearance of new disciplines. The progressive differentiation of knowledge provides the philosopher with new data; the new disciplines are new subjects of study for the epistemologist as a new species of insect is a new subject of study for the biologist.

If we can establish a sound philosophical theory of knowledge, it will be an indispensable tool in the reconstruction of culture and the reintegration of human knowledge; indeed, it is itself one form of integration, for, if fully and properly carried out, it is an ordering and an interordering of all our knowledges.

WAYS OF KNOWING

The fundamental option here is between a theory of one formal intellectual discipline and one formal valid methodology and a theory which allows for many formally different disciplines and recognizes formally different and valid methodologies. Of the first type Descartes is the first modern proponent; as he had succeeded in uniting geometry and algebra into a single discipline so he thought he would be able to connect all human knowledge in a single concatenation, homogeneous in method and formality, thus achieving a single human science of all things. This dream has haunted modern philosophy and is the ideal proposed by many contemporary thinkers. There would not be different kinds of knowledge, only knowledge of different things. On the other side is the Aristotelian and the Thomistic tradition which sees in the whole of human knowing a unity in formal diversity. Aristotle gives us a neat example of this sort of theory in the first part of the *Physics* where he discovers an intrinsic difference between the mode of defining used by the mathematician and that used by the philosopher. This difference gives rise to two formally different conceptual schemes, which cannot simply be added together or translated into each other. It seems to me that the facts of human knowing experience demand and dictate a pluralistic epistemology.

It is quite common to pose general cultural questions, as does the title of this article itself, in terms of dichotomies: "Science and Religion"; "Science and General Culture"; "Science and Common Sense"; and so on. We cannot, however, really make a fundamental approach to the basic problem as long as we think of it within the limits of any simple dichotomy like the title of this article, "Science and the Humanities." These dichotomies set the problems inadequately and, in their very statement, already exclude or confuse elements essential to a solution.

Moreover, the general terms used bear so many vague meanings and are used, by university administrators, by educational theories, by others, to include such a variety of actual disciplines that we are forced to begin with a fresh division. If I may be allowed to anticipate a bit, the term "humanities" is used to include things like plays, literary criticism, philology, and so forth, which cannot be put in the same epistemological category. Again, when one talks of "Science versus the Humanities," sometimes "philosophy" is thought of as falling within the "humanities," sometimes as falling within "science," sometimes it is simply ignored.

I propose to extricate myself entirely from all these confusions and these vague, preconceived groupings of individual disciplines by attempting to identify the basic formal differences in modes of knowledge withing our refined culture. This will give us, then, an epistemological tool for classifying the various given disciplines and for determining their interrelationships.

I suggest that we can identify at least five formally distinct refined[16] ways of knowing (the order of presentation is irrelevant):

1. The Humanistic way of knowing
2. The Scientific way of knowing
3. The Philosophical way of knowing
4. The Mathematical way of knowing
5. The Theological way of knowing.

I propose this division as a generic one only. There may be formal differences within these types (e.g., "ethical" and "metaphysical" within "philosophical"; "biological" and "physical" within "scientific") which give rise to a multiplicity of individual disciplines. Moreover, at this point I am prescinding from practical and applied knowledge. Again, these modes are all modes of knowing the "real." "Formal logic" is, therefore, not being considered.

I am maintaining that these five ways of knowing are irreducibly different, that they, therefore, give rise to formally different groups of disciplines which involve formally different methodologies, that these disciplines are radically autonomous, though not wholly so, that they are independent yet are interrelated in a variety of different ways. The nub and the rub of the situation lie in the fact that these differences are formal, not simply material; that there is an overlap of subject matter under a difference of form. This may well be illustrated by asking where in the University we can find out about "man"? The philosophy department offers a "Philosophy of Man"; there are courses on human anatomy, human learning, culture, and so on. "Man" appears to be split up and divided throughout the University; he is subject matter for many different disciplines. Having merely indicated that there are the mathematical mode and the theological mode, I will leave these in the background without giving them further attention. I will attempt to give a brief description of the other three modes since some understanding of these differences is essential for our purpose here.

---

[16] The word "refined" is not just a chance piece of rhetoric. I use this term to designate the knowledge elaborated by and in formal disciplines as opposed to the matrix of "natural" knowledge which arises as undifferentiated but genuine knowledge in man's unreflective encounter with reality. Out of this basic matrix all refined or disciplined knowledge develops by reflection and by systematic return to and extension of experience.

THE HUMANISTIC MODE

Here I am discussing the kind of knowledge and understanding we possess through the experience of reading a novel, watching a play, contemplating a painting, meditating on a poem. I am limiting myself here strictly to the knowledge aspect of this experience and I am dealing with the experience itself, not with subsequent analysis or conceptual reformulation of the experience.

As a kind of knowing we can describe this experience both subjectively and objectively. Subjectively it is characterized by an integral and unified operation of all man's conscious powers; understanding of this sort arises only in a context of imagination and emotion, of intellect and will operating in mutual interdependence. Whereas emotion impedes philosophical thinking, it is a necessary condition for humanistic understanding; whereas scientific definition aims at exact and purely intellectual terms, humanistic insight requires the rich flow of creative imagery.

If we now examine the kind of object which correlates with this humanistic knowledge experience, certain common characters can be identified. Whether the object is a painting, a song, or the imaginative experience evoked in the reading of a novel, the object is, in the main, particularized and concrete. It is not man but this man, Oedipus or Hamlet, that strides across the players' stage; it is not red and purple in general, but these reds and these purples that integrate into the object of artistic contemplation. Moreover, the object is precisely object here insofar as it is sense-presented, as in painting or imaginatively held before consciousness, as in a novel. The object is not a pure intelligibility, consciously and reflectively removed from the conditions of sense and imagination.

In humanistic experience, the object is created essentially within the sensible and sensitive activities of man. To isolate any aspect of the object from this level of presentation, to translate it into purely intelligible characters, is precisely to submit it to scientific or philosophical treatment and so to terminate the humanistic experience as such.

In this brief description, I am really pointing to a very rich sort of knowledge experience which we all have had to a greater or lesser extent. Reflection on this sort of knowledge reveals, I submit, that this description is a valid one and that in this experience we attain an understanding which cannot simply be translated into purely intellectual knowledge. Humanistic knowledge cannot be reduced to purely abstract conceptual knowledge, nor can any purely intellectual discipline substitute for it. The understanding of human life we derive from Homer or Shakespeare can never be substituted for by psychology or philosophy or theology.

THE SCIENTIFIC AND PHILOSOPHICAL MODES

These two ways of knowing show at least one common difference from the humanistic mode. Both of them seek the pure intelligibility, extracted from the context of the here and now, of the sensible, of the imaginative and the concrete. Hence they develop into purely intellectual conceptual systems.

In order to deal briefly, and somewhat superficially, with the distinction between the philosophical and the scientific mode, let us consider a rather simple paradigm of a conceptual system of this sort. If we examine any purely intellectual discipline we will find that (1) the discipline has a distinctive set of terms and of definitions, of conceptual meanings; (2) it expresses itself in a set of generalizations (principles, laws, formulas); (3) it attempts some kind of "explanation," some level of general theory which organizes the data, the concepts and the generalizations of the discipline, and (4) it employs some sort of methodology taken in the broad sense to include the intellectual attitudes and habits as well as the characteristic technical procedures. We can discern a certain homogeneity between the parts of the discipline. The generalizations will employ the concepts appropriate to the discipline. Physics will generalize about "mass" and "force"; philosophy about "essence" and "existence." The generalization and the concepts will be logically related as data and as deductions to the explanatory level of the discipline. Finally, the methodology will condition all three levels and, in turn, will be determined by them. Philosophical problems require philosophical methods; chemical methods yield chemical generalizations.

I intend now, using this paradigm as an analytic tool, to assert two fundamental differences between the type of discipline I am calling philosophical and the type I am calling scientific.

If we examine the philosophical disciplines we find that the effort is to transpose to the purely intellectual level the ontological characteristics of the given reality. A philosophical concept is the result of an effort to understand things in their own nature, not, of course, adequately, but without substitution, addition, or distortion.

Such concepts I call "ontological." They can be illustrated in ordinary natural knowledge by such an understanding as that of "oblong," not mathematicized but viewed simply as a quality of a body, the way we can all perceive it prior to our learning geometry. The non-mathematical concept of "oblong" is simply an understanding of the way oblong things really are; there is an exact correspondence between the character understood and the character realized in things.

It is, however, typical of science that its distinctive concepts are not thus "ontological." These concepts are the result of a method which indeed manipulates data drawn from reality but which adds to the resulting concept something not simply imposed by reality, or substitutes something for the original deliverance, by a sort of redefining process. Thus the concept of time actually used in mechanics is not a concept which is intended to reveal intelligibly the nature of time; it is rather a measure of time, resulting from some system and device for measurement and, therefore, bypassing the vexed question of the real nature of time. Such are the concepts of "mass," "center of gravity," of "economic cycle," of "species" in zoology, and so on.

A very simple illustration is afforded by a concept like that of "intelligence quotient." When I say, "John has an [I.Q. of 110]," I am not thinking directly and solely of some ontological qualification of John as I am when I say "John is a rational being" or "John is a substance." There is no "110" written into his intelligence, nor does a "quotient" form part of his reality. The concept, of course, relates to John but only through a complex set of operations which are, at least partially, arbitrary and which leave results within the final concept itself. Such concepts, then, express reality obliquely, as inextricably bound up in selected operations; they are "constructural."

A parallel distinction can be drawn between the generalizations of science and those of philosophy. In philosophy principles must arise through a grasp of their intelligible ground. Thus, the metaphysical principles of finality and causality must be empirical in the sense that their ground is found in experienced reality but not in the sense that an unknown connection is factually established indirectly. Where no intelligible grounds can be discovered, generalization must be empirical in this second sense. The law of gravitation is just such a generalization. By a complex series of observations, measurements, and correlations it is established that "Every particle of matter in the universe attracts every other particle with a force which is directly proportional to the product of the masses of the particles and inversely proportional to the square of the distance between them." Newton did not so generalize because he saw any intelligible necessity why this rather intricate mathematical relationship should obtain. He simply established that it did obtain. The ontological ground remains hidden. As Ernest Mach wrote:

> The Newtonian theory of gravitation, on its appearance, disturbed almost all investigators of nature because it was founded on an uncommon unintelligibility. People tried to reduce gravitation to pressure and impact. At the present day gravitation no longer disturbs anybody; it has become a *common* unintelligibility.[17]

It is altogether appropriate that where the conceptual scheme is only an oblique transcription of the real, a sort of radar-conceptualization[18] of the real world, the generalization should typically be of this factual-empirical type. Thus a homogeneity is discernible in the paradigm; constructural concepts (—) factual-empirical generalizations in constructural terms (—) explanations derived from and connected with reality through constructural patterns (—) an indirect, oblique methodology.[19]

---

[17] Ernst Mach, *History and Root of the Principle of the Conservation of Energy*, English translation by Jourdain (Chicago, 1911), 56, in James B. Conant, *On Understanding Science*, 115.

[18] *Time* for May 16, 1955: 73, quoted Carl Anderson as saying that there is no way to see the atom or examine it at first hand. "It must be studied by indirect evidence, and the technical difficulty involved has been compared to asking a man *who has never seen a piano* to describe a piano from the sound it would make falling downstairs in the dark." (Italics added.)

[19] For a fuller explanation see my *A Thomistic Explanation of Relations Between Science and Philosophy*, Bulletin of the Albertus Magnus Guild, 3, no. 4: 4–6. Cf. also, E.F. Caldin, *The Power and Limits of Science* (London: Chapman and Hall, 1949); Jacques Maritain, *The Degrees of Knowledge* (New York: Scribner's, 1959); Gavin Ardley, *Aquinas and Kant* (New York: Longmans, Green and Company, 1950); George Klubertanz, "The Doctrine of St. Thomas and Modern Science," *Sapientia Aquinatis* (Rome: Officium Libri Catholici, 1955), 98–104.

SOME CONCLUSIONS

On the view which I have just briefly reported, certain important observations can be made about those disciplines which employ, at least typically, the "scientific" mode of knowing.

a. Such disciplines cannot be expected to yield an ultimate explanation of reality. They cannot do duty for metaphysics. The factual results of scientific inquiry can be inserted in a metaphysical framework, but they cannot determine that framework.

b. For the same reason they cannot supply the formal principles of structure of an ethics. Their findings may be relevant to ethics (e.g., a scientific psychology may make the determination of responsibility more accurate), but they cannot generate an ethical system.

c. Taken in a strict sense, a science is a homogeneous abstract system of concepts, laws, theories, and explanations, a pure intellectual system intrinsically self-contained and autonomous. A science, therefore, cannot be formally made into a humanity; the distinction is imposed by the fact of two disparate modes of knowing. This is science formally taken.

d. Though scientific disciplines are constructural in their conceptual schemes, they are nonetheless knowledge of the real world and are in constant touch with the world of "fact."[20] Scientific knowing moves from fact and forward to new fact; it progressively uncovers facts. The total result of several centuries of scientific investigation has been a vast accumulation of facts, observed facts, inferred facts, tested facts. Now, to a certain extent, it is possible to separate these facts from the formal scientific system. Thus we can teach children the general pattern of the solar system without teaching them astrophysics. It is thus possible to put these facts together into a sort of "scientific story" or "scientific picture" of the world in which we live. When we put the facts together in a chronological order, presenting the dynamic evolutionary movement of the universe, we can call the result a sort of "story." When we take a static view of the universe and expose it in terms of scientific fact, we can call the result a sort of "description" or "picture." In determining detailed factual content of this "story" and this "picture" science has the commanding role.

---

[20] I realize the rather naive use of the highly ambiguous term "fact"; I would beg the reader to take it in a very simple way as the illustrations indicate.

e. Because science is correlated with reality in an exact, detailed, and controlled way, and because it is a fact-finding, fact-controlling, fact-organizing enterprise, it is also a superb instrument for the control and reconstruction of man's environment. I do not mean this simply in regard to "physical" realities; science has important technical applications to man, to his emotions, his thinking, his social life, and so forth. It thus gives rise to or serves technology, techniques, and various professions.

f. We can also think of science not as a formal system, nor simply as a way of knowing, nor even as a vast theory for practical achievements, but now as an enterprise of human beings, like mountain climbing, falling in love, or fighting wars. So seen, it is an activity that arises out of the enthusiastic questing of man, springing from his imagination and his creative insights, carried on despite opposition, discouragement, even repeated failures, by dogged persistence, by hard work and hard thinking to high achievement. Thus viewed it is indeed a human thing, a revelation of the spirit of man.

A PROGRAM

We are now prepared to return to the general problem of the place of science in modern culture. From the viewpoint of the history of culture, the scientific mode has given us a whole set of new disciplines by which we can extend our knowledge. But our epistemological examination indicates that while these disciplines cannot be dispensed with, they must be put alongside of, not in place of or over, the other disciplines which arise from other valid and autonomous ways of knowing: humanistic, philosophical, mathematical, theological. A complete modern culture must find places of honor for all these disciplines.

What I have called the scientific "story" and "picture" of the universe, since it is the most accurate and complete factual account of the universe in which we live, should become part of the common knowledge of all adults in our culture. This can be done, even though we cannot provide that all adults will have a mastery or even, for that matter, an introduction to all the sciences which contribute to this story. The educated adults of the fourteenth century had some such factual picture; they conceived that the world, for example, was spherical and at rest in the center of the material universe, although many of them knew little of the scientific arguments for these factual conclusions. To present our modern story to all adults is all the more feasible since we have reached a point where a fairly coherent, complete, and certain account can be offered.

On the other hand, it must be remembered that this account, distilled from the sciences, cannot be the total account. No matter how detailed and how accurate the account of science may become, the ultimate questions of the ontological status and meaning of the totality and of each thing viewed existentially remain beyond reach of the scientific mode. Yet, again the scientific "story" lies open to a completion within a larger general framework drawn from philosophy and theology. However much one may disagree with the methods of du Noüy and Teilhard de Chardin, they have in fact show that the factual conclusions of science do lie open to integration into the parallel framework set forth by other disciplines. Moreover, contrary to the hasty conclusions of some modern writers, theology and philosophy contain within them insights and principles adequate to realign their syntheses with the factual determinations of science.[21] This integration and this realignment will give our culture a common world view that can belong to both specialist and nonspecialist.

A truly humanistic acceptance and understanding of the entire scientific enterprise will amount to a reintegration of science into our total society and culture. But this effort has not been made and is, I think, largely responsible for the bipolarization of which Snow complains. The humanists have not applied humanistic understanding to the

---

[21] Some, like Burkhardt, see the progress of science as forcing the retreat of religion or philosophy from one position after another: "But this dualistic view never quite established peace—even after western religious creeds gave up their attachment to specific astronomical and cosmological beliefs" (*Science and the Humanities*, 24).

The truth of the matter is that theology and philosophy in the West have been able to shift from one scientific "story" to "another" because both were open to relationships with any factual determination of the universe. The principles were already clearly formulated in the two greatest theologians of the West, Augustine and Aquinas. It is often forgotten that the Aristotelian astronomy to which Scholasticism was attached was accepted as against systems which factually seemed closer to the biblical account. One need only read St. Thomas, *S.T.*, 1, 66–74, to find a constant exposition of theology in relationship to the *opiniones* of men, of philosophers, geographers, and so on, and various expressions of the indeterminacy of theology in reference to such matters. Theology is constantly prepared to renovate what it borrows from human learning. It is, of course, true that individuals and schools have not carried on this work in a constant and enlightened manner. And, of course, there lies across the beginning of the modern period the shadow of the Galileo case. However unfortunate this case was, it remains atypical of the Church and of theology.

industrial, technological, and scientific revolutions. Until they do, science will remain outside and alongside a large segment of our culture.

The reconstruction of that dimension of our culture which is the product of the humanistic mode of understanding must always be under way. Humanistic culture is, to be sure, traditional; it maintains the insights of the great writers, the great artists, the creatively thoughtful and expressive humanists. But it is the task of humanistic workers not only to maintain this tradition but to bring the whole of contemporary human life under humanistic consideration and to transmit this contemporary understanding to the men of our time in novels, poems, biographies, historic paintings, and so on.

Science as an activity of human beings as well as a vast technological movement is a truly human concern which falls under this sort of consideration. The humanistic mind can deal thus with science and scientists without itself becoming scientific just as the humanistic tradition has dealt with mystics and mysticism without becoming mystical theology and with statesmen and wars without becoming either a political theory or a theory of military strategy. I agree with Snow and Holton that our humanists have not yet so interpreted science and scientists to us. There is a large measure of truth in Holton's remark:

> This view of modern man as a puny, irrelevant spectator lost in a vast mathematical system—how far this is from the exaltation of man that Kepler found through scientific discovery: "Now man will at last measure the power of his mind on a true scale, and will realize that God, who founded everything in the world on the norm of quantity, also has endowed man with a mind which can comprehend these norms!" Was not the universe of Dante and Milton so powerful and "gloriously romantic" precisely because it incorporated, and thereby rendered meaningful, the contemporary scientific cosmology alongside the current moral and esthetic conceptions? Leaving aside the question of whether Dante's and Milton's contemporaries, by and large, were really living in a rich and fragrant world of gladness, love, and beauty, it is fair

to speculate that if our new cosmos is felt to be cold, inglorious, and unromantic, it is not the new cosmology which is at fault *but the absence of new Dantes and Miltons.*[22]

Allied to the humanistic understanding is another one of which I have said all too little in this article, namely, the historical. I have not given it a place alongside the five modes listed earlier because I do not think history makes use of any generically different ways of knowing. In fact, it can move in various modes, though its commonest form is the humanistic.

But history is a unique discipline; in one sense different from all others, in another sense embracing them and all their subject matters, for even the most abstract and timeless theory has a history, and, indeed, a human history. History, therefore, can be thought of as a sort of universal dimension which measures all other disciplines in its own peculiar way.

Thus, science in all its aspects lies within history and is subject to historical investigation.[23] Some excellent work is now being done in the history of science, in the United States. But there remains a great deal to be done before we achieve a truly integrated history of culture within which science can find its place. The elaboration of such a history will again be a unified interpretation of our culture to ourselves and will thus contribute to the removal of radical divisions.

Finally, I return to what I have asserted is the central problem—the epistemological one. I have only suggested in this paper the main lines of what I conceive to be a valid basic approach. A great deal remains to be done here. I have argued elsewhere[24] that our current theories of knowledge are too narrowly conceived to ground an epistemology adequate to this twentieth century of Western and world culture. While I would maintain the soundness of the basic approach here advocated,

---

[22] Holton, "Modern Science," 1192 (italics added).

[23] I. Bernard Cohen, the eminent historian of science, is quoted as saying that in the history of science he sees "a unity of *all* human creativity and a medium in which science can regain the humanizing dimensions so often lost in purely formal presentations in *The Birth of a New Physics*, I. Bernard Cohn (New York: Doubleday, 1960), front fly-leaf.

[24] "Philosophy of Knowledge and Theory of Learning," *Educational Theory*, 8, no. 4 (October 1958): 193–199.

I would equally strongly urge that our epistemology must remain open, open to new developments not only in correlative sciences but in all disciplines insofar as they are subject matter and problems for the epistemologist.

SOME EDUCATIONAL SUGGESTIONS

I said earlier that the problem to be discussed was not directly an educational one. However, any program for the reconstruction of culture necessarily entails some educational directives.

If the "story" and "picture" of the universe given us by science is to be the common possession of all adults, the scientific story and picture should be taught throughout elementary and secondary education as we have taught, say, the geography of our own country.[25]

The humanistic studies should be expanded throughout the educational system so that a wider range of matters are included. I would think here of a range between an extreme "literary" kind of humanism on the one side and a rich cultural anthropology on the other side.[26] The humanistic assimilation of science could be transmitted within such a range.

While we cannot expect to give those who do not specialize in science an extensive quantitative grasp on a scientific discipline strictly as a formal discipline, genuine experience of scientific knowledge (methodology, conceptual systems, laws, and explanations), systematically and purely conducted, should be part of at least every collegiate education. This experience, however, will remain sterile and without meaning unless it is brought under reflective and comparative study through epistemological analysis. Within collegiate education, final interpretation of the disciplines and of our culture should be achieved in at least two general courses—a theory of knowledge and a history of culture. Many institutions have attempted to do something of this sort in survey or general-problem courses in freshman or sophomore year.

---

[25] Dr. Carlton W. Berenda at the University of Oklahoma has been developing just such a presentation for elementary and secondary teachers.

[26] For a fuller explanation of why I think cultural anthropology can be intimately related to humanistic learning see "A Philosopher's Interpretation of Anthropology's Contribution to the Understanding of Man," *Anthropological Quarterly*, 32, no. 1 (January 1959): 22–40.

I am convinced that neither of these things can be done effectively until after the college student has covered a range of systematic disciplines and has achieved some degree of specialization in at least one discipline. I would suggest that we reorder our collegiate program so that the student completes most of his specialized major in sophomore and junior years rather than in junior and senior years, thus leaving ample time in senior year for serious work in epistemological and historical interpretation and integration.

To round out these comments, which have been largely directed to science, every collegiate student should have some sound personal experience of each of the great modes of human knowledge as well as a personal grasp on the main substantive results of each mode. The senior year envisioned above could then be a year of balanced integration and personal conquest of intellectual maturity.

II

PHILOSOPHICAL METHOD AND THE CULTURAL CRISIS OF OUR TIMES

New Introduction: In 1961 the American Philosophical Association announced a special Inter-American Conference on philosophy to be held in San Jose, the capital of Costa Rica. A call went out to the whole hemisphere for papers to be delivered at that meeting. I thought that this would be a good opportunity for me to become acquainted with the philosophical trends in Latin America and to meet some of the most representative philosophers of that area which I was especially interested because at that time of my life I was beginning to do a great deal of consultation with the Catholic University of Latin America. Moreover the government of Costa Rica announced that any foreign philosopher who delivered a paper at the conference would have all his expenses paid by the government and would be a guest of the government during his stay. So I wrote this article,[1] submitted it, and it was accepted for presentation. Meanwhile the American Philosophical Association announced that any American philosopher who had a paper accepted for presentation at the congress could apply for a travel grant. I did this and also got my travel paid for by the American Association. I delivered the paper to a small seminar group at the Congress. It was very well received. In fact some of the seminar people wanted to prolong the discussion of my article because

---

[1]First published in *ACTAS Segundo Congreso Extraordinario Interamericano de Filosofia*, 22–26 Julio 1961 (Costa Rica: *Imprenta Nacional*, 1962), 257–260.

they considered that I had raised an extremely important point with regard to modern culture.

This article might be regarded as a corollary to article I. It picks up on the exclusive claim that the scientific method is the only method by which truth can be attained or anything that remotely resembles truth. What I tried to point out in this article is that as a result of the wide acceptance of that exclusivity there was a crisis in modern culture because of the conflicting claims and the fact that a sort of scientific elite were coming to conclusions which the vast majority of the human race did not and would not accept. I still believe that this crisis exists and that it will continue to exist until a broader epistemology is more widely accepted.

* * *

It is a plain fact that the application of scientific methodology has, in many fields, resulted in a dramatic expansion of human knowledge and an explosive acceleration in the rate of this expansion. Yet, it is also plain, though not so obvious, that the limitation of intellectual disciplines to scientific methodologies—or, expressed differently, the complete identification of scientific methodology with sound intellectual and rational methodology—has resulted in a progressive impoverishment of man's insight into himself and the world.

(I here use "scientific methodologies" to denote the methods developed in modern Physics, Chemistry, et cetera, and analogous methods in modern Sociology, Psychology, et cetera.)

I would like to advance two sets of extrinsic evidence for this statement. First of all, it has become a recurring theme in modern discussion, repeated by reflective thinkers in many different fields. To cite just a few. Early in our century, Bergson challenged the adequacy of scientific concepts to express reality.[2] Maritain, in his magistral *Degrees of Knowledge,* analyzed the nature of scientific knowledge and displayed its intrinsic limitations.[3] Davenport asserted that the limitation of knowledge to scientific knowledge leads to a loss of fundamental

---

[2] *An Introduction to Metaphysics* (New York and London: Putnam's, 1912).

[3] *Les Degres du Savoir*, 5e ed. (Paris: Desclee De Brouwer, 1946).

insights essential to human society.[4] Joad linked scientism with the "decadence of our age."[5] Polanyi has argued that, as scientific method takes over more and more areas of knowledge, certain things which we as men know *to be facts* are excluded from the official area of "knowledge."[6] In similar fashion, Schrodinger argues that the effort to fit all knowledge into the scientific world-view creates great gaps in our knowledge which the scientific method cannot fill.[7]

In the second place, men, whether ordinary non-specialists or trained scholars, have simply refused to accept the limited knowledge-universe of the scientific method. *The Critique of Reason* was the first systematic effort to identify reason with mathematical-scientific reason. It failed and, likewise, all subsequent efforts have failed. In short, the first law to be inferred from philosophical experience is *"Philosophy always buries its undertakers."*[8] Kant saw that, if he was to eliminate Metaphysics as a science, he had also to explain why men persisted in being metaphysicians. Only thus could the human mind be exorcized of the demon of Metaphysics. In this, too, he failed and, I believe, Polanyi has pointed out the reason for the failure. Quite aside from science or cultural tradition, there are things which men know and know they know which cannot be purged from their minds and which cannot be fitted into "science." *This* knowledge needs an elaboration of a kind quite different from that available through scientific means. *This* knowledge contains the basic natural insights of human beings within which all their knowing and acting take place.

I offer these considerations not as proofs but as indications that not all aspects of reality or all areas of human knowledge can be brought under the control of scientific knowledge. Some other kind of human encounter with reality and some other type of human interpretation are necessary to give an account of the whole of human experience.

---

[4] *The Dignity of Man* (New York: Harper and Brothers, 1955).

[5] *Decadence* (New York: Philosophical Library).

[6] "Scientific Outlook: Its Sickness and Cure," *Science*, 125, 15 March 1957.

[7] "On the Peculiarity of the Scientific World-View" in *What is Life* (Garden City: Doubleday, 1956).

[8] Etienne Gilson, *The Nature and Unity of Philosophical Experience* (New York: Scribner's, 1946), 310.

Without renewed cultivation of this other way (or ways) of knowing, human knowledge and culture will be perhaps vastly increased while yet being steadily impoverished. Not to attempt this renewal is to run a risk of losing even the values of scientific method: "Scientific stringency, inflexibly resolved to denature the vital facts of our existence . . . *may yet issue in a sweeping reaction against science as a perversion of truth.*"[9]

If the thesis so far presented is true, if a universal extension of scientific methodologies leaves wide gaps in our intellectual knowledge, what remedy (Polanyi speaks of a "cure") can be offered.

Many take refuge from the grim depersonalization of science in the so-called "humanities." Here, we can find life in full concrete richness as against the schematic models of science, the individual as against the universals of science, personality and values as against the moral and esthetic indifference of science. I do not in the least wish to discount the value of the humanities for our intellectual, as well as for our volitional and moral life.[10] Indeed, had we no other recourse, the humanities could serve as a sort of balance-wheel. But, in truth, the humanities cannot really fill up the gaps in our intellectual knowledge or supply the sort of intellectual elaboration demanded by many aspects of reality. The mode of the humanities (poetry, drama, novels, music, art) retains something of the confusion of actual experience; it is not wholly re-ducible to intellectual factors or to rational control. The humanistic manner cannot elaborate the immediate arid concrete insights into an intellectual discipline, though literature and art may well be the matrix of such an elaboration.

Is there, then, another method that can give the sort of elaboration needed to establish fundamental human insights in a true intellectual discipline?

I am taking the position that there is such a method and that it has, in principle, been practiced by the philosophers of the western tradition and that it has been lost by large numbers of modern thinkers.

Philosophy is frequently grouped with the "humanities." This classification, I think, implicitly denies that Philosophy is a substantive

---

[9] Michael Polany, *Personal Knowledge* (London: Routledge and Kegan Paul, 1958).

[10] See my "Science and the Humanities," in *Thought* 35, 139, (Winter 1960): 513–536.

intellectual discipline in its own right and plays directly into the hands of scientism.

On the other side, Philosophy today is often reduced to a sort of summarizing commentary on science, or an analysis of the structure and method of science, or even, simply identified with the highest level of scientific theorizing.

Against this dual devaluation of Philosophy, we must reaffirm at least a triple division of disciplines—1. the scientific disciplines, 2. the philosophical disciplines, and 3. the humanities—if we are to re-establish the internal health of modern intellectual culture

If we examine the methods of the great philosophers, we find in most of them an effort to achieve an insight into or an intellectual penetration of raw reality, of given and ongoing experience, to achieve this by reflection and meditation on fact, rejecting hypotheses, postulates, constructs, methodological "nets" or sieves,[11] striving, on the contrary, to take in, fully and only, the *given* intelligibility of reality. From this basic *intellectual* encounter with reality an encounter involving, either explicitly or implicitly, a phenomenological reflection, philosophers have tried to elaborate concepts which would display the genuine intelligibility of things insofar as this can be grasped by man's mind.[12]

The philosophical encounter with reality, which is, in the first instance, an intellectual-existential experience, is fundamentally different from the experimental-observational encounter which lies at the

---

[11] *The Philosophy of Physical Science* (Cambridge: Eddington, 1949), 16–17.

[12] Cf.: "Nada más lejos del propósito de Ortega que comenzar con una definición de la caza. ¿Por desdén de la definición? Al contrario: hace ya bastante tiempo que la filosofía ha vuelto a estimar las definiciones y a considerar que una de las principales funciones del intelecto es llegera ellas; pero esa misma estimaciòn hace que se las tome en serio y proceda con circumspección, sin tomar por definiciò cualquier fòrmula apresurada. Es menester primero tomar contacto con la realidad objeto de nuestra indagacion, aprehenderla en su immediatez, de un modo directo, sin interposiciòn de teorias. Se trata, ante todo, de señalar hacia la caza, pnerla presente, encontrarse con ella; luego se intentará decir qué es aquello que se tiene delante. Pero lo decisivo, no se olvide, es tenerlo delante. Si, por el contrario, se parte de un esquema conceptual—y por tanto ya abstracto—, se corre el riesgo probable de que ese esquema no coincida con la realidad en cuestion, y ésta—o al menos grandes porciones suyas—quede fuera de nuestro conocimiento." Julián Morias, *La Filosofía Española Actual* (Buenos Aires: Espasa-Calpe, 1948).

base of science. The elaboration of philosophical understanding employs a mode of conceptualization that likewise differs radically from the operational-constructural mode of defining typical of science. It is thus irreducible to science and not subject to the limitations of the scientific method. Yet, because it does elaborate the fruit of its intellectual-existential brooding into intelligible concepts it is sharply distinguished from the concrete, imaginative elaboration of humanistic reflection and creation.

Precisely because of what it is, this method alone enables man to put into a controlled and common discipline the basic insights of human experience and so make them architectonic in structuring human culture. Without this discipline, these insights will be lost to sophisticated culture, and the "intellectuals" will become humanly and indeed *intellectually* impoverished. This is precisely the crisis of culture to which the thinkers, of whom I have offered a sampling above, refer.

We are called to nothing less than the restoration of a true Philosophical method which can be made as universal as the scientific method itself. This is no easy task. Philosophical method is exacting and makes heavy *personal* demands on the individual thinker, much as artistic creation does. It requires, too, a long and grueling training, a schooling under demanding masters, as well as a hard self-discipline.

Here, then, is a task for our times; a task demanded by our cultural crisis. It is our task as philosophers to restore a truly philosophical method and to train a generation of true philosophers.

III

A THOMISTIC EXPLANATION OF THE RELATIONS BETWEEN SCIENCE AND PHILOSOPHY

New Introduction: This paper[1] was presented at a meeting of the American Associations for the Advancement of Science in Saint Louis, Missouri, 1952. The discussion became controversial and indeed somewhat heated since two Dominicans present at the meeting declared flatly that neither Fr. Klubertanz nor I were true Thomists. The result was that we had to do two things simultaneously, namely, we had to establish our authenticity as Thomists and at the same time present some important epistemological differences between modern science and Thomistic philosophy.

The essential point is the recognition of two basically different kinds of concepts, namely, the ontological concept and the constructural concept. The position we took is that typically modern science uses constructural concepts while Thomist philosophy uses ontological concepts.

* * *

It is an honor to have the privilege of participating in this discussion on the philosophical problems raised by the existence of modern science. I have been asked to enter this discussion as a representative of "Thomistic" philosophy. My first obligation, therefore, to this panel and to you is to clarify my position as a representative of

---

[1]First published in *Bulletin of Albertus Magnus Guild*, 3, no. 4 (October 1956): 4–6.

Thomism. In the first place, I will not be merely repeating a theory or doctrine which may be read in the works of Saint Thomas or of the older Thomists. No such theory exists there. Saint Thomas was not faced in the thirteenth century by the precise problems of modern science, for, though in the learning of that time, rudimentary antecedents of modern science existed, there was no body of knowledge scientific in the modern sense. So true is this that in that Latin which was the thirteenth century language of the learned, no word can be found to translate our modern term, "science." Moreover, it would be absurd to assume that any past thinker, whether Aristotle, Saint Thomas, Leibnitz, Kant, or anyone else, completed and closed philosophical development, and it would be contrary to the facts to assert that Saint Thomas had something to say about all philosophical problems.

Nor will I be presenting a position which is accepted by all modern Thomists. And I here include even the other members of this panel. What then is my claim to the term "Thomistic"? In the history of any field of knowledge there are certain definitive achievements which represent a permanent gain and which can be definitely dated. Thus, the behavior of the column of mercury noted and described in the seventeenth century by Torricelli is a definitely determined fact in the history of science and no change of scientific theory will remove this observed fact. In the same way, there are certain facts and principles rationally described, accepted, and developed by Saint Thomas which are definitive and final philosophical achievements. I have attempted to deal with the problem of modern science in the light of these philosophical achievements of Saint Thomas; in this sense my position has been inspired by him and in this sense I propose it as Thomistic. But I will not place the responsibility for this theory on Saint Thomas or any other Thomist. I accept the full responsibility.

Now in any discussion between philosophers and scientists there are fruitful and rich sources of possible misunderstanding. There are also established attitudes, on both sides, of mistrust and even of antagonism. These attitudes are not without foundation, for both scientists and philosophers, victims no doubt of occupational prejudice, have talked a great deal of nonsense about each other. Moreover, to bring the difficulty closer to home, when a philosopher approaches these problems he is going to claim a certain special competence with regard to problems of knowledge which may seem like sheer arrogance to a man who has practiced the scientific method all his life. For all these reasons

I come to this discussion with a certain trepidation. Yet I have very willingly accepted the role of participant because I am convinced of three things: (1) that we are facing here one of the crucial problems of our time, (2) that this problem can only be solved through the cooperation of philosophers and scientists, and (3) that prerequisite to this cooperation is mutual understanding.

Our problem has a long history for it first presented itself in acute form through the intellectual revolution of the seventeenth century, the century in which modern science came to birth in a struggle with the older learning. It is true indeed that history knows no absolute beginnings and that modern science is in continuity with the rational ideals of the Greeks as well as of the medieval thinkers. Yet the beginning of the scientific movement in the seventeenth century was in a true sense a revolution. It was a revolution which liberated a whole group of disciplines from the overlordship of philosophy and by which these disciplines—astronomy, physics, chemistry, and the rest—won a charter of autonomous existence. Thus there has been established a set of more or less clearly defined bodies of fact and explanation which are distinctly new and definitely different—and this despite the fact that rudimentary beginnings of these disciplines can be found in previous history. Thus, though certain chapters in optics drawn from the thirteenth, the seventeenth, and the twentieth centuries are found almost to coincide, the movement from the Aristotelian physics of Saint Louis's University of Paris to the atomic physics of today's Saint Louis University is a movement not to a more highly developed form of the same thing, but to a differently developed and differently constituted discipline.

Now the struggle of the seventeenth century began in astronomy and physics and thus appeared as a direct opposition between the physics of Aristotle and the new physics of Galileo and Newton; yet because the older worldview had been so highly integrated and so long established, it seemed that a complete opposition was developing between the totality of the old learning and the new science. The apologists of the older view defended the celestial spheres of Aristotle by the same means and with the same zeal as they defended their metaphysics and their theology. On the other side, many of the practitioners of the new methods proposed to apply them to all fields of learning. They had a new total method and philosophy which was to supersede the old, unproductive, outworn philosophy inspired by Aristotle.

The subsequent tremendous success of science seemed to give the decision of history in favor of the new learning. Yet even so and despite the fact that the scientist has largely assumed a dominant role in our civilization, the struggle is not over. We have not yet succeeded in placing science within the totality of human learning and we have not yet reached agreement as to the nature of science as a kind of knowledge and as to its relationship to other disciplines. There are those who maintain that philosophy is myth and emotion rather than knowledge, that science is the only true knowledge and that its methods alone are the touchstone for all truth and certitude. Others believe that philosophy is reduced today simply to a reflection on scientific method and that it has no other legitimate field of operation. Still others would make philosophy a sort of super-science, unifying the results of the particular sciences at a higher level of generality and would limit it therefore to the same theoretical methods as science. Now these questions are not mere academic questions, for the position which we take in this matter will determine the kind of intellectual culture, the kind of morality, the kind of education and consequently the kind of political and social institutions which our civilization will have. The problem is current and crucial.

In order to understand and assess the conflict of the seventeenth century as well as to answer the questions I have just placed, the primary necessity is to determine what sort of knowledge science is and what sort of knowledge philosophy is.

The problem therefore presents the old questions as to the nature of knowledge and the kinds of knowledge. It must be noted that these are not scientific questions in the sense that they fall within the competence of any particular science. There is no such thing as a chemical analysis of knowledge. A chemist may report what he thinks, how he proceeds, and what techniques he uses, but his methods can yield no answer to the question: what sort of knowledge chemistry is, any more than his analysis of a painting can ground a decision as to its artistic value. Moreover, the very question puts the inquirer outside of the sciences; he must approach each science as a totality and place it with regard to human knowledge in general, while the chemist or the physicist is, by his very profession, located within the science, and the questions which he asks and answers, as a chemist or physicist, must be asked and answered within the framework of his own science.

However, there is no pat or *a priori* solution that can be worked out in the abstract. The philosopher must look at and reflect upon every variety of human knowledge; he must see what the scientist does, how he proceeds, what his methods and techniques are. As in any inquiry, here also experience is the primary source of knowledge.

In studying this problem, therefore, I have tried to stay close to factual evidence; I have developed solutions and checked conclusions in discussion, with actual working scientists. I have tried to catch them in the very act of being scientists, observing them, so to speak, at ease in their native habitat.

As I pointed out above, I cannot, in so short a space, present the full evidence or attempt a proof of the positions which I now hold. What follows is in the nature of a schematic outline aimed at clarity rather than proof. I hope therefore that I will be forgiven if I now proceed in a dogmatic expository manner.

Historically and systematically, both the sciences and philosophy arise from and are rooted in human experience. Now, philosophers have done an exceptionally fine job of obscuring the idea of experience by involving it in curious and far-fetched abstractions. For my purpose here I simply mean whatever falls under our awareness taken together with that awareness itself. Thus, when you are out stone-cold, unvisited even by dreams, you have no experience; when you are at all aware, even as in dreams or mild intoxication, you have experience. This seems to me simple enough for us all to begin without prejudging the content or meaning of experience. Now I further maintain that it is obvious that in experience we are aware of *something* and that among the *somethings* which we experience is a world distinct from us, really existent and no mere creation of our subjective experiencing. I am a frank realist; but I am so not by assumption or postulation or even argumentation but because of the internal self-evidence of our experience itself. This is not the place to discuss the realistic position in philosophy. But it must be asserted as it is fundamental in this explanation. Moreover, this realism further includes the conviction that in our experience the external world reveals some of its true objective characters.

Within the experience of every man there develops an undifferentiated spontaneous knowledge which is sometimes called "common sense" but which I prefer to call unrefined knowledge. It is from this unrefined knowledge that the refined knowledge of both science and philosophy arises. It is the fashion to talk as though philosophy or science could begin somewhere in the air with a set of unprovable assumptions. From this standpoint I am unfashionable. For the unrefined knowledge, grounded in human experience, is essentially necessary for the erection of this philosophical and scientific structure of knowledge; there is an essential continuity between the first spontaneous movement of the human intellect and the most elaborate scientific theory or the most far-reaching philosophical insight. We are human knowers before we are scientific or philosophical knowers, and this priority is both temporal and logical.

Out of our experience and on the basis of our natural unrefined knowledge the whole range of intellectual disciplines is developed by a reflective effort to understand, to extend, to elaborate, and/or to control experience. Now the various disciplines are not differentiated simply in the sense that they stake out different parts of experience as their fields of application. Rather the differentiation arises because of the essentially different ways in which experience can be handled and elaborated reflectively.

A full treatment would require an exposition of the progressive elaboration of unrefined knowledge from its first moment to the refined stages of science or philosophy. But I must short-cut my presentation and I shall therefore select an end-product of this elaboration and use it as a touchstone to differentiate scientific and philosophic knowledge.

One of our indispensable intellectual tools for understanding and managing experience is the concept, and this is the touchstone I shall use. I shall distinguish two different types of concepts, one of which I shall call "ontological," the other "constructural." Concepts roughly verifying these two types are to be found in unrefined knowledge, in ordinary common sense, but, in refined knowledge, the types are sharply distinguished and become formally characteristic of philo-sophical and scientific knowledge respectively. Now I shall roughly illustrate the two types. Let us start at the level of common sense. When I think—at the level of ordinary knowledge and not of mathematical knowledge—"this paper is rectangular," a concept of "rectangular" func-tions within the unity of this judgment. What is this concept? What is its content? The concept here is an intellectual understanding and grasp of a character of the paper as *it is*, as it really is and as it is therefore presented in experience. Its content is such that it answers, in intellectual understanding, the question: what sort of shape is here, and because it answers this question it enables me to distinguish—qualitatively—the what-sort of shape of this paper (rectangular) from the what-sort of shape of that paper (triangular). This appears to be a very simple sort of experience but I would ask you to reflect upon it, for these reasons especially: (1) this experience has been obscured by abstract and *a priori* theories of knowledge and (2) a full realization of the nature of this experience is crucial to our solution.

We have here an objective or ontological *fact* and its transference, through understanding, to the intelligible level of a concept and the unity of a judgment. The concept is, in this case, an understanding of a fact; not a statement that such and such *is* a fact but an expression of the "what" of the fact. It is the intelligible grasp and expression of the intelligible nature of the fact. The concept in this case is a direct transcription of what is to be found in the thing itself.

Now I know that this raises extreme difficulties for anyone trained in certain modern systems of thought, but I would submit that if one approaches experience without the *a priori* prejudice of a philosophic system or an exclusive attachment to scientific method, he will find this to be the fact of the matter, verifiable in the experience of any human being and as truly verifiable as any scientifically controlled experiment. However, since I am engaged primarily in exposition, I would ask you to bypass for the present the difficulties which may arise from your own points of view. This type of concept which is simply the intelligible transcription or grasp of some nature or "what" as it actually is, this I call ontological.

Let us take a different type of concept, not drawn this time from common sense but from economics. Let us think of an index, for example, of an index of the "cost of living." I am talking about the content of the concept itself as it may be expressed, to use a fictitious example, as "1.9." When we think this precise concept, what sort of content are we thinking? We are not thinking of anything that can *be*, can *exist*, or can *be given* in any concrete experience. There are real concrete instances which truly embody the intelligibility of rectangular or triangular or of "being" or of the ontological principle of contradiction. There are no instances of an index of living costs. Yet, on the other hand, this concept of an index is not a purely fictitious one, an arbitrary construct, the product, so to speak, of the intellectual imagination. On the contrary, if constructed according to the principles of the practicing economists, it bears a determined relation to experience and to ontological reality. Lines of reference move down from the concept to concrete facts—actual wage payments, individual human beings working, bushels of real wheat, actual motor cars, and so forth. The index formula is a sort of algebraic manipulation of all these facts and their mutual relationships with which the formula is statistically and indeed very usefully correlated.

Now if we reflect on these examples of the two types of concepts, it will be seen that they are elaborated by two very different methods. The index concept is derived by a selected process which in turn presupposes a number of statistical unifications of the data. These statistical results are not themselves transcriptions of the ontological intelligibility of the data but relate to them through simple measurements. This process acts as a sort of screen which sieves out precisely the ontological intelligibilities of the men, products, and so forth, upon which it is built. This concept therefore, precisely because of the process by which it is constructed, is only indirectly related to the intelligible facts as intelligible. Now it is my contention that it is this type of concept, the constructural concept, which is characteristic of science as such. And if we look over the range and reach of the various sciences we will find that there are many kinds of constructural concepts because there is an indefinite variety of indirect processes by which reality may be handled.

On the other hand, the first type of concept is elaborated (at least in the initial concepts of this type) by a direct consideration of experience itself and of the reality therein revealed. The ontological concept is elaborated by using that power which we all have, of understanding presented reality directly. This power of directly understanding reality, this power of transcribing onto the intellectual level the intelligibilities contained in the facts and realities of experience, I call insight. Philosophy proceeds and develops by a conscious deepening through reflection of this intellectual insight. Thus the intelligibility of being which is already present, though obscurely, in unrefined knowledge, can be consciously taken possession of; insight into it can be deepened and sharpened by reflective meditation, and it is through this process that the metaphysician lays down the initial grounds of his study. The initial moment of philosophy is thus contemplative and reflective and is precisely a deepening of insight into reality itself. The ontological concept which results from this reflection and which is characteristic of philosophy is the product, not of some indirect correlation, whether by measurement or by other means, but of a refined direct insight into reality.

Insight, intuition, and similar words are today evocative of an unfavorable reaction in men's minds. But, I repeat, the existence of insight as I have described it and its functioning in human knowledge are facts, primary facts, discoverable by reflection. That the insight process is a fact has been obscured in the minds of men today by two factors: (1) For many minds, an epistemological prejudice based upon an *a priori* set of difficulties has directed attention away from it. But the fact of insight, just because it is a fact, is more durable and impregnable than any abstract argumentation against it. (2) Those who like Bridgman and Eddington have largely been concerned with scientific method have overlooked "insight" because it does not have a formal primary function within scientific method. But this is only an accident resulting from an exclusive preoccupation with one form of knowledge.

To extend our investigation, we must note that refined knowledge does not consist merely of initial concepts or definitions. Science develops through generalization and the formulation of laws; philosophy through the elaboration of principles. Here again the methodological difference is found to be parallel to that discovered in the elaboration of concepts or definitions. Both philosophy and science derive their principles and laws from experience and both therefore use an inductive process. But the induction, in the case of the philosopher, is based upon insight into the intelligible characters of reality. The necessities expressed in philosophical principles are found to be intelligibly present in reality and to permit of generalization parallel to the intelligible ground of these necessities. Thus, it is seen in any existing thing that its very existence makes impossible its simultaneous non-existence. The ontological intelligible ground of the necessity here expressed is the actual existence of the thing itself. Hence the ontological necessity of the principle of contradiction can be generalized to any existing thing, to any being. The ground of this generalization is insight into the given, actual, intelligible necessity seen in the cases presented for contemplation in real experience. But the scientist sets up generalizations by an elaborate and very ingenious method of experimentation involving constructural definitions and constructural processes. No amount of experimentation, or correlation or scientific observation, can verify in the slightest degree a formal law of logic or the metaphysical principle of contradiction. On the other hand, there is no insight which will reveal the properties of penicillin. The therapeutic value of penicillin can be asserted only on the basis of repeated controlled clinical tests. The validity of a physicist's formula can only be asserted on the basis of controlled experimentation which reveals an indirect correlation with the facts to which it applies. In the one case the principle is asserted on the basis of intelligible necessities seen, of a grasp of intelligible necessities inherent in reality itself; in the other case the generalization is made because of a factual (not *de jure*) correlation, but the ontological ground of the correlation is not intelligibly grasped.

Thus given initial concepts and laws or principles both the scientist and the philosopher can argue to unexperienced realities. The strictly formal character of the argumentation involved is, of course, the same in both cases, yet the specific nature of the process taken in its entirety is different for science and for philosophy. The philosopher must begin with insight into reality itself. His argumentation depends on the continuous maintaining of this insight, for through it he comes to conclusions which assert intelligible and ontological characters of unexperienced realities. Scientific argumentation begins and moves with constructs and correlations, and for this reason concludes formally only to constructs. Since the precise secret of the success of the scientific method lies in the fact that it has been able to bypass the fundamental questions concerning intelligibility, insight into intelligibility of the facts need not function throughout the argument. It is for this reason that large sections of scientific argument can be reduced to a mechanical method, given to assistants to work out, or even put on a machine. The philosophical argument can never be so handled, for insight is the vitalizing force of the argument and we cannot use another man's insight nor can we evaporate the insight so that the residue may be entrusted to a machine however ingenious. As has been said, the argument must conclude to new realities under that formality which is imposed by the specific nature of the argument. Thus, the astrophysicist argues to the existence of a new planet as to a focal point of forces. This involves all the constructural thinking of physical theory and so touches reality only indirectly. The philosopher argues to the existence of God as an ontological reality with intelligible ontological characters.

I shall now conclude with summary points:

(1) Both philosophy and science begin with experience. Both deal with reality; both therefore presuppose that reality is intelligible or in some sense rational, for on the one hand philosophy deals directly with the intrinsic intelligibility of reality and on the other hand science manages reality through rational and intelligible correlations.

(2) But experience yields different data to philosophy and to science in virtue of the fact that the methodological handling of experience is different in each case. Philosophy must draw from experience the intrinsic intelligibility of reality and must take possession in a precise and ordered way of the intelligibilities and intelligible necessities of reality. Science however applies to experience a method of indirection which precisely bypasses the intrinsic intelligibility there presented and sets up a correlated pattern of constructs through which it organizes and manages experience and reality. A physicist, for example, involves time in his constructs, but he does so through the medium of measurement, and since time may be measured—a clock may be read—without adverting to the real nature of time, the physicist need never raise this question. The philosopher, however, cannot handle time in this manner; he must meditate the problem of the real nature of time. Thus we have two formally distinct types of knowing, the one ontological, the other constructural.

(3) Because of this formal differentiation both in method and in starting point, neither discipline depends upon or can modify the internal structure of the other. Philosophy cannot be derived from science. Some modern thinkers have attempted to develop philosophy by the scientific method; others have attempted to build philosophy on the highest generalizations and theories of science. In either case philosophy is ruined and science misrepresented.

(4) Again, because of the formal differentiation of the two disciplines, the kinds of questions which they can handle are necessarily different. This very fact imposes limits on them. For philosophy can be developed only in those areas where intelligibility can be grasped and used. These areas are very limited especially with reference to the external material world. Philosophy has never yielded control of the detail of the material world because that world in so much of its detail is opaque to the direct light of the human intelligence. It is precisely in these areas where direct insight is not open to us that science has had its

most fruitful application and most astonishing success for here it has developed an ordered control by resorting to the vast and ingenious resource of indirect methods. On the other hand, where a strictly ontological question is asked and where strictly ontological answers are necessary, science is, on its side, impotent. Thus because of their very formal nature, philosophy will bake no bread and will never discover a cure for cancer, and science will never answer the ontological riddles of man's nature or the existence of God. This view also makes clear why scientific explanations and theories may pass and change without prejudice to the development of the scientific enterprise. The constructural theories of science do not attempt to state the ontological character of the real world; they are in a sense artifacts, ingeniously devised to order and control the factual data gathered from that universe. Rather than a transcription of the nature of reality, they are a means of rationally manipulating reality, and so may be reconstructed or discarded when more efficient or more inclusive means are discovered or devised. But in philosophy, an insight that is once gained cannot be changed or discarded. The true insights of Plato or Aristotle or Augustine or Descartes are still essential to the substance of the *philosophia perennis*. On the other hand, the theory of the four elements, of phlogiston, of the vortices, are no longer part of the substance of science. They are outworn and discarded instruments.

In this explanation, therefore, the question concerning the nature of science and philosophy as knowledges is answered thus: Philosophy and science are two valid, autonomous, and independent types of knowledge formally distinct throughout because of their methodology. Philosophy occupies a privileged position because of its ontological orientation, but this characteristic imposes a severe limitation on the applicability of philosophy; science, on the other hand, through its ingenious indirect methods, is able to handle an indefinite reach of reality where philosophy is wholly useless, but it cannot pronounce the ultimate verdict on ontological reality.

To the historical question we can give this answer: What was actually discovered in the seventeenth century was the secret of indirect handling and control of nature and the wide efficiency of this method. But neither side in the controversy realized the true nature of the new methods and so their defenders overstated their own case while the opponents denied even their valid use.

And so I have presented in a schematic way and very inadequately a Thomistic theory of science and philosophy. The additional papers and the discussion will no doubt clarify and perhaps correct what I have tried to say.

IV

MAN'S KNOWLEDGES OF PHYSICAL REALITY

Few Introduction: I think that I established direct realism with regard to knowledge of the material world in article V (The Basis of Philosophical Realism Re-examined), but the human mind approached knowledge very creatively and we have developed specific methods and strategies for understanding and controlling particular parts of the universe. In this article[1] I attempt to set forth some of these methods and strategies.

For instance, statistical methodologies are now used extensively in economics, sociology, and psychology, although the Greek scientists and scholars did not use statistical methods as we now know them.

This article was being considered as sort of an exploratory investigation of various individual ways in which we know physical reality. It does not conclude any generalization with regard to these various methods of knowing. But I think in the course of this study there is one interesting thing that emerged, namely, that individual colors like green, blue, yellow, pink, and so on do not have a per se intelligibility of their own, which can be elaborated and expressed in a concept. For example, there is no intelligibility of redness which can be abstracted from an individual case of concrete red and expressed in an intellectual concept.

We can indirectly recognize the difference between red and green

---

[1]First published in *Essays on Knowledge and Methodology*, ed. Edward D. Simmons (Milwaukee: Ken Cook Publishers Company, 1965), 73–86.

47

as concrete instances, but there is no redness that we can generalize abstractly and intellectually. When we deal with redness, the red color, we must do so either by two experiences of cases, that of present redness or of images of red. This is to say of course that we cannot move our experience of red from the order of sensibility to the order of intelligibility. Of course we can study colors from the aesthetic point of view, namely, looking at the harmony, the contrast, and their beautiful extrinsic beauty. Scientifically we can correlate individual, red specific colors with an electromagnetic wavelength.

I think this consideration sharpens our realization of the great difference between the order of sensibility and the order of intelligibility.

* * *

1. *Introduction: The Basic Problem.*

The topic of this paper could be interpreted so as to be a question "within" the discipline of physics. Once physics is developed as an independent science, it can be considered as a body of rational knowledge enclosing within itself its own "objects" and its own "principles" and being independent of other "objects" as well as of other disciplines. As it grows, it becomes more and more "self-defining" and "self-determining."

When then a question is raised about "physical reality," it can be understood as a question pertaining to physics alone. In this sense, the question of reality will deal with that which is a formalized part of physics, and the physicist alone can declare whether or not something is part of the "reality" defined by physics.

Such an answer lies wholly within physics; it does not and cannot determine the status of this reality in relation to anything outside of physics. No question is raised and no answer given as to a reality lying outside of physics, on which the science of physics depends as on a material object. On the other hand, it is likewise impossible to determine the nature, the limits, and the value of the "knowledge" within physics, without going outside physics and attempting to see it in the total context of all man's experiences and knowledges.

When this step is taken the question of physical reality and of physical knowledge now lies outside of the totality of physics; it escapes the methods of physics since it is now the whole of physics which lies sub judice. At this point, philosophy is reached; physics becomes a "specimen" for the epistemologist and that physical reality which lies outside of the formalization of the science of physics must now be discovered and described by the metaphysician.

To ask what kind of knowledge physics is is not to ask a "physical" question, for physics has no method to deal with any knowledge as such.

This paper therefore begins outside of physics within the broadest possible matrix of human experience and of human knowledge.

2.   *The Primary Description of Physical Reality.*

Since I will be talking about that reality to which physics is related as a form of human knowledge, I must first indicate what this reality is. I will describe it in a rather experiential and neutral fashion without appealing to the conclusions of physics or any other developed discipline. What is this reality as we find it in immediate experience, in our direct contact with whatever is given?

Within this framework we can describe physical reality as that part or those parts of reality which we find characterized by being spread out in space, extended, quantifiable, "occupying space," located within dimensions, or, as the old description puts it, having parts outside of parts. This physical reality is likewise "temporal." From one standpoint, this means that it is a changing and shifting reality, existing in the midst of process. Things come and go. There are events; there are happenings. From another standpoint—a more metaphysical but still quite primary one—this means that physical reality exists moment by moment, momentarily; its existence, too, may be said, metaphorically, to be spread out over time, not had in one permanent "moment" of existence; it is never *tota simul.* Let me simply say then that I shall be talking about the reality which can be thus circumscribed or pointed to.

3.   *The Primary Matrix of Human Experience.*

The primary form of human experience which is at the same time the primary content of human consciousness is a concrete encounter with a complex object or set of objects. This encounter is experiential and conscious; it is a knowledge encounter as well as an encounter with objects.

Now it is true that in human beings who have had past encounters, who are "experienced," this encounter is never just itself. As a knowing encounter it is enriched (or, perhaps, deformed) by past experiences and past elaborations of experience. But, even so, reflection can uncover within our present experience the basic and primary given of the encounter.

Among these given is this: that the objects which are thus encountered are things, that they exist in themselves, not merely in or for me; that, in some absolute sense—that is to say in some non-relative sense—they *are*.

This immediately reveals to further reflection something of the nature of this encounter as a "knowing encounter." This "knowing" must be such as to be able to understand independent self-exercised existence; the very meaning of "exist" taken in a most brutal simplicity.

The encounter is not just the physical collision of objects, nor the object-stimulation of subjective sensitivities. Objects are here brought within the ambit of awareness which can recognize and express, independently of and beyond its own limited reality and the relativity of its own experience, objective existence—and this not merely as a fact but as an *understood* fact, a fact *understood* at two levels.

This encounter is through-and-through a conscious one not only in the sense that there is an on *awareness centered on objects* which lifts the encounter to a level of objective knowing, but also, in the sense that the entire concrete encounter takes place within the ambit of an embracing, unified, and self-illuminating awareness which taken together with a wealth of actual content is the true matrix for each successive encounter. Within this larger awareness the objective existence of objects is understood in its fullest "objectivity," for it is seen in opposition to the existence and the activity of the knower within whose awareness the encounter takes place.

In this encounter "objects" are seen to be not merely "objects" but existing things.

4.   *The Independent Existence of Physical Reality.*

But objects do not present themselves as unknown subjects of the quality of "existing"; they present themselves as characterized by various traits. Objective existence is not abstract. It is the existence of these given individual things here and now encountered; nor is it the sole character presented by these things. In fact, the objects are presented within a kaleidoscope cloud of qualitative experiences. Here again analytic reflection can discover that the objects so presented do, as things and not merely as objects, possess this peculiar ontological characteristic of *being extended.*

I am asserting that we can find our direct experience giving us a world of existing extended entities which *are* independently of our awareness and which are extended independently of our awareness. Of physical reality we can know that it is independently real and extended.

I am speaking of extension here as a qualification of things both intelligible and ontological, as a sort of quality prior to its proper quantification by subjection to measurement and to geometrical idealization.

5.   *The "Sense-Context" of Immediate Experience of Physical Reality.*

The immediate context of the encounter with any physical object is a varying set of what are commonly called sensations and sensible qualities. These are the sounds and smells and flavors and colors and feels which accompany and enrich our experience.

Here we touch on a matter which has been the subject of endless controversies since the very beginning of Western thought. I cannot here run through a dialectical resolution of these controversies or present a full argumentation for a substantive position. I will simply make a series of assertions necessary to the simple integrity of my statement.

These sense experiences have always resisted both complete conceptualization and complete ontological objectification. The specific "quality" of these sense experiences can be understood according to certain intelligible characteristics (as "sound" can be understood to be different from "taste"), but the full quality, say, of "red" cannot be intellectually isolated and encapsuled in a concept.

On the other hand, a simple absolutizing of such qualities into independent characteristics of existing physical things seems to be meaningless. This is clearest in the case of a sound. It is meaningful to speak of a low sound; but what would it mean to say of an objective thing that it possesses a "low sound" as it possesses existence or extension?

Moreover, under reflection, the very qualities of sense experience can be seen to be relative to the subject of the encounter as well as to the object encountered. I have pointed out that by discovering and asserting the independent existence of an entity, the knowing subject thereby escapes from its subjective relativities and reaches an absolute ground. Nothing of the sort is possible for the awareness of sense qualities. These are relative to the nature of the experiencing subject and reflect in themselves the changing conditions of the subject. On the other hand, within the larger context of experience of objects, they can be seen to be relative to the entities encountered in experience, changing also as these entities themselves shift and change.

The epistemological situation is then as follows: We can know and understand that physical reality exists as a plurality of different independent entities with certain understood general traits such as extension. But the sense-qualifications of experience do not reveal an intelligible ontological characteristic of the existing entities encountered in the particular experience. Because they are relative to the entities encountered, they do enable us to infer that this physical world consists of entities with many differentiations, and which are in movement and activity and change. They do not, however, enable us to grasp directly or to infer directly what might be the ontological intelligibility of the specific characteristics of physical entities.[2] The sense qualities, therefore, reveal themselves as correlates for generically definable but specifically unknown ontological qualities, activities, or events.

As our experience grows we find that the sense qualities not only correlate with objects but also with each other. Moreover, we find that this complex set of correlations is ordered and repetitive. Hence, for practical purposes in dealing with entities of the physical world, these sense qualities, in themselves, in their intercorrelation, and in their interpretations from past experience, become clues for prediction and for purposeful action.

6.   Two Different Types of Knowledge of Physical Reality.

We may pause to point out that we have now identified two

---

[2]When I speak of ontological knowledge as containing the proper and direct intelligibility of the object, (1) I do not mean that it contains *all* the intelligibility of the object, but only that *all* that is contained in the knowledge is to be found ontologically in the object. (2) I do not mean that the intelligibility is gotten by direct insight or immediate experience, but only that the intelligibility grasped in knowledge directly expresses the reality of the object without any reinterpretation or reformalization of the reality expressed. The "directly" here refers to the mode of expression, not to the manner of acquisition.

different conscious ways of reaching and dealing with physical reality. In the one case we grasp the intelligibility of the ontological characteristic itself—thus we know the *existence* of the physical entity. In the other case we do not know the intelligibility of the ontological situation; we have immediate access only to certain correlates and clues. Systematic approaches to physical reality can be developed along both lines. Thus, by insightful reflection upon the act of existence given in physical reality, a metaphysics directly applicable to physical reality can be developed.

On the other hand, a systematic classification of certain types of physical entities and their interactions can be developed in terms of sense qualities. A great deal of the non-mystical alchemy of the Middle Ages is a systematized science of this type. To describe sulfur as "a yellow powder which when heated irritates the nostrils" is not to give a direct ontological understanding of the nature (if any) of sulfur. It is to describe, and so define, sulfur in terms of natural sense correlates.

In the unphilosophical and comparatively unreflective knowing of everyday life both sorts of knowledge are blended together in a sort of unprecise, practical approach to physical reality. But as soon as we attempt to refine knowledge, to set up reflective, systematic, and formally coherent disciplines, we find it necessary to distinguish knowledge that is in ontological terms and knowledge that is in terms of correlates. Thus a true metaphysics cannot employ a definition that formally con-sists in descriptive smells and tastes.

7.   *Enrichment of Experience by Past Experience.*

I pointed out that the matrix of experience is constantly enriched by past experience. This happens in at least two ways. Experience leaves with us a growing knowledge content upon which we constantly draw to illumine each new encounter. In addition, in our effort to understand, to order and organize, to use and deal with experience we not only deepen available insights by repetition and reflection but we devise ways of imposing structures upon reality where too little is directly supplied us by reality itself. These structures may be purely intellectual as, for example, when we form the concept of a "hole" or of any privation and so deal with it as though it were a positive reality. Here we have a very simple sort of "construct" which is common enough in even the sim-plest intellectual life.   In other cases, however, the imposition involves an operation which results again in a constructural type of knowledge. Thus the devising of a system of measurement and of a way of measuring results in an intellectual expression of size or amount which is not simply ontological but which includes in its intelligibility a reference to the system and mode of measurement. The quantity which I designate as 15–1/2 inches does exist in physical reality but 15–1/2 inches as such do not so exist. Briefly, we find it useful and indeed necessary to supplement our ontological concepts with contrived *entia rationis* of many different sorts.

Again, we may note that in practical everyday knowledge onto-ogical concepts and *entia rationis* blend and intertwine without dis-turbing thought or action. As soon as, however, we attempt to systematize our knowledge, it becomes imperative to become fully aware of the modes of our conceptualization and to distinguish those modes which are mutually incompatible. Metaphysics, for example, could not rest a proof for the existence of a first cause upon a con-catenation of constructural concepts.

8. *Knowledge of "Connections" in Physical Reality.*

The physical reality, the physical world, which we discover through continuing encounters, is not only a world of existing extended beings; it is a world of movement and change, of interaction and interrelation. At one level, and this is the more primary both logically and historic-ally, the connections, the changes, the patterns are seen in a purely empirical fashion as simply facts to be understood and reported. But insightful reflection and inference bring us to see that the existence and activity of the physical world must be understood within a framework of causes and of causal explanation. Here again, levels of knowledge develop. In some broad ways, as in the question of contingent existence, the necessity of causes is an intelligibility discovered in experience and ontologically grasped. But as far as the detail of individual event and happening is concerned, connections are presented, for the most part, purely empirically. Some events remain so, no significant connection being seen or guessed. But in other cases, the accumulation of cases, each quite empirical, brings the connection beyond the possibility of accident, and, in the light of the larger insight into an actively changing world, beyond the level of the empirical. And so we establish rough generalizations, rules, and, finally, laws which, on the one hand, presuppose necessary and causal connection, and, on the other hand, do not reveal or express the intelligibility of the causal connection. Here we have innumerable cases where the fact of connection is known but the nature of the connection is unknown. For centuries, the native doctors of India used the rood *rauwolfia serpintina* to calm madness without knowing why the root effected tranquilization. They knew the effect was no accident; they knew *that* the root was truly *effective*; they did not know *why*.

Again, we may point out that in ordinary knowledge there is a confused mixture of purely empirical and factual knowledge with insights into causes and reasons and inferences to unknown causes and reasons.

9.   *The Elaboration of Refined Knowledges.*

Out of the total matrix of knowledge and experience, which I have been describing, arise the more sophisticated disciplines, the knowledges which are deliberately elaborated as *knowledge*.

There is a sort of knowledge which begins with direct experiential insight and is elaborated by continued insightful reflection and insightful inference. Here, we reach ontological intelligibilities; we discard description in terms of the sense qualifications of experience, we reject constructs, surrogate intelligibilities and mathematical relations. Here, we must grasp the ontological reality, express it intelligibly as it is; we must see the *per se* relationships and connections, understanding them to be ontologically necessary and because ontologically necessary, therefore, intelligibly necessary.

Physical reality becomes subject to this sort of knowledge in its broad lines as consisting of existing entities, qualified as extended and interacting. Existence, extension, change, causality, the transcendental attributes of being are examples of the themes so developed. So the disciplines of metaphysics and of natural philosophy are elaborated. But these disciplines, though dealing with matters of ultimate significance are powerless to penetrate into the intelligibility of material entities in their specific natures or in their particularities. It is of high moment to know that physical reality is a contingent existence demanding a *per se* cause of existence beyond itself, but from this nothing about gravitation, or electricity, or nuclear energy can be deduced or extracted.

Outside of a few direct insights, we have no immediate grasp of the specific intelligible natures which constitute physical reality. *Essentiae rerum materialium sunt nobis ignotae.*

But this does not mean that our resources for exploring and knowing physical reality are exhausted. There is first of all the continuous revelation of the physical world through the sense qualities of our encounter with it. True, these do not simply express ontological or even intelligible features of reality itself, but their natural correlation with the shifting events and entities of the world supply us with a set of natural surrogates, susceptible of refinement to high precision and of organization so as to reflect physical reality and afford prediction and control. Thus, definitions of some chemicals, such as sulfur and gold, in alchemy incorporated not only certain ontological qualifications of extended objects (as, for example, solidity) but also sense qualities of experience like color and taste. These sense qualifications form the basis of taxonomy in botany and ornithology and are used, to a greater or lesser extent, in chemistry and in many other disciplines.

These definitions can be rendered fairly precise by careful observation, description, and selection of traits. Moreover, rules, patterns, and models, reflecting the relationships of reality itself, can be empirically established in terms of such definitions and brought to the level of genuine generalizations though the ultimate *per se* ground of the generalization remains unknown.

In effect, we thus build disciplines out of definitions, laws, and explanations which are surrogates for the *per se* intelligibilities we cannot reach. Yet such knowledge structures are neither false nor arbitrary. To be sure they are a move away from the ontological reality, but they are related to it and, to a large extent, determined by it.

10. *Knowledge Through Mechanical Explanation and Mechanical Models.*

A second type of knowledge which falls short of ontological intelligibility and yet reveals a great deal about physical reality is understanding through mechanical explanations and mechanical models.

I take a machine to be essentially a combination of physical parts so arranged as to use the qualities and/or forces or the parts and/or force transmitted from without in order to achieve some effect. The essential intelligibility of a machine lies in its design. If I know the design I have a *per se* knowledge of the functioning of the machine, the "why" of its operation or effect. But I understand the machine only on condition that beyond the design itself I stipulate the necessary qualities of the specified materials and the necessary forces—none of which are in themselves ontologically intelligible to me. For example, a combustion engine which makes use of a gravity feed can be understood, provided we stipulate the force of gravity. But we do not grasp the intrinsic intelligibility of that "force." Thus, as Mendeleeff said, "Without knowing the cause of gravitation, it is possible to make use of the law of gravitation."[3]

I know of no discipline which makes exclusive use of mechanical explanation, but it is clear that there are mechanisms in nature and that we have discovered a large number of them. Thus the circulation of the blood, the movement of the tides, the flowing of springs, etc., involve at least some moments of mechanical intelligibilities. It lies, however, in the very nature of mechanical explanation that it will always be superficial, never complete, never ultimate. No single mechanical model nor any combination of mechanical explanations can exhaust the intelligibility of physical reality.

11. *The Development of Modern Physical Sciences.*

Finally, there remains that sort of knowledge of physical reality in which the most spectacular successes have been achieved. I refer to the development of scientific disciplines in which the mode of conceptualization is a brilliant extension of the ability of our intelligence to create viable and effective constructs when ontological insights are lacking, in which the typical constructs result from the quantification of experience and the operational control of experiential data through imposed experimental methods.

Here then, in the physics of Galileo and Newton, and, more so, in contemporary physics, is a discipline in which the conceptual description of physical reality avoids both ontological intelligibilities and the mixed constructs of sense quality descriptions. Because of its use of mathematics, it is more purely intelligible than the latter, but, perhaps, less ontological. In any case, however, the concepts are still controlled, to a large extent, by reality as selected by the experimental method. The laws, which express patterns of activity or correlation in physical reality, are likewise, based on constructs and experimentation, not on insight. The type of explanation is, therefore, different as well.

---

[3]Quoted in Gerald Holton, *Introduction to Concepts and Theories in Physical Science* (Cambridge: Addison-Wesley, 1952), 423.

At the level of first generalization or laws, the effort is to express relationships in mathematical formulae, to substitute numbers and mathematical relationships for any concept of nature. Thus, as this effort succeeds, the expression of qualitative traits—whether in purely ontological terms or in the sense-quality descriptions, tend to disappear, and their physical correlates become more and more only points of reference for measurements. Thus, to take a simple example, in mechanics time and motion are dealt with in various mathematical formulae, but no qualitative definition of either is intrinsically necessary to the movement of the discipline or the understanding and use of the formulae. When "t" appears in a formula, only a highly ludicrous situation would result from attempting to substitute a definition instead of a number. Really, one needs only a way of measuring time; he need have no insight into the nature of time, just as a clock maker can make an accurate clock without even worrying about what time really is.

Thus, by accepting a methodological use of constructs, modern physical science has rendered itself independent, logically and epistemologically, of the ontological insights of common sense, of metaphysics, and of the philosophy of nature. To the extent that it succeeds in restating its concepts in mathematical and operational terms, it moves away from the semi-constructural type of definition offered by sense-quality description.

The first level of mathematical generalization and those higher in mathematical formulae, which are logically derived from the first level, express physical reality in such a way that that reality can be controlled and events predicted, but without affording the intellect an insight into the underlying nature of physical reality. Hence, viewed as theoretical knowledge, it is somewhat like the knowledge given by a simile when only one side of the comparison is known.

Now, this first level of generalization arises immediately out of the experimental data and is controlled by them. At this level, then, we can predict according to the generalization, provided the new situation repeats the conditions under which the first data were given. In other words, we go up to the generalization and return to physical reality by the same methodological path.

But no discipline can be content to rest with empirically imposed laws. There is always a pressure to push on to higher generalization, to explanation and broader theoretical construction.

In the early period of modern science, this pressure had a strong ontological orientation, and, in the seventeenth century moved, by preference, toward mechanical explanation. To achieve an explanation in nature the scientist steps back, as it were, and asks himself what sort of structure or nature reality could have in order to yield a measurable correlation such as he has discovered. Hence, at this point, there is a logical break in the upward movement; there is a leap of imagination through the opaque methods he has used into the realities beyond.

In his experimentation with gases, Robert Boyle discovered a correlation between volume and pressure. This yields simply a mathematical equation, which can yield only further mathematical equations. But, here the scientist stopped mathematics and asked himself—what is the nature of a gas, such that it could yield this correlation? In answer to such questions, the scientist has frequently proposed what is called a "mechanical model." Imagine gas to be structured in such and such a way; then, from a mechanical standpoint, it is clear why this correlation would result; indeed would be expected, indeed necessitated. But the model, being a concrete mechanical pattern, can be seen to have yet other deductive possibilities; not only must Boyle's law result, but such and such other empirical observations should be forthcoming. So a fruitful experimental verification begins, the original model is changed as verifications are extended, or perhaps entirely rejected when finally it becomes impossible to adjust it to the increasing data.

But the important thing here is the logical break, for the upward movement is logically broken. We cannot say, "If Boyle's law is correct, gases must have this structure"; all we can say is, "if gases have this structure, Boyle's law is inevitable." And each new verification, by experimental testing of deduction, must be added to the conditionatum; the model remains, always hypothetical, as long as there is no direct independent observation of it.

This kind of theory was not unknown, either, before the seventeenth century. In fact, ancient astronomy provided an excellent example. The reduction of the phenomenal movements of the heavens to compositions of circular motions of various orientations, velocities, and sizes, first worked out in Plato's Academy, as an excellent example of a mathematical theory joined to a mechanical model. The theory functioned as "accounting for" observed phenomena, enabled accurate predictions, and was flexible enough to adjust to more precise or more extended observational data. Aristotle, of course, made of this mechanical model an ontological fact (a mistake parallel to the reifaction of "ether" in the nineteenth century); however, the Greek theorists recognized precisely the fact that this was in the nature of a supposition and Simplicius clearly described the logical status of such hypotheses. Thomas Aquinas adopted and repeated the identification of this type of "*ratio*" or theoretical reason.

It should be noted at this point that the logical break in the upward movement was to a large extent ignored. Not only did the scientific workers imagine that their hypotheses were genuine efforts to describe reality but they came to consider well-tried theories as being a statement of the actual situation. There are reasons in the history of ideas, why such views prevailed, but, in more recent times, the hypothetical and purely functional character of model-theories has been clearly recognized. For the most part, as components of, or moments in, a scientific discipline, mechanical models or metaphysical theories have the same logical and epistemological function as mathematical theories.

We may call the sort of hypothesis used by Robert Boyle an hypothesis *of fact*. It was intended to be a theory about how gases really are structured, a theory which could be verified as a fact, if and when independent observation became possible. Hypotheses of fact have been used in many areas of the study of physical reality, not only as matters of general theory (as was the hypothesis of ether for those who thought of it as proposed natural entity) but as explanations of individual situations. The discovery of Neptune may be cited as an illustrative case.

In the first half of the nineteenth century, astronomers were confronted by an apparent violation of the law of gravitation in the anomalous motion of Uranus. Various explanations were offered—a deviation from the law of gravity, an unseen resisting medium, an unseen satellite and others. Adams and Leverrier, however, assuming that Newton's law held even in that remote part of the solar system, calculated the position of an unknown planet which could account for the anomaly. Galle, following this directive, searched for the planet and actually observed it. Neptune had been added to the map of the solar system.

This case illustrates a very important epistemological point.

I have observed that the basic structure of physical scientific knowledge translates data into measurements and mathematical relationships and so moves away from the sense-quality-descriptive sort of knowledge. When, however, a hypothesis of fact is introduced at an upper level of theory, in most cases its verification requires a return to the sense-quality level of experience. When Adams and Leverrier calculated the position of the new planet, they did not logically deduce a planet as this is understood from ordinary observation. Logically, they merely located a point as a subject of measurements. The movement to the descriptive idea of a planet was easy because of habitual correlation but epistemologically it was a leap from one sort of knowledge to another. Once the planet was observed and described *observationally*, it could then be geometrized and incorporated into astrophysics.

Now, while explanation-by-hypothesis-of-fact continues to be used in many fields, especially in the more descriptive disciplines (geology, geography, etc.), the tendency of modern physics has been rather to bring the first level generalizations under the deductive control of higher mathematical generalizations or laws.

This can happen two ways. A higher mathematical formula can be drawn, logically and mathematically, from a number of different first-level formulae. In this case, the same formal rigidity and neatness characterizes the derivation of the higher formula as well as the subsequent deduction of the lower formulae.

Or, on inspecting a group of lower formulae or laws, the mind may envision a broad mathematical model, including but extending beyond the known cases. Here, again, there is a leap of insight, a creative flash of imagination, but the resulting formula lies open to rigid deduction to new experimental situations and so to a very pure type of systematic verification.

I have been describing a kind of knowledge of physical reality which begins with experience out of which brute facts, which can initially be described and identified by a sense-quality-observational description, are selected as subjects for contrived operations which yield mathematical and/or operational concepts, laws, and theories. The tendency in some areas like modern physics is to purify the discipline more and more of any intrinsic use of sense-quality knowledge, yet without destroying the correlations maintained through experimental contact with sensibly discernible fact. It seems to me that this purification is particularly evident at the highest level of theory in current physics.

On the other hand, many sciences maintain an intrinsic and disciplined use of sense-quality description sometimes with little or no quantification (as for example in descriptive botany) but sometimes with a correlation between mathematical theory and sensible fact which is intrinsic to the discipline.

Of this latter I think chemistry offers some excellent examples. Descriptive definitions of the elements which include sense-quality data as formal and intrinsic parts are still part of the science itself. But these definitions are now correlated with the periodic table which is itself formally established on quantitative grounds.

12. *Summary: Three Basic Kinds of Knowledge and Their Elaboration into Disciplines.*

I have been saying that we can discover three fundamentally different types of knowledge which arise from our experiential discovery and exploration of physical reality. All three of these types are found in various combinations and rudimentary developments in man's natural knowledge life.

They come to be formally distinguished and formally interrelated only as we undertake to develop knowledge for its own sake.

The grasp of fully ontological characters by an intellectual experiential encounter with physical reality can be elaborated into various philosophical disciplines through insightful reflection and insightful inference. These disciplines are ontological, that is, the intelligibilities dealt with are intellectual expressions of reality, intellectual transcriptions of what really is. But this sort of knowledge is limited both intensively and extensively.

We can have this sort of knowledge only of a few traits and relations of reality. As a philosopher, I would maintain that, from the speculative standpoint, these are the most important traits of physical reality—but undeniably this knowledge is limited in its extent. But it is also limited in depth. Though what I can understand of the act of existing is literally and directly true of physical beings, I can never attain a full comprehension of the act of existence of even the humblest of physical realities. This would be a divine vision, and it is the original sin of the rationalist to think that *he* has this vision.

Next there is the knowledge of real things grasped in and expressed in the sense qualities of experience. Here we can no longer speak of genuinely ontological knowledge for this knowledge is precisely in terms of qualities which are subjective-objective correlates and which cannot simply be understood as ontological characters of physical reality. This is knowledge—an obscure and mysterious knowledge—of reality—but a "constructural" knowledge. Hence, when our ontological insights are elaborated into disciplines, they must be disentangled from the sensible qualities. Metaphysics must be purely intellectual.

In addition to these primitive knowledges, we readily elaborate our knowledge by all sorts of manipulations, constructions, etc., the most important mode being that of operational-mathematical definitions and method. Knowledge of this sort is epistemologically formally different from either of the previous types, but while it cannot be formally incorporated in an ontological discipline as a theoretical knowledge, it can be combined with sense-quality knowledge in various disciplinary ways. Through these various elaborations a vast extension of our knowledge of physical reality has been possible.

We are then faced with a certain radical and irreducible pluralism in our knowledge of physical reality. Epistemology can order these knowledges, and new ways of elaborating and exploiting them can no doubt be devised, but there is no way, finally, to translate an ontological concept into a sense-quality descriptive concept into an operational concept into a purely quantified concept.

13. *A Final Question.*

I would like to close with a glance at one last question. Can the elaboration of the non-ontological disciplines, for example, modern physics in its highest theoretical range, yield any new ontological knowledge and so substantively contribute to philosophical knowledge?

It seems to me quite clear that it has not and cannot do so directly. No "piece" of physics can simply be taken over and inserted in metaphysics. Yet, since physics, no matter how constructural it may be, is still knowledge of the world, can it ever be brought under philosophical reflection so as to yield new clues to the ontology of physical reality?

Frankly, I do not know. It seems to me that there has been no case in which this has happened, but I am not prepared to exclude the possibility.

BIBLIOGRAPHY

Caldin, E. F. *The Power and Limitations of Science*. New York: Harper, 1949.

Collins, James. "Philosophical Discussion in the United States: 1945" *The Modern Schoolman*, 24 (1947), 65–81.

Crombie, Alastair C. *Augustine to Galileo: The History of Science, A.D. 400–1650*. London: Falcon Press, 1952.

Hawkins, Denis John Bernard. *Causality and Implication*. New York: Sheed and Ward, 1937.

____. *The Criticism of Experience*. New York: Sheed and Ward, 1945.

Henle, Robert J., "A Thomistic Explanation of the Relations Between Science and Philosophy," *Bulletin of the Albertus Magnus Guild,* 4 (1956), 4–6.

Lee, Otis. *Existence and Inquiry*. Chicago: University of Chicago Press, 1949.

V

THE BASIS OF PHILOSOPHICAL
REALISM RE-EXAMINED

New Introduction: Having taught the history of modern philosophy for a good number of years and likewise an annual course in Epistemology, I am naturally brought up to face the problem of realism and idealism in modern philosophy. Since I have given a great deal of thought to this problem in my life and I finally came to the conclusion that I have discovered a fundamental solution which would not only explain natural realism that is the universal conviction of all men untainted by philosophical thought, that there is a real existing material world, etc., and with answers of philosophical problems as well. Without that conviction, I decided to present my final position in this article.[1] Furthermore I had presented a position at some length in my *Theory of Knowledge*. I have been disappointed that so few people seem to consider this solution as important as I do. In fact in my own mind I consider the identification of the integral touch experience as my greatest contribution to Philosophy.

I consider my identification and analysis of the integral touch experience to be my most important contribution to neo-Thomistic epistemology. I have been very disappointed that it has not been more widely recognized as an intuitive basis for direct realism. I believe that it furnishes a certitudinal intuitive basis for both a natural and philosophical realism.

---

[1] First published in *The New Scholasticism,* 56, no. 1 (Winter 1982): 1–29.

* * *

In order to make the exercise of this article easier and more open to discussion, I am going to ask you, by a self-denying act, temporarily to divest yourselves of the philosophical positions and categories which you now use in dealing with our primary experiences and to do a fresh, perhaps a new and different, reflection on that experience.

The experience with which we start is the consciousness or awareness of adult normal people. I am not talking about introspection or the awareness of our own subjective acts, I am talking about the open, comprehensive awareness which we have in dealing with our world—which indeed does include but is not limited to our subjective activities.

I am not thinking of "inside" and "outside" our awareness. Such language surreptitiously imposes spatiality on our consciousness and distorts all subsequent analysis.[2]

---

[2]Cf. Kenneth T. Gallagher, *The Philosophy of Knowledge* (New York, 1964), 44–46.

"Any evaluation of Descartes should center not on his methodic doubt but on the accuracy of his description of consciousness. Give or take a few nuances, the employment of the methodic doubt is inevitable in epistemology, for it is simply the critical method self-consciously used, and criticism is the business of epistemology. The real question is whether Descartes, in turning the light of criticism upon consciousness, has really succeeded in tracing its authentic outlines. Contemporary philosophers, who by and large disagree with the Cartesian viewpoint, concentrate their fire on his analysis of the structure of consciousness and the present chapter will follow suit.

By way of preface, we may begin with an admonition which is elementary, but whose usefulness extends much further than its application to Descartes' thought. For, concealed at the base of all subjectivism, including Descartes', is a false image of consciousness which thwarts all attempts to break through to realism. This is the image of consciousness as a container "in" which reality is present. Only rarely, of course, would things be stated quite this baldly, but the attitude is operative even when it does not find its way into verbal formulation. It is a perfectly natural attitude, as is evidenced by our everyday manner of stating the relation between consciousness and its object. What I am aware of, I am prone to say, is "in" my awareness; what I am not aware of is "outside" my awareness. Reality as present to me at any given moment is "within" my consciousness. Sometimes we go on to say that it is "in my mind." And sometimes the image is pushed to the clearly untenable limit of saying that it is "in my head."

However spontaneously we may fall into this way of speaking, it is nonetheless ruinous. For, having posed matters in this way, I am stuck with the image and with its consequences. The consequences are dire indeed. For the briefest reflection will give rise to an inevitable question. If what I know is "in" my consciousness, then how does

Before going to the point of this article, I have to lay down certain preliminary results which I can only indicate to you here. These results are not, in my view, assumptions or postulations but insightfully established results. I can not validate them here. You may already agree with them. If you do not I ask you to accept them, as assumptions. The first of these is that we find two radically different kinds of apprehensive awareness of objects, sense and intellect. Epistemologists call both of these knowing powers. Sense is to the sensible as intellect is to the intelligible; thus they can both be called "knowing" but, since every element in this equation is qualitatively different from its corre-

---

it ever allow me to make contact with what is "outside" my consciousness. My consciousness is *my* consciousness, a subjective occurrence in me; it is within me, and my knowledge therefore leaves me locked up inside itself. There is no need to think that Descartes proceeded according to this explicit image (if he had, its shortcomings would have been more evident). The point is that his way of stating the problem, his way of describing consciousness, is only possible if the image is implicitly operative in his thought. His problem is that of winning through to the "other," and certifying the varied status of the "other." This must mean that he does *not regard the other* as a primitive datum for consciousness, and hence that reality as present primitively to consciousness is not present as other but as "within" the consciousness of the subject: its credentials of otherness have still to be verified. Many a modern philosopher has been trapped into a similar subjectivist beginning by this implicit conception of consciousness as a container. Once the image is identified, it may be summarily dealt with. For if anything is clear, it is clear that we cannot seriously compare consciousness to a container or receptacle.

To demonstrate this we need only contrast the manner in which a contained thing is literally in a container with the manner in which the known thing is "in" the knower. A literal relation of container and contained is a relation between two spatially external objects. When an orange is in a crate, it makes perfect sense to say that the orange is from one standpoint still *outside* the crate. That is, the orange is not within the wood of the crate; it is surrounded by it, but it is nevertheless still spatially juxtaposed to it. Orange and crate are touching one another, and hence externally related: it is perfectly possible to mark off the limits of each to say just where the crate stops and just where the orange starts. Now obviously this is not so with the relation of consciousness to its object. When I am aware of the orange I cannot tell where my awareness "leaves off" and where the orange "begins." I cannot point to some point in space and say "Here I, as knowing subject, stop, and here the object as known begins." My awareness is not juxtaposed in space to this orange, not touching it, not outside it. True, my head and the orange are spatially related to each other—but this only proves that consciousness in not going on "inside my head." My consciousness does not stop at the limits of my head, at my eyeballs, or halfway between my head and the orange. My consciousness is not spatially related at all to the orange."

sponding element, knowledge-language can be used of them, only analogously.

The second presupposition is that we have only one consciousness and that this unified consciousness is completely penetrated by intellectual awareness. The materialist and the reductionist break our knowing into a system of material parts connected by a material process. But traditional scholastic analysis has also tended to give the impression that achieving knowledge is a sort of spiritual mechanical process. I would ask you to forget all that for the moment and reflect on your consciousness.

Intelligence penetrates, englobes, includes the whole of our awareness. At any moment we can direct our attention to any "part" of our awareness and instantly express what we experience in a judgment, that is, in an intellectual grasp and expression.

To put this in terms of formal objects: The formal objects of the specific senses formally exclude each other—one cannot taste color or hear odors—and also formally distinguish sense from intellect. But the formal object of intelligence encompasses all the sense formal objects. I can only see colored objects. I can only hear noises. But I can intellectually recognize both colors and noises and *intellectually know* that I see colored objects and hear noise and this by immediate reflection.

To put the same thing in terms of level of powers: St. Thomas says that the higher power can do all that the lower power can do but in a more excellent way. Or as Cajetan says the higher power working with the lower power "*coatingit*" the object of the lower power.

I am using these more sophisticated expressions only as a means of pointing to the fact I am here stressing. The actual pervasiveness of intellectual awareness is a fact which can be intuited by direct reflection.

The next presupposition is a corollary of the previous one. It is impossible to study sense knowledge, qua knowledge, i.e., epistemologically, in separation from intellectual knowledge. There is no way to establish the "validity of the senses" in themselves. The task is meaningless and impossible.

Against the background of these assumptions, I now approach the main point of this article. If we sit back and look around, letting our attention wander through our total awareness, we find that we are aware not only of those things which I can see—the wall in front of me, the people within visual reach, but also of the room and building in which

I am, the wall back of me, the back of my own head. I am aware of, recognize, and place many sounds—a car going by, the wail of an ambulance. . . . But also with regard to the things of which I am aware because I see them—I am aware of much more about them than arises from just the present perceptual experience. I am aware of the people I perceive, as human beings. I cannot see, hear, taste, smell humanness.

Ordinary people who are neither philosophers nor scientists never have a doubt about the objective reality of their habitual world. This prephilosophical realism is at least an ineradicable subjective certitude. Even Hume admitted that when he descended to the dining room all skeptical doubts disappeared. And Descartes thought it so firm that he could use it to argue that thereby God, being the author of this natural certitude, guaranteed the existence of a material world. But I do not believe that even for ordinary people this realism has only a subjective certitude. On the contrary, it is an objective certitude resting on massive evidence. I never use the term "naive realism" because there is no such thing.

The purpose of philosophical reflection is to turn this objective certitude of the ordinary person into a philosophical realism and to raise and deal with questions which rarely, if ever, arise in the commerce of ordinary affairs. To do this, we must reflectively examine our integral awareness in order to find the evidence the existence of which is attested to by the universal conviction of all ordinary people. This universal conviction is, of course, not self-justifying and, *a priori*, it conceivably could be wrong. But any philosophy that makes nonsense of such a universal view is at least highly suspect.

Certainly, it is clear that what I have called our habitual awareness of self and world or of self with the world contains many things for which there is no immediate justification. There is no immediate justification for saying "I hear a fire engine going up Grand Avenue" or "That dessert looks delicious." We learn to judge distance and size, we learn to associate disparate experiences and to use clues. If such things are to have an objective validation, we must probe our total experience to find the first principle of realism, the undeniable evidence on which all the rest of our habitual and actual awareness is founded. We come thus to the decisive moment in the philosophical treatment of realism. It is here, I am convinced, that most epistemologies have gone astray, never to return to the right path. I cannot inductively present my position through all the laborious efforts of the *via inventionis*.

Brevitalis studio, I am forced to adopt at this point a more didactic procedure. I will simply state the position.

The certitudinal evidence for philosophical realism is to be found in the perceptual acts which consist of cooperative sense and intellectual awareness and in which the "sense" is an integral touch exploration.

Important points should be noted. (1) "Touch" is the sense that puts us in direct and immediate intentional contact with the real world. (2)"Touch" must be taken in its fullness as a "perceptual system." I am not talking about touch "sensations," but about perception. James J. Gibson makes this point very clear.

> It has always been assumed that the senses were channels of sensation. To consider them as systems for perception, as this book proposes to do, may sound strange. But the fact is that there are two different meanings of the verb *to sense,* first, *to detect something,* and second, *to have a sensation.* When the senses are considered as perceptual systems the first meaning of the term is being used.[3]

Touch viewed as a perceptual system is "active touch": it must

---

[3] *The Senses Considered as Perceptual Systems* (Boston, 1966), 1. Gibson found this basic distinction in Thomas Reid:

"The external senses have a double province; to make us feel, and to make us perceive. They furnish us with a variety of sensations, some pleasant, others painful, and others indifferent; at the same time they give us a conception, and an invincible belief of the existence of external objects. This conception of external objects is the work of nature. The belief of their existence, which our senses give, is the work of nature; so likewise is the sensation that accompanies it. This conception and belief which nature produces by means of the senses, we call perception. The feeling which goes along with the perception, we call sensation. The perception and its corresponding sensation are produced at the same time. In our experience we never find them disjoined. Hence we are led to consider them as one thing, to give them one name, and to confound their different attributes. It becomes very difficult to separate them in thought, to attend to each by itself, and to attribute nothing to it which belongs to the other" (*Essays on the Intellectual Powers of Man,* II, p. 17).

Reid was certainly right in making this distinction and right in accepting the validity of our perceptions. Unfortunately, he was content to accept this validity as "natural" and never displayed the basic evidence for it.

explore objects and this implies movement.[4] (3) As "active" or "exploratory" touch can be directed by intelligence and monitored by intelligence. Recall what I said above about intelligence permeating all awareness. (4) "Touch" is not simply a fifth sense; it is a genus and therefore includes a variety of specific sense experiences. But in any integral touch exploration all these subsidiary senses are interrelated so that the skin, muscles, and tissues can be viewed as the "organ" of "touch."

Now I am going to ask you to do three reflective "experiences."

The First Experience. (It helps to focus attention if the participant is blindfolded or, at least, closes his eyes.) Grasp any solid object that can be held in the hands and explored by them. First focus on the internal muscular tensions in the hands and the arms. You may emphasize these experiences by squeezing the object. You are aware of these experiences as being within your hands, muscles, tendons, etc. No one objectivates these experiences; no one thinks that there might be a reality in the object corresponding to the feeling of tension in the muscles. Now, note that I not only "feel" these tensions; I am immediately aware of them also intellectually. I can immediately say, "I know that I feel tensions in my hands." This knowledge is judgmental; it is intellectual.

---

[4]The phrase "active touch" is the title of a book the subtitle of which is "The Mechanics of Recognition of Objects by Manipulation." Unfortunately, it does indeed deal with "mechanics," the physiology, anatomy and psychology of touch recognition. Yet it does include some clinical evidence confirmatory of my position. *Active Touch*, ed. George Gordon (Oxford, 1978). If one remembers that the book deals with "mechanics," interesting support can be found in the following from p. xiii:

" 'If I could only move my hand about I should know what the things were.' This was said to Victor Horsley (1909) by a patient who was asked to identify various familiar objects placed in his hand three weeks after the arm area of his precentral gyrus (the so-called motor area') had been removed surgically. He could feel himself being touched; he knew approximately where he was touched, and the position of his fingers; but he had an enduring disability in moving them. This showed 'what the real basis of the stereognostic sense is—namely, merely a complex of tactile, muscular and arthric memories of movements, which are, in fact, the compound experiences of grasping and feeling objects.' This is a view few would disagree with today; saving only the word 'merely,' because the detailed mechanisms underlying manual recognition, some of which we now have the methods to study, are by no means simple."

T. A. Quilliam shows how the fingertips are specially adapted for exploration ("The Structure of Finger Print Skin," pp. 1–18). Montague also emphasizes the special sensitivity of the hands and of the mouth for exploration.

Now, secondly focus on any feeling you might have of hot or cold. This focus can be emphasized of the object has been warmed or cooled in advance. Depending on the circumstances you will be aware if a feeling of warmth or coolness *in your hands*. You can also be aware that you have immediate intellectual awareness of this feeling. But the feeling of hot or cold, the cold or hot feeling is consciously found in the hands. This can be made clearer if one places the hand flat and fully down on a hot surface for a time. On removing the hand one continues to be aware of the "hot" but is no longer aware of an external surface.

I pause here for an anticipatory reflection. I need not go into the evidence that feelings of hot and cold are not only subjective ("in the hands") but relative. But I do want to point out two things. (1) Neither the relativity nor the subjectivity of the hot-cold feelings in any way attain the objectivity of touch perception. Whether I find an external surface through a feeling of warmth or through a feeling of coolness makes no difference to the objectivity of the total perception.[5] (2) With regard to the temperature sense, one cannot defend the traditional doctrine that the proper formal objects of each sense respectively "exist formally in reality."[6] This theory ignores the facts of experience and misinterprets the epistemological meaning of "formal object." I will return to this later. Now, back to our exploration of the object. Do you feel what we normally call "smooth" or "rough"? Again, you cannot only focus on the feeling of "smooth" or "rough" but you can make an immediate judgment based on the immediate intellectual awareness of the situation. Here we are closer to the surface of the object; we are dealing with a real qualification of the surface, though just the awareness of "smooth" or "rough" cannot fully reveal the real surface. We must notice that *the degree* of awareness can be subjectively modified. If the fingers are sandpapered (as in safe-cracking) or heavily callused or if the participant has taken certain drugs, sensitivity to

---

[5] It is astonishing how often the relativity of the hot-cold sense is used to eliminate any consideration of touch as a basis for philosophical realism. Thus Joseph De Vries, *Denken und Sein* (Freiburg in Breisgau, 1937), 180.

[6] "With the same clarity the senses actually witness to and reveal the formal existence in reality of both the common and the proper sensibles. In fact, perception of the common sensibles presupposes perception of the proper sensibles. Hence, the proper sensibles exist formally in reality." Reginald F. O'Neill, S.J., *Theories of Knowledge* (Englewood Cliffs, NJ, 1959), 44.

"smooth" and "rough" will vary. Yet, the subjectivity is not as clear as in the case of the temperature sense. One cannot retain the feeling of smoothness immediately after removing the hand from a smooth surface as one can retain the feeling of warmth after removing the hand from a hot surface.

Now we come to the crucial aspect of this experience. Through this complex of conscious experiences and beyond them you are intellectually aware of an object that is external and distinct from you. You can be aware of this as soon as you grasp the piece of wood; you can make your awareness clearer by moving your hands over the wood. There is no specific sense experience or internal sensation that corresponds to or mediates this awareness of an object. Through and in this complex of active-passive experiences you become clearly and certitudinally aware —intellectually with direct and unmediated intellectual awareness—of an object that is distinct from you and really existent. Move your hands over the wood; you immediately understand (grasp intellectually) the object as distinct from yourself, extended in three dimensions, resistant (you cannot put your hands through it or squeeze it together), having a determined shape and size and, at least for the moment, stable and unified. There is no barrier of sense images or sense impressions standing between your intellectual awareness and the object. Your intellectual awareness reaches the object directly through and with the sense awareness involved.

This experience is not esoteric, unusual or contrived. It is a sample of natural human experience which has been multiplied into a thousand instances in everyone's life. This repetition of a basic realistic experience explains the massive conviction of all men that they deal with a real world. Note that the requisite experience is an integrated sense (touch) and intellectual (insight) awareness, that it involves movement and exploration and that it requires an expanded contact. It is simply the same kind of exploration that we see babies and young children do. It is difficult to analyze this experience accurately. And so I ask you to do a second experience.

The Second Experience. Place your hand flat on the top of a desk or table, then move it about. Reflect carefully. You are aware of changes in your hand, of the very surface of your hand in contact with the top. But you are just as aware of the surface as distinct from you. As you move your hand about, you immediately recognize the difference between the stationary surface and your moving hand. Now move your hand over to the edge and slowly move your hand off the surface (not upward). The clear awareness of the external surface is emphasized by your awareness of the end of the surface and your gradual loss of contact. Vary the contact. Move your hand off the edge then bend it to fit the top and side. Play your hand back and forth in various ways. Concentrate now on your awareness of your hand and now on your awareness of the "other" surface. This experience is well described by Katz:

> The fact seems to be that touching a solid object one can attend either to the external resistant or to the impression on the skin. The reader should try it. Within limits, you can concentrate either on the edge of the table, say, or on the dent it makes in *you*. It is as if the same stimulating event had two possible poles of experience, one objective and the other subjective. There are many possible meanings of the term *sensation*, but this is one: the detection of the impression made on a perceiver while he is primarily engaged in detecting the world.[7]

As I have repeatedly pointed out, this reflection requires one to approach experience in a new and fresh way, to break through the usual categories, theories, classifications and habitual interpretations to apprehend this experience in its given reality.

The Third Experience. Place your hands together, palm to palm, rub them together in different ways, separate them, then place them surface to surface and move each hand differently. You will realize what Katz is describing.

In these experiences we have found not only the fact of a real world but also our primary and primitive definition of a real world.

First of all we discover intellectually the basic and ordinary meaning of "exist," of existential being, which we express in our immediate judgment of perception. We hereby understand independent subsistence. We can define "material" as extended in three dimensions and solid (that is, as resisting and maintaining a comparatively stable three dimensional shape). We find thus structure, interrelationship, and

---

[7]*Der Aufbau der Tastwelt*, D. Katz (Leipzig, 1925), 19, quoted by Gibson, *The Senses,* 99.

multiplicity. Moreover, all this is presented to combined sense and intellectual awareness with physical, sensism, and intellectual immediacy.

If we have correctly reported what we ineluctably find in this reflection, we have identified and defined the objective certitudinal evidence upon which realism rests. *By this operation, natural realism has been turned into philosophical realism.*

This can be confirmed by the fact that there are *no illusions* of *objective existence* in touch-intellectual perception. The illusions alleged by skeptics from the beginning of philosophy are mostly within visual experience. The reason why there are, as a matter of fact, no illusions in the touch-intellect perception is clear if one reflects on the total experiences just described. The existence of an external object is an essential *sine qua non* for those experiences.[8]

One can simulate the clutching of an object and thereby generate inner muscular sensations without any perception of an external object. One can artificially excitate "hot" and "cold" sensations without any awareness of an object. But the difference between these experiences and the integral operational exploration of an object is sharply defined in awareness.

Any psychologist may immediately retort that there are illusions of touch. The finger immersed in mercury does not "feel" the continuous increase in pressure downwards. If this is an illusion, it is not an illusion with regard to the objectivity of existence. One cannot have this experience without really touching real mercury. If one places a pencil or stick between two fingers, he will seem to be aware of *two* objects. This situation, noted already by Aristotle, if illusory, concerns only the number, not the existence of real objects. An external object is a *sine qua non* of this experience. Besides, any haptic exploration removes the error (if there is one).

There are no illusions of objective existence in the touch-intellect experience. If our analytical reflection is correct the reason for this fact

---

[8]What Yves Simon says of all external sensation is absolutely true of integral active touch: "L'universal est dans l'âme; une fois que sa forme y est imprimée on peut oublier la manière dont elle y a eté deposée: l'absence physique de l'objet n'importe, sa forme demeure dans l'âme et ne cesse de la rendre apte à s'unir intentionnellement à lui. Le singulier sensible est dans la réalité extérieure, *l'âme ne peut s'unir à lui que sous l'influence toujours présente de la réalité extérieure.*" (Emphasis added). *Introduction a L'ontologie du Connaitre* (Paris, 1933), 165

is that illusions in touch-intellect perception are impossible. The reason *for this* is the epistemological/physical direct contact; the immediacy of the subject-object relationship.

Now we go on to the next part by laying down a didactic thesis: No sense other than integral touch, whether taken singly in itself just at the sense level, or as a complete "perceptual system" including intelligence, or in conjunction with one or more other senses (other than touch) provides a certitudinal basis for realism. To counterbalance this thesis I assert that once we have developed our habitual awareness of the real physical world we can use all the senses to detect things and aspects of things in this world and express them in perceptual judgments that are generally valid[9] or easily subject to correction.

The basic problem in the history of realism is that most attention has been given to the sense of sight. Touch has indeed been studied and discussed by both philosophers and psychologists but rarely in respect to its fundamental role in realism. Thus Ashley Montague remarks,

> One would have thought that the remarkable versatility of the skin, its tolerance of environmental changes, and its astonishing thermostatic and tactile capacities, as well as the singular efficiency of the barrier it presents against the insults and assaults of the environment would have constituted conditions striking enough to evoke the interest of inquirers into its properties.
>
> Strangely enough, until relatively recent years, this has not been the case. Indeed, most of what we know about the functions of the skin has been learned since the 1940s. Though much knowledge has been acquired, of both the structure and the physical functions of the skin, much more remains to be learned.[10]

But even when psychologists have dealt with aspects of touch their

---

[9]Note that I am maintaining the general validity of these perceptual judgments only as long as they are within the familiar context of one's habitual awareness (the complex group of phantasms which combine with present sense experiences to give a full perception of any situation). The plainsman easily errs in judging distance when first he travels in the mountains.

[10]*Touching: The Human Significance of the Skin* (New York, 1971), 3–4.

findings have had little value for epistemology.[11] There have been notable exceptions such as D. Katz, Ashley Montague, James J. Gibson, and A. Michotte.[12] Philosophers have treated the sense of touch either in dependence on the general theory of the senses or with reference, not to realism as such, but only in respect to special problems like Molyneux's question.[13] Occasionally the certitudinal value of touch is recognized but it is rarely given specific substantial epistemological treatment. Thus Yves Simon remarks in a *footnote*:

> The strongly asserted presence of the heteronomic passion in touch has, no doubt, something to do with two well-known characteristics of touch sensations: on the one hand, they are rough, clumsy, generally unable to achieve fine discrimination. On the other hand, they enjoy unique certitude. When we wonder whether what we apprehend is physical reality or illusion, we trust our hands more than our sight or hearing.[14]

---

[11]What Gibson says of "sensory physiology" is true of most "sensory psychology" as well and refers to all the senses. "A vast literature of sensory physiology has developed and a great deal is known about the receptors. It is a highly respected branch of science. But all this exact knowledge of sensation is vaguely unsatisfactory since it does not explain how animals and men accomplish sense perception," *The Senses*, 3. The most comprehensive presentations of the data, experiments and theories of psychologists and physiologists with reference to the senses are the works of H. Pieron, *The Sensations*, tr. by M. H. Pirenne and B.C. Abbott (London, 1952), and F. A. Geldard, *The Human Senses* (New York, 1953). Despite the vast learning of these books, they have very little to offer the epistemologist.

[12]*Der Aufbau der Tastwelt* (Leipzig, 1925), a neglected pioneering book; Ashley Montague, *Touching: The Human Significance of the Skin* (New York, 1971); James J. Gibson, *The Senses Considered as Perceptual Systems* (Boston, 1966); A. Michotte, *The Perception of Causality,* tr. T. R. Miles and E. Miles (London, 1963). Gibson refers also to Ivo Kohler of Innsbruck, *The Formation and Transformation of the Perceptual World* (International Universities Press, 1964), and Gunnar Johansson of Uppsala, but I am not acquainted with their positions. Gibson provides an extensive bibliography, *Senses,* 322–329.

[13]Molneux's question, addressed to Locke, was greatly discussed and debated through the eighteenth century. The most recent comprehension treatment of the matter is Michael J. Morgan, *Molneux's Question* (Cambridge, 1977).

[14]"An Essay on Sensation" in *Philosophy of Knowledge,* ed. Roland Houde and Joseph P. Mullally (Chicago, 1960), 60.

One of the few philosophers who has given touch perceptions the primacy they deserve is Ortega y Gasset:

> Now, as I have said, touch differs from all the other senses or modes of presence by the fact that in it two things are always present at once and inseparable; the body that we touch and our body with which we touch it. The relation then, is not between a phantom and ourselves, as in pure vision, but between a foreign body and our body.[15]

And again:

> And if this is so, touch and contact are necessarily *the most conclusive factor in determining the structure* of our world.[16]

The point may be illustrated by the famous penny so dear to the British analysts. The penny is constantly "seen" as having a variety of shapes; there is only one (or two) viewpoint from which one actually "sees" the "true" shape of the penny. If examined by touch, however, there is only one perception of its shape, and that an irreducibly valid perception. But the analysts do not make this appeal to touch. Instead, they work out complicated theories of "sensa" or whatever and then extend their theory to all the senses.

Thus, Pappas says, "The penny case is used by Broad as an example, and the points it serves to bring out and the conclusions reached concerning it are supposed to be applicable to other perceptual cases. Accordingly, the results reached with respect to the penny case are held to be generalizable across all other *visual* cases, and *further generalizable across the other sense modalities*"[17] (emphasis added).

The modern empiricist (phenomenalism—linguistic analysis, etc.) approach to perception by way of analyzing visual experience is generally traced back to Descartes (whose rejection of sense as a principle of knowledge was based largely on visual illusions), yet this approach antedates Descartes and has beginnings far back in classical culture.

---

[15]*Man and People* (New York, 1957), 72.

[16]*Ibid.*

[17]"Broad, Sensa, and Explanation" in *Studies in Perception*, ed. Peter K. Machamer and Robert G. Tumbull (Columbus, OH, 1978), 414.

Ancient skepticism appealed to many of the same phenomena as modern empiricists—color experiences such as the multitude of colors on the neck of a pigeon, double vision, after-images, etc. In the fourteenth century Peter Aureolus collected a series of such "experiences" as a basis for his study of perception. Every one of his "experiences" relates to the phenomena of vision. In fact, his list is a summary of the examples of this sort adverted to in classical, Arabic, and early medieval philosophy.[18] Hume and others simply repeat the classical list.

> I need not insist upon the more trite topics, employed by the sceptics in all ages, against the evidence of *sense*; such as those which are derived from the imperfection and fallaciousness of our organs, on numberless occasions; the crooked appearance of an oar in water; the various aspects of objects, according to their different distances; the double images which arise from the pressing one eye; with many other appearances of a like nature.[19]

Thus, the skeptical attack on realism has almost always proceeded from an analysis of the sense of sight and the transposition of this analysis to all the senses, though more often than not, the other senses are ignored or cavalierly dismissed.[20]

---

[18]For a brief summary of his positions see Julius R. Weinberg, "The Problem of Sensory Cognition," in *Essays in Knowledge and Methodology*, ed. Simmons (Milwaukee, 1965), 29–40. For a more extended treatment see Michalski, K., "Le Critique de la Scepticisme dans la Philosophie du XIVe Siecle, *Bulletin International de l'Academie Polonais des Sciences et des Lettres*, An. 1925 (Cracow, 1926), 41–122.

[19]*Enquiry Concerning Human Understanding*, Sec. XII, Pt. I. Hume however seems not to have used the argument from illusions as a conclusive disproof of realism. Rather he argued from an *a priori* subjectivism: "But this universal and primary opinion of all men is soon destroyed by the slightest philosophy, which teaches us, that nothing can ever be present to the mind but an image or perception, and that the senses are only the inlets, through which these images are conveyed, without being able to produce any immediate intercourse between the mind and the object" *(Ibid.)*. For a full discussion of these points see Maurice Mandelbaum, *Philosophy, Science and Sense Perception* (Baltimore, 1964), 123–170.

[20]De Vries is typical. He "disproves" immediate realism by analyzing an example of visual perception. "Die Frage, um die es sich handelt, ist eine ganz audere: Ist das Gegebene, wie es als weiß, ausgedehnt, bewegt, in einem bestimmten Abstand von

Since, however, the universal conviction of the ordinary man does not rest upon visual experience but upon the massive, pervasive and almost unnoticed tactile experiences and, since this realism can be turned into philosophical realism and given objective certitude (reflective evidential certitude) only be a thorough examination of our cumulative tactile experience, the whole discussion of the "illusion" and "errors" of visual experience is simply beside the point.

It is true that a polemical argument can be made that the face of our ability to discover and correct illusions indicates that we do have some objective knowledge, but it does not uncover the basic evidence for realism.

---

meinem Körper befindlich unmittelbar gegeben ist, so such als an sich seiend (existierend) unmittelbar gegeben? Das ist keineswegs ohne weiteres klar. Denn daβ etwas weiβ, rechteckig, bewegt, auβerhalb meines Körpers ist, das sind zunächst alles nur Soseins-bestimmtheiten; all das antwortet nur auf die Frage nach der kategorialen Beschaffenheit des Gegenstandes (quale, quantum, ubi sit usw.), nicht aber auf die Frage nach dem Sein schlechthin (an sit). Ohne Zweifel kann mir die Phantasie, z. B. im Traum, das alles in ganz ähnlicher Weise vorstellen. Auch da erscheint der geträumte Gegenstand auβerhalb des eigenen Körpers; aber der eigene Körper, insofern er gesichtsmäβig vorgestellt ist, gehort eben mit zum Trauminhalt. Das zeigt deutlich, daβ mit dem, "auβerhalb des eigenen Körpers sein" das Sein schlechthin, d. h. das bewuβtseinsunabhängige Ansichsein, noch nicht unbedingt gesichert ist. Es ist damit noch keine unmittelbare Evidenz gegeben, daβ nicht etwa das Sein all dessen, was uns da unmittelbar erscheint (mitsamt dem eigenen Körper), nur ein "percipi," d.h. nur ein Vorgestelltsein im Bewuβtsein, ist. Und das ist in der Frage nach dem unmittelbaren Realismus das Entscheidende: Die Seinsweise des durch die Sinne unmittelbar Gegebenen (ob nur vorgestellt oder anischseiend) ist nicht unmittelbar evident. Die These des sich also." Joseph De Vries, *Denken und Sein* (Freiburg in Breisgau, 1937), 177

All this can be conceded, if one takes this visual experience in isolation. All De Vries shows is that the infallible evidence for philosophical realism is not to be found in an abstract consideration of visual "phenomena." He does indeed take brief note of the sense of touch, but he quickly dismisses it on the ground of the relativity of the temperature sense and the temporary mislocation of pain in amputees. "Auch die Einschrankung des unmittelbaren Realismus auf den Tastsinn hilft nichts. Denn auch der Tastsinn erfaβt nicht das Seiende als solches; auch bei ihm gilt, daβ die Phantasie im Traum ganz ähnliche Vorstellungen hervorbringen kann; und schlieβlich kommt es such bei ihm vor, daβ der Gegenstand anders erscheint als er ist (jedenfalls kann nicht dasselbe Wasser zugleich warm und kalt sein). Ebenso beweist die Möglichkeit von Trugwahrnehmungen in Bezug auf den eigenen Korper—man denke etwa an die Trugwahrnehmungen von Amputierten 12—, dab auch der eigene Korper nicht in wesentlich anderer Weise gegeben ist als aubere Körper." *Denken*, 180. For another example see O'Neill, *Theories*, 38–47.

On the other hand, the discussion and defense of realism has almost always likewise centered on the sense of sight.

Thus, Joseph de Tonquedec, in his masterful exposition of Aristotelian and Thomistical positions, in dealing with the major objections against the objectivity and veracity of sense knowledge, under the rubric "*Les objections 'Scientifiques'*" discusses almost exclusively objections from visual phenomena (color phenomena, illusions, hallucination). Some objections are drawn from the "scientific" account (physics, physiology, psychology) of sensation but of touch proper only the relativity and specificity of the isolated tactile sensations are mentioned.[21]

Another point must here be made. Unsophisticated people are quite certain that they "see" real things, where they are, and, in some respects, as they are. I am not going to say that they are completely mistaken. On the contrary, I will maintain that we do see real things within an integral perception based on sight. The position I will take is that this valid objectivity is ultimately in function of our integral touch experience and not because of any objectivity intrinsic to vision. To be sure the "common man" may find our explanation surprising, but his inability to provide an adequate explanation for himself leaves him open to the manipulation of the skeptic.[22]

It is perfectly obvious that many of our perceptual judgments in sight are partially or wholly based on learned skills, associations, clues, etc. For example: Watching for a train on a straight run of track, I see first a tiny speck which grows larger as it approaches. I don't say: "The

---

[21]Joseph de Tonquedec, *La Critique de la Connaissance* (Paris, 1919), 91–132.

[22]"He [the "common man"] reads the idealist and positivist out of court when it comes to the *conviction* that things exist. But should the idealist persist in his questioning, he will probably win the day. Any idealist who knows his business can trick the non-professional realist into a blatant contradiction. The man of common sense, strong as he is on judgment, is often weak on reason.

The man in the street is positively certain that things exist; his knowledge signifies the real world; his knowledge is *representative* of reality. Therefore—he is asked by the idealist—do you say that knowledge is a representative of reality? Knowledge—answers the realist—*must* be a representation of the thing known; knowledge, most certainly, is a copy or an image of what really exists outside the mind. And when the realist has gone this far (prodded by the skilful questioning of the idealist), he has talked himself right out of realism." Frederick D. Wilhelmsen, *Man's Knowledge of Reality* (Englewood Cliffs, NJ, 1956), 76.

train is getting bigger," but "The train is getting closer." When I blow up a balloon I don't say, "The balloon is getting closer" but "The balloon is getting bigger."[23]

All such "learned" uses of sight to "detect" things in the actual world must be ignored for the time being. I will first examine the apprehension of "colors." It has of course been recognized from the earliest times that the quality of color experience is relative. In fact every sighted person is aware of it. The peasant knows that the play of color in his fields is different under full sunlight and under lowering storm clouds. It didn't take Hegel to tell us of the night in which all cows are black. The changes of light, illness, eye injury, or congenital defects all modify the quality of color experience. Tinted glasses change the color appearance of the world. Stage lights dramatically modify the colors of settings and costumes. And so on. The skeptic has used these facts to prove that color experience is purely subjective and purely relative, without objective representational value or objective correlation.

The realist has often contended that, while color experience is relative to many factors, there is a set of "normal" or "natural" conditions under which the senses (and therefore sight) attain their proper objects as they really are. There is therefore a "true" color existing *formally* in the object which the "normal" eye apprehends and so the color-blind person learns from the testimony of most other people that his color experience is defective and false.[24]

On reflection, however, we find that the relativity of our quality-color experience is present not only in what we call abnormal situations but also in normal ones. It is quite possible that some evolutionary change in human genes could produce almost universal color-blindness. Then the sighted few would have to accept, on the testimony of the

---

[23]It is possible to set up an artificial experimental situation in which it is impossible to interpret an apparent change in size. In ordinary experience our learned interpretations depend on an integral context.

[24]"Let us now try to determine where error lies in those "falsified" apprehensions of sense qualities. If a color-blind person asserts that there is no difference between what normal people call a red light and what they call a green light, his error resides in a judgment. This sort of error can be corrected, without improvement of vision, provided the color-blind person is willing to trust the majority of his fellow men and to concede that he is unable to perceive a difference that others hold obvious." Yves Simon, "An Essay on Sensations," *L'ontologie du Connaître,* 85.

majority, that their color apprehension was defective and false. It is possible that an evolutionary development could produce in us a faculty of vision that would have a range of color experiences qualitatively totally different from our present range. These changes could take place without any change in the constitution of objects. Also, possibly, a large strange body could come hurtling through space and plunge into our sun, permanently changing the constitution of sunlight. Everything would look differently in "daylight" than things look now. The so called "true" or "real" color is only a statistical normality or usualness.

Note here that the thorough-going relativity of color experience in no way destroys or even lessens the possible objectivity of vision itself. I look at a colored object. The realist question is not, "Do I see a real quality of 'red' in the object" but "Do I detect a real thing by means of the 'red' color."[25] I look at a red object. I "see" my French Dictionary. I put on green glasses, I "see" my French Dictionary. I put a square of transparent purple glass in front of the object. I still see my French Dictionary. Whether I "see" it as green, red, purple, muddy, or whatever, I can still "see" the object. As a knower, using the sense of sight, I attain the object by means of experienced color. This is the very definition of the "formal object" of a knowing faculty; it is that way or means by which I attain, come to know, an object. Change all the colors in my room and I will still see my room, recognize my things and detect the structure and organization of the room and of its contents. Once this is realized, all the skeptical objections based on color, collapse. The pigeon is real no matter what his color, and the horse "of a different color" in *The Wizard of Oz* remains the same horse despite his color phantasmagoria.

By the same token the argument for the formal reality of colors based on the fact that we see extended things only because of color disappears.[26]

---

[25]Chisholm is close to this distinction when he reduces apprehension of "red" to being appeared to redly. See *Person and Object* (La Salle, IL, 1976), 47–50.

[26]"*Common Sensible Grasped Through Proper Sensible.* This explanation, however, does not yet determine clearly enough just how the quality is said to be in the object, whether formally or merely causally. It has already been seen that the common sensible is truly objective, and the same should be said of the proper sensible, since I do actually perceive both. In fact, I *see* extension precisely insofar as it is colored, and the loss of the ability to see a colored thing involves the loss of the ability to see an extended thing,

Do not think that I am in any way depreciating color as an intentional means of gaining knowledge about the world and dealing with it. But the use of color to see objects of itself yields no infallible certitude about the real existence of a material world.

An experience of "red" viewed as a sensation (i.e. as a subjective modification) can be reflected upon as a psychological event,[27] and thus treated as a "thing" (just as we can reflect on our concepts as psychological realities), but as such it neither represents the real world nor yields knowledge of that world (except insofar as we can establish a physical causal link between objects in that world and the sensation). Thus there is indeed both a psychological and physical aspect to our color experience. But when we consider colors as they function epistemologically, we see that they are intentional signs which we learn to use to identify, distinguish, and locate sensible objects. We intentionally project the seen color in the point of origin.[28] So that we see the color

---

because it literally means the loss of the ability to see. The senses, in other words, witness to and reveal what is; and their witnessing reveals not only the common but also the proper sensible. Hence both are objectively or formally in reality. This does not mean that my knowledge of proper sensibles presupposes my knowledge of common sensibles or that I establish the objectivity of the proper by reliance on the common. Rather, what has been said of the objectivity of the common sensibles can also be said, even *a fortiori*, of the proper sensibles, since in my grasp of sensibles the latter have a priority." O'Neill, *Theories of Knowledge,* 42–43.

[27]Note that this reflection is highly selective. "Sensation" is thus an abstraction. Cf: "The worst difficulties of the present subject originate in our inability to achieve the experience of a sensation free from association with images, instinctive judgments, memories and thoughts. If it were possible for us to suspend no matter how briefly, all such associated representations and processes, if it were possible to elicit pure sensations and yet to watch ourselves sensing, the understanding of sensation would, no doubt, be greatly facilitated. But sensation is the center of a complex, and from this complex it cannot be extracted, except by rational analysis. Experientially considered, sensations always exist in the vital unity of wholes. By reason of this unity, we attribute to senses the apprehension of things which are neither sense qualities nor modes of sense qualities." "An Essay on Sensation," Yves Simon, *Philosophy of Knowledge,* 56.

[28]This is very like the projection of awareness in using a probe.

"A similar projection takes place in the use of tools and probes, and the process can be studied here more easily, since the stimuli that are projected here can be fairly well observed in themselves. The relevant facts are well known. The rower pulling an oar feels the resistance of the water; when using a paper-knife we feel the blade cutting the pages. The actual impact of the tool on our palm and fingers is unspecifiable in the same sense in which the muscular acts composing a skillful performance are

where that point of origin putatively is. This is perfectly clear in reflection. It is a scandal to materialists, for this fact cannot be explained or in anyway accounted for by physicalistic causal theories or neurological-brain event description.

This intentional projection of a color and identification of it with a material object is valid, only on the assumption of the existence of a material world. Once we have discovered the real world, through integrated touch exploration, and developed our gross habitual awareness of that world, we can then learn to use sight objectively and fruitfully to "detect" that world.

The basic reason why sight has no independent and self-justifying apprehension of really existing things is that visual experience "of objects" can be duplicated without the presence of the appropriate objects. The ancients thought of magicians' acts and of staging. Today we can think of three-dimensional movies and of TV presentations. But the most modern confirmation of the fallibility of sight with regard to object is the new holography.

The director of the Cincinnati Art Museum leans forward, squinting in the darkened room for a glimpse of his favorite sculpture. A needle of ruby-red light stabs the blackness and

---

unspecifiable; we are aware of them in terms of the tool's action on its object, that is, in the comprehensive entity into which we integrate them. But the impacts of a tool on our hands are integrated in a way similar to that by which internal stimuli are integrated to form our perceptions: the integrated stimuli are noticed at a distance removed outward from the point where they impinge on us. In this sense impacts of a tool on our hands function as internal stimuli, and a tool functions accordingly as an extension of our hands. The same is true of a probe used for exploring a cavity, or for a stick by which a blind man feels his way. The impact made by a probe or stick on our fingers is felt at the tip of the probe or stick, where it hits on objects outside, and in this sense the probe or stick is an extension of our fingers that grasp it." Michael Polany, *Knowing & Being* (Chicago, 1969), 127.

For intentional adjustment within our integrated perceptions, cf. Polanyi's description of the "upside-down" glasses. "The normal way of seeing objects 'right way up' satisfies our self-set standards of coherence between visual and tactile, as well as proprioceptive, clues. Spectacles which invert our retinal pictures make us see objects 'upside down.' But after a few days' habituation to the spectacles the eye restores coherence once more by seeing things now *right way up through the spectacles.* On removing the spectacles, objects now appear *upside down, without the spectacles,* but eventually coherence is restored again by the re-establishment of *normal vision*" (I. Kohler, *Die Pyramide,* 5 [1953], 92–5; 6 [1953], 109–13). *Personal Knowledge,* 97.

a shimmering image leaps into life, a small Fourteenth Century religious work of Mother and Child. Its delicate lines and exquisite form draw even the casual observer. Three dimensions—height, breadth, and especially, depth—need no imagination. They exist. The director stands in total concentration. His eyes search every square millimeter of the familiar image. He bobs and weaves his head, seeing everything, missing nothing. He straightens in the still-dark room, turning to his unseen companion. "But why did you light my sculpture with that silly red lamp?" Room lights snap on, blazing, and the art expert winces. The ruby beam dies. He blinks now, not in reaction to the brightness, but in amazement. His lovely little sculpture has disappeared. In its place, a sheet of smoky glass betrays no image, only swirls in the gray-green color, where seconds before stood the work of the unknown Spanish artist. The museum director did not see a solid statue. He saw a hologram, so lifelike that a viewer can distinguish it from solid reality only by trying to touch it—and ending up groping at empty air. . . .

A hologram is a three-dimensional image stored on a high-resolution photographic plate, exposed with a laser. After Wuerker develops his film and lights it with another laser, it recreates the image of space.[29]

Thus, the putative perception of existing material objects by using sight alone is not self-justifying.

A further confirmation of this is the fact that, even after we have learned to rely on sight, in the last analysis, we naturally turn to touch to resolve a doubt. Even the author of the excerpt above on Holography, who is not a philosopher, naturally refers to touch as the test of the holograph.

We awake at night. Is that a person, a being, looming up by my bed? I strain my eyes only to become more frightened; I watch for movement; I listen for breathing—finally I reach out—empty space, shadows, a natural holograph. Touch is the determinative test.

---

[29]"Holography: Photography in the Round," Don Bane in *The American Way* (Oct. 1979), American Airlines, 90–91.

Thus it is through exploratory touch and movement that we discover our real material world. In this process we correlate all our senses as perceptual systems; we learn to actively use them to detect the world. Gibson describes this process of "learning" with clear accuracy:

> If the senses are perceptual systems, however, the infant does not have sensations at birth but starts at once to pick up information from the world. His detection equipment cannot be exactly oriented at first, and his attention is imprecise; nevertheless, he looks at things, and touches and mouths them; and listens to events. As he grows, he learns to use his perceptual systems more skillfully, and his attention becomes educated to the subtleties of stimulus information. He does learn to perceive but he does *not* have to learn to convert sense data into perception.
>
> On the assumption that the senses are channels of sensation, the process of learning has been thought of by stimulus-response psychologists as an attaching of new responses to a fixed set of possible inputs. On the assumption that the senses are perceptual systems, however, the emphasis is shifted to the discovery of new stimulus invariants, new properties of the world, to which the child's repertory of responses can be applied. This is perceptual learning as distinguished from performatory learning. Both kinds of learning occur in the child, but perceptual learning is the more in need of study because it is the more neglected.[30]
>
> These five perceptual systems overlap one another; they are not mutually exclusive. They often focus on the same information—that is, the same information can be picked up by a combination of perceptual systems working together as well as by one perceptual system working alone. The eyes, ears, nose, mouth, and skin can orient, explore, and investigate. When thus active they are neither passive senses nor channels of sensory quality, but ways of paying attention to whatever is constant in the changing stimulation. In exploratory looking, tasting, and touching the sense impressions are incidental

---

[30]*Senses,* 5–6.

symptoms of the exploration, and what gets isolated is information about the object looked at, tasted, or touched. The movements of the eyes, the mouth, and the hands, in fact, seem to keep changing the input at the receptive level, the input of sensation, just so as to isolate over time the invariants of the input at the level of the perceptual system.[31]

Thus, when we have developed the use of these "perceptual systems" into a complex intentional system for detecting and discovering real things and real properties, we can normally rely on the intentional objectivity of our perceptual knowledge. In many cases of doubt we do not have even to go back to touch, since we have learned to explore and to cross-check by active exploration with all our senses.

Thus we learn to judge distances and sizes. We learn to locate the source of sound and to "hear" (intentionally) the sound at *the point of origin*. Thus, I hear a noise *downstairs*, a car *in the street*, or the telephone ringing *in my outer office*.

In all this learning, we are being guided and controlled by the objective structured material world which we are constantly (if unconsciously) rediscovering through integral touch perception.

Much of the interpretations, projections, and skills disappear in any given complete act of perception. They become intentional means, almost pure formal signs. Polany calls this "subsidiary" knowledge. Since Polany summarizes, in his own striking way, much of what I have been saying I wish to quote at some length.

> Ames and his school have shown that when a ball set against a featureless background is inflated, it is seen as if it retained its size and was coming nearer.[32] This illusion seems to be due to the fact that in this case we accommodate our eyes to a closer range, even though in consequence the object gets out of focus. Worse still, we simultaneously increase the conver-

---

[31] *Ibid.*, 4.

[32] This is Polany's footnote: A. H. Hastorf, "The Influence of Suggestion on the Relationship Between Stimulus Size and Perceived Distance," *J. Psychol.*, 29 (1950), 195–217. Cf. W. H. Ittelson and A. Ames, "Accommodation, Convergence and Their Relation to Apparent Distance," *J. Psychol.*, 30 (1950), 43–62; W. H. Ittelson, *The Ames Demonstration in Perception* (Princeton, NJ, 1952).

gence of our eyes so that the two retinal images are displaced from corresponding positions, which would normally make us see the object double. Those defects of the quality and position of our retinal images are accepted here by the eye, in the urge to satisfy the more pressing requirement of seeing the object behave in a reasonable way. Since tennis balls are not known to blow themselves up to the size of footballs, a ball which does so must be seen as approaching us, even though in shaping this sensation the eye must override standards of correctness which it would otherwise accept as binding.

The rule that we follow in shaping the sight of the inflated ball is one that we taught ourselves as babies, when we first experimented with approaching a rattle to our eyes and moving it away again. We had to choose then between seeing the rattle swelling up and shrinking alternately, or seeing it change its distance while retaining its size, and we adopted the latter assumption. By this way of seeing things we eventually constructed a universal interpretative framework that assumes the ubiquitous existence of objects, retaining their sizes and shapes when seen at different distances and from different angles, and their colour and brightness when seen under varying illuminations. . . .

In a larger perspective, the present experience of seeing the inflated ball come nearer to our eyes appears merely as the last of a life-long chain of experiences encountered and shaped by us, to each of which we reacted to make sense of it as best we could, and which are now all subsidiarily effective in the shaping and comprehension of our present experience. The sensory clues offered by the inflated ball thus appear to be evaluated together with an immense array of past clues, gone beyond recall—but *not* without effective trace. . . .

We owe Gestalt psychology much of the available evidence showing that perception is a comprehension of clues in terms of a whole. But perception usually operates automatically, and gestalt psychologists have tended to collect preferentially examples of the type in which perception goes on without any deliberate effort on the part of the perceiver and is not even corrigible by his subsequent reconsideration of the result. Optical illusions are then classed with true perceptions, both being described as the equilibration of simultaneous stimuli to a comprehensive whole. Such an interpretation leaves no place for any intentional effort which prompts our perception to explore and assess in the quest of knowledge the clues offered to our senses. I believe this is a mistake. . . .[33]

To sum up, any epistemological approach to perception must view it as a combined activity of sense and intellect in which intellectual awareness encompasses and penetrates the sense deliverance and activity. We must treat a sense faculty not as giving rise to "sensations" but as an active perceptual system. When we so examine perception as it involves all the senses we find our actual perceiving to be in function of the basic natures of the senses and the intellect and of learned skills largely in the intentional order but not limited thereto, and of a habitual awareness of a total sensible and existential context of the world around us.

When we analyze this complex perceptual activity we find that the objectivity of our judgments of sense perception rests ultimately on the integral touch perception wherein alone we reach sensuously and intellectually an existing material world and discover some of its basic structure. Reflection on the integral-touch-perception reveals that it is indubitable evidence, the undeniable grasp of reality, a first principle of our knowledge of being and of an existing material world.

---

[33] Michael Polany, *Personal Knowledge* (Chicago, 1958), 96–98, *passim*. It should be noted that Michael Polany, despite his brilliant analyses and his remarkable contribution to epistemology, does not find an essential difference between animals and men and, like so many others, places primary emphasis on sight with little attention to touch.

VI

AN EXPERIENTIAL APPROACH
TO REALISM

Now Introduction: When it was announced that a book as a tribute to Etienne Gilson should be planned, in view of my great admiration for him and the great intellectual debt I owed him, I was anxious to contribute to that volume. So I wrote this article[1] on something on which Gilson and I were in basic agreement, namely, direct realism. Gilson always held direct realism in its purity, but to my knowledge he never analyzed the basic evidence for direct realism as I have tried to do. And so I felt that I would be adding additional support to one of Gilson's major positions.

* * *

It is the purpose of this paper to present an approach to that evidence upon which, ultimately, philosophical realism as well as the realism of the common man rests. It is never an easy matter to bring basic evidence under personal philosophical reflection; a steady and, indeed, courageous effort is always indispensable.

The climate of contemporary thought is, however, particularly unfavorable to the sort of realism I am proposing. Hence, before going on to the evidence itself, a preliminary discussion of some of the assumptions which, from the start, rule out realism and prevent any serious consideration of its case is necessary.

---

[1]First published in *An Etienne Gilson Tribute* (Milwaukee: Marquette University Press, 1959), 68–85, as "A Phenomenological Approach to Realism."

Anti-Realist Assumptions

When a discipline reaches a certain maturity, having attained an inner homogeneous structure of fact, concept, and argument, an investigation of its methodology becomes possible. We isolate the methodology and set it down as a prolegomenon to the study of the discipline itself. Thus we are able to dictate beforehand the conditions of proof, the range of competency, and the criterion of legitimacy for the discipline. In a highly sophisticated intellectual culture like our own, which has been long preoccupied with questions of methodology, we come to think of the methodology as prior to and determinant of the discipline, and, when generalized, as prior to and determinant of all intellectual effort. No doubt, from the standpoint of logic, this sort of analysis of disciplines is legitimate, even indispensable, but to absolutize this priority is to limit intellectual legitimacy to those conditions already recognized in whatever disciplines we consider established. We come to forget that in the order of discovery we cannot determine conditions of proof until after we have solved the proposed problems. We actually discover the logic of mathematics, for example, only by examining successful mathematical thinking. I do not mean that we accept this logic *because* it succeeds in a pragmatic sense; but that, on inspection of successful mathematical thinking, we see such and such procedures and we see, by inspection, their validity. Without examples of mathematical thinking, there would be no method to perceive. I am saying that in all cases of evidence, we either do or can come to see its validity by intellectual insight. Consequently, there is no way of laying down, *a priori*, an exhaustive list of the types of legitimate evidence. Yet, we have come to assume and to demand evidence of a certain type.

It is part of the heritage of Cartesianism that, on the side at least of rationalism and idealism, genuine philosophical proof is expected to be of an abstract kind. It is only since Descartes that we have had a series of efforts to *prove,* in an abstract sort of way, the existence of an external material world. The assumption that only such a proof will be valid is to be found in all types of rationalism, even in certain rationalistic types of Thomism. Unless one is willing to reconsider this assumption, the case for realism is closed before trial.

On the other hand, we have an empirical tradition which demands proof within the limits of a certain type of factual evidence, often identified with the type of evidence proper to experimental science.

Within the framework of Humean epistemology or of logical positivism, there is no evidence for realism.

In short, the present situation in philosophy makes it necessary to request a suspension of accepted ideas of evidence prior to the examination of the case for realism. In this sense, realists must ask for a "fresh start," an open-mindedness in the matter of proof and evidence, not merely to establish their case but also to obtain a hearing at all. If the conditions of proof which realists must meet are laid down from current philosophical positions, realists will have nothing to say. A sympathetic attention to realist arguments requires then a powerful reflective effort to escape (at least temporarily and for the sake of argument) from the pervasive assumptions regarding conditions of proof—an effort all the more difficult, since, as Gilson pointed out, the non-realist is so unaware of the vast gulf which here separates him from the realist.

Modern thought commonly presents the possibility of only two types of philosophical structure. The great rationalists—Spinoza, Wolff, Hegel—present us with the idea of a philosophical system, logically interrelated, deductive, and, in a sense, closed and complete. Those who rebel against the vast ambitions of such systems tend, on the other hand, to see philosophy as constantly evolving, tentative, really without a single certitude that can claim any permanence. A realistic philosophy is neither of these; yet, in the face of current modes of thought, it is difficult even to explain what sort of structure it has. Since it is experiential, it cannot be *a priori* and deductive; since it is an effort to understand reality, it cannot be complete and closed. Since it is evidential, it will establish insights, arguments, and understandings with definitive though not exhaustive conclusiveness. It is difficult to categorize its structure in current terms, since it lies wholly outside of the assumptions of contemporary philosophy. It mediates the entrenched dichotomies, but not by a theoretical compromise. Rather it destroys the dichotomies at the start by a more comprehensive approach to evidence and by rejecting, on evidential grounds, the assumptions common to both sides of the dichotomies. If realism is expected to follow the patterns set within modern philosophy by Descartes or Locke or Spinoza or Hume or Kant or Hegel or Dewey, realism will have nothing to present. It is in the paradoxical position of being more experiential than empiricism yet intellectual, of being certain yet not concluded.

There is another pervasive modern influence which has conditioned our mentality against realism. The modern scientific movement, because of its vast success, both practical and theoretical, has penetrated all our thinking. It has seemed to discredit all other modes of knowing and has brought us, consciously or unconsciously, to accept the scientific mode of thinking as the univocally ideal one, if not the only valid and fruitful one.[2] It supplies the principal models for epistemological analysis and establishes the principal criteria for judging validity. Philosophers themselves have accepted these models and standards, have tried to make philosophy dependent upon science and conformed to its ideals of method.[3] I do not think any of us has escaped the pressure of this absolutizing of scientific method. But, again, unless we are willing to consider, at least, the possibility of other valid methodologies, realism need not be heard; it will be condemned out of hand.

Thus, realism does not compete on equal terms with other philosophies in the arena of modern thought. It cannot play the game according to the rules commonly assumed for philosophical discussion. It cannot join the discussion at the purely theoretical level, for it is opposed, in its very origins and foundations, to basic contemporary assumptions. This is why I have thought it necessary to prefix this brief and inadequate discussion of assumptions as a sort of prolegomenon.

The Method of Inquiry

And so we return to the problem of making a "fresh start." In a sense, of course, men must always make a fresh start in order to become philosophers, for philosophy is essentially a personal understanding and depends upon personal grasp of evidence. In this respect philosophy is quite unlike science. Scientists can build on the work of others without forever repeating the experiments and deductions others have made. It is enough that the experiments have clearly been shown to be repeatable, under controlled conditions, by competent practitioners. But, if a scientist need not reproduce all the experiments upon which his science

---

[2] For an extreme example of this attitude, see Homer W. Smith, "Objectives and Objectivity in Science," *The Yale Scientific Magazine*, 23 (February 1949): 2.

[3] *Cf.* Hans Reichenback, *The Rise of Scientific Philosophy* (Berkeley: University of California Press, 1951).

depends, the philosopher must personally repeat all the essential experiences on which philosophical understanding depends. He cannot build on the insights of other men any more than he can grow by another's digestion. Much less can he accept and peddle the conclusions, the phrases and terms, of another's philosophy. Surely he needs the aid of others, the guidance and inspiration of the great thinkers of the world, but this essentially consists in discovering for himself, under their guidance, the same experiences and the same reflections. Philosophy is essentially personal, yet, for all that, it is not subjectivistic, for we do indeed have essentially similar experience and share a common intelligence.

It is for this reason that scientific exposition, once the difficulty of technical terms is overcome, is essentially easy while philosophical exposition remains always difficult. The philosopher must aim to induce in his readers the same experiences and the same reflection as he himself has. Perhaps exposition is not the proper mode of philosophical communication and teaching. Plato's description of philosophical inquiry seems to me still the best.

> For in learning these objects it is necessary to learn at the same time both what is false and what is true of the whole of existence and that through most diligent and prolonged investigation, as I said in the beginning; and it is by means of the examination of each of these objects, comparing one with another—names, definitions, visions, and sense perceptions proving them by kindly proofs and employing questioning and answering that are devoid of envy—it is by such means, and hardly so, that there bursts out the light of intelligence and reason regarding each object in the mind of him who uses every effort of which mankind is capable.[4]

We must approach the enterprise of a "fresh start" as far as possible unhampered by assumptions, postulates, or preconceptions, but, above all, with a determination to take into account the evidence, all the evidence, the evidence in its fulness. I realize, of course, that, in speaking of "evidence," I am already using a sophisticated term which immediately raises the haunting specter of methodological disputes.

---

[4]*Epistle* 7.344b.

Even if we substitute a seemingly undetermined word like "fact," this, too, turns out to be a chameleon sort of term, taking its shading from backgrounds of epistemological theory. Yet somehow we must get behind or beyond theory to the underlying "given," the irreducible data which are prior to all theorizing.

It seems to me that the very fact that we are able to communicate at all—and we do so communicate—shows that we have some common experience and some basic common convictions. At the level of highly sophisticated theory, we become, often enough, mutually unintelligible, and our criticisms ineffective, yet there remains a basic communication between the adherents of even the most diverse theories. In this basic communication, our experiences of knowing, of thinking, of intelligence are, at least, very similar, and, however divorced from common ways our systems may seem, there are common points of fact which none of us can, in fact, ignore. We are men before we are philosophers and philosophers because we are men, and we cannot forget, as philosophers, those things that are experiences common to all of us as men.

And indeed it seems obvious that, in the history of human culture, all theories relate somehow to something encountered, unavoidably, in experience. No science or theory has even been elaborated as an explanation of something with which man has no contact of any kind, real or imaginary. People find plants and develop botany; man observes the spots of moving light in the night skies and begins to be an astronomer; we find ourselves reasoning and, reflecting on this process, discover the laws of logic. So also all discussions of knowledge relate to a certain experience or set of experiences—a certain "given" which men have found and, even prior to all theories, called by a distinctive name—the experience of knowledge.

Monsieur Jourdain of Molière's *Le Bourgeois Gentilhomme* was delighted to learn that, without knowing its definition or laws, he had actually been speaking prose all his life, however imperfectly. Thus, any man, who comes to a philosophical understanding of knowledge, must be able to see that *this is* what he had been doing all his life, however imperfectly.

Where, then, and how does any man make contact with this "given"? Where does he first discover it in human experience? It would seem obvious that knowledge is first discovered within personal experience by "reflection" on "acts" of spontaneous knowledge which even the child and the untutored savage (the mediaeval *rusticus*) have or make or suffer. For all our experimentation, no one has isolated "knowledge" from conscious experience. We may build up a collection of centipedes; capture and cage the platypus; produce pure hydrogen and cap it in a test tube. But knowledge cannot be chopped out in objective chunks, or cabined, cribbed, and confined outside of conscious experience. We first make contact with knowledge there, and there we must look if we would observe it in its natural habitat. This would seem to be an irreducible starting-point from which no one has ever wholly freed himself and to which, in the last analysis, we must all return. It is clear, then, that the very "given" of knowledge dictates a certain approach to it. If it "exists" or is "given" only in conscious experience, we must "look" at it there and this "looking" we call "conscious reflection."

Does this bring us, right at the start, to the "discredited" method of "introspection"? Well, what if it does? If there is no other place to look directly at the experience all the world has called "knowing," then introspection it must be. It may well be that, for certain purposes of experimental psychology, introspection has proved an inadequate and unreliable instrument, but this does not necessitate abandoning all use of it. And indeed we cannot. Even those who have attempted to study knowledge solely on its "objective" or "external" side really know what they are talking about and what they are explaining only from a pre-philosophical introspection. Without this, their whole effort to make knowledge the object of external observation would be meaningless. Introspection and reflection must be used at least to identify that which is being discussed; only through it is the specific and concrete "given" of knowledge discovered and a *common* basis for explanation established.

We must, therefore, "look" at knowledge as it goes on or is given, and this "looking" we shall call conscious reflection. This reflection must not be a casual interior glance, a mere "identifying" of the "given," but rather a prolonged gaze, a continuous and concentrated effort to "see" what knowledge is really like, for, as Chesterton has said, it is not easy to see something as it really is, even (or perhaps especially) when it is pervasive and obvious. On the other hand, we must abstain, initially, from all efforts to theorize, to infer, or to "explain." We wish, at first, only to report what is seen. Thus an examination limited exclusively to the "given" brings us to a first methodological stage which approximately coincides with the "phenomenology" described by Professor Wild, . . . the disciplined attempt to describe and analyze the immediate data of awareness as they are given."[5]

It is an indispensable peculiarity of this kind of description that we do not here report facts beyond others' experience, as a traveler does in describing foreign countries to his home folk. We are not trying to communicate through vicarious experience; rather, the method sets up, through its reportorial description, pointers and guides which will enable others to find and identify and "see" the same data within their own personal experience. By the same token, the process is not a demonstration, a logical proof, but a "monstration," a pointing-out. We have analogous experiences. "See that cloud there?" "Where?" "Up there, to the left of the large mass." "Yes, yes." "See how it resembles a camel, the hump toward the north and down there the four feet." "Yes, yes, I see it; it is indeed very like a camel." So two experiences are found to agree; a common "given" is established. This is our purpose: to sift experience and our descriptions of it until we reach a common agreement on a mutually and truly discovered given.

Derivative Knowledge

When an adult begins—when, let us say, he moves from being just a man to being a philosopher—to reflect upon the pieces of knowledge which he possesses or fancies he possesses, he readily discovers that

---

[5]*The Return to Reason* (Chicago: Henry Regenery, 1953), vii. The phenomenological method here described must not be identified with the philosophy of Husserl. Thomism itself stands in need of a thorough but preliminary phenomenology. As a living philosophy, it has suffered many of the same pressures as other modern philosophies and too often has allowed itself to be forced into a rationalistic framework. Faced by the modern type of problem, Thomism has had no way, without a phenomenology, to maintain its unique grounding in experience. In this situation rationalistic Thomists have become far less experiential than was either Aristotle or St. Thomas. A phenomenology will not only ground Thomism in its own right here and now, not only open up intercommunication between all modern thinkers, but will also make it more loyal to its historical origins. Professor Gilson has noted that traditional metaphysics has lacked a phenomenology which it needs.

"Mais il n'est pas moins nécessaire à la métaphysique de l'être de s'appuyer sur une phénoménologie qu'elle dépasse sans pourtant s'en séparer. C'est pour avoir manqué de ce lest salutaire, qu'elle s'est si souvent perdue dans le vide de l'abstraction pure et qu'elle a cru pouvoir user du concept comme d'un équivalent du réel." *L'être et l'essence* (Paris: J. Vrin, 1948), 728.

these pieces display marked differences. He knows that the world is round, that Columbus landed in the West Indies, that his little girl likes candy, that $f = ma$ is a formula of physics, and so on. Obviously, a great deal of his "knowledge" is derivative and second-hand. He has never had first-hand experience of the shape of the earth; he knows it because he learned it in school, or because he knows the proofs developed by geographers and astronomers, but he only understands what it means and accepts it as fact because of prior knowledge. Let us exclude from our first investigation all the knowledges which are obviously derivative and if one makes trial of this, he will find, I think, the greater part of his knowledge is in this category.

Direct Acts of Underived Knowledge

We thus find ourselves reduced to instances of origins of understanding as well as factual acceptance, to instances that seem to display an immediacy and directness not characteristic of conclusions or elaborations. Let us take, then, a simple case. I take a block of wood in my hands and examine it. Before I found this block of wood, before I saw it and handled it, I knew nothing of this block of wood. True, before it entered my experience, I knew, somehow, something which I subsequently use to understand it. I may, for example, say at once that it is a "book end." I previously knew something of books and how they are held upright. I may call it "wood"; I previously knew this strange noise "w-o-o-d" and its significance—certain characteristics by which I recognize the sort of thing meant. I come to this piece of wood equipped with, so to speak, ready-made "understandings" which I apply to it. As I consider this concrete experience, I see, however, that this previous knowledge equipment is usable only because here and now, as this piece of wood enters my conscious experience, I know it directly. It is this direct knowledge of the piece of wood which determines my selection of previous knowledges and my application of them to this wood. Thus, by reflection, we can distinguish these two kinds of knowledge and can set aside, for the moment, the previously acquired knowledge. Obviously, as it functions in this instance, it is derivative and lacks the immediacy we are looking for. What we are interested in is my direct knowledge given or gained in *this* experience.

Sense and intellectual Awareness

As I hold the wood in my hand and reflect upon the concrete experience, I become aware of the high complexity of this simple, everyday act of knowing. I can, in fact, distinguish different layers or aspects or factors within the concrete unity of the act. I can distinguish an experience in which I am immediately aware of certain "qualities": the wood is "smooth"; the wood is "cool"; the wood is "hard"; and so on. This awareness itself is double: I am aware in a sort of "feeling" way, I shall call this the level of "sensing." At the same time and in the same concrete act I am aware at a level of consciously and self-consciously possessed recognition. *I feel* that the wood is cool; *I know* the wood, the coolness and the feel of it. I shall designate this level as the "intellectual level."

I am here merely pointing to a primitive distinction within awareness. That sense-awareness and intellectual-awareness are radically different kinds of awareness, and what these differences are can only be "seen" by continued reflection and by a similar use of many different sorts of knowledge experiences. Since I am only schematizing the line of reflection, let me simply assert the fact of these two types of awareness and let this rough characterization serve for the present.

Here I must point to a difficult but extremely important fact. The level of intellectual awareness is not related to the level of sense awareness, as an inference to a premise, or even as a second-step to a first-step. There is an experiential interpenetration of the two levels, such that the intellectual awareness (with its accompany-self-awareness) is in as immediate contact with the objects of sensing as is the sense awareness itself. It is very difficult to express or describe this unique and concrete experience which is unlike any other experience we have. Perhaps nothing in the data of our knowledge experience has been so obscured and disfigured by theory. Sense and intellect were sharply not merely distinguished but separated, by Descartes, for example; the intellectual was reduced to the sense, by Berkeley, for example; the intellectual was ignored, by Hume. It seems to me obvious that, in the direct act of knowing a material thing, the sense and intellectual levels interpenetrate, maintaining distinctive characteristics indeed, being, that is, what they are, yet not compartmentalized, not operating like successive stages in an assembly line, but together in a mutual immediacy.

Let us return to the experience itself, for we must remember that our method requires us to examine the complexity of the act while maintaining its concreteness and its experiential unity. No facet or factor can be allowed to assume, in our reflection, an abstract and independent status.

The Immediacy of Knowledge in Direct Acts

Now, we find that within this experience we can say of the wood, "This is a thing" and "This is an extended thing." Let us reflect upon this situation. The awareness, at both the sense and intellectual levels, which is (partially) expressed in these statements, depends upon the presence of the wood in my hands. Remove it and I cannot so speak because I am not so aware. Place it there and I am able confidently to make these assertions.

When I am directing my attention to the wood I hold in my hand, I find that the experiential awareness is not an awareness, initially and simply, of some concept, idea, image, or feeling—some modification of myself. On the contrary, in the immediate experience of the wood, I am quite *unaware* of whatever concepts, images, or subjective modifications may be present. The experience itself in its concrete totality presents itself to my reflection as an awareness of an existing extended thing. It is factually false to say that by my direct acts of underived knowledge I immediately know only concepts or ideas from which I must, somehow, infer an existing object. On the contrary, in my direct acts of underived knowledge, my knowledge and the attention of my mind terminate immediately at the existent thing.

Since the seventeenth century it has been widely accepted that we know first and immediately subjective modifications of our own minds or bodies, concepts or ideas. This assumption was common to both rationalists like Descartes and empiricists like Hume; it was taken over, almost without examination, by Kant. It has reached the status of an obvious fact. A genuinely independent examination of our knowing experience yields quite different report. The assumption stands in contradiction to the facts. Reid and others have pointed this out. Thus Professor Joad has gone so far as to say, "Almost I would go to the length of maintaining that we never know our own ideas."[6] What Professor Joad asserts is true of our immediate acts of underived

---

[6]C.E.M. Joad, *Decadence* (New York: Philosophical Library, n.d.), 130.

knowledge. It requires an interruption of the act itself, a realignment of activities and indeed discursive argumentation to discover the concepts and ideas through which we know. What is obvious is that we know directly an existing thing. Since it is the *thing* that we *know*, the activities *by which* we know are no part of *this knowledge*.

The realist, therefore, challenges the assumption that in acts of underived knowledge our awareness is limited to the immanent products or operations of our own consciousness. And he challenges it, not on another assumption or because of philosophical consequences, but as a matter of fact and experience.

Partial Subjectivity of Sense Experience: Objectivity of Direct Intellectual Knowledge

Let us describe the factual situation from a slightly different standpoint. The sum-total of "objects" which, in this experience, stand over against awareness are not adequately reported as an assemblage of sense data, of coldness, smoothness, roundness sensed. Reflection on experience shows that this is a distorted description:

(1) because our awareness does not terminate at sense qualities but at a thing ("this feels cold" is a report of immediate experience); (2) because our awareness of the thing is not simply a sense awareness; intelligence penetrates to the object through the sense awareness; (3) because what is immediately understood of the wood is not only sense qualities but non-sense aspects—"This is a thing," "It exists," "It is extended." The sense data description is an abstraction which ignores evidence and omits precisely the crucial evidential facts.

The complex apprehensions within our awareness as we consider the piece of wood in our hands cannot be expressed in a single statement. We must say: "The wood feels cold"; "This is a thing"; "This exists"; "This is extended"; and the like. I have already pointed to the distinction between sense-apprehension and intellectual-apprehension. I have tried to point to the sense-apprehension by describing it as a sort of "feeling" experience. The wood "feels" cold; it does not "feel existently" or "thingly." The very expressions we use for the sense-level experiences convey (what I reflectively discover with clarity) that these "felt" qualities involve a subjective factor. We find that there is, indeed, a certain subjectivity and relativity in strict sense-apprehension. This fact was recognized from the very beginning of philosophy.[7] Wine, said the Greeks, tastes sweet to a well man, but bitter to the diseased man. What feels cold to the warm hand feels warm to the cold hand. But, in the concrete experience, the relativity of sense-experience is seen to be immaterial to the objectivity of our apprehension of an existing thing. The relativity is in the quality of sense-experience, not in the total concrete object of the sense-intellect apprehension. Whether the wood feels hot or cold to me, whether at first it feels hot and later cold, I nonetheless apprehend a thing existent and extended. The quality of the sense experience does not touch the immediate intellectual-apprehension.

If we reflect now on the content of intellectual apprehension, we find that we discover in the immediate apprehension of the wood itself what we express by saying: "This is an extended existing thing." We use *these* words and, if one wishes to speak logically, we apply *these* corresponding concepts, because we find, in this case, an existing extended thing. The meaning of the words and the content of the concepts are verified or realized in the piece of wood of which I am aware. These meanings (which are here simply "understandings" of the wood) do not reveal (as did "coldness," for example) any relativity or subjectivity; they are the very expression of a *discovered objectivity.* The act of immediate knowledge is an encounter with an "other," a really existing extended thing; it is an encounter which is not merely physical or material but conscious; it is an encounter the meaning of which I immediately grasp. It is from this encounter (repeated a thousand times in daily experience) that there arises my understanding of "objectivity," of "existence," of "thing," of "extended." All of these are seen to be non-relativistic; they are in some sense "absolute," unqualified by subjective experience.

Intellectual Knowledge and Intelligibility

Here we can increase our understanding of intelligence. For here it consciously apprehends precisely an "existent," in its own existence, in its otherness and independence. This cannot be and is not *sensed;* it is intellectually understood. The act of knowing takes conscious posses-

---

[7]*Cf.* D.J.B. Hawkins, *The Criticism of Experience* (New York: Sheed and Ward, 1945), 24–41.

sion of a thing which is not the act of knowing, not its subjective qualifications and not existentially a part of my consciousness. The understandings of things, which cannot be sensed, I call intelligibilities, because they are apprehended by operations at the level I have called intellectual. Intelligibility is not some added magical property of the things presented in my experience; it simply names the objective reality of the thing as I find it open to my intellectual apprehension. The intelligibility of things is simply the objective reality of things: the intellectual understanding of things is simply the grasp of their objective reality.

To summarize: What I am saying is that, if a man maintains a prolonged meditative reflection on any simple instance of the sort here described, if in doing so he washes his mind of all theories, abstractions, and preconceived expectations, he will find that in this experience he immediately encounters an independently existing extended thing; that this encounter is an immediate intellectual awareness, however partial and fragmentary, of an objective reality; that his intellectual awareness goes beyond subjective states, indeed, through them as through transparencies to the objective.

Further, I am saying that in this instance (and a thousand others) the nature of intelligence is seen to be not a qualified way of experiencing, but a power of understanding realities and hence a power correlative to reality or existence.[8] One does not *assume* that reality is intelligible; one *finds* that it is intelligible. The full elaboration of the intelligibility of the real requires other reflections and other experiential facts, indeed, inference and argumentation, but the basic point is found here in any simple immediate act of underived knowledge. It is from this starting-

---

[8]Intellectual awareness displays a great versatility and variety of operation and occupies a commanding position in our conscious life. In order to distinguish sense from intellect, philosophers have made use of various facets of intellectual activity, many of them more clear-cut than the characteristic pointed out in the text. For example, a very common method is to appeal to the universalizing power of intelligence which is not displayed by sense. This yields a sharp distinction but it has several disadvantages. First, it is inadequate, since it uses only one achievement of intelligence; secondly, it points to an activity at a second level of reflection, not to the presence of intellect in immediate knowledge of the individual; thirdly, it tends to reify the "universals" and to give priority to universality over intelligibility and so artificially creates the problem of universal knowledge versus singular realities.

point that a realist moves to a full metaphysical understanding of the traditional dictum *ens est verum*.

Special Difficulties of This Procedure

I should like to pause here and call attention to several difficulties in this method. It is inherent in our descriptive technique that attention can be called, only step by step, part by part, to the elements, moments, or factors which are found in interrelated unity in every moment of the experience on which we are reflecting. Our purpose is not to isolate and consider separately the various elements, but to point to them in the complexity of experience. Unfortunately, while it is possible to apprehend them simultaneously, it is not possible to talk about them simultaneously. Hence, the piecemeal descriptive analysis employed should not itself be reified but should be related to and checked by the experience itself. Unfortunately, by the same token, a certain amount of repetition is unavoidable since each aspect is actually interrelated with all the others and must constantly be tied back into the total concrete picture.

Secondly, I am fully aware that what I am trying to do will appear to many, at least at first sight, to be superficial, non-philosophical, and perhaps naive. If I may inject a personal note, I am also aware how extremely difficult it is for anyone nurtured in the main lines of the modern philosophical tradition to immerse himself in this sort of experiential reflection and (an even harder thing) to take it seriously. I have myself lived through these difficulties, held to the search by puzzling over why men as men and often enough as philosophers have been, as a matter of fact, tenaciously and incorrigibly realists while modern philosophers in general have been unable to find any adequate grounds for it and have found themselves constantly driven from realistic positions. Having struggled with all these difficulties, I am now convinced that the reason for the situation is threefold: (1) the evidence for realism has been systematically ignored and indeed *a priori* excluded—through assumptions—from consideration; (2) the experiential data have been in modern times described in an inadequate and falsifying way; (3) in the resulting absence of evidence, the numerous apparent difficulties against realism have become real and insoluble difficulties. (To illustrate briefly from history, once the problem had been set as it was by Descartes and Locke, the appearance of a Hume became, logically and psychologically, possible—indeed almost inevitable.)

The Intentionality of Knowledge

To resume our reflection. When, in this complex but unified act of knowledge, I encounter the external real existent "this," which is the piece of wood, and express my awareness, "This is a real thing," I see, by reflection, that all the activities of knowing are indeed my activities, the awareness is indeed the awareness of a determined individual subject—myself. Yet my awareness goes immediately, through these activities yet without making them part of the object known, to another "this," thus transcending the activities and the determinations of the self. This characteristic of knowledge which is factually discovered in experience has been called its intentionality. Notice that this is a primitive characteristic which knowledge displays in its simple and direct form; yet it is to be found in its more elaborate exercises. For example, when I am speaking of Paris with a friend, recently returned, and I ask whether Paris is still gay under spring skies, whether Notre Dame still has its glorious glass, whether the taxis still drive madly about, I am thinking not of images or concepts but of the real Paris, the Paris so many miles away, so independent of me. My mind, through its concepts, "intends" a real object. Obviously, were knowledge not "intentional," all this would be sheer fooling; we would indeed be closed in like miners buried in a fall-in, left to groundless inference and guessing. Knowledge is intentional whether the data and evidence for the knowledge are immediately apprehended (as in the case of the piece of wood) or are indirectly grasped, not being now immediately present to awareness (as in the case of Paris). Indeed, knowledge displays its intentional character even when no decisive evidence is at hand, either immediately or indirectly. When we suppose an objective state of affairs as merely possible, it must be conceived intentionally, i.e., as a possible state of *real* affairs. Thus, were not knowledge intentional, the detective in our stories could not propose his first (and, by the rules of such stories, therefore most certainly wrong) reconstruction of the crime.

We come to see that intentionality is a primitive character of knowledge, then, by a prolonged and ever-deepening reflection on cases of immediate apprehension, such as ours of the piece of wood. Since it is thus discovered experientially as a fact, a thousand theoretical difficulties may indeed deepen our understanding of and our wonder at its uniqueness but cannot bring us to reject it. *Contra factum non valet illatio.* Once again, if we approach knowledge not experientially but abstractly, after the manner of the idealists and the rationalists, intentionality will be sieved out through abstract logic and be forgotten. Unfortunately, this is what actually happened. For intentionality was almost forgotten in the logicizing decay of scholasticism and was theoretically ignored (it was employed practically, of course) through most of the subsequent modern development. Brentano was one of the first to call attention to this oversight and thus to restore to certain modern thinkers some conscious recognition of intentionality.[9]

The Intelligibility of Being[10]

I have already rather briefly pointed to the meaning of the term "intelligibility" and given some examples of a discovery of intelligibilities in direct knowledge. Among these was the intelligibility of "existent thing." If I may again repeat, we find this intelligibility in the piece of wood itself as presented in experience, and, indeed, it is from the immediate experience that we gain, by intellectual insight, an understanding of this intelligibility. I know what "existent" means only because I encounter "existents" in experience. The fact is that I do have such an intelligible grasp on the "existent," on the determinate individual existent in its own objectivity. It is perfectly true that "existent" cannot be analyzed into prior concepts since it is itself a primitive intelligibility. It cannot be logically located in prior categories, since it is radically unique and hence either denatures or is denatured by any category we attempt to apply to it. Yet all the world knows, however vaguely and imperfectly, what "existent" means. It is not the business of the philosopher to get rid of this primitive understanding, impatient with it because it is recalcitrant to logical manipulation or the clarifying simplifications of reductionism. There it is: the primitive intelligibility, given in experience, forced upon us at every turn and constantly intruding itself into philosophy even after a neat naturalism has thought its exorcism final. It is our business to accept what is thus given and by

---

[9]Cf. L'intentionalité et les reductiones," *La Phénoménologie et la Foi,* ed. Revmond Vancourt (Paris: Desclée, 1953), 31–39.

[10]For a longer effort, likewise at least partially phenomenological, to present the basis of a realist metaphysics. see my *Method in Metaphysics* (Milwaukee: Marquette University Press, 1951).

long, hard meditative reflection to deepen our understanding of it and to describe its full wealth.

In short, immediate experience lays open to human intelligence the primitive and inclusive intelligibility of (now merely to transpose our terminology) being, not the a *priori* and empty concept of the rationalists, rightly derided by empiricists, but the understanding of being as it is in real things, an understanding that can never be closed and neatly catalogued. The development of realist metaphysics is simply a long intellectual effort, first, to see ever more deeply into the myriad experiences which reveal beings and to deploy the full richness of these ever-growing insights. Thus, the principle of contradiction, as a metaphysical principle, is only a statement of the intellectually recognized absolute character of a concrete existence. The elaboration of the transcendentals —the classic one, true, and good—of the realist tradition is only an unfolding of the full meaning of being as it is found in experience. The inferences and argumentations of metaphysics all proceed from the seen implications of concrete existents. Obviously, a detailed justification of realist metaphysics would demand a complete exposition of this discipline, a task impossible here.[11] I have attempted merely to point to those pieces of evidence which force one to realism and to indicate by what loyal meditation on experiential reality one moves along the road (always arduous but especially for those who must rebuild their own step by step) to realism.

Conclusion

In this paper, I have attempted to point out by taking one of a thousand possible instances where one must look for evidence of the sort which establishes realism. I have given a kind of minimal schema of that evidence. It is perceived in a thousand such experiences perhaps inaccurately, unreflectively, confusedly. But it makes every man a common sense realist and even keeps every philosopher a practical realist. It is this evidence, massive in its immediacy and pervasiveness, which, when examined by critical reflection and probing meditation, presents

---

[11]For a systematic presentation of realist metaphysics, see George P. Klubertanz, S.J., *Introduction to the Philosophy of Being* (New York: Appleton-Century-Crofts, 1952); and *cf.* Wild, *Return to Reason*, 36–37.

the groundwork of both a realistic epistemology and a realistic metaphysics.

Realism does not present itself as one side of an "option," which distinguishes temperaments: the "tough-minded" from the "soft-minded," the naive from the critical, the crude from the refined. It does not present itself as a system structured on reasonable or useful postulates which work out well, in theory and practice, and, without imperative urgency, simply recommend themselves to sensible people. It presents itself as the result of the data of experience, of ineluctable evidence, primitive, massive, all-pervasive, which, while never adequately describable, yet grows all the stronger and firmer as critical reflection tests and examines it. It is not an assumption; it is not a postulate; it is not an option; it is the acceptance of things as they are.

SCHOPENHAUER AND DIRECT REALISM

New Introduction: This article[1] is a result of a conversation with one of my students. I was teaching Epistemology and one day after class a student came up and said that he had been reading Schopenhauer and that he had found places in Schopenhauer that sounded very much like what I was teaching. I immediately felt betrayed and I said firmly, "I don't believe it." The next day the student came to me with photocopied passages from Schopenhauer. When I read them I had to admit that they sounded somewhat like me. So I got the book to which the student was referring and examined the passages carefully in context and I concluded that Schopenhauer indeed had lucid moments in which he permitted the eminence of reality to overcome his inherited idealism. My own suspicion is that the reason for these lucid moments was that Schopenhauer had studied in the medical school for a time and therefore perhaps had to confront the experiential evidence more carefully then most idealists had to do. The result was these lucid moments of realism in the midst of an orthodox but somewhat weird idealism.

I think this article is still valid and stands in its own right. It needs no correction or addition. What it shows I think is what idealists need to do is to carefully examine the experiential evidence and if they do so they may find themselves having lucid moments of realism.

---

[1]First published in *The Review of Metaphysics*, 46, no. 1 (September 1992): 125–140.

SCHOPENHAUER AND DIRECT REALISM

I

The main thesis of this study[2] may be summarized as follows: (1) In Schopenhauer's earliest work, *The Fourfold Root of the Principle of Sufficient Reason,* two different lines of philosophical thought can be identified, each arising from a different source. (2) The first of these is the a priori Kantianism and idealism heavily emphasizing the function of the a priori principle of causality, and the forms of time and space. This line comes from Schopenhauer's study of Kantianism. (3) The second line of thought consists of an implicitly realistic analysis of perception which seems to arise from Schopenhauer's personal reflection on perceptual experience. This experiential analysis seems to be partially due to his medical studies, as his use of medical rather than philosophical authorities indicates. (4) This realistically oriented element can be extricated from the totality of Schopenhauer's philosophy with the result that it can furnish new insights valuable for the understanding and confirmation of philosophical direct realism.

A secondary conclusion might be that a similar analysis might be usefully applied to other philosophers resulting in better understanding of the philosophers themselves and with the contribution to philosophical thought itself.

II

In order to provide a philosophical basis for the identification of the realistic theme it is necessary to set forth some of the definitions and positions of philosophical direct realism.

"Realism" as used in this discussion may be defined as the conviction that there exists, independently of human knowledge or willing, a more or less structured world containing material entities, that is, entities extended in three dimensions, existing in space, resistant, gen-

---

[2]This paper is based entirely on Schopenhauer's earliest work, *Ueber die Vierfacke Wurzel des Satzes Vom Zureichenden Grunde (Schopenhauer's Sämtliche Werke)*, ed. Arthur Hübscher, vol. 1 (Wiesbaden: F. A. Brockhaus, 1911). The English translation used in this paper is *On the Fourfold Root of the Principle of Sufficient Reason*, trans. E. F. Payne (Lasalle: Open Court, 1974).

erally shaped, and possessing a variety of qualities; and that human beings can gain considerable objective knowledge of these entities.

Realism may be "natural" or philosophical. Philosophical realism may be direct or indirect. Natural realism is the universal conviction all people have that they are living in a really existing world of material entities. It is generally admitted that this conviction is so strong that no philosophy can eradicate it. Descartes made the absolutely permanent character of this conviction an essential part of his indirect argument for a limited realism.[3] But Descartes maintained that philosophically this limited realism has to be justified by a reasoning process. He was thus an indirect realist.

On the other hand, direct realism is the philosophical position that holds that this conviction cannot be demonstrated and needs no demonstration because it is immediately evident from personal human experience. This is the sort of realism implicit in Schopenhauer.

The philosophical problem for the direct realist is to discover, analyze, and make explicit the precise human experience that justifies direct realism and puts it beyond all doubt. Some direct realists present their evidence, often forcefully, but without detailed analysis.[4] For the purpose of this study a more precise analysis is necessary. That analysis reveals that the basic certitudinal evidence for both natural and philosophical direct realism lies in the intellectual perceptual awareness of the active and exploratory general touch experience.[5] It is this type of direct realism that Schopenhauer describes and to which he gives additional personal insights.

A brief example may explain that type of evidential experience just referred to. Take a piece of wood about a foot long and two or three inches wide or thick. Now explore the wood with your hands moving them around the wood. You are immediately aware that there is an

---

[3]René Descartes, *The Meditations Concerning First Philosophy*, trans. Lafleur (Indianapolis: Bobbs-Merrill, 1961), 125–126.

[4]See for example Etienne Gilson, *Réalisme thomiste et critique de la connaissance* (Paris: Tequi, 1939).

[5]For this analysis see R. J. Henle, "A Phenomenological Approach to Realism," *An Etienne Gilson Tribute* (Milwaukee: Marquette University Press, 1959), 68–85. See also R. J. Henle, "Basis of Philosophical Realism Re-examined," *The New Scholasticism* 56 (Winter 1982); and R. J. Henle, *Theory of Knowledge* (Chicago: Loyola University Press, 1983), 80–128.

object outside your hands. Your hands move; the surface of the wood does not move with them. Put the wood between your hands; you cannot join your hands. Put the wood down. You cannot reproduce that experience as you can the image of a green tree in your imagination. You cannot produce a sensation that resembles that experience. You may have hot or cold sensations. They are irrelevant to the fact that you have direct experience of an external resistant, shaped object that is in no sense part of you. In such integral touch experiences there are no illusions of objectivity,[6] no possibility of error. The experience includes sense *and intellect.* There is not a sensation or a group of sensations which are examined intellectually, but rather the entire experience is saturated with intellectual awareness.[7] Thus arises a quite different definition of "perception." Perception is a complex knowledge process by which through combined sense and intellectual activity, we come to know an object presented here and now in sense experience. Through hundreds of such experiences do we develop our habitual awareness of the real material world.

Within this habitual awareness we learn to use the other senses as sources of information and as guides to action. The senses thus act together as a system[8] through which the senses other than general touch (especially sight) obtain a derived objectivity of their own. Schopenhauer especially clarifies this latter point.

A brief account of four main sources of skepticism about the existence of a real material world may also be useful for the identification of Schopenhauer's Realism. First, most attacks on the reliability or objectivity of the senses begin by concentrating on the sense of sight. Stress is laid on the numerous illusions, "deceptions": hallucinations and dreams, the bent oar, the two suns, varying colors on the necks of pigeons, the relativity of color vision, and so forth. After rejecting sight as a source of reliable knowledge of an external world, this rejection is simply extended to all the senses, including touch. Sometimes a general

---

[6]There are some cases of alleged illusions, for example, if one puts a pencil between two fingers and closes one's eyes, it may seem that there are two objects. This is an illusion with regard to number, not to objectivity. The experience is impossible unless there is an object between the fingers.

[7]See Henle, *Theory of Knowledge,* 84.

[8]See James J. Gibson, *The Senses Considered as Perceptive Systems* (Boston: Houghton Mifflin, 1960).

sense of touch is dismissed because of the relativity and subjectivity of the specific temperature sensations. Descartes, after a brief reference to dreams and the deception of the senses,[9] simply dismisses any consideration of sense as an original source of objective knowledge. Schopenhauer does not make this mistake. He *begins* his discussion of the senses with the objectivity of the sense of touch. This seems to be a personal discovery of Schopenhauer's.

A second common mistake, especially of early modern philosophers, is the belief that in all cases of perception there is always some subjective element which is the true object of awareness. This element may be an impression, a sense idea, a sensation, an image. Somehow whatever we know of the external material world must be derived from these subjective objects. In Descartes, sense ideas, which are characterized by obscurity and confusion, are created by God and only because of His veracity do they reveal to some extent the real material world. In Berkeley ideas (sense ideas) are created by God and, in themselves, constitute the world people call real. There is no objective correlate. For Hume impressions are produced by unknown causes and all knowledge is at the sense level. In Leibniz the ideas are precreated by God and unfold during time in preestablished harmony with the real world. Thomas Reid clearly identifies this mistake and effectively criticizes it.[10] In the case of the complex general touch experience described above, awareness, both sensitive and intellectual, terminates cognitionally at the external object.

A third source of skepticism is the confusion concerning the nature and activity of the intellect and the nature and activity of the senses. Sometimes intellection completely disappears in a philosophy. Thus, in Hume, all conscious activities must be explained at the sense level by impressions, ideas, feelings, and so forth. As a result, all intelligibility and necessities disappear in sense experience. In such a system nothing can be known of an external world. There can be no realism. Schopenhauer maintains a radical distinction between intellect and sense.

---

[9]Descartes, *Meditations,* 76–77.

[10]See Thomas Reid, "Reflections on the Common Theory of Ideas," in *The Intellectual Powers of Man* (Cambridge: MIT Press, 1969), 211–286. Cf. R. J. Henle, S.J., "Thomas Reid's Theory of Signs," in *Semiotic* 1983, ed. Jonathan Evans and John Deely (Lanham, Md.: University Press of America, 1987).

Sometimes intellection is recognized but almost completely separated from sense experience. In Berkeley the (sense) ideas have no intrinsic intelligibility or connections; only the notions are intellectual. In direct realism there is a clear radical distinction between intellection and sensing,[11] but intellectual awareness pervades all sense awareness so that cognitionally the intellect is in direct contact with the external objects. When a person places his hand on the surface of his desk, he is immediately aware that he is feeling a smooth external surface and he immediately understands he is so doing. Without any reasoning or intervening cognitional elements he can immediately express the intellectual judgment, "I am feeling a smooth external material surface." This analysis is implicit in Schopenhauer's realism.

A fourth source of skepticism is a confusion between perceptual judgments based on *per se* perceptions and those based on *per accidens* perceptions. If a person picks up a rock and says, "I am holding a hard object in my hands," this is a *per se* perceptual judgment because the total evidence is being presented in this experience. If, on the other hand, a person says, "I hear a fire engine," this is a *per accidens* perceptual judgment based partially on previous experience and associations. Though such judgments of the latter sort are generally correct, they can be mistaken because most sounds for example, can be reproduced without the presence of the usual source. Descartes' reference to what he saw when looking out the window of his study is an example, though he used it as a basis of skepticism.[12]

Schopenhauer appears to be quite aware of the importance of this distinction, though his terminology is different.

III

As already stated, the texts for this study are taken exclusively from Schopenhauer's earliest work, *On the Fourfold Root of the Principle of*

---

[11]Descartes illustrates the difference between sense and intellect in a striking example. He says he can both conceive a triangle and imagine a triangle, but he cannot imagine a thousand-sided figure, though his concept of it is perfectly clear and distinct. See Descartes, *Meditations* 6.

[12]Descartes, *Meditations* 2, 89.

Sufficient Reason.[13] More precisely, these tests are drawn from section 21, "The A Priori Nature of the Concept of Causality. Intellectual Nature of Empirical Intuitive Perception. The Understanding" (pp. 52–121).

Within section 21 there appear to be two different sets of ideas and, correspondingly, two different sources of evidence. These two philosophical themes sometimes intertwine and sometimes stand almost side by side in apparent contradiction.

One source of thought, which is the basic one for the entire treatise, is doctrinaire Kantianism according to which the empirical world is "constructed" by the understanding applying the a priori concept causality to the sensations—which contain nothing resembling their causes —with the aid of the a priori forms of inner sense, time (the possibility of change), and of outer sense, space (the possibility of bodies appearing in space). These texts will be referred to as *K*.

The other set of ideas appears to result from Schopenhauer's personal reflection on and analysis of experience. These ideas will be referred to as *S*. Included in *S* are Schopenhauer's reference to medical texts and anecdotal accounts (of blindness, and so on) from newspapers and other publications. In fact, it seems clear that the appearance of *S* in the midst of *K* is due to the fact that Schopenhauer early on studied medicine, a study which tends to be realistically detailed. Hereafter the key texts will be numbered for easy reference.

IV

The basic specific text is found in section 21, pages 75–120. The first part of this text (pp. 75–79) is devoted to an explanation of the Objective Intuitive Perception, strictly in accord with K. The Objective Intuitive Perception is the process by which the understanding "constructs," "brings into being" the objective world of bodies; or it is the way the "beautiful world arises." The process begins with "sensations" which are "modifications of the body," "lie under the skin," and have nothing resembling their external causes. Next, the understanding— wherein there lies ready-made, prior to all experience, the law of causality—goes to work on the sensations and turns them into "effects,"

---

[13]Payne, ed. *On the Fourfold Root.* Hereafter, page numbers given in the text will refer to this volume.

and so refers them to their causes out of which the understanding, with the help of the a priori form of inner sense, time, and of the a priori form of outer sense, space, constructs the empirical world.

The intellect is constituted by the understanding and the reason. The understanding is intuitive and simply applies the law of causation. The reason is the faculty of abstract thinking (it alone deals with concepts) and is the faculty of logical reasoning. Thus these two together constitute the intellect which is simply identical with the brain. Schopenhauer makes the following important points: Perception is intellectual, intuitive, and makes no use of concepts. Now, since Schopenhauer here gives the most comprehensive explanation of "sensation" according to K, and since it is in such sharp contrast to some of what follows, the entire text is here quoted.

Text 1

For what a poor, wretched thing mere sensation is! Even in the noblest organs of sense it is nothing more than a local specific feeling, capable in its way of some variation, yet in itself always subjective. Therefore, as such, this feeling cannot possibly contain anything objective, and so anything resembling intuitive perception. For sensation of every kind is and remains an event within the organism itself; but as such it is restricted to the region beneath the skin; and so, in itself, it can never contain anything lying outside the skin and thus outside ourselves. Sensation can be pleasant or unpleasant—and this indicates a reference to our will—but nothing objective is to be found in any sensation. . . . Yet it remains mere sensation, like every other within our body; consequently, it is something essentially subjective. (pp. 76–77)

Schopenhauer concludes the first part of this section by saying, "I will now show in more detail the great gulf between sensation and intuitive perception" (p. 79). In view of this, the very next paragraph in which S appears is, to say the least, surprising. The next text is the basic one for S.

Text 2

Properly speaking, only two senses, touch and sight, are of use to objective intuitive perception. These alone supply the data,

and on their foundation the understanding enables the objective world to come about through the process just
mentioned. The other three senses on the whole remain
subjective; for it is true that their sensations point to an
external cause, but yet contain no data for determining its
spatial relations. (p. 79)

As Schopenhauer begins his study of the senses, he makes a capital
distinction between touch and sight on the one hand, and between the
other three senses of smell, taste, and hearing on the other. These three
latter senses remain subjective even after the operation of the Objective
Intuitive Perception. Only touch and sight have a degree of objectivity
and supply specific data to the understanding, or later to empirical
intuitive perception. In this objectivity, as will be seen, touch holds the
primacy—a primacy of infallible objectivity. This is most striking in
view of the almost universal, previous practice of early modern philosophers of beginning with an analysis of vision and a rejection of its
objectivity, and therefore of all sense objectivity.
     Now, as if he has given too much to touch and sight, he quickly
repeats K:

Text 3

. . . However, what touch and sight supply is still not by any
means intuitive perception, but only the raw material for this;
for perception is so far from being found in the sensations of
these senses that, on the contrary, they do not resemble at all
the qualities of things presented to us by means of them, as I
shall show in a moment. (p. 80)

The objectivity asserted in Text 2 cannot arise from sensations but
rather from immediate intuitive contact with the objects. Later, in Text
11 below, Schopenhauer will base the infallibility of touch on the fact
of direct "contact" with the object. Schopenhauer constantly repeats his
position that sensations remain subjective and cannot contain anything
resembling their causes. Yet he will assert that touch yields very
specific and objective data (see Text 10 below).

V

At this point the consideration of touch must be interrupted in order to study the subjective senses. Schopenhauer's treatment of these senses is enlightening in itself and is a necessary prelude to the completion of the primary discussion of touch.

In Text 2 Schopenhauer distinguished taste, smell, and hearing as senses which are mainly subjective and remain so. The temperature sense, which Schopenhauer identifies as part of the data of touch, should be classified with these three. In this Schopenhauer is clearly mistaken. Temperature has often been included in touch since it usually arises within the integral touch experience. But it has a distinctive content, a subjective sensation that is radically different from the data of the general sense of touch. If one explores a round object with the hands, the shape discovered is a quality of the external body. Whether that body is hot or cold is totally irrelevant to the discovery of its shape. If one holds a hot ball in his hands for a short time and then puts the ball down, he will continue to feel heat in his hands. That is, felt heat is a subjective sensation, while the awareness of a round object ceases at once. Moreover, the sensation of heat does not resemble or disclose the nature of the external activity that stimulates the temperature sense. Therefore, the temperature sense is analogous to taste and smell. Hence hereafter the temperature sense will be classified with the subjective senses, thus raising the number of such senses to four.

Schopenhauer says very little about taste and smell, but that little is very important and is expanded in the subsequent more extensive treatment of hearing:

Text 4

The other three senses on the whole remain subjective; for it is true that their sensations point to an external cause, but yet contain no data for determining its *spatial* relations. . . . Therefore those three senses can, of course, serve to announce to us the presence of objects already known to us in another way; but no spatial construction and thus no objective intuitive perception is brought about on the basis of their data. We can never construct a rose from its perfume, and a blind man can hear music all his life without obtaining the slightest objective representation of the musicians, the instruments, or the vibrations of the air. (p. 79)

Implicit in this Text is a distinction of great importance which Schopenhauer does not express with precision. In fact, he has no terminology for dealing with it. This distinction is the standard scholastic one between *per se* and *per accidens*. *Per se* these senses terminate at a specific kind of sensation which is a subjective event. The qualities or data which they attain by their very nature are *per se* qualities of the sensations. Thus we always and *per se* taste flavors, smell odors, hear sounds. We smell an odor; it can be strong, sweet, or have a distinctive quality such as that produced by Lysol or lilacs. These qualities bear no resemblance to any outside body. We learn from experience, both our own and that of others, how to connect specific odors with specific kinds of things. These connections are *per accidens*, not arising out of the *per se* qualities. If on entering the dining room one smells a very distinctive sharp odor, he knows that sauerkraut is on the menu. This was learned "in another way," that is, by past association, not by *per se* analysis of the particular odor. The *per accidens* use of these senses is of great importance for dealing with the real world. For example, experience and reflection can vastly extend use of these senses. A chef can recognize many more spices by smell than the ordinary diner. Tea tasters and wine tasters show how delicately discriminatory the sense of taste can become.

In the *per se* use of these senses, there can be no deception. We smell the odor we smell. We taste the taste we taste. In the *per accidens* use, however, mistakes can be and are made. One may smell lilac and really do so. He looks about for lilac bushes, although the source was actually the strong perfume of a passing lady. In addition, the senses may be modified by illness, so that sweet milk will taste sour. But most mistakes are easily corrected.

<h2 style="text-align:center">VI</h2>

As pointed out above, Schopenhauer said very little about taste and smell; but of hearing he gives a somewhat more extended and careful analysis. Like taste and smell, hearing is a subjective sense and yields no data concerning the nature of external bodies:

Text 5

A blind man can hear music all his life without obtaining the slightest objective representation of the musicians, the instruments, or the vibrations of the air. (p. 79)

Moreover, in hearing there is a very definite and clear sensation, namely, the sound or the tone itself. Sound is an internal event of which we are clearly conscious. *Per se* we experience only sound and its proper qualities of volume, pitch, and quality.

Text 6

But the tone never indicates spatial relations, and never leads us to the nature of its cause. On the contrary, we stop short at the tone itself; consequently, it is no datum for the understanding that is constructing the objective world. (p. 80)

Schopenhauer cites music as one of the great values of the sense of sound, since music is an artistic product in our sensitive-intellectual consciousness arising from a planned stimulation of the various qualities of sound itself. Even though we *per se* "stop short" at the tone, what is true of the other subjective senses is true of hearing namely, that it can "announce to us the presence of objects already known to us in another way." This means that we have an enormous use of sound through *per accidens* connections. Through experience and investigation we learn to identify an incredible number of things "known to us in another way."

This extended use becomes so second nature that instead of saying, for example, "I hear a noise made by a police car," I say simply, "I hear a police car." The sound becomes almost a formal (or pure) sign;[14] and so sound becomes a constant source of information and of protection.

Of course, as in all *per accidens* connections we can and do make mistakes. I think I hear shots when, in fact, it is a radio drama next door or backfiring in the street. I think I hear thunder but it's only a large truck passing by. Such mistakes can easily be corrected and, besides, the usefulness of sound far outweighs them.

One remarkable thing about hearing, to which Schopenhauer does not allude, is this. We learn immediately to project familiar sounds to

---

[14]The classical systematization of the formal sign comes from John Poinsot, *Tractatus de Signis,* ed. John Deely (Berkeley: University of California Press, 1985). For contemporary application see John Deely, "Towards the Origin of Semiotic," in *Sight, Sound and Sense,* ed. Thomas Sebeok (Bloomington: University of Indiana Press, 1978), 1–30; Henle, *Theory of Knowledge,* 54–55, 60–61; and Frederick D. Wilhelmsen, *Man's Knowledge of Reality* (Englewood Cliffs: Prentice-Hall, 1956), 86–87.

the point of origin of the vibrations. Thus, I hear shouting *in the street*. I hear hammering *next door*. I hear someone walking *in the corridor*. Of course, because this is learned, that is, is *per accidens*, mistakes can be made. Ventriloquists and echoes can mislead us.

Schopenhauer points to spoken language as one of the great contributions of hearing.

Text 7

On the other hand, the sense of hearing is of great value as a medium of language, whereby it is the sense of *reason* or of the rational faculty. (p. 79)

Schopenhauer has said (in *K*) that sensations is a poor thing that requires the application of the a priori forms of the understanding to give rise to the beautiful empirical world. Schopenhauer's own analysis in *S*, however, shows that the sensation which is the sound is rich in itself and in its many uses. The understanding supplies only intellectual awareness; it supplies nothing of the proper nature of sound (that is, from sense experience), nor does it "refer the sensation" to its external causes. If it did, we would all be aware of the vibrations of the air which are the external cause of sound. We have to discover sound waves by experimentation and reasoning.

Schopenhauer is correct in saying that in the subjective senses our sensitivo-intellectual awareness terminates initially and *per se* at the sensations. As he points out, we can use the qualities of these sensations, which we intuitively apprehend, for useful ends such as the production and enjoyment of music. More important than all this, however, we learn to use these very sensations to transcend them, as it were, and enable us to make objective judgments of the real world which we know in another way, namely, through touch and sight.

VII

The sense of touch, which is quite different from the three (or four) senses just discussed, must now be more thoroughly examined. In Text 2 Schopenhauer says that only touch and sight supply objective data for the Objective Intuitive Perception. What data does touch supply?

Text 8

Touch, on the other hand, immediately supplies the data for the knowledge of size, shape, hardness, softness, dryness moisture, smoothness, temperature and so on. (p. 81)

It has already been shown above why temperature does not belong in this list. The other data are qualities of external bodies, not the content or qualities of sensations. It should also be emphasized that these data furnish knowledge—not feelings, or pleasure, or sensations, but knowledge. Moreover, touch *immediately* supplies these data. This is a crucial difference, and it indicates the complete objectivity of the sense of touch. Pitch is a quality of sound and not of any external body. Hardness is a quality of an external body, not of the hand or of a subjective sensation or of the imagination. Taken as S this description exactly corresponds to the integral touch experience, for there are no sensations corresponding to these data. As one places his hand on the surface of a desk, he is immediately aware of the external surface. This experience cannot be analyzed into (1) a sensation, then (2) the application of the principle of causality, and then (3) the perception of an extended material surface.

Text 9

On the other hand, it is true that touch is restricted to *contact*, but its data are so *infallible* and varied that it is the most radical and thorough sense. (p. 81, emphasis added)

Touch is in direct contact with the material object, and then establishes its infallibility. In contrast, in hearing, our sensitivo-intellectual awareness stops short at the "tone," the sensation. In touch, our sensitivo-intellectual awareness is in direct contact with the material body and so immediately reports the qualities of material bodies. This is confirmed by the very next text.

Text 10

Indeed perceptions through sight ultimately refer to touch and sight can be regarded as an imperfect touch extending to a distance and making use of the rays of light as long feelers. It is therefore exposed to many deceptions just because it is limited entirely to qualities that are brought about through the medium of light; and so it is one-sided. (p. 81)

The objectivity of sight depends on the objectivity of touch. The fallibility of sight taken in itself is due to the fact that there is a *medium* in sight perception, namely, light. There is no medium, physical or cognitional, between the sensitivity of the hand and the surface it touches or the ball it holds. Touch is the ultimate test and guarantee of the objectivity of sight. Psychologists and psychiatrists know this. If you can put your hand through the pink elephant, there is no pink elephant. If you cannot grab the shadow by your bed with your hand, it is just a shadow.

Text 11

In this it [touch] is assisted by the shape and mobility of the arms, hands, and fingers from whose position the understanding by touching bodies, derives the data for constructing them in space; it is also aided through muscular power by means whereof it knows the weight, solidity, toughness, or brittleness of bodies; all this with the least possibility of deception.

Movement and exploration by the hands are essential parts of the integral touch experience. Although Schopenhauer's understanding of the contribution of the hands, and so forth is somewhat different, his account is closer to *S* than to *K*. Again he emphasizes the infallibility of touch:

Text 12

If in the dark I put my hand on a flat surface . . . or seize a ball of some three inches in diameter, then in both cases it is the same parts of the hand which feel the pressure. Only from the different position, assumed by my hand in the one case of the other, does my understanding construct the shape of the body, contact with which is the cause of the sensation and it confirms this sensation for itself by varying the points of contact. (p. 82)

In this text Schopenhauer identifies a number of internal sensations and explains that by a complicated sort of calculation from which we discover the shape of the ball. These sensations are not sensations of touch, nor is there any experiential or reflective evidence that we employ any such inferential process. This may be an effort by Schopenhauer to justify his a priori assumption that in all sense knowledge there are intermediate sensations. This is contradicted by his description of, and emphasis on, the direct and immediate "contact" of touch with the external object (see Text 9 above). Moreover, these sensations are not caused by the external bodies. Our effort to grasp and explore generates tensions and conscious use of muscles. When, blindfolded, we attempt to determine the shape of an external object, our focus is entirely on the outside body. We can, of course, change our focus and ultimately reflect on the internal kinesthetic sensation, but we do not use them to calculate the shape of the external body. In Text 11 Schopenhauer is much closer to describing the role of exploration by hands and fingers and of movement in our acquisition of objective knowledge through touch.

As stated above, Schopenhauer assumes that in all sense experiences there are sensations that function in the Objective Intuitive Perception. It was shown above, both from experience and from Schopenhauer's own S description, that there are no touch sensations, no conscious or cognitive medium between human sensitivo-intellectual awareness and the external object. We are immediately aware of an external object, and through external exploration immediately grasp its shape.

VIII

We are now ready to relate our conclusions concerning touch to our original project. If we extricate all the S elements from the K context, we can enumerate the following points:

(1) Perception always involves intellectual activity as well as that of sensitivity.

(2) The touch experience involves "grasping," holding, movement, exploration by hands and fingers. (Thus the elements of space are already given in immediate touch experience; there is no need for an already existing a priori form of "space.")

(3) Initially no deductive reasoning is involved in perception ("Reason" functions later.) Perception is "intuitive."

(4) Through touch we are in immediate, direct contact with external bodies. There are no touch sensations and no cognitional intermediates.

(5) For the reasons stated in (4), perceptions based on touch are infallible and beyond doubt.

(6) For the same reason, the data supplied for perception through touch are size, shape, hardness, softness, dryness, moisture, smoothness, and so forth. These are all real qualities of real external bodies, not of sensations (as loudness is a quality of the sensation "sound"); and they are not "modifications of the organism."

(7) The combination of all these points amounts almost to a description of the Integral Touch Experience. Thus the combination, contrary to K, presents the infallible intuitive evidence for the existence of, and our knowledge of, an extended material world of bodies—that is, the evidence for direct realism.

The integral touch experience is the test and guarantee of the objectivity of sight and of the objective use of the other three (or four) senses. Another more general conclusion is this: This is another instance that confirms the belief that all idealisms imply realism, that idealism is a pathological function of realism.

VIII

METHOD IN METAPHYSICS

ew Introduction: This article[1] was the 1950 annual Marquette
University Aquinas Lecture. Since it was my first important
publication since my dissertation I decided to deal with a
central point in my understanding of Thomism, namely, the experiential
and intuitional origin of metaphysics. I took up a position which excluded all forms of a priorism in metaphysics—Kantian, Barclay's
idealism, transcendental Thomism (before the fact).

I have always maintained that we obtain our understanding of being
and of its principles either from immediate intuition of the real world or
by arguments depending upon those original intuitions.

* * *

Some twenty-two years ago, the eminent Père Maréchal opened a
series of lectures at the University of Louvain in which he intended to
deal with the problems of the transcendental value of metaphysics.[2] The
crux of the problem he crystallized in what he called the question of the
gate to metaphysics, that is to say, the passage from sense knowledge
to metaphysical knowledge strictly so-called. It is with this problem that
I am here concerned. I do not intend to deal directly with the question
of the transcendental applications of metaphysics but rather with the
crucial issue of its origin in human knowledge from sense experience.

I do not intend to give either a complete and total explanation or

---

[1]*The Aquinas Lecture*, 1950 (Milwaukee: Marquette University Press, 1951).

[2]Maréchal, "Au seuil de la métaphysique: Abstraction ou intuition," *Revue Neo-
scolastique*, 31 (1929): 27–52, 309–342.

129

one that is entirely new. Much of what I will say has already been discovered and said by those before me, notably by the patron of these lectures, Thomas Aquinas. But above all I am fearful of falling into the fallacy which I have called the fallacy of "only." It is dangerous temptation to which most philosophers yield at some point or other, to mistake some positive discovery or explanation for a total explanation—to say, for example, that because they have found one method of knowledge which is valid and intelligible, it is the only method of knowledge. Whenever we insert an "only" in a statement it becomes really two statements, one positive and the other negative. If we say, for example, "the only way to travel from Saint Louis to Milwaukee is by train," we are saying first that we can travel from Saint Louis to Milwaukee by train, which is obviously true, and secondly, that there is no other way we can travel from Saint Louis to Milwaukee, which is obviously false. Moreover, while it is quite possible to prove the positive element in such a composite statement it is extremely difficult to prove a negative statement which almost has the force of a universal exclusion. This is the error of those who say, for example, that only the scientific method can yield valid knowledge or that only one type of science is true science.

Nor will I pretend to give an explanation which will constitute a "system" in the meaning which that term has acquired in modern thought. A system pretends to be complete and closed, and to be complete and closed a body of thought must have achieved an exhaustive transcription of its object into intelligible expression. For the philosopher whose object is the intelligibility of the whole of the real such a pretension would be equivalent to the deification of his own mind. Consequently any philosophical explanation, however sound and certain its positive elements may be, must remain open to deepening insight and the advancing conquest of reality. I hope that I shall be able to indicate at least how those discoveries and formulations which constitute the definitive contribution of historical Thomism to philosophy will remain within the framework of my proposed explanation.

I shall try therefore to avoid fallacious exclusion as well as specious and over-simplified completeness. While it is true that certain basic characters run through all our knowledge, there is, within the complexity of this knowledge, an almost endless variety of differences. The human mind has rich resources and a fecund creative power from which arise the astonishing devices and means—the metaphors, theories, abstractions, correlations, concepts, constructs, and so forth —by which it attempts to understand and control reality. A vast field of investigation lies open here which the Thomists have perhaps cultivated with too little effort. It may be that our failure here explains in part why there is so little Thomistic contribution to the theory of art, or of rhetoric, to the philosophy of history and to the explanation of post-Renaissance science.

Now when a science puts forth a claim to be both an independent science and a science of the real, this claim must be justified by establishing an immediate source of data which is proper to this science and not open to any other science or discipline. If metaphysics then is an independent, self-constituted science of the real, there must be a point at which it is in a privileged contact with reality and at which it takes its origin. This moment which I thus designate as a necessary moment in the construction of any independent science of the real, I shall call experiential for it is from human experience that metaphysics must draw its sustenance.[3] *Our problem may be now described as that of the experiential moment of metaphysics.*

For the purposes of the present discussion I shall make two presuppositions.

While a conscious study of method may precede a science in its pedagogical presentation, logically and historically, reflection on method follows at least the partial constitution of a science. I have therefore been able to limit my problem to a question of method because I am convinced that a body of valid metaphysical knowledge is in existence and may serve as a laboratory specimen for our investigation. I am presupposing that there is such a metaphysics which is, as a matter of fact, different from the body of knowledge in any other

---

[3]I use the word "experiential" to designate a wider area than that covered by "experimental" or "empirical." These latter words have been appropriated to indicate the methods of physical science. If they are allowed to cover all the modes of immediate contact with reality, then there is no room for an independent philosophy and metaphysics. The positions would be determined by an assumption which, however widespread and currently respectable, remains a mere assumption. If metaphysics does not have an initial (and continuing) contact with concrete reality independently of the methods of so-called scientific methodology, then it cannot be an ontology, an independent science of being, but rather a meta-physics, a meta-mathematics, or some other sort of discipline at two removes from experience and subject to the limited sciences upon which it depends.

science and which is, moreover, not distilled from other sciences by any process of super generalization or universal analysis. The metaphysics to which I refer is existential Thomism, the metaphysics of being (*ens*) and existential act (*esse*).[4] At the point where this investigation begins, the problem of the possibility of metaphysics is, as a simple matter of given fact, already solved. Yet, though a valid metaphysics is given, it is neither whole nor complete now nor will it ever constitute a closed and circumscribed system to which no addition can be made or in which no further depth is possible.

The existence of a valid metaphysics is then the first presupposition. It must be pointed out, however, that this is not a mere assumption. Thomistic existential metaphysics contains its own evidence and its own justification, though the examination of that evidence does not fall within the limits of this discussion.

Secondly, I do not intend to be led astray by the so-called "critical" problem, that mirage of speculation which has led so many modern philosophers to die of intellectual thirst in the arid desert of epistemology. I accept as certain that knowledge can be and, as a matter of fact, often is a knowledge of things as they are and of things which are. I do not presuppose for one moment that knowledge is a platonic vision of reality, that the intellectual object or even the sense object is given whole and entire, actuated, that is, in the order of knowledge, independently of the faculties which we possess and the modes of knowing which are ours. But to admit that knowledge involves subjective limitations is not to deny the massive fact, the common intuition, the objective evidence, that to know is to know something, and that in the first instance, to know is to know some sensible thing. Consequently, in what I have to say, it is presupposed that realism in a large sense is a sound philosophical position, though it is not to be understood as a naive realism or as the absolute realism of Plato. The basic position is that of a true realism that can find objectivity within human knowledge, an objectivity which is *per se* independent of the subjective

---

[4]The best general view of Thomistic existentialism in English is to be found in Etienne Gilson, *Being and Some Philosophers* (Toronto: Pontifical Institute of Mediaeval Studies, 1949), 154–189. See also, Gilson *L'être et l'essence* (Paris: Vrin, 1948), *Le Thomisme,* (5th ed., Paris: Vrin, 1944), especially 42–68; 497–523. Thomistic existentialism is, of course, profoundly opposed to the current existentialisms of Sartre, Jaspers, etc.

modifications which make knowledge possible as well as of the emotions and other factors which may, indirectly, affect our knowledge. The validity of realism is therefore the second presupposition, though this, like the previous one, is no mere assumption or hypothesis.[5]

The problem before us can now be stated thus: *What is the experiential genesis of Thomistic existential metaphysics, viewed as an independent science of the real?*

We are therefore investigating the experiential moment of a certain kind of knowledge. Unfortunately the discussion cannot be conducted on so narrow a basis. It is necessary first to understand intellectual knowledge and its genesis in a more universal way before we can grasp this particular type. We must examine knowledge in itself.

Here a number of different approaches are ready at hand. Experimental psychology—or perhaps we should say experimental psychologies—use various indirect approaches: Intelligence, knowing, and knowledge are measured and their manifestations correlated among themselves or with accompanying processes, neurological, physiological, and so forth. Knowledge is treated simply as a fact and the mystery of its nature abstracted from. Sometimes it is reduced to categories of physical processes (e.g., "reaction to environment") which methodically obscure what is peculiar to it. Because of the great variety of methods, it is difficult to characterize the whole body of experimental psychologies; yet, in the main, the approaches are "indirect" and leave the nature of knowledge in itself untouched.

For our purposes, it is necessary to study the unique and specific and, even mysterious, nature of knowledge as such, to grasp it in its own peculiar intelligibility. The approach must be direct, though we are confronted by an ultimate and almost inexpressible reality. The method must therefore be a philosophical one.[6]

---

[5]See Gilson, *Réalisme thomiste et critique de la connaissance* (Paris: Vrin, 1939); Maritain, "Le réalisme critique," in *Les Degrés du Savoir* (5th ed., Paris: Desclée, 1946), 137–263. The remark of Gilson with regard to modern thought and Thomistic realism needs emphasis: "Hence in the first place we see that modern critics of scholasticism do not so much as suspect either the nature or the depth of the gulf that divides them from it." *The Spirit of Mediaeval Philosophy* (New York: Scribner's 1940), 238.

[6]The treatment here presupposes a distinction in methodology between the philosophical and the physical sciences. In the philosophical sciences ontological intelligibility is dealt with directly; consequently contemplative insight and induction-through-insight are essential to philosophical method. In the physical sciences

Yet even philosophers have handled the nature of knowledge in different—and nonetheless-legitimate ways. The philosophy of knowledge being a direct science of a nature and hence ontological in character allows easily of a metaphysical prolongation. Those whose minds are peculiarly adapted to metaphysical consideration pass rapidly to this stage of philosophical explanation. Knowing and knowledge are viewed at this point as a kind of becoming and of being. Thus arises the strangely exhilarating theory of the *esse intentionale*, the order of intentional being and becoming.[7] While the uniqueness of knowledge does not disappear when it is thus translated into terms and conceptions (*esse*, act, etc.) which are proper to metaphysics, yet this way of understanding knowledge is not the simple and concrete view of its nature as given. The introduction of these higher and deeper insights of the metaphysician, while fruitful and valid, often tends to obscure the concrete peculiarity of the data to which they are being applied.

The metaphysical approach is, therefore, not the one we need here, however magnificent the sight to which it leads. We are interested in precisely the concrete richness of knowing in its own immediate and direct intelligibility.

Another traditional part of "rational psychology" (or "philosophy of man") has to do with the analysis of knowledge in terms of its efficient causes. The analysis begins with facts of experience in the order of knowledge. It requires a certain moderate measure of intelligent introspection to discover within consciousness, as moments or elements of our knowing, the sense image and the concept. It is quite easy to become aware of the elaborated sense-presentation of an object; somewhat less easy to identify the concept of an object. Yet the concept was historically one of the earliest discoveries in the theory of knowledge; Socrates and Plato clearly identified it and distinguished it from the sense data, though neither of them was fully aware of what he had

---

ontological intelligibility is not primary; indirect understanding and control of certain aspects of reality is achieved through constructs and induction-by-inference. Thus the concept of "mass" in physics is typical of the physical sciences; the understanding of the substantial unity of a living organism is typical of philosophy. Certain points of this distinction may be found, in a somewhat exaggerated form, in Ardley, *Aquinas and Kant* (New York: Longmans, 1950). See also Hawkins, "Induction and Hypothesis," *Causality and Implication* (London: Sheed and Ward, 1937), 107–122.

[7] Cf. J. Maritain, *Les Degrés du Savoir*, 215–230.

discovered. Aristotle further examined conceptual knowledge and laid down some of its definitive characteristics. Since then consideration of the concept has rarely been absent from philosophical discussion.

Because of the ease with which the image and the concept can be recognized and distinguished, Thomistic rational psychology has taken them for a starting point. Both image and concept stand out in the fluid processes of our knowing as clear-cut and formed terms; consequently, in using them, Thomists have concentrated attention on the terms rather than on the processes of knowing. Taking certain characteristics (e.g., particular—universal; concrete—abstract) of image and concept, their natures are sharply and specifically distinguished, the one is found to be material the other spiritual. The question of their genesis is now placed in the order of efficient causality, within which the whole elaborate structure of agent and possible intellect, and of the *species impressa,* is set up. When the line of causality is followed according to this analysis, at only two points does it necessarily fall within consciousness. It begins with the elaborated sense presentation—the phantasm—which is discovered in consciousness and terminates at the full-formed concept, the *verbum,* which is also consciously possessed. In between, the process, as far as this argument goes, is wholly below the level of consciousness and consequently only virtually in the order of knowledge as such.[8]

This reduction of knowing to its underlying efficient causes is of course valid and philosophically necessary, but there is a strong tendency at this point to commit the error of the "exclusive only." We so stress this part of the analysis that we are tempted to say that this is the whole story of the genesis of intellectual knowledge and the only causation to be considered. If we do so however, several very inconvenient results follow. By resting our case so exclusively on a "formed" result of intellectual activity—a "term"—namely the *verbum, "cogitatio formata,"* the fact of a process of formation is overlooked and a certain artificial cleavage introduced into our consciousness. By relating this term to a set of ontological and fundamentally general principles of activity, we give the impression of a certain mechanical rigidity little in keeping with the plasticity and mobility of our intellectual experience. There are other insufficiencies, some of which

---

[8]E.g. Remer, *Psychologia* (Westminster: Newman, 1942), 134–196.

will appear in the course of the discussion, but at the moment it is more important to return to the main line of our argument.

The kind of investigation which I am proposing can now be described more closely. The approaches of the experimental psychologists fail us because they are extrinsic to the very nature of knowledge itself. The metaphysical consideration of knowledge does not reveal the immediately perceived unique character of knowledge but, presupposing this, moves on a more profound and generalized plane. The causal analysis rests mainly upon the material and spiritual character of the image and the concept and these characteristics are ontological rather than noetic characteristics. Having selected from directly perceived evidence these convenient facts and characteristics, it leaves the order of knowledge itself to establish ontological principles of operation.

The consideration we must employ must be centered on the immediately perceivable nature of knowing and knowledge. Our own knowing lies open, in its process and products, to immediate introspection and reflection. Hence, to remain wholly within the order of knowledge we must remain within consciousness where alone knowledge is formally present and discoverable.[9] The reflection needed is not a hasty glance sufficient to identify a *fact;* it must be contemplative in character, a gaze concentrated and held steady until we penetrate the *nature* of knowing. We may then describe our procedure as a study of knowledge as such in its own unique and directly perceivable "intelligibility."

The introduction of the word "intelligibility" points up a seeming paradox in our procedure and at the same time leads directly to our next problem. We are attempting to achieve a knowledge of knowledge and are so led to speak of the intelligibility of intelligibility. But, however cumbersome such expressions may be and however verbally puzzling, there exists no real difficulty, since we are capable of intellectual reflection, in which knowledge is, in a sense, transparent to itself. All

---

[9]This procedure is in no sense to be confused with that of Descartes. Descartes begins within a *closed* consciousness wherein he finds *thought* and *ideas* and from which he must argue to external realities. In a true realism, reflective consciousness discovers *knowledge* of *things* and finds itself in *immediate contact with reality.* This *knowing* must, however, be studied by reflective contemplation.

confusion can be avoided if we remember that "intelligibility" appears at two different levels in our discussion.

Intellectual knowledge involves an object (since knowledge is always knowledge *of*) and this object must be intelligible.[10] Consequently to understand knowledge, we must understand "intelligibility." Thus intelligibility is part of the subject matter of our investigation in which we must therefore inquire "What is intelligibility?" This is the first level at which intelligibility is involved.

Our approach to the problem of knowledge and intelligibility, as has been indicated, is direct and immediate, that is we are inquiring into intelligibility under the aspect of its intelligible nature. Thus at this second level, intelligibility is a formal constituent of the viewpoint from which we are considering knowledge.

For a proper understanding of both of these levels we must now attempt to understand what intelligibility means.

Considerable time must be devoted to this attempt for precisely here, both extreme reationalism and sensism have conspired to conceal "intelligibility" from the view of modern philosophers. We are at a point of crucial disagreement, and of irrevocable choices. "Choose" says the philosophical Queen; a fatal choice will be avenged by philosophy's own inexorable Furies.[11] Our method will imply an appeal to the immediate intellectual experience of each man and must amount to a pointing out through examples, rather than a description in alien terms, for we are up against a unique and ultimate reality that can be compared justly to nothing else in the world.

The obvious dialectical definition of understanding *(intelligere)* and the intelligible in terms of each other is thus of no service, for it is meaningless without an awareness of the immediate experience in which the two are found together. We can compare them in the line of act and potency, explain them in terms of general categories, as object

---

[10]D.J.B. Hawkins, *The Criticism of Experience* (New York: Sheed and Ward, 1945), 11–23.

[11]Both Hume and pre-Kantian Rationalism agree in denying intelligibility to sense-given objects. Sensism uses this to destroy the entire order of intelligibility and with it all rational necessities. Rationalism asserts the independent and *a priori* character of thought. In either case reality as given is opaque to the eye of intelligence. See J. Maritain, *Réflexions sur l'intelligence* (Paris: Desclée, 1930), 9–77. Maréchal, *Le point de départ de la métaphysique* (Paris: Alcan, 1923), Cahier II, 179–185.

and subject, as being or becoming, or illumine them by metaphors, scientific or literary, drawn from sight and the visible, from light and image, but the peculiar reality of intellection and intelligibility escapes all these devices and remains in its own nature unique and ultimate.

The difficulty is increased by the distortions which philosophy and scientific theory have introduced into the whole question of intelligence and its operations. Philosophical reflection and analysis has, in many cases proceeded as though there were, in the whole of man's conscious activity or in large areas of it, no such thing as intelligibility.[12] I do not mean to say that any thinker has been able to work without intelligibility, but I do mean that many thinkers have excluded it in whole or in part from their formal theoretical explanations, or have misinterpreted and disfigured it. It goes without saying that any crude materialist would do so. An example of an attempt to explain knowledge without considering either intellection or intelligibility is the naturalistic theory of Ralph Barton Perry.[13] To one who practiced intellectual reflection, Professor Perry's explanation appears incredible, an amazing feat of sustained ignoring—and the theory can only be seriously regarded when one remembers the theoretical presuppositions which entail such an explanation. The history of philosophy offers many examples. To find Berkeley reducing the intelligibility of concepts to sense images in the very example in which he is unmistakably describing the fact of an

---

[12]"Psychologists, following the biologists, who are themselves following the physicists, feel that at all costs they must be objective. Therefore they study man in a detached sort of way, as if they were not men themselves. Mr. Sidney Hook has seriously wondered (in *Education for Modern Man*) whether man is intelligent. He says this is an empirical question on which considerable evidence has accumulated. One would think that Mr. Hook, having made the acquaintance of some men, would know whether they are intelligent or not. But no. Scientific reserve demands the cautious statement that "evidence has accumulated." But how does evidence accumulate? Does it lie around in a sort of dust pile, or does it accumulate in minds, and if so, don't men have to be intelligent in order to take in the evidence? Perhaps it would not be too outrageously daring to conclude that "at least some men possess at least some intelligence." Mr. Hook might have come to this conclusion by contemplating himself. But here is the point—by the rules of the scientific game, he is not allowed to contemplate himself. To do so would not be objective. It would be subjective. It would be using *introspection*, a procedure which is regarded with the darkest suspicion by all true scientists." Anthony Standen, *Science Is a Sacred Cow* (New York: E.P. Dutton & Co., 1950), 118–119.

[13]Ralph Barton Perry, *Present Philosophical Tendencies* (New York: Longman's, 1919), 271–328.

understanding of a common nature is at least amazing.[14] It is as though a detective were to establish the non-existence of a murderer by the very argument in which he clearly identifies and convicts a living criminal.

In order to capture intelligibility in the moment of its experiential presentation the practice of intellectual reflection to an uncommon degree is therefore requisite, accompanied by an ascetic abstention from obscuring theories and theoretical interpretations. Intellection and intelligibility are pervasive in our conscious living, yet, as Chesterton has said, it is the vast and obvious thing that a man overlooks. A man may gaze at grass in safety ninety-nine times; the hundredth time he may see at last that grass is green!

Let us suppose a person who has no experience and no knowledge of rectangularity, a person to whom both the word "rectangularity" and the content which it expresses are as yet unknown. In order to induce in him the knowledge of "rectangularity," I present to him a rectangular card. The card enters his consciousness in the elaborated phantasm (the unified sense presentation). A variety of characters are, of course, here re-presented for the card has a certain roughness or smoothness, a definite color, size and location. By a series of rhetorical eliminations and "pointings" I focus the person's intellectual attention on the shape of the card. He not only senses the shape, he intellectually sees the peculiar type of shape which I am designating as rectangularity. He sees it thus in the card itself and in the re-presentation of the card in the phantasm which is a transparent revelation of the card itself. The very moment in which he sees the rectangularity, he begins to assimilate it intellectually, he begins to understand what is meant by rectangularity, to possess this meaning and to express it to himself in a concept. The full actualization of this understanding (intellection) is reached only when he manages to express it in an articulated definition. There is nothing unusual about this experience; it is the common experience of learning from sense presentation of real objects. The understanding which begins with the first active moment of seeing the rectangularity in the card and reaches its first completion in a conceptual definition is what we mean by intellection. It is contemporaneous with the sensible experience though different from it. Reflecting upon it we see that it can be called an active assimilation of the rectangularity of the card, an

---

[14]Berkeley, *The Principles of Human Knowledge* (La Salle, Ill.: Open Court, 1940), "Introduction," 14–19.

expression in intellectual knowledge of the same rectangularity, an insight into the presentation of sense and the experienced card. The rectangularity in turn is called intelligible because it can be thus the object of intellection. Now, just as the act of intellection reveals in itself in a continuous series of stages, so does the intelligibility of the object. There is the point before the card is presented; there is here no act of intellection with regard to rectangularity; the card is presented and attention focused, the intellection begins by an active insight stimulated by the sense re-presentation; it reaches perfection only when the rectangularity *of the card* is expressed by the intellect to itself and possessed in a definition transparently present to intellectual consciousness.

So also with the rectangularity *of the card*. Before the card is presented, it is not understood but it can be understood—for it is the rectangularity *of the card* that the intellect will assimilate. Though *intelligible* (can be understood), at this point the card is not within the order of intellectual knowledge at all; hence it is said to be potentially intelligible. When it is presented in sense experience, it enters the field of knowledge; it can be understood, but it is still not within the order of intellectual knowledge, it is still potentially intelligible, and it is still the intelligibility *of the card* which is being "carried" and re-presented by the phantasm. Only when the rectangularity begins to be "seen" by intelligence does it move into intellectual knowledge, and only when it is expressed in a concept is it wholly actuated within intellectual understanding. At this point therefore the rectangularity *of the card* is understood and actually intelligible.

In knowing the rectangularity of the card, we see that its intelligibility is not another reality or character super-added to rectangularity; it is the rectangularity itself. The rectangularity is a reality in the card and, to exactly the same extent, an intelligibility of the card. At every stage in the process so experienced, it is the intelligibility *of the card* which is in question, and in the final stage, completed in a direct existential judgment, when we say "This card is rectangular," it is the real rectangular card which is understood expressed and asserted.

This instance reveals to reflection the meaning of intellection and intelligibility. It has the additional advantage of exposing the stages in which an intelligibility may exist as potentially intelligible, actually intelligible, and actually understood. Moreover it is the type of intellection which is basic in human knowledge for it begins with sense data and moves to pure intellection without ever cutting itself, epistemo-logically, from the concrete object.

Yet the same active power of insight is found in many different processes. We might take a case in which we are no longer dealing with the intelligibility presented by a sense phantasm. Whenever the intellect follows a line of reasoning and constructs a formal syllogism in which it assents to a conclusion because it sees it flowing from or involved in two premises, the intellect perceives a relationship which exists between the premises and the conclusion. The perception of this relationship is an understanding, an *intelligere*. The relationship itself, since it can be perceived in this peculiar intellectual way, is said to be intelligible. It is actually intelligible because it does not have to be transferred from a buried sort of existence in sense data to the actualization of pure intellectual knowledge but can be immediately perceived as soon as the premises are set up. Given the premises, the mind perceives the necessary connections and assents to the conclusion. The intelligibility of the connection is immediately seen, and, again, this character of intelligibility is not simply superadded to the relationship but is iden-tical with it in so far as the relationship is, in its very nature, transparent to conscious intelligence.

These instances should suffice to indicate where intelligibility is to be found in experience and how contemplation of it is to be carried on. I do not mean to say that the account just given does not raise many questions and difficulties. Much less would I pretend that anyone who has been accustomed to approach knowledge through the selective abstractions and in-directions of experimental psychology or through the obfuscating theories of non-realistic or anti-intellectual philosophies will readily perceive the content of this experience or its meaning and bearing.

However, though these instances would suffice for our immediate purpose, I intend to treat yet another case, for this special case, besides emphasizing the nature of intelligibility, will supply a necessary groundwork for later developments.

Let us suppose again that I am holding up a card before your eyes. I then draw a line dividing the card. The card, I tell you, with reference to this division, is called "the whole," the divisions as divisions are called "parts." I point out that I could indicate parts by drawing com-plete lines anywhere on the surface. By a process similar to that in the case of rectangularity, I thus induce an understanding of "whole" and "part" in a quantitative sense. As in the previous case, you can continue to contemplate the "whole" and the "parts" *in the card*. As you continue to do so, the question is put, "Is the whole greater than any part I indicate?" Yes. "Is it in the nature of the case that it must be so?" Yes. Observe the card. Observe the "whole" and the "parts." It is immediately obvious *in the card* that the whole card must be larger than any indicated part. Not only is the intelligibility of "whole," "part," "larger" intellectually perceived in the card itself but the *intelligible necessity of the relationship is likewise seen in the card itself*. This may go against the doctrinal grain of all those who have been accustomed to think of the necessity of principles as involving some *a priori* element or as being derived from conceptual analysis. I would suggest that at no point have preconceptions more thoroughly obscured the true state of the case.[15] The necessity is first of all an intelligible ontological necessity; the necessity is in reality experienced; it is an intelligible necessity just as rectangularity was an intelligible modification of the card. Consequently, it can be and is directly understood in the sense-experienced data, in the reality itself. Because it is found in reality and there understood, it can be expressed in knowledge. The necessity of the principle does not arise from intellect but from reality; necessity qualifies the expression in the order of knowledge because the necessity is ontological and being determines knowledge.

The necessity is already in the singular judgment as a *de jure* and not merely *de facto* necessity. It requires only a reflection—that in fact adds nothing—to purify the proposition of accidental elements and express it as a principle of continuous quantity in general: "The whole is greater than any of its parts."

---

[15]Both extreme sensism and extreme rationalism agree in denying any intelligible necessity to the sense-presented object. Along with Kant, a great deal of modern thought has worked under this restrictive assumption. Cf. Kant, *Critique of Pure Reason*, trans. Smith (London: Macmillan, 1933), "Introduction," 43–45; Smith, *A Commentary to Kant's 'Critique of Pure Reason'* (London: Macmillan, 1930), xxxiii–xxxiv. The simple fact is that some necessities can be seen in the sense-experienced reality. The absolute opposition of contingent and necessary is not verified as between experience and intellectual knowledge. "Respondeo. Dicendum quod contingentia dupliciter possunt considerari. Uno modo, secundum quod contingentia sunt. Alio modo, secundum quod in eis aliquid necessitatis invenitur; *nihil enim est adeo contingens, quin in se aliquid necessarium habeat*. Sicut hoc ipsum quod est Socratem currere, in se quidem contingens est; sed habitudo cursus ad motum est necessaria; necessarium enim est Socratem moveri, si currit". *Summa Theol.* I q. 86 a. 3.

It will be recalled that instances of understanding were introduced here in order to guide intellectual reflection to the discovery of intellection and intelligibility. The central point in the instances is that peculiar activity which is understanding. If we have been able to recognize the existence and character of this activity, we now see how it permeates intellectual knowledge, no matter how diverse the mode of knowing or the things known.

Anything, therefore, which can be known intellectually, which can fall under intellectual activity may be designated as intelligible, whether potentially or actually. Intelligibility is not a character or reality added to the thing known; the thing as such can be known and its intelligibility is therefore, in the first instance, concretely identical with it. The thing however as knowable or as known can be re-presented in the order of knowledge; all the "carriers" or "expressions" of the knowable and the known are simply, in the first instance, expressions and carriers of the intelligibility *of a thing which is known*. Consequently, whether the intelligibility be on an ontological mode of being (as rectangularity) or a necessary ontological relationship (the whole is greater than any of its parts), it is always the intelligibility found in the real order that continues to be understood and reflected upon in intellectual operations.

Two further points must be noted here. The reflective contemplation and the analysis (of experiential data, not of concepts) we have just conducted leads to the broadest possible extension of meaning for the term intelligible; indeed, a great deal of our remaining task will be taken up by filling in the matters to which it can be applied and exploring the diversity of intellection.

Though the instances were introduced to illustrate intelligibility, a review of our discussion will reveal that we have actually described in the first and second case the process of induction through insight. We maintained ourselves strictly within a noetic consideration, contrasting the known and knowing, the intelligible and intellection. When an intelligibility is brought to full act, in the pure intellectual state, if it contains an understood ontological necessity, this necessity is seen to be potentially multiple to the exact extent to which the intelligibility in which it is, is potentially multiple. That is to say, if the ontological intelligibility is capable of being in other instances, the understanding of that precise intelligibility in pure intelligible form will be seen, on reflection, to be universal; that is, it can be used as a means of understanding and expressing further instances.

Certain important conclusions can be drawn here: (1) The opposition of knowledge and the known is not an opposition of thing and thing, or of particular and universal, but of thing and that thing's actually grasped intelligibility. (2) Universality is not a *per se* characteristic of knowledge as such; it attaches to certain kinds of human knowledge because of the conditions, subjective and objective, under which human knowledge takes place. (3) Consequently, to state the problem of knowledge as primarily involving a tension of individuality and universality or of contingency and necessity is to set up a pseudo-problem and to repeat both the Platonic and Kantian error. In other words the problem of induction is fundamentally solved as soon as the fact and nature of inductive insight, that is of the movement of intelligibility from a potential to an actual state within intellectual knowledge, is discovered and realized. The reflection we conducted above can bring us to this discovery and, slowly indeed, to this realization.

The facts which we have reviewed would be impossible if there were a sharp and absolute break between sense and intellect. The openness of sense to the active insight of intelligence is a central and often overlooked fact. The expression "potentially intelligible" designates the sense re-presentation as it thus falls under the activity of intellect. The Thomistic doctrine of potential intelligibility is therefore not a theory resulting from an *a priori* application of act and potency but is the expression of immediately observed facts.

The moment a sensible object enters consciousness through its re-presentation in the phantasm it falls within intellectual awareness. The phantasm, epistemologically speaking, initiates the activity of intellectual knowledge and the moment of attention and awareness is the first moment of the causality of sense with reference to intellectual knowledge. *The phantasm is object of awareness for the intellect and, qua object, a mover.*[16]

All this is merely an explication of the content of our previous analysis. Yet it will appear to many Thomists to be an intolerable paradox. The limited analytic procedure by which phantasm and concept are sharply distinguished and related to independent and essentially diverse faculties tends to obscure the vital unity of sense and intellect.

---

[16]For a fuller development of this point as it refers to conceptual knowledge, see B. Lonergan, S.J., "The Concept of *Verbum* in the Writings of St. Thomas Aquinas," *Theological Studies*, 7 (1946): 372–380, especially the valuable footnote on page 373.

Sense and intellect are, of course, essentially diverse, and the sense faculties cannot be the efficient cause or seat of concepts. Yet experience reveals that we are intellectually aware of the phantasm and that there is a conscious continuity within the integral act of human knowing.

The facts may be approached from another angle. Thomistic philosophers, in establishing the unity of man, have frequently made use of the immediately perceived unity of consciousness. Our experience does not reveal two distance consciousnesses, each cabined, cribbed, and confined in itself. Sense consciousness and intellectual consciousness may be formally diverse but they are experientially conjoined; intellectual awareness permeates all our conscious life.

Doubtless, unity of consciousness is evidence of a unity of substance; the ontological ground must be found in one substance. Boswell may cling as closely as he wishes, pad and pencil in hand, to Samuel Johnson, yet his sense consciousness can never merge with the intellectual consciousness of his idol and master. The argument is metaphysically ineluctable—but what is frequently overlooked is that the very evidence for it is a *unity at the level of operation*, the permeation of the whole of consciousness by intellectual awareness. The self-aware light of intelligence is not focused solely on the limited area of concepts or of judgments, but spreads through the more obscure places of sensation and emotion.

If one finds it difficult to discover this fact in conscious experience, we might point it up by asking how we can intellectually assert the distinctive characteristics of the phantasm and rationally conclude to its formal diversity from the concept. Are not these characters—and consequently the phantasm itself—immediately open to intellectual reflection?

The phantasm therefore is itself an object of intellectual awareness. As such, it re-presents to intellectual insight the ontological reality known through it; that is, it carries the potential intelligibility of that reality. As soon as it becomes object of intellectual awareness and attention, it is engaged in the causality of knowledge. Yet, though it is an intelligible object, it is not a wholly satisfactory object; intellect cannot grasp its intelligibility purely and spiritually until, as we have pointed out before, it possesses this intelligibility in a pure intellectual and intelligibly transparent way. The potential intelligibility of the object, both thing re-presented and phantasm, must be moved to the actual intelligibility of pure intelligence. Again, the fact of a process within consciousness is indicated.

If we review the instances of "rectangularity" and the principle of "whole and part," we see that the process begins precisely with an intellectual "looking," a contemplation of the sense data in which there is a growing understanding, a progressive and active assimilation of intelligibility.[17] In many cases the process is relatively simple and rapid; in others there is definitely an effort, a conscious effort to understand and to express. The effort to express what is seen in the sense re-presentation is, in many cases, the effort to form a concept and to articulate a definition.

I should like to point out again that, if the analysis of knowledge into its ontological efficient causes were the whole story, the process and effort within consciousness (and within the formal order of knowledge) would be wholly unintelligible, for the transition from phantasm to concept or definition would lie below the level of consciousness. Experience reveals that this latter is not the true account.

There is another experience to which we can appeal to bring out the point that I am making. There are two very clear ways in which conceptual knowledge of any object may be increased. We can learn for example that this is a man. We can extend this knowledge by discovering that man is rational. We can further extend it by discovering and stating that he is an animal. In this extension of our understanding of man we are expressing distinct intelligibilities to which logicians often refer as notes. These notes can be held apart in distinct concepts or they can be brought together in a composite concept. They can be thought of as simple objects of the understanding or they can be used as

---

[17]"Unde intelligit quidem immaterialia, sed inspicit ea in aliquo materiali." *Contra Gentiles* II 73, ed. Leonine, 13: 462. ". . . finis autem potentiae intellectivae non est cognoscere phantasmata, sed cognoscere species intelligibiles, quas apprehendit a phantasmatibus, et in phantasmatibus secundum statum praesentis vitae." *Summa Theol.* III q. 11 a. 2 ad 1, ed. Leonine, 11: 160. ". . . Quando aliquis conatur aliquid intelligere, format sibi aliqua phantasmata per modum exemplorum, in quibus quasi inspiciat quod intelligere studet." *Summa Theol.* I. q. 84 a. 7, ed. Leonine, 5: 325. "Intellectus noster et abstrahit species intelligibiles a phantasmatibus, inquantum considerat naturas rerum in universali; et tamen intelligit eas in phantasmatibus," *Summa Theol.* I q. 85 a. 1 ad 5, ed. Leonine, 5: 332. "Non potest secundum eas (species intelligibiles) actu intelligere nisi convertendo se ad phantasmata, in quibus species intelligibiles intelligit, ut dicitur." *Summa Theol.* I q. 86 a. 1, ed. Leonine, 5: 347.

predicates, but the point is that the extension of knowledge here is *by way of addition of distinct intelligibilities or notes.*[18]

The extension of knowledge in the way just described obviously involves an increase in distinct intelligibilities within the order of quiddity. There is, however, another way in which knowledge may be extended. This way may be characterized, in opposition to the previous type just described, as a deepening of insight. The concept or the intelligible note or the pure expression of intelligibility is never exhaustive and may consequently vary not only between different individuals but also within the development of any single individual's knowledge.[19] It is a common experience of those who have engaged in intellectual work or study to find that with increased experience, after viewing, for example, a number of divergent instances of the same intelligibility or after constructing in the imagination metaphors or symbols of the same intelligibility or after constructing in the imagi- nation metaphors or symbols of the same intelligibility, there is an increase of understanding so that a person says, "Now I see what that meant" or "Now I appreciate the full meaning of that." For example, the very experience of intellectual life itself constantly adds to our understanding of the intelligibility expressed by the word "rational" in the definition of man. In this type of extension of knowledge there is no question of an added note, no question of a new intelligibility. Consequently, we frequently find ourselves unable to express the increased depth by the simple addition of a new term. It becomes necessary for us to indulge in an indirect rhetorical or psychological method, utilizing sense experiences and metaphors and so forth, in order to bring home to anyone the new understanding which we ourselves have achieved and now enjoy. Clearly in this case there is a conscious relationship between the expression of the intelligibility in the concept and the experience of the sense data which gives rise to the deepening of understanding. The concept is not a mechanical expression of something which has appeared on a different level or in a different con-

---

[18]*Summa Theol.* I q. 85 a.5.

[19]*Summa Theol.* I q. 85 a. 7.

sciousness, but it is worked out and elaborated, it grows from the very intellectual contemplation of the sense data themselves.[20]

The importance of insight into the phantasm is pointed up also by another fact. Even after we have elaborated a concept, we find it necessary to return, as it were, to the phantasm, to re-embody the intelligibility in a sense presentation in order to understand fully the intelligibility expressed. In the same way, when attempting to understand something, we often create phantasms in which to read the intelligibility we are trying to grasp.[21]

From these few indications and this brief review of cognitive experience we find: (1) that the phantasm is an object of intellectual awareness, (2) that as such it initiates the active movement of intelligence, (3) that it is potentially intelligible in the order of conceptual intelligibility, (4) that as object of awareness and as potentially intelligible it is object also of an active insight through which we read, with varying depth and fullness, the intelligibility it contains and as a result of which we express, with varying degrees of effort, its intelligibility in a pure conceptual state. The intellect, using a concept as a formal *signum quo,* returns to the sense, therein to contemplate the intelligibility understood through the concept—at this point knowledge is rich, real, accurate.[22]

If all this is true, the initial ontological insights are all dependent upon sense, in the first instance, and derivative from it, not by

---

[20]"The Scotist rejection of insight into phantasm necessarily reduced the act of understanding to seeing a nexus between concepts; hence, while for Aquinas, understanding precedes conceptualization which is rational, for Scotus, understanding is preceded by conceptualization which is a matter of metaphysical mechanics. It is the latter position that gave Kant the analytic judgments which he criticized; and it is the real insufficiency of that position which led Kant to assert his synthetic *a priori* judgments; on the other hand, the Aristotelian and the Thomist positions both consider the Kantian assumption of purely discursive intellect to be false and, indeed, to be false, not as a point of theory, but as a matter of fact." B. Lonergan, S.J., "The Concept of *Verbum* in the Writings of St. Thomas Aquinas," *Theological Studies,* 7 (1946): 373, footnote.

[21]"Quilibet in se ipso experiri potest, quod quando aliquis conatur aliquid intelligere, format sibi aliqua phantasmata per modum exemplorum, in quibus quasi inspiciat quod intelligere studet" St. Thomas, *Summa Theol.* I, q. 84 a. 7.

[22]For a description of "formal sign," see J. Maritain, *Les Degrés du Savoir,* 228–235.

argumentation or inference but by immediate insight.[23] It follows that the fundamental concepts are neither given *a priori* in the intellect, nor formed from sense experience by a quasi-automatic "natural abstraction" which guarantees their exhaustive and perfect character and eliminates contemplation and effort. If this is true in general, it is eminently true of that most realistic, most ontological of all the sciences, metaphysics. Its content, its intelligible necessities must be drawn in the first instance from sense data by inductive insight.[24] Its method in origin must therefore be inductive, not deductive. Since the intelligibilities so derived are not exhaustive and never complete, the metaphysician must at every step resort to the sense data, must continue to employ inductive insight at every point where his science rests boldly on the real.[25]

---

[23]"Non autem manifestantur nobis principia abstractorum, ex quibus demonstrationes in eis procedunt, nisi ex particularibus aliquibus, quae sensu percipimus. Puta ex hoc, quod videmus aliquod totum singulare sensibile, perducimur ad cognoscendum quid est totum et pars, et cognoscimus quod omne totum est majus sua parte, *considerando* hoc in pluribus." *In I Post. Analyt.* Lect. 30, ed. Leonine, 1: 259, no. 5.

"Ad 2ᵐ dicendum, quod iudicium non dependet tantum a receptione speciei, sed ex hoc quod ea de quibus iudicatur examinantur ad aliquod principium cognitionis, sicut de conclusionibus iudicamus eas in principia resolvendo . . . Sed quia primum principium nostrae cognitionis est sensus, oportet ad sensum quodammodo resolvere omnia de quibus iudicamus." *De Veritate* q. 12 a. 3.

[24]"Dicendum quod in qualibet cognitione duo est considerare, scilicet principium et terminum. Principium quidem ad apprehensionem pertinet, terminus autem ad iudicium; ibi enim cognitio perficitur. Principium igitur cuiuslibet nostrae cognitionis est in sensu, quia ex apprehensione sensus oritur apprehensio phantasiae, quae est motus a sensu factus, ut dicit Philosophus, a qua iterum oritur apprehensio intellectiva in nobis, cum phantasmata sint intellectivae animae ut obiecta, ut patet in III de Anima." *In lib. Boethii de Trin.*, q. 6 a. 2, ed. Paul Wyser, O.P. (Louvain: E. Nauwelaerts, 1948), 63.

[25]"Ad quintum dicendum quod phantasma est principium nostrae cognitionis, ut ex quo incipit intellectus operatio, non sicut transiens, sed sicut permanens, ut quoddam fundamentum intellectualis operationis, sicut principia demonstrationis oportet manere in omni processu scientiae, cum phantasmata comparentur ad intellectum ut obiecta, in quibus inspicit omne quid inspicit vel secundum perfectam repraesentationem vel per negationem. Et ideo quando phantasmatum cognitio impeditur, oportet totaliter impediri cognitionem intellectus etiam in divinis. Patet enim quod non possumus intelligere Deum esse causam corporum sive supra omnia corpora sive absque corporeitate, nisi imaginemur corpora, non tamen iudicium divinorum secundum imaginationem formatur. Et ideo quamvis imaginatio in qualibet divinorum consideratione sit necessaria secundum statum viae, nunquam tamen ad eam deduci oportet in divinis." *Ibid.*, ad 5 (65).

With some few exceptions what I have said up to this point would seem to presuppose that concepts express all that insight can discover in sense-presented reality and that human knowledge reaches its fullness and final perfection in conceptual knowledge. Our next investigations will show that this is not so.

Let us take the direct judgment "This card is rectangular." Several points must be noted:

1. We are talking about and thinking about a thing, an actually existing being. We are not talking about concepts, or about the content of concepts *qua* conceptual content, or about phantasms. The judgment is and expresses knowledge of reality; the epistemological term of this act of knowledge is the existing rectangular card. The psychological and/or epistemological media are here transparent in the order of knowledge; in technical terms, they here function as pure formal signs. There is a vital connection within the order of knowledge between this judgment and the card.

2. The judgment is itself an intellectual act. It is formally constituted and unified by an intellectual assent, an affirmation which englobes within intellectual vision and acceptance all the knowledge expressed in the judgment, whether this knowledge is wholly actuated in the intelligible order or not.

3. According to the causal analysis of knowledge, the ontological efficient cause of the act of judgment is the intellect itself. To seek the cause however *within the order of knowledge itself*, the true cognitional cause, is to seek the evidence upon which the judicial assent rests. But to seek this evidence in the case of a direct judgment like "This card is rectangular" is to ask for the source of the knowledge.

What is the complete knowledge expressed in the judgment?

In this judgment there are quidditive conceptual elements which can be considered separately as actual intelligibilities, the quiddity of "card" and the quiddity of "rectangularity." Conceptualized in their actual intelligibilities, these elements are knowledge of formal constituents and reveal the characteristics of all such knowledge. They are abstracted from the concrete "here and now" and from existence. In such cases the intellect has assimilated itself to the formal nature of the thing known, living its life by sharing the determination of its form, but according to its own spiritual mode.[26]

But besides these elements the judgment englobes a knowledge of the concrete individual, for it is not merely "card," it is "*this* card" that is known and expressed in the intellectual act which is the judgment. While there is no opposition between the abstract form "card" and its individualization in this card, the concept neither contains nor expresses the individual. This is to say that the concrete individual cannot be distilled into pure intelligibility. On this point experience is definitive, and this has been rather consistently recognized throughout the Thomistic tradition. Yet, it is part of the intelligibility carried by the phantasm, read there by the intellect and expressed in the judgment. Hence, the intelligence can only bear upon an individual as it is presented or re-presented in sense. A vital operational continuity *(continuatio)* of sense and intellect is thus necessary for the concrete existential judgment.[27]

---

[26]"Unde, cum similitudo rei quae est in intellectu nostro, accipiatur ut separata a materia, et ab omnibus materialibus conditionibus, quae sunt individuationis principia; relinquitur quod intellectus noster, per se loquendo, singularia non cognoscat, sed universalia tantum." *De Veritate* q. 2 a. 6.

[27]It is clear in St. Thomas that when *intellectus* is correlated with conceptual knowledge, an understanding of the individual is excluded. Yet, in order to form the judgment "Socrates is a man," intellectual knowledge of the individual is necessary. (*Summa Theol.* I q. 86 a. 1). Moreover, the same power must be aware of both the "universal" applied and the individual to which it is applied. ". . . Ita etiam non possemus cognoscere comparationem universalis ad particulare, nisi esset una potentia quae cognosceret utrumque. Intellectus igitur utrumque cognoscit, sed alio et alio modo." *In III De Anima* lect. VIII (ed. Pirotta, no. 712).

St. Thomas describes the mode in which intellectual knowledge attains the individual by various expressions, *Indirecte, per quamdam reflexionem, per quamdam continuationem*. In any case the actual sense presentation of the individual is required. "Et ideo singularia non cognoscuntur in sua absentia nisi per universalia," *In VII Metaph.,* lect. 10 (Cathala no. 1496); ". . . illa, quorum est definitio cognoscuntur per suam definitionem; sed singularia non cognoscuntur nisi dum sunt sub sensu vel imaginatione," *ibid.,* (no. 1495.)

The sense powers are said to assist the intellect in knowing the singular ("adminiculo inferiorum virium," *In lib. Boethii de Trin.,* q. 5 a. 2 ad 4). The term *"indirecte"* is reduced to the idea of union; "in quantum [intellectus] coniungitur phantasiae, quae repraesentat sibi phantasma: et sic indirecte cognoscit [singularia in materia]," *Quodlibet.,* q. 12 a. 11.

The same results may be obtained by a consideration of concrete time[28] and place, but above all, by a consideration of concrete existence. Reflection on pure conceptual intelligibility reveals its neutrality with regard to being; it expresses the *rationes* of things, not their existence. Or again, among material things only the concrete individual exercises the act of existence; concepts, because of their very mode, abstract from the material individual. It is equally impossible to express an existing material individual in a concept and to *derive* actual existence from concepts.[29]

Consequently, the concrete existential judgment requires wider and deeper insight into the phantasm, quite independently of the distillation of concepts. Actual existence cannot be expressed in conceptual intelligibility; only a vital *continuatio* between intellect and sense can underlie the judgment expressing it. Neither the concrete individual nor

---

The *"reflexio"* is explained as a *continuatio*. "Inquantum ergo intellectus noster per similitudinem quam accepti a phantasmate, reflectitur in ipsum phantasma a quo speciem abstrahit, quod est similitudo particularis, habet quandam cognitionem de singulari secundum continuationem quamdam intellectus ad imaginationem." *De Veritate* q. 2 a. 6.

We therefore have a situation in which the intellectual knowledge of the individual involves the presence of a phantasm, of which the intellect is aware and in which it finds the material singular. Whether the context concerns the application of a universal to the particular, the operation of ethical knowledge in particular cases or the experiential knowledge of an individual, the description is basically the same. This description outlines an operational unity of intellect and sense in which the intellect uses the sense powers. The key word, *continuatio,* was already a technical term in Arabian philosophy for just such an operational unity of diverse powers. A judgment concerning a material individual (e.g., "Socrates is a man.") is possible only through an intellectual awareness of and an operational unity with the sense powers in which the individual is presented. Both the texts of Saint Thomas and experiential reflexion used in our text lead to the same conclusion and reach agreement in the same description of the facts. For a significant collection of pertinent texts see G. Kennard, S.J., *The Intellect Composing and Dividing According to St. Thomas Aquinas* (unpublished thesis, Saint Louis University, 1949), chapter 3, "The Necessity of Composition for Knowledge of the Temporal and the Particular," 58–90; G. P. Klubertanz, S.J. *The Vis Cogitativa According to St. Thomas Aquinas: Sources and Doctrine* (unpublished thesis, University of Toronto, 1947), 393–400, 428–435, 441–446; Klubertanz "The Unity of Human Activity," *The Modern Schoolman* 27, (1950): 75–103.

[28]Cf. *De Veritate* q. 2 a. 7.

[29]Cf. R. J. Henle, S.J. "Existentialism and the Judgment," *Proceedings of the American Catholic Philosophical Association,* 21 (1946): 40–52.

its act of existence is in the order of form. The intellect assimilates itself to the existing thing through the exercise of a corresponding act within the order of knowledge, that is in a vital act of judgment in which the intellect lives the life of the thing in the "is"—no longer a colorless copula but objectivated and energized by assent through intellectual insight and transparently expressing the *existing* thing.

The intelligibilities and intelligible necessities which are expressed in the direct existential judgment are therefore known in the object and carried by the phantasm. The formal intelligibilities and formal necessities do not however cover the whole of this knowledge and consequently quidditative concepts are inadequate as expression of it. Intelligibility appears in two orders, that of form or essence and that of *esse*, the act of existence. Our intellectual knowledge overflows the limits of conceptualization and is fully grasped only in the judgment.

Let us turn then to metaphysics. The basic insight and intelligibility of Thomistic existential metaphysics is that of the *esse*, the act of existence. Metaphysics does not ignore the order of essence or the total structure of beings, but all its contemplation, all its effort to understand is carried on in the light of this act, *esse*. By this metaphysics is differentiated from all other sciences, for esse as intelligible does not command the formal considerations of any other science. By the same token, metaphysics is a philosophical science, since it deals with direct intelligibilities.

The experiential moment of metaphysics is therefore the moment of vital contact with reality in direct existential judgments. The primary necessities and insights of metaphysics are not deduced from concepts, nor added by *a priori* forms in the mind but are already contained in the existential judgments we constantly make.[30]

Yet to possess this knowledge in a series of such judgments is not to be a metaphysician or to possess a metaphysics. The necessities are

---

[30]Une métaphysique de l'être en tant qu'être "consignifie" l'existence, elle ne la "signifie" pas, à moins précisément qu'elle n'use de la deuxième opération de l'entendement et mette en oeuvre toutes les ressources du jugement. Le sentiment, si juste en soi, que le concept universel d'être et le contraire d'une notion vide, trouvera là de quoi se justifier. Sa richesse est d'abord faite de tous les jugements d'existence qu'elle résume et qu'elle connote, mais plus encore de sa référence permanente à la réalité infiniment riche de l'acte pur d'exister. C'est pourquoi la métaphysique de saint Thomas poursuit, à travers l'essence de l'être en tant qu'être, cet existant suprême qu'est Dieu. Étienne Gilson, *Le Thomisme,* 67.

there in the object known, in the phantasm, in the judgment; the intelligibilities are there. But in the direct judgment they are not possessed in their pure intelligibility nor in their full depth. By what process can this knowledge be moved from a stage of direct understanding to a stage of full explicit possession, without adding thereby to the knowledge itself any intrinsic modification? Since knowledge is transparent to itself and subject to self-direction the means lie ready to hand in reflection. We have already seen in the case of the principle, "The whole is greater than any of its parts," an instance of the operation of reflection in achieving a scientific status for knowledge of what is seen in the object. A similar procedure is necessary here. Reflection must be exercised upon the knowledge expressed in the judgment (not upon the judgment as a psychological act or a *form* of knowing) for two purposes: (1) to *direct* and focus contemplation of the reality itself with which the judgment is in living contact; (2) to order the intelligibilities of the judgment and understand them in their purity. The first is a process of deepening insight, a nourishing and enriching of the mind with the strong food of reality; the second lifts the knowledge to the level of consciously possessed intelligibility, that is, to the level of philosophical science. There must be a continuous movement between the two phases; thus metaphysics becomes ever deeper, ever more firmly grasped.

Metaphysics therefore cannot proceed by analyzing concepts. There are, in the first place, no concepts clear and exhaustive after the Cartesian pattern either given initially or infallibly produced by an automatic abstraction of the mind. Moreover, even given such concepts, existence, either concrete or purely intelligible, could never be derived from them. A metaphysics of conceptual analysis could never extend roots into the rich soil of reality.[31]

Nor can metaphysics arise from a reflection upon the forms of knowing, since as forms they would be empty of real content; the contact with reality would not be maintained.

Metaphysics must therefore be derived from experience, through a constantly purifying reflection. Nor does this refer to a single starting-point; the fundamental necessities and intelligibilities with which meta-

---

[31]Lonergan, *ibid.*

physics deals and on which it builds must be continually discovered in concrete experience.

We can once more illustrate by briefly examining a basic principle—that well worn, much-maligned principle of contradiction. Often it is presented as an inference from the concept of being or as primarily a law of thought. Sometimes we do think and speak as though it were a pattern laid up in an intellectual heaven with which we must force things to agree or as though it were a mental mold by which neutral and fluid experience must be shaped and formed. But, as a matter of fact, its intelligibility is present in the first and in any direct existential judgment. Any uneducated person recognizes the concrete intelligibility and necessity of the principle and rejects as absurd and laughable any suggested instance of its violation. The principle is, in fact, merely a recognition of the necessity of being in a given act of existence. "When Socrates sits, he sits with necessity." Reflection upon this intelligibility merely releases it in its purity, so that the scientific statement of the principle is an intelligible transcription of the necessities of concrete *esse*.

The example of the principle of contradiction is introduced here to supplement and recall the example of the principle "The whole is greater than any of its parts." Both can be seen, on reflection, to illustrate induction through intellectual insight. But the principle of contradiction expresses an intelligible necessity of the *act of existence* while the other principle is limited to the order of form and quiddity. Once we have discovered that intelligibility extends beyond quiddities and conceptualization, it becomes evident that metaphysical principles and insights depend likewise upon an induction through insight. The illustration of the principle of contradiction serves merely to summarize all our results in a strictly metaphysical principle.

At the beginning of the discussion we placed our question as that of the origin of metaphysics from sense-experience. We were dealing with an existing valid and realistic metaphysics, the metaphysics of being and its act, esse. We then asked, with more precision, what the privileged experimental moment of this metaphysics was and by what method metaphysics was derived from this experiential moment.

We have discovered that the privileged experiential moment of metaphysics lies in the experience from which arise the concrete existential judgments which we all make; from this experience metaphysics is derived by induction through intellectual insight and a purifying reflection. The experiential moment is privileged in the sense that metaphysics keeps always in view the intelligibility of *esse*, while all the other sciences attend, by direct or indirect means, to quidditative intelligibilities and, at most, presuppose existence or treat it as a fact and not as an intelligibility. Moreover, the concrete and realistic character of metaphysics is evident, since its insights and principles are found directly in reality. Finally, its position at the peak of philosophical science is clearly validated, for it deals not merely with quidditative or formal intelligibilities but with the intelligibility of that most intimate and ultimate of acts, *esse*, in the light of which it and it alone considers all things.

IX

MARITAIN'S METAPHYSICS: A SUMMARY PRESENTATION

Ｎew Introduction: When we were preparing for the Fourth Annual Meeting of the Maritain Association we decided that instead of issuing a general call for papers dealing with Maritain's thought we would select one work of Maritain and concentrate the whole meeting on that one work. We would lay the groundwork for the discussion by inviting different people to write papers on different parts of the book. The book we selected was the *Degrees of Knowledge* and I was invited by the committee to do the paper on Maritain's note of understanding the nature of metaphysics. This article[1] answered that request. The meeting was a great success. Everybody enjoyed concentrating on one book, which of course we had asked them all to re-read before they came to the meeting itself. At the end I collected all the papers and published them in a book entitled *Selected Papers from the Conference-Seminar on Jacques Maritain's "The Degrees of Knowledge."* As a general assessment of Maritain's metaphysics I would say that Maritain is thoroughly existential and authentically Thomistic. His metaphysics is incompatible with transcendental Thomism and incompatible with all forms of *a priori* philosophy. Toward the end of the article I began to deal with a

---

[1]First published in *Selected Papers from the Conference-Seminar on Jacques Maritain's "The Degrees of Knowledge,"* Proceedings from the Fourth Annual Meeting of the American Maritain Association, Saint Louis University, May 9–10, 1980, eds. R. J. Henle, S.J., Marion Cordes, and Jeanne Vatterott (St. Louis: American Maritain Association, 1981), 32–54.

controversial issue, namely, whether we can have a concept of an existance or being. Gilson, Brunan, Bourke, and I myself all maintain that we cannot have a concept of being or of existence when Maritain insisted in talking about the concept of being. While he maintains there is a concept of being, by the time he explains why this is a privileged concept and really unique it no longer appears to be a concept at all.

In recent years Maritain's reputation as a Catholic philosopher has been diminished, I think, largely because of his conservative attitude to Vatican II. And that I believe is a great loss to Catholic intellectual life. Maritain is a very insightful and profound philosopher.

* * *

As we all know, *The Degrees of Knowledge* is primarily directed toward an analysis and critique of our modes of knowing. One cannot expect, therefore, that even in the sections explicitly devoted to a discussion of metaphysics, Maritain would attempt to give even an outline of a complete metaphysics. For this reason, although my paper is based primarily on The *Degrees of Knowledge,* I have used, by way of interpretation and supplement, several other closely related works. Maritain himself, in the postscript to the third edition (*Degrees,* xvi), referred to his *Quatre essais sur l'esprit dans sa condition charnelle* as, ". . . in certain respects, a supplement to *The Degrees of Knowledge.*" I have made extensive use also of *Existence and the Existent* and of the *Preface to Metaphysics.* Both of these works are closely related to the metaphysical expositions given in *The Degrees of Knowledge.* For the text itself, I have used the fifth French edition and the Phelan English translation.[2]

While *The Degrees of Knowledge* cannot be considered as having an exposition of a total metaphysical doctrine, it is itself, in one sense, totally metaphysical. Maritain divides metaphysics (that is to say, metaphysics fully formed and presented didactically) into three parts, namely, a critique of knowledge, a basic ontology, and a natural theology.[3] Epistomology, in Maritain's view, does not exist outside of or

---

[2]Jacques Maritain *Les degrés du savoir* (Paris: Desc de Brouwer, 1948). Trans. Gerald B. Phelan in *The Degrees of Knowledge* (New York: Charles Scribner's Sons, 1959). Hereafter referred to as *Degrees.*

[3]*Degrees,* 80.

separately from metaphysics. Metaphysics is precisely the locus for epistemology and for critique because it is the highest natural wisdom and, therefore, has as its function not only reflection on, and justification by such reflection of, its own principles, but also reflection on the basic forms or modes of knowing which are formal to all other disciplines. It belongs to the wise man to order all knowledge.

In a sense, therefore, this entire conference is dealing with the first part of metaphysics, namely the critique of knowledge. Therefore, in my presentation, I will concentrate on the second and third parts of metaphysics.

The analysis of metaphysics into these three phases or parts is not, of course, in the order of origin; they are parts of a constituted and developed metaphysics. We do not begin to develop a metaphysics by starting with a critique of knowledge. We start with some perception of being.

Maritain stands in the line of the great philosophers of being for whom metaphysics is a true science, a true wisdom and substantive knowledge, which deals with being as being. Of course, no neat and clean explanation is universally accepted as to what this time honored phrase "being as being" means. The first task, therefore, in understanding metaphysics, is to determine the philosopher's conception of being as such.

Maritain's philosophy is a thoroughgoing realism, in which things, as they are, present themselves to us an are the source and measure of all knowledge, and therefore of truth. His metaphysics then, is likewise a realistic metaphysics, and its roots must be in the reality which we all know. Consequently, at the origin of metaphysics, we must reflect upon our direct and ordinary knowledge, which arises from our immediate experience of the real world. Maritain uses the term "common sense" to refer to this kind of pre-philosophical, pre-scientific and pre-reflective knowledge of things. Here, in the first intellectual contact of the human mind with the really existing sensible world, an understanding of being is immediately and spontaneously generated. At the first awakening of the intelligence, the first spontaneous understanding englobes a concept of being.

I find it everywhere, everywhere itself and everywhere varied.
I cannot think anything without positing it before in my mind

> . . . it is being which is first known and into which every object of thought is resolved for the intellect.[4]

This grasp of being in common sense is not simply an acceptance of a given or of a factually present, or simply of a particularized thing. In this initial understanding of being, there is, though implicit and not recognized as such, the very intelligibility of being itself and of its first principles. This first concept implies or necessitates all the primordial intelligibilities of being, including even its analogical character.

> For being is a primordial and common object of concept . . . which . . . is itself and right from the start essentially diverse in the diverse objects in which the mind meets it.[5]

This common sense grasp of being includes the intelligible necessities of being to such an extent that even the non-philosopher, operating only within the realm of common sense, is able to reach true pre-philosophical conclusions concerning fundamental problems. These conclusions include a pre-scientific, pre-philosophical knowledge of God, of human personality, of free will, and of other most vital practical conclusions.[6] Though at the common sense level the metaphysical concept of being is not disengaged but "disguised, invisible,"[7] its intelligible force is fully present.

The spontaneous process, by which the intellect, at this common sense encounter, immediately generates a concept of being, is a natural total abstraction which is opposed, as we shall see to the formal abstraction that is involved in the metaphysical intuition of being itself. Borrowing a term from Yves Simon, Maritain calls this abstraction an "extensive" abstraction.

> . . . we perceive the notion of being to be the most extensive, the widest of all notions. But we have not yet disengaged the

---

[4]*Degrees*, 210–211.

[5]*Degrees*, 211; 214.

[6]Jacques Maritain, *A Preface to Metaphysics* (New York: Sheed and Ward, 1948), 29. Hereafter referred to as *Preface*.

[7]*Preface*, 33.

properties of beings as the primordial source and focus of intelligible mystery.[8]

The understanding of being as the most extensive of all concepts is not merely implicit, it is explicit in the knowledge of common sense.[9] Common sense puts all objects into this concept. The common sense grasp of being is therefore as universal or as extensive as the metaphysical understanding of being itself. Common sense, then, is more general, more extensive than the particularized, individual sciences which are subsequent to it.[10] Moreover, since the initial grasp of being is spontaneous and immediate, common sense grasps what it does grasp without flaw or error, for being, at this stage, "cannot deceive us, since, being the first, it cannot involve any construction effected by the mind nor, therefore, the possibility of faulty composition."[11]

It must be emphasized, as I have already said, that the intelligibilities of being and their intrinsic necessities are discovered spontaneously by the human intellect in the sensible world, even though this world is, indeed, a world of contingency and change. Despite the contingent character of the sensible world, there are stabilities and necessities in that world which are immediately open to intelligence. Maritain well understood that contingency and necessity are not purely and totally opposed in the real world, and, therefore, are not always mutually exclusive. On the contrary, he saw that the real sensible world is a world of contingent necessities, thus eliminating the original sin of Platonism, Kantianism, and Transcendental Thomism, namely their assumption that no necessary and universal knowledge could be derived from the sensible world.

The concept of being which I have been describing up to this point is not, of course, the subject or the formal object of metaphysics as a scientific discipline. This concept which we all possess at the level of common sense is called by Maritain the "vague" concept of common sense. In our ordinary, everyday common sense knowledge, we do not

---

[8]*Preface*, 31.

[9]*Preface*, 32.

[10]*Preface*, 29.

[11]*Degrees*, 214.

disengage being—"real being, in all the purity and fullness of its distinctive intelligibility—or mystery."[12]

I have emphasized and re-emphasized the content of the vague concept of being found in common sense, even though this concept is not the subject of metaphysics as such. It is important to understand that at the level of common sense the intelligence has already implicitly and blindly, as it were, grasped the basic intelligibilities which become explicit in metaphysics as we move from the vague concept to the philosophical concept. Thus is established what Maritain calls the second phase of metaphysics, in which we identify being as the "subject" of metaphysics, that which metaphysics studies and for which it seeks explanation and causes.

As already pointed out, the vague concept arises without any *a priori* imposition of the mind on reality, without any intellectual re-structuring of experience. Rather, there is a grasp of the intelligibility that is found in the diverse entities presented to the mind in ordinary experience. When we pass from this vague knowledge to the explicit knowledge of metaphysics, it is likewise important to note that, for Maritain, what happens in this movement is not the addition of some new intelligibilities of being to existence and the principles of being and existence as they are found in the vague notion, and, therefore, also in the real world.

Common sense attains the same objects as metaphysics,[13] but in a different way,[14] and is, indeed, an "incomplete" knowledge.[15] The act by which we disengage being from its immersion in common sense is called by Maritain "an intuition." His formal definition of this intuition is "the intellectual perception of the inexhaustible and incomprehensible reality thus manifested as the object of this perception."[16] He adds, "It is this intuition that makes the metaphysician." Since this is a disengagement of what exists englobed in common sense, the intellectual perception includes the perception of being and its properties, the

---

[12]*Preface*, 44.

[13]*Degrees*, 214–215.

[14]*Preface*, 229.

[15]*Preface*, 31.

[16]*Preface*, 44.

perception of its transcendental character and its analogical character.[17] This intuitional disengagement is achieved by formal abstraction which is distinguished, of course, from total abstraction.

Maritain proposes to call abstraction "visualization" rather than "abstraction" because of the misunderstandings and the various connotations attached to the word "abstraction." Therefore, total abstraction is called "extensive visualization."[18] In extensive visualization, the intelligible object is there (and this is the case in the common sense grasp of being), but is "wholly implicit or blind." Formal abstraction, or intensive visualization, places before the mind universal types and essential intelligibilities explicitly abstracted and laid bare.[19] In the case of metaphysics, intensive visualization, or formal abstraction, yields a concept of being in which being is understood in its purity, not as found in sensible objects alone, but as open simply to the world of intelligibility and of real or possible existence.

Thus, at this level of visualization, it can be seen that being does not imply sensible being, that being as such, in its pure intelligibility, abstracts from all matter. Because of this purification or disengagement of the concept of being from the sensible beings in which we initially find it, the second phase of metaphysics, which now deals with this disengaged concept of being, is called "transensible." It is the realm of the trans-sensible, now being itself, even when found in sensible beings, is seen to transcend the sensibility of the object and to exist in a realm of pure intelligibility.

For the same reason, this intensive visualization is identified with the third degree of abstraction of traditional Thomism, and is at the highest level of conceptual immateriality.

It should be noted that Maritain identifies all three degrees of abstraction as being intensive visualizations and formal abstractions. Thus we read in the *Preface*:[20]

---

[17]*Degrees*, 214–225; *Preface*, 44.

[18]*Preface*, 75.

[19]*Preface*, 76.

[20]*Preface*, 84.

There is thus a series of successive courts of scientific jurisdiction corresponding with successive levels of intelligibility.
We must pass from one to another, drop one veil after another,
and so ascend to increasingly pure degrees of formal visualization so long as there is still something left to see in the
object, something which could not be seen hitherto, because on
the level which had been reached it was still hidden, lay
beyond the jurisdiction to which appeal was made. We are thus
made conscious at one of the indigence and the greatness of
the human mind which can enter the being of objects only by
gradual stages, by divesting them first of this, then of that
objective determination, of this and that stratum of know-
ability, sensible first, then intelligible-physical, then intelli-
gible-mathematical, which conceals what still awaits our
perceiving. For a pure spirit there could be no question of
degrees of abstraction or visualization. It would not abstract.
It would see everything in an object from within and as
involved in its being itself, down to the final determinants of
its singularity. The vision of an Angel represents a knowledge
at once and indivisibly metaphysical, mathematical and
physical, and which even comprises the intellectual equivalent
of sense perception. All these things are distinct for us only
because we are intellects that derive from material things
themselves by means of the senses, the objects on which they
feed. To reject abstraction is to refuse humanity.

It is essential to note that this movement from the vague concept to
the intuition of being is achieved not by way of additional content of
knowledge, not by way of induction, not by way of demonstration, but
simply by a reflective disengagement of being in its trans-sensible
intelligibility. It simply drops all that flows from or pertains to the
materiality of corporeal sensible being. It is, therefore, ontological
knowledge, an understanding of real being, whether existent or possible.
This concept of being, which is the result of the metaphysical intuition,
provides the subject of the second phase of metaphysics, namely, that
which metaphysics studies and for which it seeks explanation and
causes. It provides also the formal object of the discipline and gives rise
to and specifies the *habitus metaphysicus*.

At this phase, metaphysics deals with the inferior analogates, in which we apprehend being *de facto*. Separated from and God, as *really existing beings,* are not yet included in the metaphysical viewpoint. However, since metaphysical knowledge at this level is trans-sensible, it is possible and, according to Maritain, necessary for the metaphysician to consider the structure of purely immaterial beings, even of infinite being, though at this point one does not yet know whether such exist or even whether they are positively possible. Maritain points out that, in the *Summa,* St. Thomas develops a doctrine concerning the Angels which rests upon revelation. Yet, Maritain also maintains that woven into this presentation is a metaphysical analysis of the structure of a finite pure spirit which can be disengaged from the data of revelation and viewed simply at a metaphysical level. In fact, he says, "He who has not meditated on the angels will never be a perfect metaphysician."[21]

By the same token, Maritain maintains that although the study of man belongs to the philosophy of nature, the soul, in its spirituality, comes also under the consideration of the metaphysician. The intuition of being which reveals its pure intelligibility likewise reveals its inexhaustible intelligible richness, richness such that we can neither grasp nor express it in a single concept, however analogous it might be. Consequently, in the second phase of metaphysics, we not only elaborate the concept of being itself and work out its internal structure in terms of essence and *esse* and its consequent analogous character, but we explicate that intelligibility in a series of concepts which deal with modes attached to being itself. Thus, we arrive at the transcendental modes, such as the good and the true, or specialized modes, such as substance. Moreover, the existential character of being involves the development of first principles or judgments which themselves reveal an additional richness. In the *Preface* Maritain himself works through the reflective and analytic explanation of the principles of identity, sufficient reason, finality and causality.[22] The first judgmental principle is the principle of identity, of which he gives a rather elaborate exposition in the *Preface.*[23]

---

[21]*Degrees,* 221.

[22]*Preface,* 91.

[23]*Preface,* 91–97.

Thus, at this level, basic intelligibilities of being are endlessly mined and elaborated. Once we have established the contingency based on the distinction between being and its act of existence, as we find it in all the inferior analogues of being which we directly know, and, further, after we have established the principle of causality, a truly philosophical search can be made for the causes of being, thereby transforming metaphysics into a true science. That is to say, metaphysics provides a knowledge of its subject through the principles or causes thereof.

The second phase of metaphysics consists of trans-sensible knowledge and analogous knowledge, but it is dianoetic in the sense that, at this level, and prior to the discovery of the causes of being, we have direct access to all the analogates which we find in experience, and we grasp them in their very being, at least up to some limit of intelligibility. Therefore, at this stage, we apply analogous concepts to the analogates because we know the analogates.

As we now proceed to the third phase of metaphysics, in which the causes of being are established and, therefore, in which not only the possibility, but the existence of God is established and brought under the formal object of metaphysics, we pass form dianoetic to ananoetic knowledge. Ananoetic knowledge is knowledge in which we have to think objects, which are otherwise unthinkable and unknown, by means of analogies drawn from the inferior analogates of the second phase and which we do know. Thus, our knowledge of God is purely and simply based on applications of analogies to a mode of being of which we have no direct understanding.

We can recall how Maritain maintains that the vague concept of being gives every man an adequate base for a certitudinal knowledge of God. Here, in the third phase of metaphysics, in natural theology, that certitude becomes a scientific one, as the proof is disengaged and laid bare.

In the *Degrees* Maritain gives a sample of the sort of demonstration we can use to establish the existence of God. It begins with the reflection on "thought," which discovers both its intrinsic value and its essential contingency, and then moves through the principle of causality to a thought "which has itself as its existence and as its object."[24] At this

---

[24]*Degrees*, 224.

point, therefore, we reverse the order of the analogates. We had to establish the inferior analogates within the second phase of metaphysics and, through them, move to the first cause of all being, so that now we see that the first cause is itself the primary analogate on which all others in the hierarchy of the analogy depend, and through which they are all ultimately to be explained. Thus, metaphysics is completed as a science. Moreover, while in the second phase we saw being as purified from material conditions and from all matter, and, therefore, had reached a trans-sensible knowledge, here we reach a trans-intelligible knowledge, since we can have no dianoetic knowledge of God.

Here, finally, is fully revealed the majesty and the misery of metaphysics, of which Maritain writes at the very beginning of the *Degrees*. Metaphysics reaches its culmination in the ananoetic grasp of God, the infinite being, the pure act of existence. Herein lies its majesty. But we reach God in metaphysics only blindly. Despite our ananoetic effort, God remains a hidden God, and we do not reach Him in Himself. Left to itself, metaphysics, in the very hour of its greatest success, seems to be a tragic failure.

At this point, not only does metaphysics become a completed science, that is, an understanding of its subject matter and its causes with scientific certitude, but it has become also a wisdom. Wisdom is "a supreme knowledge having a universal object and judging things by first principles." Above all the human disciplines, metaphysics is the only one that judges all things; that is, only metaphysics has an object so universal that it is transcendent and exercises this judging in the light of the highest of first principles. Beyond it lie only the two supernatural wisdoms which Maritain recognized, namely theological wisdom and mystical wisdom. These, indeed, surpass metaphysics in the line of wisdom. At last all three wisdoms will give way to the final vision of God.[25]

Looking back now, we can see why metaphysics, according to Maritain, includes a critique of all knowledge. As the highest knowledge and as a wisdom, it judges not only its own first principles epistemologically, but also the principles and the hierarchy of all other human disciplines. This, then, is an outline of Maritain's metaphysics. Several points, however, require special treatment.

---

[25]*Degrees*, 24–54.

Maritain has spoken constantly about the "concept" of being. He also maintains that there is a "concept" of existence. He has repeated over and over again the fundamental Thomistic doctrine that being is the first apprehension of the mind and is that into which all other apprehensions are ultimately to be resolved. In the *Degrees*, the emphasis lies on the concept of being or simply on "being." The act of existence is indeed emphasized and discussed, but the importance of the act of existence does not seem to come out as clearly as it does in some of his other works. I think the reason for this is that in the *Degrees of Knowledge,* where he is doing epistemology, or the first part of metaphysics, he is heavily dependent on John of St. Thomas, whose epistemology rests likewise heavily upon the nature of the concept. Therefore, to supplement the meager treatment of existence as we find it in the *Degrees,* we have to turn to some of the other interrelated presentations.

Our question is this. Given Maritain's emphasis on the "concept" of being, and even on a "concept" of existence, does he not risk losing the unique Thomistic understanding of the very act of existence itself, of the *esse*?

Being is what is first in our knowledge. How is this to be understood? Maritain tells us:

> The intellect . . . in the initial upsurge of its activity out of the world of sense, in the first act of self-affirmation accomplished by expressing to itself any datum of experience, it *apprehends and judges in the same instant*. It forms its first idea (that of being) while uttering the first judgment (of existence), and utters its first judgment while forming its first idea.[26]

In the first contact with reality, whatever the particular experience may be in which that contact takes place, the intellect is actuated both in simple apprehension and in the judgment, actuated simultaneously by a reciprocally caused and mutually related grasp of the subject of the act of existence and the actual exercise of the act of existence itself. The latter is not grasped through simple apprehension. Yet the intellect does intentionally grasp the very act of existing of the entity discovered outside the mind. It not only grasps this act, but it expresses it by

---

[26]Jacques Maritain, *Existence and the Existent* (New York: Pantheon, 1948), 23. Hereafter referred to as *Existence*.

affirmation and projection.[27] Grasp of existence as the very act of existence, as *existentia exercita*, is proper to the judgment and cannot be reduced to a concept or an essence. "But existence is not an essence; it is shut off from the whole order of essence."[28] "It is *judgment* which the act of existing confronts."[29]

Being is that which exercises the act of existence. It can be grasped in simple apprehension and, therefore, in a concept. But this concept is a privileged concept which transcends the order of essence and overflows simple apprehension because of its relationship to the act of existence;

> ... a privileged idea which is not the result of the process of simple apprehension alone but a laying hold of that which the intellect affirms from the moment it judges, namely the act of existence.... The ideas of being ... precede the judgment of existence in order of material or subjective causality; and the judgment of existence precedes the idea of being in the order of formal causality.[30]

> The abstraction proper to metaphysics does not proceed from a "simple apprehension" or an eidetic visualization of a universal more universal than the others. It proceeds from the eidetic visualization of a transcendental which permeates everything and whose intelligibility involves an irreducible proportionality or analogy—A is to its own act of existing *esse* as B is to its own act of existing *esse*....[31]

Although Maritain does indeed admit a "concept" of being and locates that concept in simple apprehension, it is like no other concept. It is "privileged" and it is "unique." Therefore, he emphatically refuses to reduce being, insofar as it is visualized in a concept, to the order of

---

[27]*Degrees*, 98, n. 3.

[28]*Existence*, 22.

[29]*Existence*, 23.

[30]*Existence*, 26.

[31]*Existence*, 30.

essence. It may be apprehended by a simple apprehension, but not by simple apprehension alone. Being, as the subject of existence, is intrinsically related to the act of existence, which is simultaneously reached, initially in the first judgment of the mind. This judgment coincides with the first act of simple apprehension. Being is differentiated from all other concepts by this intrinsic relationship.

Moreover, Maritain asserts the reality of essences and their act quality within their own order. The intelligibility of the essence is fundamentally a structured potency for the act of existence. Therefore, while he calls the act of existence a super-intelligible with reference to the intelligibility of essence, he also indicates that the true intelligibility of the order of essence is derived from the super-intelligibility of the act of existence itself. We know potency through act. Essence is not pure potency; it is a structured potency having its own intelligibility. Yet this intelligibility is derived from the act of existence.

Thus, in the very first grasp of being, acquired from the contact of the intellect with sensible reality, being and existence, or the subject of existence and the act of existence, are seen to be really distinct in the inferior analogates of being. They are seen to be in a relationship which differentiates and yet binds them together, a relationship which is unique to each being and yet common to all beings, so that the analogy of being is one of proportionality.

> The very notion of *essentia* signifies a relation to *esse*, which is why we have grounds for saying that existence is the primary source of intelligibility. But not being as essence, or an intelligible, this primary source of intelligibility has to be a super-intelligible. When we say that being is *that which exists or is able to exist, that which exercises or is able to exercise existence*, a great mystery is contained in these few words. In the subject, "that which," we possess an essence or an intelligible—insofar as it is this or that, insofar as it possesses a nature. In the very "exists" we have the act of existing or a super-intelligible. To say "that which exists" is to join an intelligible to a super-intelligible; it is to have before our eyes an intelligible engaged in and perfected by a super-intelligibility. Why should it be astonishing that at the summit of all beings, at the point where everything is carried to pure transcendent act, the intelligibility of essence should fuse in an

absolute identity with the super-intelligibility of existence, both infinitely overflowing what is designated here below by their concepts, in the incomprehensible unity of *Him Who is*?[32]

It is the judgment which first grasps, expresses, and intentionally apprehends existence as a true act of an external being, and therefore according to its proper nature. Nevertheless, Maritain maintains that besides this judgmental understanding of *existentia ut exercita,* there is a concept of *existentia ut significata.* This, he holds, is truly a concept in which existence is conceived *per modum quidditatis* after the fashion of a quiddity,

> presented to the mind not insofar as a subject has it, but, rather, insofar as it can be conceived *per modum quidditatis* as constituting a certain intelligible object . . .[33]

> There is a concept of existence. In this concept, existence is taken *ut significata,* as signified to the mind after the fashion of essence although it is not an essence.[34]

Therefore the metaphysician deals with the act of existing as the act par excellence. "It is everywhere the act and the perfection of all form and all perfection. . . . The act of existence is that which is most actual and most formal. . . . God contains within Himself all the perfection of being because He is being itself or the very act of existing subsistent by itself."[35]

Despite Maritain's insistence on the conceptualization of being, as well as the conceptualization of existence *ut significata,* there can be no doubt that his metaphysics is existential to the highest degree, but without dissolving essences either into pure limits, or otherness, or an emptiness which is posterior to existence itself.

Finally, there are two appendices that I would like to add to this presentation.

---

[32]*Existence,* 34–35.

[33]*Degrees,* 98, n. 3.

[34]*Existence,* 33.

[35]*Existence,* 36–37.

The first of these concerns "subsistence." In his analysis of the structure of beings, Maritain accepts the *modus subsistentiae* as a distinct part of that structure. The *modus subsistentiae* terminates the essence in the order of essence and makes it a true supposit. By so terminating it, it also makes it capable of receiving the act of existence. I feel obliged to add this to the general structure of his metaphysics because he insists on it, even to the extent of writing a special appendix for the *Degrees*, "On the Notion of Subsistence," consisting of pp. 434–444, but I confess that I can neither explain nor defend the *modus subsistentiae*. I do not understand it, and I think it violates the fundamental Thomistic analysis of the metaphysical structure of being.

A few additional comments on Maritain's intuition of being are in order.[36] In the course of this paper I have given what I consider his technical definition, a definition which seems to me to be quite reasonable, namely, a direct and immediate intellectual apprehension of intelligibility, or a super-intelligibility, if you will. Yet Maritain frequently speaks in almost ecstatic terms about this intuition as an event which sometimes is like a sudden illumination, occurs to different people as a result of different sorts of shock or experiences. At times, he describes it almost as though it were some sort of natural mystical illumination, or even a sort of grace.

I would handle these descriptions by distinguishing between a strictly philosophical epistemological presentation of this particular intuition and a humanistic approach to it as it occurs actually in people's lives. I, myself, think that his epistemological explication of the intuition itself is sound. I also think that his humanistic and poetic descriptions of the intuition are sound but must not be taken to be philosophical, and must not be subjected to metaphysical or epistemological criticism. I think that the full realization, the express, direct insight into the act of existence, or into being, can be an experience that is emotional, profound and very, very personal. It is in the nature of a realization or of a sudden seeing, like the flashing out of an understanding, of which Plato speaks in his Seventh Letter. It is something like the real assent that Cardinal Newman described. It would be parallel to a situation in which what Newman describes as a

---

[36]In the *Preface*, footnotes on pp. 59–60, Maritain takes notice of some of the criticisms directed against his intuition of being. This text contains some very important clarifications.

notional assent suddenly becomes, for some individual, under some kind of stress or special motivation, a real assent.

I believe that in my own almost lifelong study of metaphysics, I have had several such moments, precisely with reference to the intuition of being, moments of sudden realization accompanied by a deepening insight and by a kind of spiritual excitement, that flowed from the insight and, in turn, enhanced it. Consequently, I think that the humanistic and poetic descriptions given by Maritain of the sudden intuition are not at all fanciful. They should, however, be taken as humanistic descriptions and not as philosophical analysis. I think, further, that his use of humanistic methods to bring out the importance and the true meaning of philosophical insights and positions is a measure of the seriousness with which Maritain lived the life of a true philosopher. You will all recall that he had a certain contempt for the professor of philosophy or for the man who dealt with philosophy as a lawyer might deal with statutes or a mathematician with tables. Maritain was dead serious about metaphysics.

X

EXISTENTIALISM AND THE JUDGMENT

Ｎew Introduction: When I was invited to give the Keynote Address at the National Convention of the Catholic Philosophical Association I decided that I would add to the very clear presentation of the existential character of St. Thomas Aquinas in metaphysics put forth by Jacques Maritaine and Etienne Gilson and an analysis of the one human act of knowledge which grasps and expresses existence, namely, the judgment. I thought this analysis had never been done before and that it was an essential part of the existential position. I think it also makes clearer the reason why existence/being cannot be reduced to a concept. There must always be some objective reference in any understanding of being. I hope this article[1] makes that clear.

I am still completely convinced that we cannot conceptualize being or existence. There is no regular concept of being, for instance, of any individual thing, only in a judgment, but that leaves open the question "How do we understand and express the universalized understanding of being?" I now think that our universal understanding of being, the understanding of pure being, is grasped by the human intellect through a special complex apprehension that is gathered from all the experiences of individual beings that we have had. In this way this special apprehension can express the tremendous richness of being. And it can be the basis for developing the first principles of being such as the principle of contradiction, the principle of identity. It is this kind of apprehension, I think, that Maritain is talking about when he talks about

---

[1]First published in *American Catholic Philosophical Association Proceedings* 21 (1946): 40–52.

the concept of being almost as a mystical experience or at least a profoundly humanistic experience.

* * *

The subject assigned to me is "Existentialism and the Judgment." The task of treating this problem I approach with great diffidence. Professor Gilson has written in his *Thomisme*[2] of the difficulty of maintaining an existential attitude in metaphysics. This difficulty arises not only in understanding metaphysical problems and positions but also in expressing them. With these difficulties in mind and in view of the fact that a good deal of our time during these meetings will be devoted to various discussions of existentialism, I have attempted in this paper to suggest lines of thought rather than to assert positive conclusions.

EXISTENTIALISM

Thomistic existentialism, as I understand it, rests ultimately upon a clear and conscious recognition that *esse* is the supreme and ultimate act, that it is—to use a metaphor—an energy at the heart of the real, in virtue of which whatever is, is actualized. Being, therefore, is no longer to be identified with a Platonic essence or formality, or even with a substance whose act is form. Being, and in it the whole world of essence, is not orientated toward a further act; all else is potential—the reality, the qualities, characteristics, and modifications of essence, substance, and individuals are being only in relation to the final act which actualizes all that they are.

Now, Platonism had indeed explored the problems of philosophy and stored up a heritage of insights and conclusions; and of this philosophical good, Christians had taken their share and themselves produced philosophical writings of depth and power. But Platonism, precisely because it missed the center of the real, was unable properly to complete the work of philosophy. It was forever in danger of dissolving the real into a phantom play of formalities or attaching it to the unintelligibility of that which lay beyond being and beyond essence. Within Christian thought, a tension was thus set up between the implicit existentialism of revelation and the alluring but essentialist direction of

---

[2]*Le Thomisme*, 5e ed. (Paris: Vrin, 1944), 67.

Platonism. Moreover, Aristotle himself, a Greek indeed and never fully free of Platonism, did not reach the one truth necessary not merely to complete what he had found but to render what he had found finally intelligible and in itself true.

When St. Thomas broke through essence to existence, when he extended act and potency to the existential order, using them to express the unique nature of the interrelation of essence and *esse*, he reached the center of philosophy because he had reached the center of reality. The tensions of Aristotelian and Platonic thought, of Greek and Christian thought were thus relaxed not by a clever compromise or a facile eclecticism but by a fundamental reorientation, that brought to light, like the application of the proper key to a half-understood code, whatever truth they all possessed. This is why St. Thomas seems always to be close to his sources and yet at no point, in metaphysics at least, merely repeats them. The goods of tradition which had attracted the harmonizers of the past are not lost in St. Thomas, but they are in a new focus, and therefore they are different.

For our purpose we may now consider a text which is indeed an illustration of what I have just said, for it is a well-known existential text found in the Commentary on Aristotle's *Perihermenias*.[3]

> Ideo autem dicit quod hoc verbum EST consignificat compositionem, quia non eam principaliter significat, sed ex consequenti; significat enim primo illud quod cadit in intellectu per modum actualitatis absolute nam EST simpliciter dictum, significat in actu esse et ideo significat per modum verbi. Quia vero actualitas, quam principaliter significat hoc verbum EST, est communiter actualitas omnis formae, vel actus substantialis vel accidentalis, unde est quod cum volumus significare quamcumque formam vel actum actualiter inesse alicui subjecto, significamus illud per hoc verbum EST, vel *simpliciter* vel *secundum quid;* simpliciter quidem secundum praesens tempus; secundum quid autem secundum alia tempora. Et ideo ex consequenti hoc verbum EST significat compositionem.

---

[3]*In Perih., c.* 3, 1. 5, *n.* 8.

The proper and principal signification of "est" is actuality in its absolute sense, *in actu esse*. Whatever its subsequent and derived uses, its primitive function is to assert the primary act, the act of existence, that act through which all other acts can be actualized, can indeed reach the status of perfection even in their own order. As Jacques Maritain has said: "The copula has a properly judicative function in so far as it expresses a *vital act of assent* made by the mind thinking formally of the act of being *as an act.*"[4] Judgment is therefore an assent through an operation of the mind to the act of being. The judicative "est," signifying act, must consequently signify *per modum verbi;* it is a word of energy and actuality. In another well-known text, St. Thomas emphasizes this primitive function of the judgment. He tells us that there are two operations of the mind; the one, the *simplex apprehensio,* looks to the essence or quiddity of the thing, but the second, the act of composing and dividing, looks to the *esse rei.* The form of the judgment is therefore basically existential.[5]

Now the processes which we discover in our intellection are not proper to intellect as such but to a definite and a low level of intellect. Precisely because our knowledge proceeds to completion by a transitus from act to potency, it must be perfected through a complex series of operations. "*Cum enim intellectus humanus exeat de potentia in actum, similitudinem quandam habet cum rebus generalibibus, quae non statim perfectionem suam habent, sed eam successive acquirunt.*"[6] Yet, the processes have a correspondence to that object which is proper to our mind, and that object in every case presents a metaphysical composition of an *id quod* and an *esse.* It is in relation to this composition that the primary form of the judgment is to be understood. The judgment as such is therefore our way of grasping and asserting, in addition to the *id quod,* the act of existence which cannot be grasped in the first operation of the mind and which therefore cannot, properly speaking, be conceptualized.

It is then immediately clear that in a philosophy which has shifted

---

[4]*An Introduction to Logic,* tr. Imelda Choquette (New York: Sheed and Ward, 1937), 85.

[5]"Prima operatio respicit quidditatem rei; secuda respicit esse ipsius." *In I Sent., d.* 19, *q.* 5, *a.* 1, *ad* 7.

[6]*S.T., I.* 85, 5, *corp.* (531b 7–12).

the center of metaphysics from the order of essences to the order of *esse*—and this precisely because *esse* is the summit and center of reality—the importance and nature of judgment will be far other than it is in a purely essentialist philosophy. In an essentialist philosophy, in a pure Platonism, for example, existence must be ignored or treated as of no importance or reduced to the status of a form or a formality. In any case, the concept will be the seat of perfect knowledge and the judgment will become a purely logical function for interrelating or combining forms. Thus, in the *Sophist* of Plato, scientific or "dialectical" judgments merely state the rigid and necessary interrelation of an immobile and eternal system of pure forms. An essentialist philosophy does not therefore look upon the judgment as the perfection of human knowledge, where alone truth, properly speaking, can be found. On the contrary, it tends to assimilate human concepts to a higher type of intellection, to the mode of an intuitive intelligence. As Maritain remarks:

Since in man the apprehension of intelligible natures (simple apprehension) by means of abstraction does not provide material for judgment or assent, this apprehension must be completed by a second operation; the composition or division of concepts, the only means by which we have—in judging—true or false knowledge. Note that this condition is due to the imperfection of our intelligence. An intelligence superior to man's which would penetrate the entire object, essence and attributes, in a single act of intuition or synthetic apprehension, would see it immediately as having or not having such and such attributes in reality, would at the same time judge instantaneously *in the same operation without having to compose or divide.*[7]

Platonism then which takes our conceptual knowledge to be intuitive, posits an exact correspondence between the concept and its object. Essence is thus identified with being and the order of essence becomes the order of absolute intelligibility. Now essences are as a matter of fact multiple through mutual exclusion; they constitute an order of limitation and thereby their secondary and derivative character is revealed. Platonism, taking essence to be the absolute principle of

---

[7]*Logic*, 92–93.

intelligibility and of being, found itself in a closed sphere of multiplicity and limitation. Hence its impotence in the face of the final metaphysical problems. It could reduce the world to an ultimate principle only by a denial of intelligibility and of being in the very source of intelligibility and of being.

In an existential philosophy, the intelligibility of essences and their importance is not denied; but they are not ultimate. Since reality, whether taken as a whole or considered in its individual beings, depends upon an act of existence, in the one case upon the *ipsum esse* which is God and in the other case upon the individuals's proper *esse,* essence depends upon existence. The *esse* is the heart of the being, its most intimate and ultimate principle, the ultimate actualizing principle of whatever perfection or intelligibility the being possesses.

Essence is thus seen to be a limitation intrinsic to the act of existence upon which it totally depends and to which it is subordinated. Essence is therefore not to be identified either with being or with intelligibility. On the contrary the act of existence is seen to be the ultimate principle of intelligibility[8] and our mode of knowing through concepts, is in turn discovered to be both a limitation of intelligence and, even in the order of human knowing, an incomplete and imperfect act of knowledge. Hence the judgment which is an assent to and an assertion of the act of existence, is necessarily the perfect term of human knowledge. In it alone can formal truth be found and through it alone can we transcend the order of essence and carry the metaphysical enterprise to its ultimate conclusion.

Let us examine several aspects of this peculiarly important function of the judgment in the construction of an existential metaphysics. Being, *ens,* derives its meaning from *esse.*[9] In considering anything as being we cannot therefore ignore its relation to the act of existence which, formally if I may say so, makes it *being.* To break the relation between being and its act in the consideration of the mind, is to be left not with being, nor even with a possible, but with a pure essence. This therefore is precisely what an existential philosophy cannot do; for its stress falls upon being as that *cui competit esse.* Yet, the act of existence cannot be grasped in a concept; it is not subject to the treatment proper to a

---

[8]Joseph de Finance, *Etre et agir* (Paris: Beauchesne, 1945), 114–115.

[9]Cf. *In I Sent., d.* 8, *q.* 1., a. 1, *corp.*

formality because it is not a formality but an existential act. It can only be affirmed, assented to, intentionally possessed in the vital act of judgment. Hence an existential metaphysics cannot carry out its enterprise through concepts alone; it must continuously maintain contact with the *esse* affirmed in the judgment. The judgment must therefore function at the inception of metaphysics and throughout its development.

It is in the light of being that all our knowledge develops, that all essences are intelligible. All concepts are resolvable into being and all knowledge into the first principles of being. Being, therefore, must be the absolute starting point not only of metaphysics, but of any human knowledge whatever, even of common sense. Now since being is not conceivable except in relation to existence and since existence is itself not subject to conceptualization, the very starting points must include a judgment. That is to say that the primitive contact of the mind with reality must give rise to a unified operation which terminates and comes to rest in a direct judgment of existence. From the first there must be present in the mind, embodied in some existential judgment, "being is." Only in such an act can being itself be grasped. If there were a break between the concept and the judgment; if the mind could be informed in the first instance by pure concepts alone, no analysis of these concepts or of the subjective conditions of these concepts would ever yield "being." The grasp of actual being is absolutely prior to the consideration of essences, possibilities, formalities.[10]

Judgment then is essential to the starting point of metaphysics. Moreover, throughout metaphysics being must be considered continuously in its relation to the act of existence. If it is once divorced from that act, if the bond which ties it to its most formal act, is broken, it becomes merely essence, the highest abstraction of essential predicates, the most empty of all concepts, an essentialist void to be filled by formalities and so determined. This is of course to cease to have an existential philosophy and to lose oneself in a world of Platonic forms or disengaged essences. Metaphysics, to maintain its own vitality, must therefore not only continuously use the judgment to maintain the proportion between essence and existence but must also return to the initial assertion of actual being. Metaphysical contemplation must be

---

[10]Cf. Rousselot, "Métaphysique Thomiste et Critique de la Connaissance," *Rev. Neoscol. De Phil.* (1910): 496.

nourished and sustained by a return to actual being, as assented to in the judgment. It seems that the greatest threat to any metaphysics lies precisely in the constant danger of breaking this contact with actual existence. And is there any other way of avoiding it except through constant experience of existence? If I may translate a remark of Professor Gilson:

> A metaphysic of being as being "consignifies" existence, it does not signify it, unless, precisely it employs the second operation of the mind and sets in operation all the resources of the judgment. The feeling, so right in itself, that the concept of being is the contrary of an empty notion, will find there its means of justification. Its richness is first of all made of all the judgments of existence which it resumes and connotes, but more even by its permanent reference to the infinitely rich reality of the pure act of existence. That is why the metaphysics of Saint Thomas pursues, through the essence of being as such, that supreme existent which is God.[11]

It is then clear that unless the metaphysician uses the resources of the judgment not only in the very inception of his science, but continuously, in the enterprise of constructing metaphysics and in the metaphysical contemplation of being, he will, either in the very beginning or by slow degrees come to the clarity, the abstract emptiness, the static rigidity of an essentialism, and he will never reach the supreme existent which is God.

Our considerations have suggested that essentialism can be called abstract in some proper and specific sense. This could be justified by saying that it abstracts indeed precisely from the act of existence and so considers pure undiluted formalities. But perhaps there is another sense in which it can be contrasted with existentialism as abstract with concrete. When a chemist deals with anything precisely as a chemist, he considers the object only under certain formalities. That the object may be alive; that it may be the the living body of Fido or of John Jones may not enter into his consideration at all. But when a metaphysician contemplates anything in the light of being, he must contemplate it always with reference to the act of existence. It is therefore impossible for

---

[11]*Thomisme*, 67.

anything in the reality of the object to escape his consideration, for it is not only a *tale quid* but the *hoc tale* which is actualized by the act of existence. Being is *id quod est*. But he cannot express this concrete being except through a relation to *esse*, for the totality of an individual being is not subject to our conceptualization; pure concepts cannot express the full concrete reality. It is only in a judgment wherein the act of existence of the concrete being is affirmed that this intellectual reference to the concrete is possible. Just as the formal object of metaphysics can only be maintained existentially by recourse to the judgment, so also, precisely because of this recourse to the judgment, the being of the metaphysician when applied to any of its inferiors, even to the ultimate individuals, must, so to speak, be formally co-terminous with the full concrete reality to which it is applied. And hence it is that in the predication of being, even as between two individuals of the same species, the analogy of proportionality is present. And it is for the same reason that being can never be properly said to be an abstract concept as opposed to a concrete one. Precisely because of the resources of the judgment therefore, metaphysics is at once the most universal of sciences and, in a certain sense, the most concrete.[12] Hence when the metaphysician as such approaches reality he does not withdraw into a remote world of abstraction; he rather penetrates more deeply into the total reality, contemplating it in its highest and ultimate meaning. Essentialist metaphysics withdraws from reality; existential metaphysics plunges into the depths of reality.

We might note here another role of judgment in Thomistic existentianism. If metaphysics is not only the ruling science but also the ultimate ground and foundation of all sciences, its starting point must be self-justifying, and the theory of knowledge must develop within metaphysics and simultaneously with it. If therefore its starting point were not existential, did it not begin with "*being* is" as justified and contained in an immediate existential judgment, the whole of human knowledge would be broken off from reality and the false problem of Descartes, the problem of the bridge between thought and thing, would

---

[12]Dans une philosophie où l'exister est inconcevable autrement que dans et par une essence, mais où toute essence signale un acte d'exister, les richesses concrètes sont pratiquement inépuisables. Gilson, *Thomisme*, 67.

arise.[13] It is precisely because the primitive judgment assents to the existence of beings, before any reflection is made upon the self or the subjective conditions of knowledge that we can subsequently analyze and reflect without losing contact with reality. We do not start with thought and attempt to extract knowledge therefrom; we start with actually existing things asserted by an immediate judgment. Again it is only through the resources of the judgment, overlooked and ignored by essentialism with its conceptual procedures, that we can maintain a philosophical realism.

We have been dwelling on the existential character of the judgment and its consequent importance in the life of metaphysics. It might seem then that we have been speaking only of judgments of existence. However, the "est" not only of judgments of existence but of all judgments signifies ultimately the *esse rei*. We shall therefore now attempt to explain this by a brief analysis of judgments in which the "*est*" is said to be a copula.

As we have seen, *esse* is the actuality of all perfections; therefore whatever structural elements are discovered in any being as being, are, in an analogous sense, merely material, potential with reference to the act which constitutes them a being. Hence, the relations which the proportion of act and potency sets up within the concrete existent do not, by themselves, constitute the unity of the being. Its unity can only be achieved in its final and supreme act. A being is one in so far as it is, and it is in so far as it is one. Since, then, the *esse* actualizes not only the essence but the very unity of a being, metaphysical analysis of the structure of being as such must always be in function of the *esse*. Once a rupture is produced between being and the *esse* proportioned to it, analysis will end either in a structure of concepts or in a structure of things. It is only by returning constantly to the luminous center of the being, to its existence, that we can successfully discover the composition of being.

If then we find that we are able to grasp both the structure of being and its unity, to reconstitute, in the intentional order, its concrete unity, this is only possible through that operation in which we affirm the act of existence. This operation is, of course, the judgment. The objective composition and unity which we find in the judgment is directly depen-

---

[13]Cf. Rousselot, *Métaphysique*.

dent on the basic nature of the judgment as an assent to *esse*. Therefore, we cannot explain the reconstitution of the object in judgment, if we allow any type of judgment to lose its continuity with the primary meaning of *est*. A copula, devoid of existential reference, set over against and sharply distinguished from an existential *est,* could never join in an ontological unity, that which the subject and predicate signify.

The function of the judgment in re-composing and intentionally reproducing the unity of the object is therefore *ex consequenti;* it depends on the initial nature of judgment as an assertion of existence.

Now the judgment, though it applies a predicate to a subject, does not assert the identity of two concepts nor, on the other hand, of two things; it asserts an identity in being of that which is signified by subject and predicate.[14] The concepts which enter into the judgment bring with them the limitations imposed upon human knowledge by its abstractive and progressive character. That is to say that they do not, like Platonic intuitions, express the full reality or possess the mode of the object. Yet there is a foundation within the thing for the structure of the judgment.

> Dicendum quod similitudo rei recipitur in intellectu secundum modum intellectus et non secundum modum rei. Unde compositioni et divisioni intellectus respondet quidem aliquid ex parte rei; tamen non eodem modo se habet in re sicut in intellectu. Intellectus enim humani proprium objectum est quidditas rei materialis, quae sub sensu et imaginatione cadit. Invenitur autem duplex compositio in re materiali. Prima quidem formae ad materiam; et huic respondet compositio intellectus qua totum universale de sua parte praedicatur; nam genus sumitur a materia communi, differentia vero completiva speciei a forma, particulare vero a materia individuali. Secunda vero compositio est accidentis ad subjectum; et huic compositioni respondet compositio intellectus secundum quam

---

[14]"L'essence et l'existence sont ainsi les éléments complémentaires de l'affirmation qui apprécie la proportion des essences à l'*esse*, les jauge dans l'être. Tel est l'être du jugement, expression de l'etre des choses. Et c'est pourquoi des idées éparses et diverses que l'appréhension lui offre, il faut un tout, une unité d'ensemble." A. Marc, S.J., *L'idée de L'être chez saint Thomas et dans la scolastique postérieure* (Paris: Beauchesne), 85.

praedicatur accidens de subjecto, ut cum dicitur, homo est albus.[15]

The judgment therefore reconstitutes the unity of being, not by joining things or formalities, but by asserting an objective identity in an act of existence. *Compositio autem intellectus est signum identitatis eorum quae componuntur.*[16] As St. Thomas has pointed out, the structure of the judgment corresponds, in a sense, to the structure of the thing. Hence, the various act-potency relationships are expressed in the act-potency relationship of predicate to subject. *Nam in omni propositione aliquam formam significatam per praedicatum, vel applicat alicui rei significatae per subjectum, vel removet ab ea.*[17] The predicate is therefore an expression of some further formal determination that is identical with the subject in an act of existence. This is obviously true in the case of essential predicates; yet even in accidents, the predication would be impossible except that the *esse* of the accident, whether conceived as an extension of the *esse* of the subject or as a distinct and secondary act of existence, nonetheless unites with the subject in the most intimate union of being. Hence predication is properly *secundum rationem identitatis.* Just as the unity of the thing is completed and rendered actual only in the *esse*, so the unity as understood is completed only in the judgment which is properly an assertion of *esse*.

Moreover, the very meaning of EST as signifying the *actualitas omnium perfectionum* makes it most fit for the precise work of stating the unity of being, which, even in the composition that is itself potential to the act of existence, reveals a tension of act and potency. The existentialism of St. Thomas, in extending the notions of act and potency from the order of essence and substance to that of existence, has found for "act" a primary analogate in the most perfect of all acts, in the act of existence. And just as this act fulfills the notion of act in the highest degree, so it is also the ultimate actuation of every other act, the ontological principle without which there would be no act and no perfection. The structure of being within the order of quiddity then becomes dependent upon the existential act. Hence, *in rerum natura* no act can

---

[15]*S.T., I,* 85, 5, *ad* 3 (531b 53–532a 20).

[16]*Ibid.,* (532a 22–23).

[17]*S.T., I,* 16, 2 *corp.* (115b–7–10).

be act even in its own order except, ultimately, through the act of existence. Therefore, since first, all unity is potential unity prior to its consummation in the act of existence, since secondly, all act depends on the act of existence, since thirdly, the primary analogate of act is the act of existence, the judicative *est* is most suited to signify—according to the mode of our own intellection—the union of any act and potency, but this always in function of its primary signification of absolute actuality.

While attributive judgments do not express actuation solely within the order of existence but more immediately some prior actuation or unity within the concrete existent, they can fulfill this function only on condition that the "est" still signifies an existential act. We can say therefore with Maritain: "Thus the verb *to be* always *signifies existence* in a proposition with a verb-copula just as much as in a proposition with a verb-predicate; and all propositions affirm or deny the *actual* or *possible, real* or *ideal existence* of a certain subject determined by a certain predicate. In other words, they either affirm or deny that this subject and this predicate are identified in actual or possible, real or ideal existence."[18]

It is clear also from this discussion not only that the judgment is based on the progressive character of our human knowledge, being necessary in as much as we do not exhaust an object by one penetrating intuition, but that it is also the condition of a growing realistic knowledge. For in a judgment we do not assert the existence merely of those particular notes which may be expressed in a given concept, but of a concrete reality. If our knowledge were only of concepts, if the judgment did nothing but assent to the content of a concept, the explication of the subject of the judgment would be limited to the explication of what is formally contained therein, and hence the series of judgments by which we come to full knowledge of anything would be a mechanical unfolding of an initial datum in the conceptual order. But the initial judgment posits more than we grasp in the initial concept, and the further explication, though it may arise from many sources, is yet added to the original subject not extrinsically but *secundum rationem identitatis*. In other words, since the judgment, in an existentialism, is not an assertion of identity within the order of quiddity (non

---

[18]*Logic,* 52–53.

enim intellectus sic componit, ut dicat quod homo est albedo,[19] but basically an assertion of identity in the act of existence, the predicates may truly add to the knowledge of the subject, extending our grasp and understanding of it while at the same time contact is maintained with the concrete reality.

> Et similiter intellectus humanus non statim in prima apprehensione capit perfectam rei cogitionem; sed primo apprehendit aliquid de ipsa puta quidditatem ipsius rei, quae est primum et proprium objectum intellectus; et deinde intelligit proprietates et accidentia et habitudines circumstantes rei essentiam. Et secundum hoc necesse habet unum apprehensum alii componere et dividere; et ex una compositione et divisione ad aliam procedere, quod est ratiocinari.[20]

This progress in knowledge is therefore through judgments enlarging our knowledge by predicates *per modum formae* and *secundum rationem identitatis*. The full reality of the object sealed by the act of existence and asserted in its existence by the assent of the judgment, comes slowly to full understanding but always in relation to the act of existence posited in each judgment. The *ens* asserted in the original judgment grows through the quiddative explication of the judgment; what is actualized in the signified subject is expressed in a succession of predicates. Hence, the full comprehension of a given subject is possible through a succession of attributive judgments which are really only explications of the being asserted in an original judgment of actual, possible, or purely ideal existence. Thus our knowledge remains always true to the unity and richness of beings themselves through the judgment which is a *signum identitatis* because it signifies the existential actuation of the object.

Let us now briefly unify and summarize these various considerations. Because existentialism rests upon the consideration of existence as an act, it understands the judgment to be "a vital act of assent made by the mind thinking formally of the act of being as act."

---

[19]*S.T.*, I, 85, 5, *ad* 3 (532a 24–26).

[20]*S.T.*, I, 85, 5, *corp.* (531b 12–b 23).

Consequently just as the emphasis in metaphysics moves from essence to the act of existence, so in the theory of knowledge emphasis moves from the concept to the judgment. Likewise, just as in metaphysics ontological *verum* and *unum* are seen to be in function of the act of existence, so formal truth is to be found in the judgment and the unity of the object is reconstituted in the judgment precisely in function of its assertion of the act of existence. Therefore, finally, the judgment through its resources as a vital assent to *esse*, first of all, maintains metaphysics as a realistic and concrete science, revitalizing it as it tends to fade into abstractions, and, secondly, maintains the realistic and progressive character of all our knowledge. And we may add as an epilogue that since we are able in an existential metaphysics to escape from the limitation which is necessarily intrinsic to the order of essence, we are therefore able, through the resources of the judgment, to break through to the discovery and consideration of the pure act of existence which is God.

XI

ST. THOMAS'S METHODOLOGY IN THE TREATMENT OF POSITIONES WITH PARTICULAR REFERENCE TO "POSITIONES PLATONICAE"

New Introduction: In order to carry out the project of my doctrinal dissertation[1] I had to analyze the methodology that St. Thomas used in dealing with Platonic positions and thesis. The result of this investigation is contained in the first chapter of my dissertation. Subsequently this chapter was translated into German and republished in *Die Methodologie des hl. Thomas bei der Behandlung von "Positiones" unter besonderer Berücksichtigung der "Positiones Platonicae"* which claims to republish all of the most significant articles on Thomistic Methodology.

St. Thomas's critique of Plato is extremely important since so many efforts have been made to reconcile St. Thomas and Plato with somewhat disastrous effects for Thomistic philosophy as well as for modern philosophy.

* * *

It has long been a commonplace among students of the history of philosophy that the thought of Plato and his followers exercised a continuous influence throughout the entire period of mediaeval philosophy. The main lines of the Platonic tradition have been defined by Klibansky, who also enumerated many of the historical problems

---

[1]First published in *Gregorianum* 36, no. 3 (1955): 391–409.

connected with it.[2] Moreover, it has also been recognized that Saint Thomas found himself in the full flow of mediaeval Platonism and was confronted by systems, principles and positions which were, to a greater or lesser extent, Platonic in origin. Now, while almost every writer on mediaeval philosophy and on Saint Thomas has referred to these facts and the problems they suggest, until very recent times no thoroughgoing scholarly investigation of Saint Thomas' relation to Platonism had appeared. Huit presented several brief and rather inconclusive articles on the subject many years ago[3] and Baeumker included Saint Thomas in his general review of mediaeval Platonism.[4] However, within recent years attention has been focused on the problem and several elaborate studies have been published by Santeler,[5] Fabro,[6] Geiger,[7] and Little.[8]

These studies, obviously the result of most painstaking research, present a number of broad generalizations concerning Saint Thomas's historical and doctrinal relationships to Platonism. Their conclusions are supported by an extensive array of textual evidence. The value of the generalizations, therefore, depends entirely upon the texts presented. The crucial and critical question, then, in estimating the correctness of these studies and their enduring contribution to Thomistic scholarship

---

[2]Klibansky, *The Continuity of the Platonic Tradition* (London: The Warburg Institute, 1939).

[3]*Annales de Philosophie Chrétienne: Le platonisme au Moyen Age* 20, 324–333, 417–431, 489–514; 21, 31–47; *Le platonisme au XIIe siécle*, 21, 160–184; *Le platonisme à la fin du Moyen Age* 22, 26–47; and also *Les éléments platoniciens dans la doctrine de S. Thomas*: Revue Thomiste, 30 (1911). A short study was also published by Lipperheide, *Thomas von Aquino und die Platonische Ideenlehre* (München: Rieger, 1890).

[4]*Der Platonismus im Mittelalter*, Beiträge, Münster, Aschendorff, Band 25, Heft 1–2 (1927).

[5]*Der Platonismus in der Erkenntnislehre des Heiligen Thomas von Aquin* (Innsbruck: Rauch, 1939).

[6]*La Nazione Metafisica di Partecipazione secondo S. Tommaso d'Aquino* (Milano: Vita e Pensiero, 1939).

[7]*La Participation dans la Philosophie de S. Thomas d'Aquin* (Paris: Vrin, 1942).

[8]*The Platonic Heritage of Thomism* (Dublin: Golden Eagle Books, 1950).

is this: Do the texts, when properly and accurately read, support the interpretations essential to the various theses of these authors?

Now, anyone acquainted with modern Thomistic scholarship knows that it is no easy or simple matter to read a given text correctly. The intricacy of the sources and historical backgrounds, the difficulties of terminology, of methods, of chronology, and so forth, make the accurate reading of a text, as well as its ultimate interpretation into a general scheme, an achievement requiring all the resources of scholarship. Laborious and slow as it is, we must yet apply this type of study to the accumulated texts of these authors before we can properly assess the value of their work.

It is the purpose of this paper to begin just such a textual examination. Since the authors mentioned above do, to a large extent, employ the same texts and since, in the nature of the case, these texts turn out also to be the fundamental evidence for any understanding of Saint Thomas and Platonism, this examination should establish a solid evidential ground in the texts both for an exact critique of the published studies and for an accurate understanding of Saint Thomas's conception and evaluation of Platonism.

When, some twelve years ago, I began an independent investigation of Platonism in Saint Thomas,[9] I found myself confronted by several apparently inconsistent series of texts. Rejection and acceptance of the same or similar doctrines seemed almost to alternate in the writings of Saint Thomas. A careful examination of these texts began to reveal a pattern of methodological techniques skillfully employed by Saint Thomas. Studies in other but similar series of texts confirmed and extended this pattern. Obviously, if Saint Thomas himself employed definite techniques in handling doctrinal positions, any proper reading of his relevant texts must presuppose an understanding of his techniques.

It is the purpose, therefore, of the present paper to present the basic methodology used by Saint Thomas in handling *positiones*. We will begin with the study of a text presented in the fifth article of the

---

[9] I hope to publish the full results of my investigations.

Quaestio de Spiritualibus Creaturis.[10] The question proposed is, "Is

---

[10]Since this text is used as a prime example, it is here given with its full context: Dicendum quod, quia nostra cognitio a sensu incipit, sensus autem corporalium est, a principio homines de veritate inquirentes, solam naturam corpoream capere potuerunt, in tantum quod primi naturales philosophi nihil esse nisi corporea aestimabant; unde et ipsam animam corpus esse dicebant. Quos etiam secuti videntur Manichaei haeretici, qui Deum lucem quamdam corpoream, per infinita distensam apatia esse existimabant. Sic etiam et Anthropomorphitae, qui Deum lineamentis humani corporis figuratum esse construebant, nihil ultra corpora esse suspicabantur.

Sed posteriores philosophi, rationabiliter per intellectum corporalia transcendentes, ad cognitionem incorporeae substantiae pervenerunt. Quorum Anaxagoras primus, quia ponebat a principio omnia corporalia in invicem esse immixta, coactus fuit ponere supra corporalia aliquod incorporeum non mixtum, quod corporalia distingueret et moveret. Et hoc vocabat intellectum distinguentem et moventem omnia, quem nos dicimus Deum. Plato vero est alia via usus, ad ponendum substantias incorporeas. Aestimavit enim quod ante esse participans, necesse est ponere aliquid abstractum non participatum. Unde cum omnia corpora sensibilia participent ea quae de ipsis praedicantur, scil. naturas generum et specierum et aliorum universaliter de ipsis dictorum, posuit huiusmodi naturas abstractas a sensibilibus per se subsistentes, quas substantias separatas nominabat.

Aristoteles vero processit ad ponendum substantias separatas ex perpetuitate caelestis motus. Oportet enim caelestis motus aliquem finem ponere. Si autem finis alicuius motus non semper eodem modo se habeat, sed moveatur per se vel per accidens, necesse est motum illum non semper uniformiter se habere; unde motus naturalis gravium et levium magis intenditur, cum appropinquaverit ad hoc quod est esse in loco proprio. Videmus autem in motibus caelestium corporum semper uniformitatem servari, ex quo existimavit huius uniformis motus perpetuitatem. Oportebat igitur ut poneret finem huius motus non moveri nec per se nec per accidens. Omne autem corpus vel quod est in corpore, mobile est per se vel per accidens. Sic ergo necessarium fuit quod poneret aliquam substantiam omino a corpore separatam, quae esset finis motus caelistis.

In hoc autem videntur tres praedictae positiones differre, quod Anaxagoras non habuit necesse ponere, secundum principia ab eo supposita, nisi unam substantiam incorpoream. Plato qutem necesse habuit ponere multas et ad invicem ordinatas, secundum multitudinem et ordinem generum et specierum, et aliorum quae abstracta ponebat; posuit enim primum abstractum, quod essentialiter esset bonum et unum, et consequenter diversos ordines intelligibilium et intellectuum. Aristoteles autem posuit plures substantias separatas. Cum enim in caelo appareant multi motus, quorum quemlibet ponebat esse uniformem et perpetuum; cuiuslibet autem motus oportet esse aliquem proprium finem: ex quo finis talis motus debet esse substantia incorporea, consequens fuit ut poneret multas substantias incorporeas, ad invicem ordinatas secundum naturam et ordinem caelestium motuum. Nec ultra in eis ponendis processit quia proprium philosophiae eius fuit a manifestis non discedere.

Sed istae viae non sunt multum nobis accommodae: quia neque ponimus mixtionem sensibilium cum Anaxagora, neque abstractionem universalium cum Platone, neque perpetuitatem motus cum Aristotele. Unde oportet nos aliis viis procedere ad minifestationem propositi. *De Sp. Creat., 5, c.* (K64–66).

there some created spiritual substance which is not united to a body?" The body of the article falls into three main divisions:

1. The *primi naturales philosophi* who acknowledged only the existence of corporeal nature;

2. The *posteriores philosophi* who arrived at a knowledge of incorporeal substances;

3. We ourselves, *"nos,"* the Christians who likewise maintain the existence of spiritual being but for other reasons.

Under the second division three philosophers are introduced; first, their argumentation is briefly indicated; then certain resulting differences in their positions [*positiones*] are pointed out. In these three cases the argumentation rests on distinctly different premises. Anaxagoras' reasoning begins with his initial mixture of all material things; Plato argues from the exigency for subsistent abstractions; Aristotle presupposes as his starting-point the perpetuity of the movement of the heavens. Now all three of these lines of argument conclude to the existence of incorporeal nature. To some extent, therefore, the conclusions may be said to agree, but precisely insofar as they flow from the premises of each philosopher they show respectively definite differences. Thus, precisely because of his first premises [*secundum principia ab eo supposita*] Anaxagoras has only one incorporeal substance. Plato, however, had to number and order his incorporeal substances according to the number and order of genera, species, and his other abstractions, while Aristotle inferred the number and arrangement from the pattern of the celestial movements.

Saint Thomas refers to the arguments themselves as *viae:*

Sed istae *viae* [= the arguments of Anaxagoras, Plato and Aristotle] non sunt multum nobis accommodae . . . Unde oportet nos aliis *viis* [=the three arguments thereafter proposed by Saint Thomas himself] procedere ad manifestationem propositi.

The conclusions of the arguments are called *positiones:*

In hoc autem videntur tres praedictae *positiones* differre [here follows the statement of the differences in the conclusions of Anaxagoras, Plato, and Aristotle].

In this text, therefore, *via* (together with various associated words) is related to a *positio* (to which *ponere*, of course, corresponds) as an argument to a conclusion.[11] The relationship is sharply displayed by various phrases:

Plato vero est *alia via* [= the argument] *usus ad ponendum* [= concluding to] substantias corporeas . . .

Aristoteles vero processit [= *via*] ad *ponendum* substantias separatas . . .

Referring to the specific conclusions of each, Saint Thomas employs the following expressions:

. . . Anaxagoras non habuit *necesse ponere* . . . nisi unam . . .

Plato autem *necesse* habuit *ponere* . . .

Aristoteles autem *posuit* plures . . . *consequens* fuit ut *poneret* multas.

Thus a *via* leads to a *positio;* the *positio* is *commanded* and *imposed* by the *via*.

This same type of analysis is conducted in many texts in which the same relationship is set up between *ratio* [or *rationes*] and *positio*. Thus:

---

[11]The best known example of this use of *via* is in the *quinque viae* of *S. T.*, 1, 2, 3, *c.*: "Dicendum quod Deum esse quinque *viis* probari potest . . . ergo est necesse *ponere* aliquam causam efficientem primam . . . *ponere* aliquid quod sit per se necessarium." Another striking and formal instance is the discussion of Plato's position in the *De Sub. Sep.* 1 (P 4–7); 2 (P 8), where we find the following pattern of terms: "Unde Plato sufficientiori *via processit . . . posuit . . . ponebat . . . ponebant . . . ponebant* ulterius . . . Unde *ponebant . . . ponebant . . . ponebant . . . ponebant* . . . Hujus autem *positionis radix* . . . et ideo Aristoteles manifestiori et certiori *via processit* . . . scilicet per *viam* motus" Cf. *S. T.*, I, 50, 3, *c.*; *In I Sent.*, 35, 1, 1, *sol.*; *In S. Pauli ad Romanos*, 1, 6; *De Sp. Creat.*, 3, *c.*; *In IV Meta.*, 10 (C 663). *Positio* may, of course, be used for any statement or assertion, not only for one which concludes an argument but even for those from which the argument proceeds (*Thomas-Lexikon, s. positio, c.*). *Positio* here, however, is being determined with regard to its use in a pattern of analysis.

Quidam dicunt quod anima, et omnino omnis substantia praeter Deum, est composita ex materia et forma. Cuius quidem *positionis* primus auctor invenitur Avicebron auctor libri *Fontis Vitae.* Huius autem *ratio* est . . . quod oportet in quocumque inveniuntur proprietates materiae, inveniri materiam. Unde cum in anima inveniantur proprietates materiae, quae sunt recipere subici, esse in potentia, et alia huiusmodi; arbitratur esse necessarium quod in anima sit materia.

Sed haec ratio frivola est, et positio impossibilis.[12]

There is here again a clear distinction between the *ratio* and the *positio.* The *ratio* leads to the *positio* and determines it.[13]

In many cases, *opinio* does duty for *positio.*[14] Thus:

Hic ponit opiniones ponentium causam efficientem non solum ut principium motus, sed etiam ut principium boni vel mali in rebus. Et circa hoc duo facit. Primo narrat eorum opiniones. Secundo ostendit in quo in ponendo causas defecerunt, ibi, "Isti quidem." Circa primum duo facit. *Primo ponit opinionis rationes, ex quibus movebantur ad ponen-dum aliam causam a praedictis.*[15]

In the cases considered above, the relationship was between a definite and specific argument or argumentation and a definite conclusion. The word *via,* however, may be used in a broader sense.

Harum autem duarum opinionum diversitas ex hoc procedit quod quidam, ad inquirendam veritatem de natura rerum, *processerunt* ex rationibus intelligibilibus, et hoc fuit proprium

---

[12]*Q. U. De Anima,* 6, c.

[13]The *ratio* [*rationes*]-*positio* pattern is extremely common. For examples see *In* I *Meta.,* 4 (C 79); *In* IX *Meta.,* 3 (C 1795); *De Sub. Sep.,* 10 P 64); *De Ver.,* 21, 4, c.; *In* I *De An.,* 6 (P 71); *In* I *De C. et M.,* 6 (S 60). For *ratio* in this sense, see *Thomas-Lexikon, s. ratio,* m.

[14]Other examples are to be found *In* I *Meta.,* 3 (C 61–63); 10 (C 151, C 166).

[15]*In* I *Meta.,* 5 (C 97).

Platonicorum; quidam vero ex rebus sensibilibus, et hoc fuit proprium philosophiae Aristotelis, ut dicit Simplicius in commento *Super praedicamenta.* Consideraverunt Platonici ordinem quemdam generum et specierum, et quod semper superius potest intelligi sini inferiori, sicut homo sine hoc homine, et animal sine homine, et sic deinceps. Existimaverunt etiam quod quid-quid est abstractum in intellectu, sit abstractum in re; alias videbatur eis quod intellectus abstrahens esset falsus aut vanus, si nulla res abstracta ei responderet; propter quod etiam crediderunt mathematica esse abstracta a sensibilibus, quia sine eis intelliguntur. Unde *posuerunt* hominem abstractum ab his hominibus, et sic deinceps usque ad ens et unum et bonum, quod *posuerunt* summam rerum virtutem. Viderunt enim quod semper inferius particularius est suo superiori, et quod natura superioris participatur in inferiori: participans autem se habet ut ma-teriale ad participatum; unde posuerunt quod inter abstracta, quanto aliquid est universalius, tanto est formalius.

Quidam vero, secundum eandem *viam* ingredientes, ex opposito *posuerunt* quod quanto aliqua forma est universalior, tanto est magis materialis.[16]

Here the *procedere* and *via* are used to refer to different types of argumentation, different general modes of arguing. Hence, if two philosophies are opposed not only in certain specific arguments and positions but also in characteristically [*proprium*] different approaches to the solution of problems [*ad inquirendam veritatem de natura rerum*], they may be distinguished as commonly employing different *viae.* Relying, therefore, on this text, we would be able to speak of a *via Platonica* and a *via Aristotelica.*

The investigation may be extended by considering the use of *radix, principium* and *fundamentum* in similar analytical contexts. In the *De Substantiis Separatis* Saint Thomas makes a careful analysis of the *via* by which Plato came to establish the existence and nature of separated substances:

---

[16]*De Sp. Creat.,* 3, *c.* (K 40–41).

Unde Plato sufficientiori *via processit* ad opinionem priorum Naturalium evacuandam. Cum apud antiquos Naturales poneretur ab hominibus certam rerum veritatem sciri non posse, tum propter rerum corporalium continuum defluxum, tum propter deceptionem sensuum quibus corpora cognoscuntur, posuit naturas quasdam a natura fluxi-bilium rerum separatas, in quibus esset veritas fixa; et sic eis inhaerendo anima nostra cognosceret veritatem. Unde secundum hoc quod intel-lectus veritatem cognoscens aliqua seorsum apprehendit praeter naturam sensibilium rerum, sic existimavit esse aliqua a sensibilibus separata.

Intellectus autem noster duplici abstractione utitur circa intelligentiam veritatis. Una quidem secundum quod apprehendit numeros mathematicos et magnitudines et figuras mathematicas sine materiae sensibilis intellectu; non enim intelligendo binarium aut ternarium, aut lineam et superficiem, aut triangulum et quadratum, simul in nostra apprehensione quid cadit quod pertineat ad calidum et frigidum aut aliquid hujusmodi quod sensu percipi possit. Alia autem abstractione utitur intellectus noster intelligendo aliquid universale absque consideratione alicujus particularis, puta cum intelligimus hominem nihil intelligentes de Socrate aut Platone aut alio quocumque; et idem apparet in aliis.

Unde Plato duo genera rerum a sensibilibus abstracta *ponebat,* scili-cet mathematica et universalia, quae species seu ideas nominabat. . . .

Hujus autem *positionis radix* invenitur efficaciam non habere. Non enim necesse est ut ea quae intellectus separatim intelligit, separatim esse ea in rerum natura; unde nec universalia oportet separata ponere subsistentia praeter singularia, nec etiam mathematica praeter sensibilia, quia universalia sunt essentiae ipsorum particularium et mathematica sunt terminationes quaedam sensibilium corporum. Et ideo Aristoteles manifestiori et certiori *via* processit ad investigandum substantias separatas a materia, scilicet per *viam* motus.[17]

Thus the same type of analysis appears here and the same relation of *via* to *positio*. The *radix* of the *positio* is precisely the *fundamental operative principle* in the first movement of the *via*. In an early text *"fundamentum"* and *"principium"* are used in a similar way:

Hortum autem omnium errorum et plurium hujusmodi unum videtur esse *principium* et *fundamentum,* quo destructo, nihil prob-abilitatis remanet. Plures enim antiquorum ex intentionibus intellectis judicium rerum naturalium sumere voluerunt: unde quaecumque inveniuntur convenire in aliqua intentione intellecta, voluerunt quod communicarent in una re: et ind ortus est error . . . Sed hoc *funda-mentum* est valde debile. . . .[18]

We may now summarize. Saint Thomas makes use of an analytical method in dealing with philosophical *positiones* in which the *positio* [or *opinio*] is reduced to the arguments or argumentation [*via-ratio-rationes*] from which it properly proceeds according to his understanding of the mind of its author. In doing so he sometimes singles out, within the *via*, a basic starting-point or operative principle [*radix-principium-fundamentum*] which commands the entire line of thought, or again he may see the *via* as involving a more generalized mode of approach characteristic [*proprium*] of a given philosophy. The terminology which has emerged in this discussion is rather common in such contexts and therefore, although the analysis is sometimes worked without benefit of all or even part of this terminology, we shall refer to this pattern of analysis [and of terms] as the *via-positio* technique for handling *positiones*.

Thus supplied by Saint Thomas himself with the technical verbal pattern *via* [*rationes*]*-positio* [*opinio*], we may now reflect upon the

---

[17]*De Sub. Sep.,* 1 (P 4–7); 2 (P 8). Cf. *De Sub. Sep.,* 7 (P 49); *In* I *Meta.,* 3 (C 61–63); *C. G.,* II, 74; *S. T.,* I, 49, 3, *c.;* 65, 4, *c.;* 118, 3, *c.; Contra Retra. a Rel. Ingr.,* 6; Averroes: "Et est *positio* falsa . . . et hoc secundum *radices* eorum quoniam ipsi dicunt (*Dest. Dest.,* 14 [119B]); . . . haec *positio* est ex *radicibus* . . ." (*Ibid.* [118C]).

[18]*In* II *Sent.,* 17, 1, 1, *sol.*; cf. Averroes: "Et hoc manifestum est ei qui considerat *fundamentum* Aristotelis," *De Sub. Orb.,* 1 (5vK).

analytic method itself thereby expressed and its meaning for the interpretation of Saint Thomas.

The *via-positio* analysis precisely relates a philosophical position, as a conclusion, to the proper philosophical premises upon which it rests, whether these premises be principles, in the narrow sense, or matters of fact, real or supposed. A *positio* is thus seen as determined both in its truth and in its meaning by its proper premises and as integral and homogeneous with them. Because Anaxagoras begins with a complete corporeal mixture he must posit a single separated substance. Plato's principle of subsistent abstractions determines the hierarchy of his separated substance, while Aristotle's number is derived from his celestial mechanics.

Thus the *via* and the *positio* taken together constitute a miniature philosophical system which is properly deployed and displayed according to the formal movement of its thought. Now, if philosophy involves a movement of rational thought by which conclusions are either reached or, if the fact of the conclusion is already given, understood through premises, the *via-positio* analysis is a proper and formal philosophical analysis. A conclusion or *positio*, divorced from the context of its principles, cannot be *philosophically* determined; it cannot even be said to be a *philosophical conclusion*.

That God exists, for example, may be asserted on human faith or because one wants God to exist. It becomes a philosophical assertion only when it is integrated into the context of philosophical principles. Thus, Kant, for example, Locke, Spinoza and Saint Thomas may all be said to assert the existence of God, but when the position is determined by the respective principles of these philosophers, a vast difference is seen to exist and the position become virtually multiple, being differently specified by the principles of each philosophy.

The *via-positio* type of analysis, therefore, is the placing of a *positio* in dependence on its proper philosophical grounds. The precise meaning of the *positio* is thereby determined and likewise its specification is determined according to the specification of its premises. The statement, for example, that physical science is a valid form of knowledge is specifically different in the epistemologies, respectively, of Saint Thomas and of Kant.

This point is of capital importance for the study of the various Platonic texts in the writings of Saint Thomas. The discovery of a consistent use of the *via-positio* technique in Saint Thomas shows that he was clearly aware of the formal relationship between philosophical principles and philosophical conclusions and, therefore, also of the specifying relationship existing between them.

Moreover, this mode of analysis, besides being properly philosophical or perhaps because it is properly philosophical, reduces a philosophical conclusion to what I shall call a "pure position."[19] For it is not the accident of historical connection or the pressure of external circumstance that is used to illumine the conclusion. A single consistent set of principles is disengaged, and it is in the light of these principles alone that the conclusion is seen. Thus when Saint Thomas, having described the mode of argumentation proper to the Platonists, points out that Avicebron entered on the same way [*eandem viam*] and arrived at a doctrine which was harmonious with Platonism and indeed consequent to it [*sequela eius*], he is concerned with the continuity of philosophical reason and not with any historical connection between Avicebron and the Platonists.

In all these cases the effort is to show how the conclusions are determined solely and purely by the given premises.

The *ratio-positio* method is, therefore, (1) a properly philosophical mode of analysis, which (2) specifies conclusions philosophically, and (3) reduces them to a "pure" position.

However, the investigation of this technique (or of parallel techniques) has by no means been completed. The *via-positio* analysis is not introduced by Saint Thomas simply for historical reasons or for a mere understanding of a given position. It regularly occurs in critical passages and serves as a basis for a critique.

The first thing to be noted is that Saint Thomas commonly maintains a clear distinction between a critique which attacks the *via* or *rationes* and one which attacks the *positio* itself. This distinction very frequently appears in his classification of the Aristotelian arguments in the commentaries.

Est ergo hic contra duo disputandum: scilicet contra *rationem*

---

[19]Cf. Geiger: "En fait, historiquement, S. Thomas s'est trouvé en présence de deux systèmes, sinon entièrement purs, du moins nettement différenciés . . . Nous montrerons qu'elles représentent des systèmes achevés, parfaitement cohérents, qui développent avec une rigueur lucide les dernières conséquences de leur position initiale," *La Participation dans la Philosophie de S. Thomas d'Aquin,* (Paris: Vrin, 1942), 30.

positionis, et contra ipsam *positionem*. Utrumque enim est falsum. Nam et *ratio positionis* istorum falsa erat, et eorum *positio*.[20]

... Circa primum duo facit. Primo enim disputat contra ipsam positionem Platonis. Secundo contra rationem ipsius, ibi, "Amplius autem secundum quos etc."[21]

It is obvious that the most sweeping attack will include arguments against both the *rationes* and the *positio*. It was this sort of devastating critique that Saint Thomas found Aristotle directing against the Platonic ideas in the first book of the *Metaphysics*. Saint Thomas himself frequently uses the same twofold attack. We have seen him in his critique of Avicebron's theory of universal matter remarking: "Sed haec ratio frivola est, et positio impossibilis." Particularly with regard to the Platonic assertion of the subsisting species of material things Saint Thomas not only destroys the rational foundation of the argument but approves and repeats many of the arguments which Aristotle directs against the positio.[22]

In some texts, however, it is the *positio* which is singled out for immediate criticism. In the discussion of Avicebron's doctrine on the multiplicity of forms, Saint Thomas shows that Avicebron is following the same *via* [*eandem viam*] as Plato but in an inverted direction. Of course, the reader knows that this identification of Avicebron with Plato is, in effect, a rejection, yet, in the context, the positive arguments advanced aim directly at the resulting *positio*. "Sed haec *positio* secundum vera philosophiae principia quae consideravit Aristoteles est impossibilis." The arguments which here follow—Primo . . . Secundo . . . Tertio—are directed not against the *via* but against the theory of plurality of forms, that is, the *positio* of Avicebron.[23]

---

[20]*In* I *De An.* (P 71).

[21]*In* I *Meta.* (C 208). Cf. *In* X *Eth.* (P 1980–1996); *In* I *Meta.* (C 210); *In* I *De An.,* 6 (P71); 9 (P 132).

[22]For critique and rejection of the *positio,* see, *e.g., S.T.,* I, 6, 4, *c.; In De Div. Nom., Prooem.,* IIa; *De Ver.,* 3, 1, *ad* 4; *C. G.,* I, 51 and 52. For critique of the *rationes,* see, *e.g., In* I *Meta.,* 10 (C 158); *S.T.,* I 44, 3, *ad* 3; 84, 1, *c.; De Sub. Sep.,* I (P 4–7); 2 (P 8).

[23]*De Sp. Creat.,* 3, *c.* (K 42–45).

The primary criticism may, however, in some cases be limited to the *via*. Thus it is the fundamental principle that commands the unfolding of the Platonic *via* which is rejected in the *De Substantiis Separatis*. "Hujus autem positionis radix invenitur efficaciam non habere."[24] It is clear, in the light of the analysis of this method, that the refutation of a *via* is, philosophically speaking, at the same time a refutation of the *positio* insofar as it formally depends upon that *via*. This Saint Thomas had remarked in his earliest analytical examination of the Platonic argument:

> Horum autem omnium errorum et plurium huiusmodi unum videtur esse principium et fundamentum, *quo destructo nihil probabilitatis remanet.*[25]

In criticizing a *positio*, therefore, Saint Thomas makes use of the following procedures:

1. He may reduce the *positio* by analysis to the *via* or *rationes* from which it results and may single out the basic starting-point or principle [*radix*] of the argumentation. A critique may then be conducted by attacking (a) the *via, rationes* or *radix*, (b) *the positio* itself, or (c) both the *via* and the *positio*.

2. He may describe a *positio* and attack it directly, without the reductive analysis.[26]

The matter, however, is not quite so simple. There are cases of *positiones* which, in certain critical contexts, are analyzed by the *via-positio* technique and rejected but are, in other contexts, apparently approved and incorporated into Saint Thomas' own thought.[27] If one accepted this as a self-contradictory procedure one could, for example, arrange a series of *discordantiae* with reference to various positions,

---

[24]*De Sub. Sep.*, 2 (P 8).

[25]*In* II *Sent.*, 17, 1, 1, *sol.*

[26]*E. g., S. T.* I, 3, 8, *c.*

[27]With regard, for example, to the Platonic *primum bonum:* (a) Rejection of *via* and *rationes: De Ver.*, 21, 4, *c.* (first part); *De Sub. Sep.*, 1 (P 4–7); 2 (P 8); *In* I *Eth.*, 6 (P 74, P 79); (b) Acceptance of the *positio: S. T.*, I, 6, 4, *c.; In De Div. Nom., Prooem.*, IIa.

among them being certain important Platonic ones. One could, too, see one side of this series as being the true or mature view of Saint Thomas and reject the other. This, in fact, seems to be what Fabro has done in commenting certain texts. An examination of this procedure will further develop and clarify the methodological points in which we are here interested. Fabro, for example, advances the following text from the *Summa Theologiae*.[28]

> Plato enim posuit omnium rerum species separatas; et quod ab eis individua denominantur, quasi species separatas participando, ut puta quod Socrates dicitur homo secundum ideam hominis separatam. Et sicut ponebat ideam hominis et equi separatam, quam vocabat "per se hominem" et "per se equum," ita ponebat ideam entis et ideam unius separatam, quam dicebat "per se ens" et "per se unum"; et ejus participatione unumquodque dicitur ens vel unum. Hoc autem quod est per se ens et per se unum, ponebat esse summum bonum. Et quia bonum convertitur cum ente, sicut et unum, ipsum per se bonum dicebat esse Deum, a quo omnia dicuntur bona per modum participationis. Et quamvis haec opinio irrationabilis videatur quantum ad hoc, quod ponebat species rerum naturalium separatas per se subsistentes, ut Aristoteles multipliciter improbat, tamen hoc absolute verum est, quod aliquid est primum, quod per suam essentiam est ens et bonum, quod dicimus Deum, ut ex superioribus patet. Huic etiam sententiae concordat Aristoteles.[29]

This text is supposed to show an increased benevolence towards Plato, and even a certain disdain for Aristotle.

The following three points should be noticed about the text itself. First, only the *positio* of Plato is given: "posuit . . . ponebat . . .ponebat . . . ponebat . . . dicebat . . . ponebat." There is no presentation of the *via* by which Plato arrived at this position, though at the time this article was written Saint Thomas was in possession of a magistral and unequiv-

---

[28]Fabro, *La Nozione Metafisica di Partecipazione secondo S. Tommaso d'Aquino*, 58–59.

[29]*S. T.,* I, 6, 4, *c.*

ocally destructive analysis of this *via*.[30] Secondly, with regard to the part of the *positio* which is here approved, the evidence is said to lie in Saint Thomas' own previous argumentation:

> ... tamen hoc absolute verum est ... ut *ex superioribus patet* ... in quantum participat ipsum per modum cuiusdam assimilationis licet remote et deficienter, ut *ex superioribus patet.*

Thirdly, in the immediately subsequent paragraph, the rational explanation is explicitly derived from the Thomistic insertion of participation into the pattern of the causes which is consistently presented, in this regard, as the Thomistic alternative to the *via Platonica*.[31]

What, then, is happening in the text itself? The Platonic *positio* that there is a *primum ens et bonum per essentiam* in which all things participate is integrated with a *via Thomistica* and explained within the context of that *via*. The *positio* is, therefore, no longer *formally* Platonic; it can only be said to be *materially* a Platonic position.

This conclusion can be indirectly verified. It has been pointed out that the characteristic meaning of a *positio* is governed by its formal premises. Now the *positio* under discussion asserts a *primum ens per essentiam*. How is the precise meaning of this formula to be determined? If it is integrated with the Platonic way of arguing, the nature of the *primum ens* must be determined according to the *modus intelligendi,* for it is precisely a transposition of the common or "universal" concept of *ens* into the real order. But this is precisely the determination which Saint Thomas has rejected. In *S. T.,* I, 3, 4, *arg.* 1, the objection is raised:

---

[30]I plan to establish this fact, with full documentation, in future publications.

[31]"A primo igitur per suam essentiam ente et bono, unumquodque potest dici bonum et ens, inquantum participat ipsum per modum cuiusdam assimilationis, licet remote et deficienter, ut ex superioribus patet. Sic ergo unum quodque dicitur bonum bonitate divina, sicut primo principio exemplari, effectivo et finali totius bonitatis. Nihilominus tamen unumquodque dicitur bonum similitudine divinae bonitatis sibi inhaerente, quae est formaliter sua bonitas denominans ipsum. Et sic est bonitas una omnium; et etiam multae bonitates," *S. T.,* I, 6, 4, *c.* For the exact opposition of this pattern to the *via Platonica,* see *De Ver.,* 21, 4, *c.*

Si enim hoc sit, tunc ad esse divinum nihil additur. Sed esse cui nulla fit additio est esse commune quod de omnibus praedicatur: sequitur ergo quod Deus sit *ens commune praedicabile de omnibus.*

Saint Thomas answers this precisely by distinguishing the *esse commune* and the *esse divinum.*[32] A longer discussion of the same point with clear reference to the *via Platonica* is to be found in the *Contra Gentiles.*[33]

If, then, the meaning of the *positio* cannot here be determined by the Platonic premises, it is clear that it is *formally detached* in our text, from Platonism and integrated into a different and, indeed, opposing philosophical doctrine.

Now this text has been analyzed at some length, not simply because, when properly read, it offers no support to Fabro's thesis but primarily because it affords an excellent illustration of the technique for handling detached *positiones.* For, if the *via* and *rationes* philosophically determine the meaning of the *positio,* a *positio* [e.g., *est primum ens per essentiam*] withdrawn from its original philosophical context becomes indeterminate. This indeterminate *positio* may thus be integrated, without adulteration of principle, into Saint Thomas' own doctrine and this he does by numerous devices varying all the way from smooth insertion into a subtly shifting context to a direct and explicit determination or rather "re-determination" of meaning.

---

[32]"Dicendum quod aliquid cui non fit additio potest intelligi dupliciter. Uno modo, ut de ratione eius sit quod non fiat ei additio, sicut de ratione animalis irrationalis est, ut sit sine ratione. Alio modo intelligitur aliquid cui non fit additio, quia non est de ratione eius quod sibi fiat addito; sicut *animal commune* est sine ratione, quia non est de ratione animalis communis ut habeat rationem, sed nec de ratione eius est ut careat ratione. Primo igitur modo, esse sine additione est esse divinum; secundo modo, esse sine additione est esse commune," *S. T.,* I, 3, 4, *ad* 1.

[33]"Adhuc. Quod est commune multis, non est aliquid praeter multa nisi sola ratione: sicut animal non est aliud praeter Socratem et Platonem et alia animalia nisi intellectu, qui apprehendit formam animalis exspoliatam ab omnibus individuantibus et specificantibus; homo enim est quod vere est animal; alias sequeretur quod in Socrate et Platone essent plura animalia, scilicet ipsum animal commune, et homo communis, et ipse Plato. Multo igitur minus et ipsum esse commune est aliquid praeter omnis res existentes nisi in intellectu solum. Si igitur Deus sit esse commune, Deus non erit aliqua res nisi quae sit in intellectu tantum. Ostensum autem est supra Deum esse aliquid non solum in intellectu, sed in rerum natura. Non est igitur Deus ipsum esse commune omnium," *C. G.,* I, 26.

Those who are familiar with previous studies in the methodology of Saint Thomas will recognize that we are here describing a technique that is parallel with the mediaeval interpretation or exposition of *auctoritates*. The historical explanation and development of this *auctoritas*-technique have been well discussed by others.[34] Mediaeval discussion was carried on under the double influence of a profound reverence for tradition and a profound respect for reason. The mediaeval philosopher or theologian was, therefore, forced to substantiate his teaching by placing it under the patronage of the great names—the *sancti et philosophi*—of the past while, at the same time, supporting it on a solid rational structure. His weapons of debate were twofold: *auctoritates* and *rationes*. Saint Thomas employed both weapons and for each he possessed a style and a technique that enabled him to move through mediaeval controversy with consummate skill and prudence. Moreover, the doctrinal alignment of Plato and Saint Augustine gave him, in view of these techniques, an unexpected advantage, By using every variation of the *auctoritas*-technique he was able to maintain his solidarity with Saint Augustine and so enjoy the protection of the same great name that his adversaries invoked. At the same time, by using the *via-positio* technique in handling Platonism he was able to attack directly the fundamental principles which were Plato's source of error and were still at work within Augustinianism. Thus it was that he could borrow the *auctoritates* of his Augustinian adversaries while, without offending the Christian veneration for Saint Augustine, he could, through Plato destroy their *rationes*.

In addition, however, the application of the *auctoritas*-technique to the free *positio* enabled him, on due occasion, to invoke the great name of Plato in witness of his own positions. His varying handling of the subsistence of Ideas furnishes pertinent examples. The *via-positio* analysis has deprived the thesis of its rational ground and, therefore, destroyed it as a formal conclusion of the *via Platonica*. However, the *positio* itself is subjected to various interpretive treatments. It can be divided into an assertion of the subsistence of ideas of sensible beings and an assertion of the subsistence of ideas of Being, Unity, the Good.

---

[34]Chenu, *Auctor, actor, autor*. Archivum Latinitatis Medii Aevi, Bruxelles, Sec. Ad. de l'Union Académique Internationale (1927), 81–86; Introduction a l'Etude de Saint Thomas d'Aquin (Paris: Vrin, 1950), 106–125; Riquet, *Thomas et les Auctoritates en Philosophie*: Archives de Philosophie III, 2 (Paris: Beauchesne, 1925) 122–155.

The first thesis is generally categorically rejected, since, even as a *positio*, it can hardly receive a benevolent interpretation.

> . . . contra rationem rerum sensibilium est quod eorum formae subsistant absque materiis. . . .[35]

> . . . sed quia videtur esse alienum a fide quod formae rerum extra res per se subsistant absque materia, sicut Platonici posuerunt. . . .[36]

In these texts the thesis, as regards forms of sensible beings, is rejected in itself, as a *positio,* since it is against reason and against the Faith.

Yet even this thesis is sometimes rescued from complete rejection.

> In quo etiam aliqualiter salvatur Platonis opinio ponentis ideas, secundum quas formarentur omnia quae in rebus materialibus existunt.[37]

The explanation which "saves" Plato's opinion is Saint Thomas' theory of the divine knowledge. This is clearly not the opinion of Plato as it derives from his own arguments and even when the opinion is taken materially hardly coincides. Hence the limitation of the "aliqualiter".

The second part of the *positio,* however, is a different matter and allows, under the *positio-auctoritas* treatment, a much different use. The statement that an absolute Being, or Good, exists is one that Saint Thomas can make wholly his own. Thus, referring to Plato's position, he says:

> . . . tamen hoc absolute verum est quod aliquid est primum quod per suam essentiam est ens et bonum quod dicimus Deum, ut ex superioribus patet.[38]

In this text, as we have seen, the free *positio* is incorporated into his own philosophy.

---

[35] *S. T.,* I, 84, 4, *c.*

[36] *S.T.,* I, 84, 5, *c.*

[37] *C. G.,* I, 54.

[38] *S. T.,* I, 6, 4, *c.*

Now, the difficulty of reading Saint Thomas aright is further complicated by the fact that both the *via-positio* and the *positio-auctoritas* technique often appear in the same context. In such cases the structure and movement of the text are very subtle and need careful study.

The article in the *De Veritate,*[39] "Utrum omnia sint bona bonitate prima" includes a straight philosophical analysis of the Platonic determination of the question, starting from the familiar Platonic principle: "ea quae possunt separari secundum intellectum . . . etiam secundum esse separata" and moving to the Platonic *positio*. Against this integral opinion he then alleges in a comprehensive and summary manner the Aristotelian arguments of the *Metaphysics* and the *Ethics*. It is particularly noteworthy that he appeals to a special argument specifically directed against the Platonic Idea of the Good.

. . . tum etiam suppositis ideis; quia specialiter ista ratio non habet locum in bono; quia bonum non univoce dicitur de bonis, et in talibus non assignatur una idea secundum Platonem, per quam viam procedit contra eum Philosophus in I Ethic.

Saint Thomas then urges with special force [*specialiter . . . apparet falsitas . . .*] the argument based upon the interrelation of the causes:

Specialiter tamen quantum ad propositum pertinet, apparet falsitas praedictae positionis ex hoc quod omne agens invenitur sibi simile agere; unde si prima bonitas sit effectiva omnium bonorum, oportet quod similitudinem suam imprimat in rebus effectis; et sic unumquodque dicetur bonum sicut forma inhaerente per similitudinem summi boni sibi inditam, et ulterius per bonitatem primam, sicut per exemplar et effectivum omnis bonitatis creatae.

At this point it would seem that the Platonic position had been rather thoroughly refuted both in its *rationes* and in itself, and, indeed, in a very special way with reference to the Idea of the Good. Yet at this point Saint Thomas adds the laconic remark: "Quantum ad hoc opinio Platonis sustineri potest." The switch from the *via-positio* to the *positio-auctoritas* technique is indicated in the brief phrase "Quantum ad hoc." For what does this mean? It means that the *opinio* [*positio*] of Plato can

---

[39]*De Ver.,* 21, 4, c.

be maintained if it is referred to and understood through the typically Thomistic argument just presented as specially destroying the Platonic position. The Platonic Good must be understood as the Thomistic Good, the exemplar and efficient cause of all goodness.

It should be noted that this is exactly the meaning given to the Platonic *positio* in *S. T.,* I, 6, 4, *c.:*

Sic ergo unumquodque dicitur bonum bonitate divina sicut *primo principio exemplari, effectivo et finali totius bonitatis.*

The approval of the *positio* is conditioned on this interpretation. "*Quantum ad hoc* sustineri potest."

We may now make a final recapitulation of Saint Thomas' methodological techniques for handling a *positio*.

1. The *via-positio* technique. A proper analysis is worked out by displaying the precise premises—principles and/or facts [*via-rationes-radix*] upon which the *positio* depends for its truth and meaning. The argumentation may be seen as following a certain typical mode [e.g., the *via Platonica*]. When carried out in a thoroughgoing and consistent fashion, this results in the reduction of opinions to "pure positions" specified by a definite argumentation. A clear-cut critique is then possible. It may follow any one of three lines: it may attack (a) the *via, rationes* or *radix,* (b) the *positio* itself, or (c) both the *via* and the *positio.*

2. The *positio-auctoritas* technique. A *positio* [*opinio*] may be detached from its proper philosophical background and become thus an indeterminate but determinable *positio*. In this case the free *positio* may (a) be such that no favorable interpretation can be given it, (b) be such that it can be vaguely and partially approved [*aliqualiter*], (c) be such that it can be determined, without qualification, into a different philosophical system [hoc absolute verum est quod aliquid est primum . . .].

In the case of (b) and (c), the precise meaning of the *positio* in its new function must be determined not from the principles of its former or original philosophical framework but from that into which it is newly inserted. A complete understanding would require the discovery of the *via* which, in its new formality, justifies and explains it.

Since then these clear-cut patterns of analysis and criticism are formally present in the methodology of Saint Thomas, it is obviously important to read his *littera* in the light of this methodological background.

It is hoped that in future detailed studies of the individual texts which are central to the current discussion of Saint Thomas and Platonism these methodological principles will be confirmed and extended.

XII

A NOTE ON CERTAIN TESTUAL EVIDENCE IN FABRO'S *LA NOZIONE METAFISICA DE PARTECIPAZIONE*

N ew Introduction: I have indicated elsewhere (Article IX) that the reading of St. Thomas requires a careful understanding of his various methodologies. I there insisted that the text of St. Thomas must be carefully interpreted according to his own methodology.

After I had written that article I came upon what I thought was a clear violation of these principles of interpretation and I thought that exposing Fabro's mistake would be an emphatic demonstration of the danger of a superficial handling of one or two texts on any subject.

I had no intention of belittling in any way the reputation of Dr. Fabro. I wanted to alert Thomistic writers in general to the danger of drawing doctrinal conclusions from a handful of texts, especially when the handful of texts is not carefully interpreted according to St. Thomas' own methodology.

I think the article[1] is both clear and correct as it stands and needs no additional development or explanation.

* * *

In a previous paper I referred to the rather recent interest in the problem of Thomism and Platonism, and pointed to the elaborate

---

[1]First published in *The Modern Schoolman* 34 (May 1957): 265–282.

studies of Santeler, Fabro, Geiger, and Little.[2] I repeat here, by way of introduction, some of the remarks made there:

> These studies, obviously the result of most painstaking research, present a number of broad generalizations concerning Saint Thomas' historical and doctrinal relationships to Platonism. Their conclusions are supported by an extensive array of textual evidence. The value of the generalizations, therefore, depends entirely upon the texts presented. The crucial and critical question, then, in estimating the correctness of these studies and their enduring contribution to Thomistic scholarship is this: Do the texts, when properly and accurately read, support the interpretations essential to the various theses of these authors?
>
> Now, anyone acquainted with modern Thomistic scholarship knows that it is no easy or simple matter to read a given text correctly. The intricacy of the sources and historical backgrounds, the difficulties of terminology, of methods, of chronology and so forth, make the accurate reading of a text, as well as its ultimate interpretation into a general scheme, an achievement requiring all the resources of scholarship. Laborious and slow as it is, we must yet apply this type of study to the accumulated texts of these authors before we can properly assess the value of their work.[3]

In the rest of the paper I summarized and presented the results of studies in St. Thomas's own methodology for the handling of *positiones*.

In this present paper it is my purpose to submit to close scrutiny certain texts advanced by Fabro in support of his own conclusions. I do not wish at the present time to evaluate or criticize the broad generali-

---

[2]Santeler, *Der Platonismus in der Erkenntnislehre des heiligen Thomas von Aquin* (Innsbruck: Rauch, 1939). Fabro, *La Nozione Metafisica di Partecipazione secondo S. Tommaso d'Aquino* (Milan: "Vita e Pensiero," 1939). Geiger, *La participation dans la philosophie de S. Thomas d'Aquin* (Paris: Vrin 1942). *The Platonic Heritage of Thomism* (Dublin: Golden Eagle Books, 1950).

[3]"Saint Thomas' Methodology in the Treatment of 'Positiones,'" *Gregorianum,* 36 (1955), 391–409.

zations of Fabro's study. My present purpose is much more modest. I propose to clear the ground by examining only that textual evidence which he advances in pages 57–64.

In these pages Fabro argues that the development of St. Thomas's thought displays an increasing benevolence toward Plato and a gradual but successful effort finally to create a synthesis by incorporating the Platonic metaphysics of participation into his own system. In support of this conclusion Fabro quotes a series of texts which we may take to constitute his fundamental evidence, for at the close of the series he says:

> It therefore appears established that, especially with regard to the works of his mature period, St. Thomas always tended toward a closer assimilation, within Aristotelian thought, of the metaphysical content of the Platonic notion of participation.[4]

And early in these pages he speaks of a "more favorable attitude toward Platonism"[5] and a more explicitly "benevolent attitude"[6] in the later works.

Obviously a general discussion of Aristotelian thought and the metaphysical content of the Platonic notion of participation would require the prior establishment of an accurate historico-philosophical definition of Platonism and Aristotelianism. Fortunately, the present discussion does not demand so difficult and laborious an undertaking. For Fabro, by using only St. Thomas's explicit comments on Plato and Aristotle, has located the immediate problem within the thought of St. Thomas himself. What Platonism and Aristotelianism are and what they mean are here taken to be that which St. Thomas understood them to be and to mean.

It seems obvious, also, that there is no question here of a total point-by-point opposition between Aristotle and Plato such that if one

---

[4]"*Pare adunque assodato* che soprattutto nelle opere della maturità S. Thommaso tendesse ad una assimilazione sempre più intima entro il pensiero aristotelico del contenuto metafisica della nozione platonica di partecipazione" (*La Nozione*, 64).

[5]*Ibid.*, 58

[6]*Ibid.*, 59.

were to construct a complete list of Aristotelian theses, a list, corresponding in thesis-by-thesis opposition, could be constructed for Platonism. Whether one takes a careful historical view or whether one looks at the divergence of Aristotle and Plato through the minds of subsequent philosophers and commentators, it is surely clear that on many points Aristotle and Plato are in at least some agreement. The real problem is to determine (and here I replace the problem within the thought of St. Thomas) where St. Thomas thought the opposition lay and how important he estimated it. If the question is placed in this fashion, it is immediately clear that we cannot simply lump texts together under the two rubrics of "approval" and "disapproval" of Plato. To strike a balance between such undifferentiated lists and so arrive at a *generalized* attitude of St. Thomas in regard to Plato and Platonism would thus confuse the entire issue. Fabro himself adopts this view in criticizing Gilson. After quoting Gilson's generalized conclusions, he remarks:

> The problem with which Gilson is faced concerns the universal hylomorphism of Avicebron in its influence on Augustinianism, on the one hand, and in its derivation from Plato on the other. *Now it seems that it is perhaps more prudent to treat problems one at a time before advancing affirmations of a general type.*[7]

Since, then, this procedure seems imposed by the nature of the question as well as stipulated by Fabro himself, I shall deal with the texts as they present different individual problems. However, it must be remembered that the texts are woven together in Fabro's presentation in such a way as to produce a cumulative general effect.

The investigation of these texts may also be considered as a series of case studies in Thomistic textual exegesis and as a contribution toward a general methodology for the reading of St. Thomas.

Fabro presents the development of St. Thomas's views in essentially three stages. First he establishes a point of departure in the

---

[7]"Il problema che il Gilson ha fra lemani riguarda l'ilemorfismo universale di Avicebron nell'influsso che ebbe sull' Augustinismo, da una parte, e nella sua derivazione da Platone, dall'altra; *ora pare che è più prudente trattare i problemi uno alla volta prima di avanzare affermazioni d'ordine generale*" [italics added] (*ibid.*, 63–64).

Commentary on the Sentences wherein he finds St. Thomas an unqualified partisan of Aristotle and Plato's determined opponent. He then presents a series of texts from later works which are intended to show St. Thomas's increasing benevolence toward Plato and his gradual incorporation of Platonic metaphysics into his own system. Finally, he finds the climax of these developments in the third chapter of the *De Substantiis Separatis*.

I. The First Stage: *In II Sent.*, d. 1, Expositio Textus

Fabro advances one text to establish the point of departure:

> Plato erravit, quia posuit formas exemplares per se subsistentes extra intellectum divinum, nec ipsas neque materiam a Deo esse habere.[8]

From this text he generalizes on the early attitude of St. Thomas:

> Truly, to be precise, and here we touch upon a crucial point of our essay, even St. Thomas seems to have arrived gradually and a little at a time at this "synthetic" interpretation of the two systems. *At the beginning of his literary activity he was wholly sympathetic toward the Philosopher.*[9]

But is one text alone sufficient to ground a generalization with regard to St. Thomas' attitude "at the beginning of his literary activity," and does this text represent the consistent attitude of St. Thomas at that period?

There are approximately forty texts in the *Commentary on the Sentences* which refer to Plato and/or the *Platonici*.[10]

Now, while these texts are similar in being all Platonic references,

---

[8]*In II Sent.*, d. 1, a. 1, *Exp. Text.* Fabro, *ibid.*, 58.

[9]"Veramente a voler essere precisi, e qui tocchiamo il punto cruciale del nostro saggio, anche S.T. sembra sia arrivato per tappe ed un po' alla volta a questa interpretazione 'sintetica' del due sistemi, *ed agli inizi della sua activita letteraria tutte le sue simpatie erano per il Filosofo*" [italics added] (*La Nozione*, 58).

[10]I say "approximately" because the determination of what constitues a unit-text is necessarily somewhat arbitrary. See Henle, *Saint Thomas and Platonism* (The Hague: Nijhoff, 1956), 7–17.

they differ widely in the doctrinal points discussed and in the use St. Thomas makes of them. Moreover, if we consider them in relation to the Platonic references found in later works of St. Thomas, we find that they fall naturally into continuity with various series of texts which often reappear in the same sort of doctrinal context in the various works and often maintain a continuity quite in isolation from the general discussions of Platonism.

Let us first examine some of these texts for what they may reveal of St. Thomas's *general* attitude toward Platonism.

One group of texts deals with Plato's definition of pleasure. The definition itself is rejected precisely on Aristotelian grounds,[11] but in several of the texts the definition is recognized as revealing some aspect of the nature of pleasure and is used as a confirmation of a point of doctrine.[12]

Again a sympathetic interpretation of Plato's *"intellectus paternus"* is offered.[13]

Two texts deal with Plato's theory of the "self-moved first mover." St. Thomas refers explicitly to Averroes's commentary on that section of the *Physics* in which Aristotle attacks this Platonic position. However, St. Thomas justifies Plato by giving a broader interpretation of the word *movere*.[14]

These are only illustrations but they are sufficient to show that St. Thomas' attitude "at the beginning of his literary activity" was far more nuanced than Fabro's use of a single text would indicate. His attitude

---

[11] . . . definitio illa Platonis non est conveniens, ut patet per Philosophum in VII et X Ethic" (*In IV Sent.*, d. 49, q. 3, a. 4, qa. 4 ad 2, in contr.).

[12] . . . delectatio autem non potest esse nisi in cognoscente: propter quod Plato dixit, quod delectatio est generatio sensibilis in naturam: (*In I Sent.*, d. 1, q. 4, a. 1). Cf. *In II Sent.*,d. 20, q. 1, a. 2 ad 3; *In III Sent.*, d. 27, q. 1, a. 2 ad 3.

[13]"Vel forte intellectum paternum nominat intellectum divinum, secundum quod in se quodam modo concipit ideam mundi . . ." (*In I Sent.*, d. 3, q. 1, a. 4 ad 1).

[14]"Ad secundum, quod Augustinus accipit large moveri, secundum quod ipsum intelligere est moveri quoddam et velle, quae qroprie non sunt motus, sed comparatione. In hoc enim verificatur dictum Platonis qui dicit: 'Deus movet se' . . ." (*Ibid.*, d. 8, q. 3, a. 1 ad 2). "Sed forte propter hoc Plato posuit quod primum movens seipsum movet, inquantum cognoscit se et amat se, ut in VIII Phys. Dicit Commentator" (*ibid.*, d. 45, q. 1, a. 1 ad 3).

already included a discriminating approach to Platonic doctrines and an independence in evaluating Aristotle's critique.

Fabro increases the apparent evidential value of this text by his exposition of its setting in the *Commentary*. He introduces it thus:

> Thus in the *Sentences*, the Master, treating of creation, sympathizes with Plato against Aristotle and in this way remains a good theologian and a faithful interpreter of the Patristic tradition.[15]

But actually, in the part of the *Sentences* in which the Master treats of creation and on which the *Expositio Textus* cited immediately depends, there is no indication of sympathy with Plato. On the contrary, Peter Lombard wrote:

> . . . Moyses . . . elidens errorem quorundam plura sine principio fuisse principia opinantium. Plato namque tria initia fuisse existimavit Deum scilicet, et exemplar et materiam et ipsa increata sine principio, et Deum quasi artificem, non creatorem.[16]

There is no effort whatever in Peter Lombard's text to mitigate Plato's error; in fact, he proceeds immediately to refute it from Sacred Scripture.[17]

Fabro now continues:

> . . . but Saint Thomas, in the *Commentary*, rectifies things quickly and dryly.[18]

Since Peter Lombard has not excused Plato, there is nothing for St. Thomas to "rectify"; and the addition of "subito secco" is quite gratuitous, for if we now compare the alleged rectification with the words

---

[15]" Cosi nelle Sentenze, il Magister, trattando della creazione, simpatizza per Platone contro Aristotele ed in cio si comporta da buon teologo e da fedele interprete della tradizione patristica" (*La Nozione*, 58).

[16]*Liber Secundus Sententiarum*, 1.

[17]*Ibid.*

[18]". . . ma S. Tommaso, nel Commentario, rettifica subito secco. . . ." (*La Nozione*, 58).

of Peter Lombard, St. Thomas, if anything, is less sweeping than the Lombard:

> Plato erravit quia posuit formas exemplares per se subsistentes extra intellectum divinum, neque ipsas neque materiam a Deo esse habere.[19]

In other words, St. Thomas, as we might expect in a passage taken from the *Expositio Textus*, simply repeats the exposition he found in the *littera* of Peter Lombard. There is some variation in the statement but certainly no "rectification."

Fabro now adds:

> ... and he [St. Thomas] enthusiastically defends the orthodoxy of Aristotle.[20]

No reference is given for this addition. Certainly there is no defense in the *Expositio Textus* itself. In the articles of the *Commentary* directly based on this part of the *Expositio*, Aristotle's opinion is twice discussed explicitly. In listing opinions on *secondary* causality, Aristotle's is cited with approval and he seems to be said to hold that matter is created by God.[21] This is a simple statement, but certainly without "calore." Aristotle's doctrine is listed among the errors in the article "Utrum Mundus Sit Aeternus" and all these doctrines including Aristotle's are said to be "falsae et hereticae."[22] This is certainly no complete defense, no direct defense, and no enthusiastic ("con calore") defense.

Thus the gratuitous annotations with which Fabro surrounds this simple text from an *Expositio Textus* gives it an interpretative coloring, completely unjustified by, and partially directly contrary to, the context.

In fine, when this first text is read in its proper immediate context as well as against the entire body of Platonic references in the *Commen-*

---

[19]*In II Sent.*, d. 1, q. 1 *Exp. Text.*

[20]". . . e difende [sc. S. Tommaso] con calore l'ortodossia di Aristotele" *La Nozione,* 58.

[21]*In II Sent.*, d. 1, q. 1, a. 4 ad 4.

[22]*Ibid.*, d. 5, *sol.*

tary on the Sentences, it simply does not support Fabro's generalization. St. Thomas, in commenting on the *Sentences*, displayed a judiciously discriminating attitude with regard to Plato's doctrines. He is not the unqualified partisan of Aristotle or the unqualified opponent of Plato.

II. The Second Stage

In order to treat the texts here presented without undue repetition, I shall divide them into interrelated groups. One text, however, stands somewhat alone and so must be considered separately, I shall begin with this text.

A   In IV Metaphys., lect. 4

Fabro presents the text thus:

Finally one meets also this curious text in the Commentary on the Metaphysics (a. 1271–1272): "Sive dicamus quod universale sit unum in omnibus secundum *opinionem* nostram, sive quod sit aliquid separatum secundum opinionem Platonis, sicut *fortassis* non est verum. . . ."[23]

The text is read as displaying a benevolent attitude toward Plato for Fabro begins his next sentence, "Quest'atteggiamento benevolo"; presumably the date of the *Commentary* is explicitly mentioned to emphasize, in line with the general tenor of Fabro's argument, the maturity of the text. Fabro's underlining of *opinionem* and *fortassis* places the weight of the text in these words.

In order to read this text aright, it must first be related to the Aristotelian *littera* on which, as a commentary, it depends. As soon as we do so, we find that the text is an *ad litteram* comment, simply a clarifying expansion of Aristotle and that the words which seem to make this a "curioso testo" for Fabro are, as a matter of fact, *in the text of Aristotle*: "Et propter hoc si ens et unum non est universale idem in omnibus aut separabile, *ut forsan non est*."[24] This is simply repeated by

---

[23]*La Nozione,* 59.

[24]The translation is taken from the text given in the Cathala edition of St. Thomas's *Commentary,* Book IV, Lectio 4.

St. Thomas as "sicut fortassis non est verum." If this phrase displays a "benevolent attitude," it is Aristotle's benevolence which the text reveals. A curious situation indeed, since there is no doubt, either in St. Thomas' mind or in anyone else's, of Aristotle's opposition to the separation of the universals. Now, the apparently surprising character of this remark did not escape St. Thomas himself, for, after laying out the amplified meaning of the *littera*, he explains:

> Utitur tamen adverbio dubitandi, quasi nunc supponens quae inferius probabuntur.[25]

Thus the expression of doubt is seen by St. Thomas not as reflecting any real doubt in the mind of Aristotle but as a methodological procedure. Nor is this simply an *ad hoc* justification of the "curious" *fortassis*. On the contrary, it is a general principle of interpretation which St. Thomas frequently uses and which involves an explicit recognition of Aristotle's method. Thus, to quote but two parallel examples:

> Et quia ipse determinabit inferius quod intelligere est quaedam operatio animae, in qua non communicat cum corpore, et non est conjuncti; ideo dicit, quod intelligere forsitan est aliquid alterum ab operationibus conjuncti. *Et dicit "forsitan," quia non loquitur definiendo, sed supponendo.*[26]

> Deinde cum dicit: Physice autem magis etc., inducit rationes naturales ad ostendendum quod non sit corpus infinitum in actu. Circa quas considerandum est quod, quia Aristoteles nondum probaverat corpus caeleste esse alterius essentiae a quatuor elementis, opinio autem communis suo tempore fuerat quod esset de natura quatuor elementorum, procedit in his rationibus ac si non esset aliud corpus sensibile extra quatuor elementa, secundum suam consuetudinem: *quia semper antequam probet id quod est suae opinionis, procedit ex suppositione opinionis aliorum communis.* Unde postquam pro-

---

[25] *In IV Metaphys.,* lect. 4 (ed. Cathala, 584).

[26] *In I De An.,* lect. 10 (ed. Pirotta, 150).

bavit in primo libro de Caelo et Mundo, caelum esse alterius naturae ab elementis, ad veritatis certitudinem iterat considerationem de infinito, ostendens universaliter quod nullum corpus sensibile est infinitum. . . ."[27]

Thus St. Thomas explicitly recognizes that Aristotle's method is to move toward a solution through a problematical study of various opinions. St. Thomas reads Aristotle's text in the light of this general methodology. Hence when the Thomistic comment is properly read within its full context, it loses its "curious" character and becomes only an instance of a common type of Aristotelian text and Thomistic comment, completely neutral and immaterial for the question of an increasing benevolence—or of any benevolence at all—on the part of St. Thomas.

If the text has any implications concerning St. Thomas's own view, it is that Aristotle had, later in the *Metaphysics*, definitively refuted the separation of the Ideas as held by Plato. This could be confirmed by a long series of texts, for on this point, at least, St. Thomas maintained a consistent opposition to Plato and consistently appealed to Aristotle's refutation.[28]

It is clear, then, that the appearance of evidential relevance for Fabro's thesis was created by citing the text in a truncated form. Had the next four lines been included in the quotation, St. Thomas's own explanation would have made the true import of the text evident even to the casual reader.

B   *In I De Caelo et Mundo,* lect. 4 (ed. Spiazzi, No. 38); lect. 6 (60–61); lect. 22 (228); lect. 23 (231); lect 29 (283). *In II De C. et M.,* lect. 1 (297–98); lect. 10 (384); lect. 12 (408); lect. 21 (490). *In III De C. et M.,* lect. 6 (584); lect. 11. *In I De An.,* lect. 8 (ed. Pirotta, 107–8).[29]

---

[27]*In III Phys.,* lect. 8 (ed. Leonine, vol II, No. 5). Cf. also *In VII Metaphys.,* lect. 16 (ed. Cathala, 1646); *In V Phys.,M* lect. 6 (ed. Leon., II, 8). Fabro adds, in a footnote (59, n. 1), a reference to *In VII Metaphys.,* lect. 5 (ed. Cathala, 1368–1370), apparently as a confirmation. This text however, is simply another Aristotelian forsan text.

[28]See Henle, *Saint Thomas and Platonism,* 351–373.

[29]Fabro refers to these texts either in the body or in the footnotes on 60–61.

The last reference to the commentary on the *De Caelo et Mundo* (Book III, lectio 11) can be immediately eliminated from discussion since it belongs not to St. Thomas but to Petrus de Alvernia.[30]

The general point of all these citations, according to Fabro, is that they show St. Thomas giving a sympathetic interpretation of a point of Platonic doctrine and thereby either saving him from Aristotle's criticism or even reconciling him with Aristotle.

These texts must be considered from three standpoints: (1) the sources, (2) the doctrinal content, and (3) attitude and interpretative method.

1. The Sources

The source which St. Thomas used extensively and consistently in his commentary on the *De Caelo et Mundo* was Simplicius. Now *in every case* the sympathetic interpretation of Plato given or suggested in St. Thomas' text *is to be found in the text of Simplicius.*[31]

2. The Doctrinal Content

Moreover, none of these texts deals with any question of participation, of the theory of ideas, or of Platonic theory of knowledge. For the most part, physical and cosmological theories of quite neutral metaphysical interest are treated;[32] and most of these points are not

---

[30]Bourke, *Thomistic Bibliography* (St. Louis: "The Modern Schoolman," 1945), 17; *In Aristotelis Libros De Caelo et Mundo,* ed. Spiazzi (Marietti, 1952), 15.

[31]St. Thomas, *In De C. et M.,* I, lect. 4 (ed. Spiazzi, 38)—Simplicius, *Com. Graeci,* VII, 12.16–29; 85.7–9; 86.8–11; I, lect. 6 (60–61)—Simplicius, *ibid.,* VII, 140.9–19; I, lect. 23 (231–233)— Simplicius, *ibid.,* VII, 306.18–7.11; I, lect. 29 (283)—Simplicius, *ibid.,* VII, 301.1–22; II, lect. 1 297–298) depends substantially on Simplicius, ibid, VII, 376.28–8.22. The attribution to Plato of the doctrine of dependence on a first cause goes beyond the immediate source in Simplicius, II, lect. 10 (384)—Simplicius, *ibid.,* VII, 435.32–6.1 (*cf. Ibid.,* 88.5–25; 91.7–20); II, lect. 12 (408)—Simplicius, *ibid.,* VII,454.23–6.6; II, lect. 21 (490)—Simplicius, *ibid.,* VII, 517.3–9.11.

[32]Paragraph 38, the igneous character of the heavenly body; 231–233, priority (temporal or not?) of unordered to ordered motion; 297–298, meaning of Plato's statement that the motion of the heavens is "contra naturam"; 384, contraries in the heavenly bodies; 408, the twofold motion of the stars; 490, revolution of the earth; 584, priority (temporal or not?) of unordered to ordered motion. 228 gives no doctrinal

touched on in early Thomistic works.[33] However, in two cases, a doctrine is reported which is also noted in the *Commentary on the Sentences*.[34] For this doctrinal area, therefore the texts do not indicate any shift in St. Thomas's attitude but only a material extension of his knowledge of Platonic doctrine and of its possible interpretation.

There is only one metaphysical doctrine that appears in any of these texts. In paragraphs 60–61, 283, 297–298, the theory of the world's dependence *in esse* on a first cause is attributed to Plato. Hence from the standpoint of doctrine these are the only texts from the *Commentary on the De Caelo et Mundo* which are germane to Fabro's thesis. This point will, however, be treated later.

3. Attitude and Interpretative Method

In order to consider this point, a brief summary of the technique of each text must be given. In paragraph 38, Plato and Aristotle are reconciled by a sympathetic interpretation of Plato. In 60–61 St. Thomas exempts Plato from Aristotle's critique by (a) determining the exact point attacked by Aristotle and (b) interpreting Plato's intention in a different direction. In 231–233 Plato is exempted from Aristotle's critique by the suggestion of a *possible* (*Potest etiam intelligi Platonem dedisse intelligere . . .*") interpretation for his doctrine; yet, the point is left undecided ("*Sed quidquid Plato intellexerit*") and Aristotle is said to have argued against Plato's words ("*Aristoteles . . . obiieciebat contra id quod verba Platonis exprimunt*"). 283 follows the same pattern (but "quidam dicunt" for the "Potest intelligi"). In 297–298 St. Thomas suggests ("sed *forte* Plato non intellexit . . . sed voluit exprimere") a favorable interpretation. In 384 a statement of Plato (which is not

determination. It simply states the conciliatory exegetical principle laid down by Simplicius and contrasts it with the procedure of Alexander.

[33]See Henle, *Saint Thomas and Platonism,* "Analytic Index to the Texts," 255–288, under appropriate headings.

[34]In paragraphs 231–233 and 584 the ordered motion of the heavens is said to be, according to Plato, from God (*a Deo*) and from the first principle (*a primo principio*); in *In II Sent.,* d. 1, q. 1. a. 5, *sol,* we read: "Alii dixerunt quod res ab aeterno movebantur motu inordinato, et postea reductae sunt ad ordinem, vel casu . . . vel *a creatore, et hoc ponit Plato.*" Here St. Thomas makes no effort to interpret away the temporal priority as, following Simplicius, he does in paragraphs 231–233 and 584; but dependence on God is introduced in all three texts.

clearly approved) is used to confirm an opinion of Aristotle. In 408 St. Thomas reports Simplicius's ("Dicit etiam Simplicius") explanation of an at least apparent contradiction between Plato and Aristotle. In 490 St. Thomas suggests two possible explanations ("et ideo potest dici . . . vel potest dici . . .") which would excuse Plato and leave Aristotle dealing with his words (". . . quia possibile erat aliquos false intelligere verba Platonis, Aristoteles removet falsum intellectum qui ex his verbis haberi posset, sicut frequenter consuevit facere circa verba Platonis"). In 584 St. Thomas reports a defense of Plato made by his followers ("Sectatores autem Platonis dicunt eum hoc non intellexisse . . .") and remarks that, in accordance with this defense, Aristotle is arguing, once again, merely against Plato's words (". . . contra Platonicorum verba, ne ab eis aliquis in errorem inducatur").

Analysis of Techniques

In this summary various techniques appear.

1. St. Thomas *suggests* a favorable interpretation of Plato (as in 297–298); this technique even to the verbal signal *forte* already is used in the *Commentary on the Sentences*.

> Vel *forte* intellectum paternum nominat [sc. Plato] intellectum divinum secundum quod in se quodam modo concipit ideam mundi . . ."[35]

2. St. Thomas uses doctrine of Plato (which may not be wholly acceptable) to confirm a positive doctrine. This procedure also appears in the *Commentary on the Sentences*. The Platonic definition of pleasure is rejected, but it is used (even in the same verbal style[36]) to confirm a statement about pleasure.

> . . . delectatio causatur ex conjunctione convenientis. Conveniens enim adveniens perficit id cui advenit et quietat inclinationem in illud. Et haec quietatio secundum quod est percepta est delectatio. *Unde Plato dixit* quod delectatio est

---

[35]*In I Sent.,* d. 3, q. 1, a. 4 ad 1.

[36]After the exposition of the doctrine Plato is introduced, in the *Commentary on the Sentences*, by "Unde Plato dixit. . . ."; in the *Commentary on the De Caelo et Mundo* by "Unde et Plato dixit . . ."

'generatio sensibilis' id est incognita, 'in naturam,' idest connaturalis.[37]

3. In four texts of *In De C. et M.*—paragraphs 38, 231–233, 490, 584 (and we might add 60–61)—Plato and Aristotle are reconciled, explicitly or implicitly, by a favorable interpretation of Plato, while, in three of them, Aristotle's critique is explained as being against "verba Platonis ne ab eis aliquis in errorem inducatur."

Now it is true that St. Thomas found an explicit formulation of this technique in Simplicius[38] and repeated the statement both in these texts and elsewhere.[39] Yet the technique is already employed in his early works. Thus in the *Commentary on the Sentences*, in two texts,[40] as we have seen Plato's doctrine on the self-moved first mover is reconciled with Aristotle's unmoved mover by an interpretation of the word "move" as used by Plato. This reconciliation becomes wholly explicit in the certainly early *Contra Gentiles*.

> Sciendum autem quod Plato, qui posuit omne movens moveri, communius accepit nomen motus quam Aristoteles. Aristoteles enim proprie accepit motum, secundum quod est actus existentis in potentia secundum quod huiusmodi: qualiter non est nisi divisibilium, et corporum, ut probatur in VI Physic. Secundum Platonem autem movens seipsum non est corpus: accipiebat enim motum pro qualibet operatione, ita quod intelligere et opinari sit quoddam moveri; quem etiam modum loquendi Aristoteles tangit in III de Anima. Secundum hoc ergo dicebat primum movens seipsum movere quod intelligit se et vult vel amat se. Quod in aliquo non repugnat rationibus Aristotelis: nihil enim differt devenire ad aliquod primum

---

[37]*In III Sent.*, d. 27, q. 1, a. 2 ad 3.

[38]Simplicius, *In L. De Caelo,* I (*Com. Graeci,* VII, 352.27–33); III (ibid., VII 587.37–588.7; 640.27–31).

[39]For example, *In I De An.,* lect. 8 (ed. Pirotta, 107–8); *in III Metaphys.,* lect. 11 (Cathala, 468–471).

[40]*In I Sent.,* d. 8, q. 3, a. 1 ad 2; ibid., 45, q. 1, a. 1 ad 3.

quod moveat se, secundum Platonem; et devenire ad primum
quod omnino sit immobile, secundum Aristotelem.[41]

Thus in certainly early works, St. Thomas already uses the
equivalent to the distinction "intentiones Platonis" and "verba Platonis."
Moreover, texts of this sort are scattered through the works; for example, In *B. de Trin., q.* 5, a. 4 ad 2; *De Pot.,* q. 10, a. 1: *Q. D. de An.,* a. 1;
In VII Phy., lect 1 (ed. Leon. 7); ST, I, q. 18, a. 3 ad 1.

It is not surprising, therefore to find this technique combined with
Simplicius's principle at a very appropriate point in the text of the *Commentary on the De Anima* which Fabro cites. For in the *De Anima* St.
Thomas found Aristotle criticizing the circular structure of the soul as
developed in the *Timaeus.* On the one hand, all of St. Thomas' sources
(including Aristotle) had presented Plato as holding a spiritual soul; on
the other hand, Aristotle here in the *De Anima* appears to be arguing
seriously against a Platonic theory which made the soul a "magnitude."
If indeed the soul were a quantitative magnitude, it would not be
spiritual; and this would be irreconcilable with all that St. Thomas knew
of Plato's theory of soul.[42] If Plato did not hold the quantitative nature
of the soul, how could one explain Aristotle's effort to refute this Platonic position?

The solution which St. Thomas uses and to which Fabro refers is
highly ingenious.

> Posita opinione Platonis, hic Aristoteles reprobat eam. Ubi
> notandum est, quod plerumque quando reprobat opiniones
> Platonis, non reprobat eas quantum ad intentionem Platonis,
> sed quantum ad sonum verborum ejus. Quod ideo facit, quia
> Plato habuit malum modum docendi. Omnia enim figurate
> dicit, et per symbola docet: intendens aliud per verba, quam
> sonent ipsa verba; sicut quod dixit animam esse circulum. Et
> ideo ne aliquis propter ipsa verba incidat in errorem, Aris-

---

[41]*CG,* I, cap. 13.

[42]On the spirituality of the soul, cf. Henle, *Saint Thomas and Platonism,* "Analytic
Index to the Texts," sub voce "anima." St. Thomas never refers, outside of the *De Anima*
commentary, to the doctrine that the soul is a magnitude, and this although he devotes
extensive discussions to Plato's theories on the soul.

toteles disputat contra eum quantum ad id quod verba ejus sonant.

Ponit autem Aristoteles rationes decem ad destruendum suprapositam opionem: quarum quaedam sunt contra eum, et quaedam contra verba ejus. Non enim Plato voluit, quod secundum veritatem intellectus esset magnitudo quantitativa, seu circulus, et motus circularis; sed metaphorice hoc attribuit intellectui. Nihilominus tamen Aristoteles, ne aliquis ex hoc erret, disputat contra eum secundum quod verba sonant.[43]

Plato attributed shape and circular motion to the soul only meta-phorically—thus Plato's doctrine of the spirituality of the soul is safeguarded; Aristotle, however, to protect those who would read Plato's metaphors literally, refutes the verbal position, not the real intention of Plato—thus Aristotle's critique becomes intelligible and his proper understanding of Plato is vindicated.

From the standpoint of technique and attitude this group of texts is, then, in continuity with a series of texts stretching back to the very beginning of St. Thomas's literary activity. What he found in Simplicius was an explicit formulation of this technique, a formulation which he accepted and cited at appropriate points. However, he continued to use it, even in the *Commentary on the De Caelo et Mundo*, with reserve and caution. Moreover, in a text cited by Fabro, we find him explicitly stating the exegetical principle of Simplicius, placing alongside it the contrary view of Alexander and concluding with this remark: "Quidquid autem horum sit, non est nobis multum curandum." This expression almost of indifference toward the conciliatory method of Simplicius is in perfect accord with the judicious use he makes of the principle and with the reserve, displayed in the texts themselves, which sometimes brings him merely to *report* the interpretation suggested in Simplicius.

Summary of the Analysis

With regard to the technique displayed in these texts, we are then forced to conclude that St. Thomas throughout maintains a judicious and discriminatory attitude toward Platonic doctrines. He is prepared to reject, to accept, to distinguish, or, through various devices, to interpret

---

[43] *In I De An.*, lect. 8 (ed. Pirotta 107–108).

benevolently the doctrines of Plato and his followers. No wholesale change in his attitude here appears; neither was he in the beginning a complete opponent of Plato, nor was he at any time determined to save and defend Plato against Aristotle. And it is noteworthy that in all these cases of benevolent interpretation and reconciliation, *it is Plato's doctrine which is re-interpreted and brought in line with Aristotle,* not Aristotle's. This fact alone makes the texts move in a direction contrary to Fabro's argument.

One last point: It might be argued in Fabro's defense that the multiplication of sympathetic and conciliatory texts is still some indication of an "increasing benevolence." However, this increase in number must be viewed against the total background of all Platonic texts. The references to Plato in general increase in the later works (there are some forty texts in the *Commentary on the Sentences*; at least one hundred in the *Summa Theologiae*); within this body of texts, those which seriously criticize or condemn Plato also increase both in number and in importance.[44] Since, then, the number of texts can be seen as a function of the total number of texts, the quantitative argument gives no strength to Fabro's position.

Consideration of the remaining texts in Fabro's second stage, must, for economy's sake, be postponed at this point.

III. The Third Stage: the *De Substantiis Separatis*

Fabro brings his argument to a climax with a consideration of the *De Substantiis Separatis*. He goes immediately to the third chapter, in which the agreement of Aristotle and Plato is developed. Now, it would seem obvious that the third chapter must be read in the light of the previous chapters, since this indeed was the order established by St. Thomas himself. If, then, we turn to the first chapter we find here the most elaborate synthesis of Platonic doctrine to be found in the whole Thomistic corpus. Here St. Thomas exploits all his sources and synthesizes the main doctrines of Plato and of the *Platonici* into a philosophical unity,[45] displaying the logical connection of ideas as well as the premises which command and philosophically specify the entire syn-

---

[44]See Henle, *Saint Thomas and Platonism*, Part Two, *passim*.

[45]See *Ibid.,* 243–244, for a listing of the main sources.

thesis. The formal structure is, therefore, what I have elsewhere called the *via Platonica*,[46] a philosophical method with specific philosophical principles. At the end of this extended exposition, St. Thomas says:

> Hujus autem positionis radix invenitur efficaciam non habere.

The basis for the position has no force; the philosophical soul of the synthesis is not viable.

This text is an echo of St. Thomas' very first analytical critique of Platonism in the *Commentary on the Sentences:*

> Horum autem omnium errorum et plurium hujusmodi unum videtur esse principium et fundamentum *quo destructo nihil probabilitatis remanet.*[47]

These two texts stand respectively at the beginning and the end of a series of texts in which St. Thomas analyzes Plato's basic metaphysics and basic epistemology, and rejects their philosophical foundations (*radix, fundamentum*). I have examined this critique elsewhere and will here assume the results of that study.[48]

This faces us with a problem in St. Thomas. How does it happen that in Chapter Three he uses and approves positions whose philosophical foundations he has destroyed in Chapter One?

I have shown elsewhere that this problem is not limited to the *De Substantiis Separatis*. I there used a solution presented by St. Thomas himself, the solution based on a distinction between *positiones* and the philosophical method and principles, the *via* and *rationes,* which ground them and *give them specific meaning in a philosophical system.*[49]

This method for handling *positiones* is almost the reverse of that found in the previous group of texts. For here St. Thomas eliminates precisely the *intentiones* and *rationes* of a position while retaining its obvious verbal formulation.

---

[46]*Ibid.,* 322–350; also "Saint Thomas' Methodology in the Treatment of 'Positiones,'" Gregorianum, 36 (1955), 391–409.

[47]*In II Sent.,* d. 17, q. 1, a, 1, sol.

[48]See note 48, *supra.*

[49]See note 48, *supra.*

In the light of this analysis of the *total* situation in the texts of St. Thomas, the third chapter of the *De Substantiis Separatis* must be read as a concordance of *positiones* which have, at least as far as Plato is concerned, been freed from their philosophical foundations and, hence, from their specifically Platonic *meaning* (at least as St. Thomas understood it).[50]

Hence, the simple appeal to the apparent meaning of the third chapter of the *De Substantiis Separatis* has no evidential force for Fabro's thesis.

We are now in a position to return to the second stage and resume consideration of the remaining texts.

A   ST, I, q. 6, a. 4 ad 12,[51] and *In De Div. Nom., Prologus*

These are very clear cases of the use of the positio treatment. Hence the texts must be read in the same way as the third chapter of the *De Substantiis Separatis*.

B   *De Spirit. Creat.,* a. 10 ad 8

This text handles an objection, developed out of Augustinian citations, against the created character of the agent intellect. It summarizes the positions of Socrates, Plato, Augustine, and Aristotle, and gives, briefly, St. Thomas's critical analysis of the *rationes* of Plato and his understanding of the dependence of Augustine on Plato. It is, in fact, a selective summary of the content of *ST,* I, q. 84,[52] with which it is wholly consistent and contemporary. The text must, therefore, be read alongside the *Summa* question. Now, St. Thomas clearly and explicitly recognizes a continuity of ideas from Plato to Augustine in regard to theory of knowledge. His procedure here is to acknowledge the relationship, to refute the *rationes* of Plato, and to end with a benign interpretation of the Augustinian citations.[53] This is exactly the

---

[50]Henle, *Saint Thomas and Platonism,* 403–418.

[51]For a full treatment of this text, see *ibid.,* 302–303, and Henle, "Saint Thomas' Methodology in the Treatment of 'Positiones,'" 402–404.

[52]For an extended examination of the question, see Henle, *Saint Thomas and Platonism,* 387–396.

[53]See *Ibid.,* "Saint Thomas' Polemical Strategy," 423–425.

procedure of the *De Spiritualibus Creaturis* text. It is the final benign interpretation which Fabro cites but with no reference to this complex background which alone makes it intelligible.[54] The text runs:

> Non multum autem refert dicere quod ipsa intelligibilia participentur a Deo vel quod lumen faciens intelligibilia.

It does not make much difference which you say. Why not? Because the Platonic interpretation is equally sound? But St. Thomas has just refuted this interpretation in the very same text as well as in the running anti-Platonic critique of *ST,* I, q. 84. In what sense then? It must be in the sense of his own theory. More than this, however, in *ibid.,* a. 5, corp., he gives the exact sense in which it can be "said" that "ipsa intelligibilia participentur a Deo." This explanation precisely eliminates the Platonic meaning of the formula while letting it stand verbally.

Fabro calls this text "una frase motto inaspetta." After one has become aware of the strategy St. Thomas follows in dealing with the Platonizing expressions of St. Augustine, one, on the contrary, regularly expects phrases of this sort.

C   *In L. De Hebdomadibus*, cap. 2

> Et nihil differt quantum ad hoc si ponamus illas formas immateriales alterius gradus quam sint rationes horum sensibilium ut Aristoteles voluit.

In this text Fabro underlines "Et nihil differt quantum ad hoc," yet puts all his emphasis on "nihil differt." The restriction "quantum ad hoc" refers to the argument that separated forms, though simple in some sense, still participate *esse* and so are not truly simple. Obviously, this

---

[54]Fabro does resume the discussion of these texts in two later sections of his work (pp. 83 and 284). He there recognizes some of the qualifications which must be made (and thereby weakens the argument of pages 57–63); but a thorough examination of his treatment would require a much broader textual base and a much more extended discussion than the limits of the present article allow.

argument holds whether Platonic or Aristotelian forms are in question, and this is all that St. Thomas is here saying.[55]

D   The "dependence on God" in *In I De Caelo et Mundo,* lect. 6 (ed. Spiazzi, 60–61); lect. 29 (283). *In II De Caelo et Mundo,* lect. 1 (297–298); *De Potentia,* q. 3, a. 5

We may also resume here the point previously postponed; namely, the attribution to Plato and/or the *Platonici* of a doctrine of creation. It is indeed clear that St. Thomas came finally to a synthesis of Plato-*Platonici* doctrines in which all the levels of being are reduced to a first "cause."[56] St. Thomas recognizes that the effort to reduce multiplicity to unity is the common aim of all philosophers.[57] The differences arise, however, from the procedure by which this unification is achieved in different philosophies.[58] Granting, then, that in the first synthesis St. Thomas sees Platonism as making all things dependent upon a first principle, the question must be asked: By what procedure and through

---

[55]To make this obvious, the entire text should be read: "Est tamen considerandum, quod cum simplex dicatur aliquid ex eo quod caret compositione, nihil prohibet aliquid esse secundum quid simplex, inquantum caret aliqua compositione, quod tamen non est omnino simplex: unde ignis et aqua dicuntur simplicia corpora; inquantum carent compositione quae est ex contrariis, quae invenitur in mixtis; quorum tamen unumquodque est compositum tum ex partibus quantitatis, tum etiam ex forma et materia. Si ergo inveniantur aliquae formae non in materia; unaquaeque earum est quidem simplex quantum ad hoc quod caret materia, et per consequens quantitate, quae est dispositio materiae; quia tamen quaelibet forma est determinativa ipsius esse, nulla earum est ipsum esse, sed est habens esse. Puta, secundum opinionem Platonis, ponamus formam immaterialem subsistere, quae sit idea et ratio hominum materialium, et aliam formam quae sit idea et ratio equorum: manifestum erit quod ipsa forma immaterialis subsistens, cum sit quiddam determinatum ad speciem, non est ipsum esse commune, sed participat illud: et nihil differt quantum ad hoc, si ponamus illas formas immateriales altioris gradus quam sint rationes horum sensibilium, ut Aristoteles voluit: unaquaeque enim illarum, inquantum distinguitur ab alia, quaedam specialis forma est participans ipsum esse; et sic nulla earum erit vere simplex. Id autem erit solum vere simplex, quod non participat esse, non quidem inhaerens, sed subsistens."

[56]The most fully developed statement is *De Sub. Sep.,* cap. 1–2.

[57]"Dicendum quod communis intentio omnium fuit reducere multitudinem in unitatem, et varietatem in uniformitatem, secundum quod possible esset" (*De Ver.,* q. 5, a. 9, corp.).

[58]*Ibid.*

what principles does he think this is done? This brings us back to the formal analysis of the *via Platonica* and the *rationes Platonis* which specify the Platonic reduction to unity. The formal philosophical principles turn out thus to be invalid, in St. Thomas's view, and to entail, in the conclusions, all those metaphysical and epistemological difficulties which St. Thomas formally points out. This, however, leaves the *positio* itself ambiguous and open to incorporation into a different frame of principles.

There is, then, a certain development on this point beyond the data of the commentary on the *Sentences*, a development in St. Thomas's knowledge of the *positiones* within the Platonic tradition, in his selective synthesis of them, and, finally, in his formal critique of the principles which he finds at the root of all of them.

Conclusion

We are thus forced to the final verdict that the texts advanced by Fabro in pages 57–62, when properly read within the appropriate Thomistic context, do not support his theses: (1) that there is, in St. Thomas, an attitude of increasing benevolence toward Plato, (2) that St. Thomas more and more assimilated Platonic metaphysics, formally as such, into his own system.

Many problems, indeed, remain; and not all the evidence on the general Thomistic-Platonic problem is yet in. Still, on the basis of present evidence we can say: (1) that St. Thomas's additude toward Platonic doctrines was, from the first, one of critical discrimination—he approved, distinguished, rejected, as seemed appropriate to each point of doctrine; (2) that his knowledge of Plato and Platonism grew through his years of literary activity; (3) that he devoted more and more attention to Plato and the *Platonici*; (4) that he developed a synthesis of the metaphysical and epistemological doctrines drawn from Plato and the *Platonici* (the most developed presentation being [for metaphysics] that of the first chapter of the *De Substantiis Separatis* and [for epistemology] that of *ST,* I, q. 84); (5) that he related these syntheses to a method of philosophizing (the *via Platonica*) and a set of principles (the *rationes Platonis*) which he carefully criticized and rejected; (6) that he used (both for Plato and for St. Augustine) a via-position technique which enabled him to reject the philosophy of a *positio* while yet retaining and approving the *positio* itself.

In addition, this short study has, perhaps, illustrated the difficulties involved in drawing generalizations from isolated Thomistic texts. No doubt, this study itself has not avoided all the pitfalls in the interpreter's path; yet it may be hoped that comprehensive and cooperative efforts of this sort may bring us to establish a more scientific methodology for the reading of St. Thomas and a more exact understanding of his authentic meaning.

XIII

THE THREE LANGUAGES OF HUME

New Introduction: This article[1] was written at the request of Professor John Deely who asked me to present a paper at the meeting of the Semiotic Society held in St. Louis in 1993. I thought that a study of Hume's effort to express his philosophy in an appropriate language would be an interesting semiotic experience. I think that this study contributes substantially to the following evaluation of Hume, namely, that Hume was not only the logical result of the philosophical movement that began with Descartes and moved through Locke and Berkeley into Hume, but he was also the *reductio ad absurdum* of that same movement.

* * *

A. Introduction

Thomas Reid wrote that if Hume's philosophy were expressed in plain English its absurdity would be obvious to everyone. I agree with this statement. However, the problem is that Hume's basic epistemological philosophy of human nature cannot be expressed in plain English or in any natural language. The reason is that Hume's positions so contradict the universal experience of mankind, on which all natural languages are structured, that the attempted expression of Hume's po-

---

[1]Eighteenth Annual Meeting of Semiotic Society of America, Presenter, Panel Member (October 1993), 21–24. This preliminary study is based entirely on Book I, "Of the Understanding" in Hume's *Treatise on Human Nature* (London: Oxford University Press, 1958 ed.), 26–274.

sition in a natural language creates an internal contradiction. In this paper I intend to do a preliminary exploration of this problem.[2]

B. The Three Languages

First I must identify the "three languages" to which I refer, namely (1) natural language, (2) specialized and artificial language, and (3) Humean language.

> 1. A natural language is one developed by a social group to enable its members to communicate with each other.

Every language has a way of saying, "I love you": "Ich bin hunrig," "mucho calor." Moreover, all natural languages reflect the real world that all men experience. Thus, all languages presuppose a three-dimensional world.

These natural languages can be made extremely sensitive and beautiful by poets and orators. It has been said that the diverse cultures of the world are simply different ways of being human. [I here prescind from any value judgments.] Language is part of those cultures and so, too, is a way of being human. All these languages are human languages and so are deeply humanized, each in its own way. They are all human and so are largely mutually translatable. Any normal human being can learn any human language. There is no half-human language such as the extreme evolutionists used to postulate.

Of course, the vocabularies of the various natural languages vary considerably. Words are instrumental conventional signs[3] and so naturally vary as do other conventions. But vocabularies not only reflect the common humanity of all people but also the special experience and situations of different societies. Thus, the Japanese had no European-type bread and when introduced to it by the Portuguese simply took over the word "pan" into their own vocabulary.

Here we are not interested in the vagaries of vocabularies but in the

---

[2]An excellent discussion of language with reference to the present subject may be found in Reid, *Essays on the Intellectual Powers of Man*, Baruch Brody, ed. (Cambridge: M.I.T. Press, 1978), 1–75.

[3]R. J. Henle, S.J., *Theory of Knowledge* (Chicago: Loyola University Press, 1983), 60–61.

common substructure of human languages as human and as based on the nature of the world.

2. Specialized and Artificial Languages

The advance of learning, especially in the West, has resulted in the creation of many formally distinct disciplines (e.g., physics, psychology, epistemology, sociology, etc.). Those working in these diverse disciplines have found that in order to express their new discoveries and to render their work more precise, it is necessary to establish special terminological systems. But these new languages have been developed within the framework of existing natural languages. No radical linguistic change has been necessary.

Also, there have been efforts to establish a universal language beyond politics and particular cultures and therefore serving to promote universal peace and understanding. Esperanto is, of course, a classic example of such a language.

But, once again, these languages are essentially the same kind of languages as are natural languages.

I mention these specialized and artificial languages here to emphasize the point that a Humean language *cannot* be an extension of or a mimic of natural language. Humean language must speak in a totally different manner.

3. The Idea of a Humean Language

Of course, there is no Humean language and Hume himself offers only piecemeal contributions and implicit directives for the development of such a language.

He was himself quite aware that he had to write using natural English, though that English does not and could not express his true positions. "I know," he wrote, "that I must talk and think like the vulgar."[4] A simple example may illustrate the difficulty of translating into a Humean mode of speech. Thus, I might say, "I see a tree." Clear enough. But since there is no self in Hume's view, the "I" would have to be dropped: "See a tree."

There are no operations in Hume's world so the "act of seeing"

---

[4]Hume, *Treatise on Human Nature,* 201–202.

becomes the same thing as the "tree." We might say then, "There is a seen-tree." But the "tree" is not the physical object it is ordinarily to be but a "perception" which is not physical, is immutable and independent of all other things. What then? Should we say, "There is a tree"? Should we say, "a tree-image appears"?

C. The Starting Point for Constructing a Humean Language

We would have to begin by understanding as clearly (as possible) what Hume means by three basic terms—Perception, Impressions, Ideas—since his use of these terms is completely idiosyncratic. This is not a matter of simply adopting a new vocabulary since, in Hume, these words express a complete reductionism of all human experience and all reality to the context of their meaning. Just as these words express Hume's fundamental view of the world, so they must command the basic structure of the Humean language.

Hume himself realizes the radical departure which his view represents when he asserts that his word "impression" has no counterpart in "English or in any other language I know."[5] The reason for this is easy to find. All that is implied in Hume's use of "perception," "Impression" and "idea" encompasses a false and distorted view of the world and of human experience.

Since this view is not imbedded in any natural language and since it is the very foundation of Hume's thought, we cannot "talk like the vulgar" and truly talk Humean.

There have been attempts to establish a standard universal language by creating an artificial language, Esperanto being one of the best known languages of this type. All artificial languages are modeled on natural languages and so may simply be classed with natural language. Hence, no model can be found for a Humean language in any of the artificial languages.

D. Hume and Natural Language

Hume, of course, uses the natural English language of which he is a master as indicated by his writings on English history. Reid himself takes note of this fact. Hume is also aware that there is a distinct

---

[5]Hume, *Treatise on Human Nature* 2, footnote.

difference between "philosophical language" and the language of the "vulgar." And occasionally Hume himself seems to make an excursion into what may be called authentic Humean language. For himself, Hume himself indicates that there is no word in any language for what he calls an "impression."

E. Characteristics of Humean Language

Since this is only a preliminary study and I do not intend to try to develop a Humean language, I will here give only some major characteristics of such a language. I will briefly describe some characteristics that would radically distinguish Humean language from all natural languages.

1. Depersonalization

Hume maintains that there is no "idea" of self since there is no "impression of self." Moreover, reflection reveals no "myself." There is no permanent self-identical substance which would be a "self." Hume's world has no "selves" and so no person. A Humean language would have no truly *personal pronouns*. Humean language would be totally dehumanized and much closer to the language of geometry. We could say, "a toothache appears" or, "There is a toothache," but we could not say, "I have a toothache."

2. Destabilization

Hume's world exists only in "consciousness" or in the "mind," but the mind is only a continuously changing collection of perceptions.[6] Perceptions are the nearest thing to a "substance." But perceptions are forever fleeting. We would need a verbal system that would work with-

---

[6]"The *mind is a kind of theater*, where several perceptions successively make their appearance; pass, re-pass, glide away, and mingle in an infinite variety of postures and situations. There is properly no *simplicity* in it at one time, nor *identity* in different; whatever natural propension we may have to imagine that simplicity and identity. The comparison of the theater must not mislead us. They are the successive perceptions only, that constitute the mind; nor have we the most distant notion of the place, where these scenes are represented, or of the materials, of which it is compos'd." [Emphasis added.] Hume, *Treatise on Human Nature*, 253.

out a primary subject (like Aristotle's "substance") and would have no implication of "staying put."

3. Activity

The world in which we live, as conceived by all people, is a world of action and activity. Through action objects affect and change each other. This universal character of reality and of thought is reflected in the structure of every mutual language and, indeed, in almost all philosophical language (PhL), generally in its verbal system. There are thousands of transitive verbs capable of expressing action, force, causality and many ways of indicating the effect of those actions.

But Hume allows for no true "operations" or forceful activities, no productivity and no true causes. Active verbs and, indeed, passive modes of expression would disappear.

F. Mind

There is one word that reveals both the difficulty of finding Hume's meaning behind the facade of natural or philosophical language and the difficulty of building this meaning into a Humean language. That word is "mind."

If one checks the [NL] usage Hume makes of "mind" it will be found to include most of the meanings listed in a standard English dictionary. But in that listing you will not find Hume's own understanding of "mind."

Mind is a "loose" fluid collection of impressions and ideas, without mutual intrinsic relationships and inhering in nothing. There is no "subject," no continuing base but simply a continual flux of perceptions. In [HL] we would have to speak simply of an accidental collection of perceptions in continuing flux. An impression cannot be said to "appear to the mind"; it simply appears in the collection. So likewise it simply disappears. "Appearing" is simply a description of the perception. Furthermore, there is nothing to perceive it. Perception is just the nature of a perception. No one perceives the perception. In [HL] we cannot say that something or someone perceives the perception nor is there an *act* of appearing. In order to make perception a Humean word we must forget about a subject, a cause, and an act. What is left is a Humean perception.

This simplified perception is the "nearest thing to a substance" that there is. Nor is it simple or spiritual. Therefore the perception has no self-identity or any identity at all. It is constantly in flux; an accidental constantly changing collection of intrinsically unrelated perceptions.

Each impression and each idea is individual, self-existent, the nearest thing to substance that there is. The only abstraction is the removal or rearrangement of distinct impressions or ideas into complex ones which themselves are individual. Properly speaking, there are no generalizations and no principles in Humean language. A generalization for Hume is simply a sequence of impressions and ideas.

G. Conclusion

This brief study of the possibility of creating a genuine Humean language suggests that Hume's true views cannot be expressed in any natural or artificial language, which would appear to be a total *reductio ad absurdum* of Hume's philosophy of knowledge.

XIV

REFLECTIONS ON CURRENT REDUCTIONISM

New Introduction: I understand reductionism in general to be the effort to identify a higher level of reality with a lower level, as when intellection is identified with sensation or the effort to explain a higher level of reality by using concepts and terms drawn from a lower level of reality, as when biological life is explained by using concepts and theories from chemistry and physics to explain biological life.

The topic dealt with here[1] is extremely important because reductionism not only distorts our whole view of the universe but in particular it falsifies our whole view of the nature of man and therefore has an influence on morals, politics, and the whole of culture.

* * *

A. Introduction[2]

In a rapid review of the atheistic character of American Naturalism

---

[1]First published in *The New Scholasticism,* 59, no. 2 (Spring 1985): 131–155.

[2]For a selected bibliography on reductionism, see: *Interpretations of Life and Mind,* ed. Marjorie Grene (New York, 1971), 149–150.

Edgar Wilson has an extensive bibliography in: *The Mental as Physical* (London, 1979), 397–427. It is heavily scientific and weighted toward reductionism.

For older materials, the references in Chapters 7 and 9 of *Further Critical Studies in Neurology,* by Sir Francis Walsche (Baltimore, 1965), and in *Minds and Machines* (Baltimore, Revised Edition, 1960), are useful.

as it was developed in this century, James Collins asserts: "[It] is reductionist in the philosophically most pregnant sense of refusing to grant the status of reality to anything which challenges the assumption of nature's inclusive self-sufficiency." And of its reductionist method he says: "The only knowledge-yielding statements about reality are those which can be publicly verified according to the canons of scientific inquiry, interpreted to support the analytic continuum of method and nature."[3] My effort here will be to take stock epistemologically and metaphysically of the reductionist position as it appears in recent identity theory and to offer an integrated critique of its principles and main arguments. I will thus present a critical examination of reductionism in its present historical development.

B. Epistemological Reductionism

1. Universalizing the Scientific Method

I propose two definitions of "reductionism" (or "reductivism"[4]); the first is epistemological, the second metaphysical.

The epistemological definition is: Reductionism is that philosophical position which maintains that there is only one valid generically homogeneous methodology for attaining knowledge, and that all valid human knowledge can be brought under this methodology and so united into a generically homogenous discipline.

In modern times, the methodology selected is, of course, the generalized version of the "scientific method." Homer Smith makes a representative statement:

> Science discovers truth the hard way: entertaining no *a priori* certitudes, she starts from ignorance and, by tested and critical procedures, little by little wrests from nature successive fragments of information which prove to be verifiable by competent observers at all times and in all places. The body of verifiable knowledge is what the scientist means by truth, and process by which science extracts it from nature is called the

---

[3]*God in Modern Philosophy* (Chicago, 1959), 272; 270.

[4]Marjorie Grene prefers "reductivism" and "reductive." See: *Interpretations of Life*, 14 and passim.

scientific method. The scientific method has been tried and tested for some three centuries and remains inviolate as the only reliable method for discovering something, or anything, that can be called "truth". . . .[5]

I have called the methodology of science "generic," since, if one merely examines the acceptable modern sciences, one finds a great number of variations. Besides, not all reductionists agree on the extent of possible reduction. There are those who believe that, in principle, physics is the one discipline into which all others will be resolved and the methodology of which is the scientific method, par excellence. Other reductionists reject "crude" reductionism, and place limitations on the reducing process.[6] All agree, however, on the main point: there is only one formally constituted methodology; it is homogeneous (=its formal object is one) and exclusive (=all other proposed methods are to be rejected) and is essentially the actual method of the physical sciences.[7]

If the scientific method were a truly universal intellectual methodology, with no intrinsic methodological limitations, this sweeping claim would hold. If, however, the scientific method is only one method-

---

[5]"Objectives and Goals in Science," *The Yale Scientific Magazine,* 23, 5 (February 1949): 2.

[6]Wilson: "Unlike previous physicalist accounts, therefore, the conventional manifestations of 'mind' are not explained *away* by this hypothesis in the reductionist manner of 'nothing-but accounts. The hypothesis thus purports or promises to satisfy both of the criteria for a solution to the mental-physical puzzle, because it is both metaphysically conservative and true to experience in so far as it is non-reductionist with respect to phenomena."

[7]Extreme reductionism holds that all disciplines, in principle, can be reduced to physics: "In the view of the reductivists, all science, and biology in particular, is reducible to physics; all the laws of science can be systematically connected with and derived from the fundamental laws of matter in motion" (Marjorie Grene, *Interpretations of Life,* 1). There are less radical positions. Thus, Edgar Wilson holds that his reductionism is more conservative: "For the present purpose it is sufficient to say that the many criticisms that have been directed against behaviouristic-scientific accounts of mind-directed action do not tell against physicalism. This is because the PO [physical-objective] model is capable of accounting for mind and min-directed action without Procrustean reduction of phenomena. In fact, it is the evidence from neuropsychology and biophysics that represents the real challenge to the OA [orthodox-animistic] model of persons" (*Mental as Physical,* 55). (Footnote omitted.)

ological development of the intellect of man, such a position simply ignores whole areas and aspects of reality. As Polany puts it, it requires men to deny things they otherwise know to be true. Or, as Gilson says, men cannot deny as philosophers what they know as men.[8]

As an example, Polanyi refers to the strange fact that many intelligent people have denied the reality of "consciousness":

> Let us look at some examples of the absurdities imposed by the modern scientific outlook. Listen to three authoritative voices denying the existence of human consciousness: (1) ". . . the existence of something called consciousness is a venerable *hypothesis*: not a datum, not directly observable . . ."; (2) "although we cannot get along without the concept of consciousness, actually there is no such thing"; (3) "The knower as an entity is an unnecessary postulate." These three statements were made, respectively, by Hebb, Kubie, and Lashley at a symposium on brain mechanisms and consciousness in 1954. It is not that these distinguished scientists really believe that consciousness does not exist. They know, for example, that pain exists.[9]

Why do they come to such absurdities? Because ". . . they feel obliged to deny the existence of consciousness, *for it eludes explanation in terms of science*."[10] (Emphasis added.)

2. Conceptual Distortions of Fact

The second way of dealing with things that escape the sweep of the scientific method is to so distort their conceptualization that they can seem to fit in the procrustean bed of science.[11]

A recent example is the elaborate explication of an identity theory

---

[8]"Pourquoi refusent-ils de penser comme philosophes ce qu'eux-mêmes ne nient pas penser comme hommes?" (Etienne Gilson, Réalisme thomiste et critique de la connaissance (Paris: 1939), 196.

[9]Polany and Prosch, *Meaning* (Chicago, 1975), 25–26. (Original footnotes omitted.)

[10]*Ibid.,* cf. Walsche's discussion of the same symposium, *Critical Studies,* 203–207.

[11]Cf. Gavin Ardley, *Aquinas and Kant* (London, 1950).

of mind and brain in *The Mental as Physical* by Edgar Wilson.[12] When thinking occurs, there is one brain event, one ontological occurrence, but there are two modes of access: one indirect through the instrumentation of neurophysiology, etc., the other direct, "from the inside." Thus, mentalling is "undergoing a brain process" (or "physical process"). Awareness of mentalling is simply the brain process seen "from the inside."[13]

At first sight, this seems simply absurd and contrary to experience. No one ever experienced, in awareness, a neurological event or a brain process or a physical process. Yet, Wilson constantly talks as though this were the case. But, he points out innocently,

> It is perhaps necessary to repeat here a point made before in the discussion of IT [identity theory]: the need to avoid the intentionalist fallacy of supposing that to be undergoing a brain process must be to be consciously aware of the brain process involved as *brain process,* that is, *to know that a brain process underlies the phenomena of consciousness.* Nowadays perhaps few people would deny that at least some aspects of the phenomenology of consciousness are identifiable as the undergoing of physical processes which the subject is immediately aware of as such, as in the case of pains.[14] (Emphasis added.)

This completely undermines the dual access theory. If we do not experience by direct observation a brain process as a brain process, we are not directly observing a brain process at all, but something else. This is emphasized by the assertion that the brain process "underlies" the phenomena of consciousness and is therefore different from the phenomena of consciousness. The phenomena cannot be whisked away by incantation of "adverbial" status or "not things!" Wilson's confusion is further displayed in his assumption that pain is identifiable as the undergoing of physical processes which the subject is immediately

---

[12]I use the *Mental as Physical* as representative of reductionism since it is one of the most recent and most elaborately argued reductionist works.

[13]*Ibid.,* 78–84; 269.

[14]*Ibid.,* 221–23.

unaware of. We know today (by "indirect" means, not by inside observation) that pain is generally caused by some bodily affliction, but we don't identify the pain of a headache with acid indigestion or the neurological connection between the two.

A more striking example of irreducibility is supplied by Wilson himself:

> For example, the identity holding between 2+2 and 4 is a conceptual identity; that is to say '2', '4' and '+' have a *purely mental* status. The identity holding between water droplets and clouds is an identity of physical composition, both droplets and clouds being entities mediated by the senses.[15] (Emphasis added.)

The mathematical identity exists only under intellectual understanding; there is no way that abstract mathematical relationships can be reduced to the material connections of physical processes. The radical qualitative difference of "status" (to use Wilson's term) or of mode of existence precludes such identification.

3.   Failure in Philosophical Understanding

People like Edgar Wilson display incredible learning in engineering, neurophysiology, physics and cybernetics, but show no realization or philosophical understanding of human consciousness and knowledge.[16] This is why Marjorie Grene calls "reductivism": "philosophically untenable and humanly intolerable."[17]

Sir Francis Walsche identified another clear example:

---

[15]*Ibid.,* 81.

[16]Cf. Walsche, *Minds and Machines,* 209: "I suggest that another dominating factor in the widespread acceptance of mechanistic biology and psychology may be seen in the very restricted sources from which we draw our ideas. . . . we may search the pages and the bibliographies of neurophysiological textbooks and symposia in vain for any mention of [Whitehead's] works, or any indication that they are known . . . The same is true of Polanyi's writings, which are equally ignored."

[17]Grene, *Interpretations of Life,* 14.

In this,[18] we read that the description by Pitts and McCullich of neuronal nets by which nervous systems know universals is—and here I quote—"of revolutionary significance for natural science, moral as well as natural philosophy, and for one's theory of the normative factor in law, politics, religion and social sciences . . ." It continues, "The basic premise of philosophical idealists and realists and of scientific naturalists and mechanists to the effect that natural and biological systems can have neither knowledge of universals nor normatively defined and behaviour-controlling purposes must be rejected."[19]

Before giving a detailed refutation of this assertion, Walsche says:

I am forced to the conclusion that a fatal weakness in the claim that nerve nets know universals lies in the failure of those who make it to understand the nature of universals.[20]

In the reductionist argument great stress is laid on the increasing knowledge in neurophysiology, neuropsychology, etc. But this increase is only quantitative. All the new knowledge, which, indeed, is vast and impressive, is of the same level—scientific knowledge using the established methodologies of science, and dealing with the physical or material world. Multiplication of knowledge at this same level creates no new evidential pressure, except for those who have already eliminated the essential nature of intelligence and are confident that the reduction will ultimately be established.

Polany's more generalized assessment of reductionism runs thus:

Unfortunately, the *ideal* goals of science are nonsensical. Current biology is based on the assumption that you can explain the processes of life in terms of physics and chemistry; and, of course, physics and chemistry are both to be represented ultimately in terms of the forces acting between atomic particles. So all life, all human beings, and all works of man,

---

[18]That is, in *Prospectives in Neuropsychology,* ed. Richter Lewis (London, 1950).

[19]Walsche, *Minds and Machines,* 165–173.

[20]*Ibid.,* 165. For Walsche's critique of the thesis of Pitts and McCullich, see 164–173.

including Shakespeare's sonnets and Kant's *Critique of Pure Reason,* are also to be so represented. The ideal of science remains what it was in the time of Laplace: to replace all human knowledge by a complete knowledge of atoms in motion. . . . It is simply this sort of mechanical reductionism that is the heart of the matter. It is this that is the origin of the whole system of scientific obscurantism under which we are suffering today. This is the cause of our corruption of the conception of man, reducing him either to an insentient automaton or to a bundle of appetites. This is why science denies us the possibility of acknowledging personal responsibility. This is why science can be invoked so easily in support of totalitarian violence, why science has become the greatest source of dangerous fallacies today.[21]

4.   Argument from the "success" of the scientific method

The usual argument for the exclusive validity of scientific methodology is that it has been "successful."[22] The only thing one can say of this argument is that science has succeeded where it has succeeded. One of the most common fallacies in the history of human culture is the transfer of a method from an area of success to an area where, in the nature of the case, it cannot succeed. Thus, the men of the seventeenth century were so overwhelmed by the fantastic success of Galileo and Newton in applying mathematics to mechanics, that they dreamed of an ethics developed *more geometrico* and even, of a theology on the analogy of Newton's *Principia Mathematica Philosophiae Naturalis*—a *Principia Mathematica Theologiae Christianae.*[23]

---

[21]Polany and Prosch, *Meaning,* 25. In a pluralistic epistemology, each discipline develops, a distinctive conceptual system and a distinctive terminology. Alexis Carrel, for example, critizes precisely reductionism as a confusion of concepts and terms. (See: *Man, the Unknown,* New York 1935, 32–34).

[22]See quotation from Homer Smith, supra, p.1.

[23]"In an essay on 'The Utility of Mathematics' Fontanelle stated a general doctrine which was coming to be widely held: 'The geometrical spirit is not so tied to geometry that it cannot be detached from it and transported to other branches of knowledge. A work of morals or politics or criticism, perhaps even of eloquence would be better (other things being equal) if it were done in the style of a geometer. The order, clarity,

The argument from "success" is illusory. The scientific method has achieved enormous success where it is applicable. But this gives no ground for extrapolating its applicability to the whole of reality and of human life. On the other hand, the history of efforts to use the scientific method where it it is not applicable is a long story of failure. Though efforts to do so have been made over three centuries, no successful ethics has ever been produced by the scientific method. All the method can do is to deny the data of human morality and destroy all intrinsic values.

Science is essentially "thing" oriented. Its efforts to give a complete account of man as such has so atrociously falsified him[24] (an insentient automaton, or a bundle of appetites—as Polany expresses it) that the result is, in Marjorie Grene's words "humanly intolerable."

5. Reductionist "Faith"

The extrinsic argument from success is counter conclusive. Some reductionists admit this, but turn their position into one of faith, for example:

> Our common meeting ground is the *faith* to which we all subscribe, I believe, that the phenomena of behaviour and mind are ultimately describable in the concepts of the mathematical and physical sciences.[25] (Emphasis added)

6. Epistemological Analysis of the "Scientific Method"

In fact, there is no even plausible argumentation that can support the epistemological thesis of the reductionists. On the contrary, any epistemological analysis of the scientific method, either as a univer-

---

precision and exactitude which have been apparent in good books for some time might well have their source in this geometric spirit . . . Sometimes one great man gives the tone to a whole century. [Descartes] to whom might legitimately be accorded the glory of having established a new art of reasoning, was an excellent geometer.'" (Quoted in II. Butterfield, *The Origins of Modern Science* [London, 1949].147.)

[24]Cf. *What Man Has Made of Man,* Mortimer J. Adler (New York, 1937), and his *The Difference of Man and the Difference It Makes* (New York, 1967).

[25]Quoted in Walsche, *Minds and Machines,* 166, from "The Problem of Serial Order in Behavior" in *Cerebral Mechanisms in Behavior* (London, 1951).

salized generic method, or in any of its sub-species, reveals that these methods are intrinsically and essentially limited.

The methods of the particularized sciences display generic similarities, but are not identical. If we examine each scientific discipline, we find a specific methodology that deals with a limited aspect of the material world. Thus, gross mechanics encloses itself in a set of measurements limited to selected aspects of motion, time, distance, velocity, etc., and creates therefrom constructs such as "mass" and various mathematical formulae. But this methodology cannot be used in embryology. Chemistry has its own set of methods developed to deal with "chemical" reactions and "chemical substances." When these methods are applied to living tissue, the quality of "living" has to be ignored.

When all the methods of the various scientific disciplines are added together, the result is a limited set of limited methods. Nowhere in this set can one find a method for making an intelligent evaluation of the *Iliad* or the Mona Lisa. There is no method to deal with the ideals of people like Confucius, Gandhi, Martin Luther King, Mother Theresa, and dozens like them. There is no method to deal with human right and wrong. When a man is pushed over a cliff, physics can calculate the acceleration of his fall, physiology can explain the function of the pusher's muscles, but no scientific method can determine the guilt of the pusher.

7. An "Adequate Epistemology"

Marjorie Grene has said that a complete answer to reductionism requires a new epistemology.[26] I agree, and I further agree that only partial developments of non-reductionist epistemology are to be found in current philosophical writings. But, I am convinced that the basis for a reconstruction of epistemology exists within the still vigorous Thomistic tradition.[27]

---

[26]Grene, *Interpretations of Life,* 14.

[27]For example, consult the magistral work of Jacques Maritain, *The Degrees of Knowledge,* tr. Gerald B. Phelan (New York, 1959) esp. 27–70, 136–246; Yves Simon, *L'Ontologie du Connaitre* (Paris, 1934); Bernard J. F. Lonergan, S.J. *Insight* (New York, 1957); Alden L. Fisher and George B. Murray, eds., *Philosophy and Science as Modes of Knowing* (New York, 1969); R. J. Henle, S.J., "Science and the Humanities," *Thought,* 25 (1960); E. F. Caldin, *The Power and Limits of Science* (New York, 1949); Josef Seifert, *Leib und Seele* (Salzburg, 1973), 25–76.

This epistemology must be a pluralistic one, one which allows for irreducible generic methodologies and therefore for disciplines that cannot be combined or formally unified. Each discipline is then seen as a special development of the basic universal power of the human intellect.[28]

The nature and reach of scientific methods cannot be determined by scientific methods. The question of the meaning of scientific knowledge is not a scientific question. Thus, the nature of chemical knowledge is not a chemical question. You cannot put knowledge in a test tube and test it with reagents. Run this analysis through the whole gamut of scientific disciplines; the result will be the same.

Problems of knowledge can be dealt with only by a higher and independent discipline: an epistemology based on philosophical reflection.

The reductionist epistemology thus turns out to rest on an unwarranted assumption of the exclusive value of *one kind* of human knowledge. It leads to absurdities and cannot survive serious epistemological analysis.

C. Metaphysical Reductionism

1. The Definition

The second definition is a metaphysical one: namely, that all reality can be explained as accidental combinations of some primary physical entities which alone are really real: the atoms of Democritus, the atoms and the infinite void of Lucretius, inert matter and local motion of the seventeenth century mechanists, sub-atomic particles and energy of today's reductionists. This definition thus rests on a long tradition in Western thought—from Leucippus and Democritus to the current metaphysical reductionists. Wilson, for example, asserts that he is in this ancient tradition:

---

[28]Thus Bernard Lonergan, S.J. sets forth as part of his epistemological investigation: "Secondly, we shall go behind the procedures of the natural sciences to something both more general and more fundamental, namely, the procedures of the human mind" (*Method in Theology* [New York, 1937], 4). It is precisely because behind all the different sorts of intellectual operations lies a unified, active, general intelligence that an epistemology, based on reflection on human intelligence as such, can analyze, locate, and judge the particularized disciplines developed by that intelligence.

The present revival of these perennial issues must be seen against a historical background of "aggression" by physical determinism that has progressively accounted for more and more of the phenomena that once were widely held to be outside the sphere of the physical-causal categories. Human mentality, rationality and purposefulness now stand among the phenomena that come within the compass of scientifically based explanations along lines already indicated by Leucippus and Democritus.[29]

2. Universal Materialism

Metaphysical reductionism rests on two assumptions. The first assumption is that all reality is material; there are no spiritual entities whether existing separately (*substantiae separatae*) or as dimensions of material entities. If all things are material, then the ontological structure of all entities must be governed by the laws of matter (ideally, by the laws of physics).

However, the position that matter and matter alone exists (is "really real") and that all things in the world can be analyzed into the ultimate components of matter, is a pure assumption with no substantial basis.

It is, indeed, a pervasive and unexamined conviction within our culture that science has somehow proven materialism. The universality of matter has been assumed, stated and proclaimed by so many eminent scientists and "scientific" philosophers, that one who questions the assumption is immediately marked as an ignorant obscurantist.[30] Materialism is part of the current modern mythology.[31]

Since the dogma of universal materialism is so widely assumed, consciously or unconsciously, few even ask the question: Just when, where, and how has science established this dogma?

If science undertakes to prove this thesis, it must do so by using some form of the scientific method. But this is intrinsically impossible.

---

[29]Wilson, *Mental as Physical,* 1.

[30]Grene, *Interpretations of Life,* 20.

[31]Cf. Gilbert Ryle: "Ingrained hypotheses do feel obvious no matter how redundant they may be." "Comments on the Physical Basis of Mind" in P. Laslett, *The Physical Basis of Mind* (Oxford, 1950), 76 quoted by Wilson, *Mental as Physical,* 11.

All forms of the scientific method *presuppose* a material universe. The scientific method was developed as the methodology of a new *Philosophia Naturalis,* of universal physics, that is, the scientific method is predetermined to be materialistic by its subject matter, its "material object." It is intrinsically limited to dealing with the material aspects of reality.

If, then, there are any non-material realities or aspects of the world, science by its very nature is precluded from having any knowledge of them. A fortiori, science cannot prove that spiritual realities do not exist. It is, thus, unscientific for a scientist to step out of his field and declare that all reality is and must be material, in Thomistic terms, that *to-be* means *to-be-material.*[32]

There are aspects of reality which have always resisted materialistic explanation. As we said above, some reductionists simply deny the existence of such recalcitrant realities (see Part B, on the denial of consciousness). Or, the reductionist distorts the description of such resistant phenomena so they can be subsumed under universal materialism. Thus, Wilson's reduction of thinking to "viewing a brain event from the inside" and his "dual access" theory permits him finally to say that the only reality is the "brain-event." The material aspects of a "brain-event" can, of course, be studied scientifically, but, even here, it is doubtful whether the scientific method can do justice to the full reality of the vital activities of the human brain.

In any case, the materialistic thesis is a pure assumption. The fact that it is widely held both in our advanced scientific culture, and in our folk culture, does not increase its intrinsic credibility.

3. Levels of Being

The second assumption of the reductionist metaphysics is that there are no radically different ontological levels of reality. In its bluntest form, this thesis merely repeats that of Democritus, "only the atoms and the void are real." The rich diversity of the world is only apparent, what appear to be different qualitative levels of being are only accidental

---

[32]See George Klubertanz, "The Meaning of Being" in *Introduction to the Philosophy of Being* (New York, 1963), 28–61; also "Characteristics of Existence" in Joseph Owens, *An Interpretation of Existence* (Milwaukee, 1968), 44–82.

arrangements of the true realities: the atoms and the void for Democritus, sub-atomic particles in interaction for his modern successors.

Of course, reductionists have always made efforts to account for the phenomenological diversity in our experience. To account for intelligence, Lucretius said that the mind is made up of very smooth atoms,[33] an explanation that has about the same plausibility as Wilson's "viewing a brain event from the inside." The mechanistic biologists of the nineteenth century explained "thought" as a "secretion" of the brain, much as adrenaline is a secretion of endocrine glands.

To repeat Wilson's claim:

> . . . human mentality, rationality, and purposefulness now stand among the phenomena that come within the compass of scientifically based explanations along lines already indicated by Leucippus and Demoeritus.

It seems to me that it is precisely in dealing with such realities that the scientific method has failed. Indeed, one of the most telling arguments against reductionism is that its efforts to ignore or explain life and intelligence invariably result in a *reductio ad absurdum*.

4. Return to Metaphysics

Marjorie Grene said that, while many convincing arguments can be brought against reductionism, only a new and more adequate metaphysics can fully answer it.[34] This we do not have at the present time; although, in common with Sir Francis Walsche, she finds Alfred North Whitehead's philosophy useful here.[35]

I agree that the only real answer to reductionist metaphysics is a well-developed valid metaphysics. However, I believe that such a metaphysics does exist in continuously developing state—the metaphysics of current Thomists.

This metaphysics holds that there are essentially (radically)

---

[33]*De Rerum Natura,* Book III, Para. 177, Lucretius, tr. H. A. J. Munro, in Vol. 12 of *Great Books of the Western World,* ed. Robert Maynard Hutchins (Chicago, 1952), 32–33.

[34]Grene, *Interpretations of Life,* 14.

[35]Walsche, *Minds and Machines,* 21.

different ontological (not merely phenomenological) levels of being.[36] This position is based on the principle that when entities exhibit qualitatively contradictory characteristics, they must be ontologically different entities, different in kind or essence, not merely in individuality. The application of this principle requires a careful philosophical examination of reality, using not only scientific data but also all available data from whatever source, especially from the full range of human experience.

5. Summary

In summary, reductionist metaphysics rests on two assumptions. The first is the dogma of universal materialism, for which there is no proof. The second is the assumption that there are no "radically" or "essentially" different kinds of levels of being. This assumption arises from an inadequate philosophical examination of reality and an inadequate philosophical education.

6. Educational Reform

"Today the young scientist gets scant opportunity or encouragement to seek any further than proximate causes in his own particular discipline."[37] According to Alexis Carrel, the cause of reductionism is overspecialization.

The intense specialization required by modern scientific training not only prevents the student from becoming aware of the vast and important learning and wisdom in non-scientific fields, but it also develops a mindset that makes it difficult, if not impossible, for him to understand and appreciate other fields.

Marjorie Grene has said that only a sound epistemology and a sound metaphysics can fully refute reductionism. I have indicated that I agree. But I am more profoundly convinced that, until we reform our high school and college education, we will continue to produce graduates with precisely the mindset that unconsciously accepts reduction-

---

[36]For a non-technical exposition of the "levels" of reality, see E. F. Schumacher, "Levels of Being," *A Guide for the Perplexed,* (New York, 1977), 15–25.

[37]Walsche, *Minds and Machines,* vi.

ism.[38] We must restore breadth *and* depth, the ideal of Newman's philosophical habit of mind."[39]

I have treated reductionist epistemology and metaphysics separately. In fact, they are ultimately connected and constitute a unified philosophical position. Philosophically, they stand or fall together.

For reasons which should now be apparent, I offer no scientific definition for reductionism. Reductionism is not a science but a philosophy, for it places upon science interpretations which are beyond the reach of science.

D. Thinking Machines

1. The issue

I said above that the vast accumulation of data on the structure of the brain, neurological activities, and so forth have brought no new argument for the reductionist position.[40]

---

[38]Charles Darwin's early education was much broader than that of most scientific specialists today, yet, in his *Autobiography* he describes the progressive narrowing of his intellect: "*My mind seems to have become a kind of machine for grinding general laws out of large collections of fact*, but why this should have caused atrophy of that part of the brain alone, on which the *higher tastes* depend, I cannot conceive. . . .The loss of these tastes is a loss of happiness and may possibly be injurious to the intellect, and more probably to the moral character, by enfeebling the emotional part of our nature." As quoted in E. F. Schumacher in *Small Is Beautiful* (New York, 1973), 86. Emphasis added.

[39]E. F. Schumacher: "What is at fault is not specialisation, but the lack of depth with which the subjects are usually presented, and the absence of metaphysical awareness. The sciences are being taught without any awareness of the presuppositions of science, of the meaning and significance of scientific laws, and of the place occupied by the natural sciences within the whole cosmos of human thought. The result is that the presuppositions of sciences are normally mistaken for its findings" (Schumacher, *Small Is Beautiful,* 81). Schumacher's Chapter II, "The Greatest Resource" presents an excellent analysis of the "metaphysical disease" of our culture and of our education.

[40]The fact is that this sort of data is exactly what Thomists have used to establish the substantial unity of man and the interrelationships of all his powers. See Klubertanz, *The Philosophy of Human Nature* (New York, 1953), 12–38. Edgar Wilson consistently reports data of this sort with expressions like "underlying" (". . . complex activity of the temporal and frontal lobes of the brain underlying memory and teleological behavior," Wilson, *Mental as Physical,* 150), "corresponds to" ("But who . . . will say that *no* physiological process corresponds to lust, fear and memory," *ibid.*) But this is a far cry

There is, however, one apparent exception to this statement which needs separate treatment. The development of sophisticated computers and cybernetics appears to have given a new type of argument to the reductionists and a very powerful one. If computers can be constructed to perform logical as well as mathematical operations, there is no reason to suppose that the realization of an artificial intelligence as powerful as or even more powerful than human intelligence is far off. Once that is achieved, all the arguments based on the uniqueness of human intellection will disappear.

Joseph Weizenbaum states the issue thus:

> Whether or not this program [i.e., of artificial intelligence] can be realized depends on whether man really is merely a species of the genus "information-processing system" or whether he is more than that. I shall argue that an entirely too simplistic notion of intelligence has dominated both popular and scientific thought, and that this notion is, in part, responsible for permitting artificial intelligence's perverse grand fantasy to grow. . . . Man is not a machine. I shall argue that, although man most certainly processes information, he does not necessarily process it in the way computers do. *Computers and men are not species of the same genus.*[41] (Emphasis added.)

2. What the Computer Really Does

It is essential to recall what a computer actually does.[42] The computer performs a series of electronic-material operations determined by its structure and its program. Viewed simply in themselves, these operations have no reference to thinking, deduction, memory, understanding or any other intellectual activity. They are as neutral in this regard as the operations of a washing machine or an automated factory.

Man makes a code out of these operations, giving them an extrinsic

---

from reductionist identification. Actually, Wilson's thesis is not "identification" but the elimination of one sort of reality altogether.

[41]Joseph Weizenbaum, *Computer Power and Human Reason* (San Francisco, 1976), 203.

[42]Cf. John Neumann, *The Computer and the Brain* (New Haven, 1958), 3–38; also Weizenbaum, *Computer Power,* 39–110.

meaning, and programming them to serve his own purposes. Of itself, the computer can serve no human purpose. When a programmer reduces a set of data to units that can be correlated with the activities of the computer and directs it to deal with the symbols of these data in some fashion or other, the computer becomes an enormously versatile tool. But this does not change the basic material and mechanical nature of its activities. It is totally unaware of what it is doing; it has no understanding of the material it deals with. It simply performs mechanical activities according to a rigidly determined mechanical pattern.

3. Does the Computer Know?

Computer scientists talk of storing information in computers. What is actually in the computer is a series of physical changes in a magnetic tape. No "information" exists there; the information is not there as "ideas," as something understood, as consciously known. It is not called forth by a conscious effort of the computer, but mechanically, according to a program or at the manipulation of an operator.

"Knowledge" is in the computer in the same way as it is in books, i.e., by physical changes which of themselves have no meaning. A book is simply a series of sheets of paper with orderly smudges of ink on them. Without the knowledge and intelligence of the person who wrote the book, without the knowledge and intelligence of the person who reads the book, and without the intellectual agreement that makes these smudges into something symbolic, the book is simply paper and ink. Knowledge can be said to be in the book only by a loose metaphor, by a sort of extrinsic denomination. Knowledge, as such, exists only in intelligent consciousness.

Likewise, knowledge can be said to be in a computer only by a loose metaphor. Obviously, there is no ground here at all for speaking of even an embryonic artificial intelligence. The computer knows nothing. It is completely unaware of the extrinsic symbolism of its operations, quite indifferent to the content of its own printouts which it cannot understand. It processes "garbage" with the same efficiency and indifference as it does sound data.

4. Does the Computer Perform Logical Operations?

But, it is said, the computer "thinks" since it performs "logical operations." Edgar Wilson repeatedly uses the term "logic" and "logical" in talking about computers. He even says: "Now nobody suggests that in undergoing the processes described by the engineer the machine is not performing logical operations."[43] One wonders what sort of poll he used to discover this alleged consensus. Surely, Wilson must know that there are dozens of philosophers who would flatly deny that computers perform "logical operations."

The computer simply goes through a series of electronic-physical operations which, of themselves, have no meaning at all. Human beings arrange these operations in such a way that they actively symbolize logical operations. The computer is unaware of, and indifferent to, this logical symbolism. It will equally efficiently follow illogical directives as logical ones. Logic is not intrinsic to computer operations.

We discover logical relations by reflecting on our deductive reasoning.[44] When we relate two knowledges together in such a way that we understand a new derivative knowledge, we have established a logical relationship that has an intelligible necessity. *It is essential that we maintain both premises in consciousness in order to simultaneously see the necessity of the conclusion.* The computer runs its operation in a mindless sequence. It has no understanding of the symbolism attached by man to its operations.

Reductionism must, therefore, try to separate consciousness from intellectual activity in order to reduce intellectual activity to the same level as the activities of a computer. Wilson tries to free logic from its essential intellectual nature.

Of course, one can form extrinsic definitions which will put men and machines in the same "species."[45] But, to do so, one has to ignore

---

[43]Wilson, *Mental as Physical,* 150.

[44]I strongly suspect that Edgar Wilson and others like him know logic only as it is presented in various modern symbolic or mathematical forms and therefore without an epistemological analysis of its nature. For a broader view see Henry Veatch, *Intentional Logic* (New Haven 1952). In pages 407–411, Veatch gives an excellent brief bibliography which would yield a balanced view of logic. Se also his *Two Logics* (Evanston, 1969). A useful textbook is Francis H. Parker and Henry B. Veatch, *Logic as a Human Instrument* (New York, 1959).

[45]W. Sluckin maintains "Machines can and do think in *some* (sic) sense of the word and cannot and do not think in other senses." See Sluckin, *Minds and Machines* (Baltimore, 1954), 198. But a careful examination of the chapter "Thought and Processes" (188–201) reveals that he is not using "thinking" in a univocal sense.

the real nature of human thinking. We consciously manipulate our previous knowledge to produce new knowledge. We are consciously aware of the validity of logical relations. In brief, unconscious logic is a contradiction.

Moreover, for reductionism to succeed, consciousness must be reduced to a passive "viewing," "undergoing," or "experiencing." Other-wise, the dual access theory would be obvious nonsense. But our continual experience of intellectual *activity* precludes this ploy.

Logical reasoning is active. We consider, compare, gain insight, set up syllogisms, organize arguments, etc. We are self-determining in our intellectual activity, because we know what "reasons" are and we know what we are trying to understand, and that we know these things. The "causes" of the new knowledge reached by deduction are fully grasped by intellectual consciousness. Though vital activities in the body and in the brain are necessary for intellectual consciousness, nothing controls the syllogistic operations except the conscious intellectual insight into the premises *qua* premises.

5. Simplistic Understanding of Human Intellection

Reductionists attempt, almost surreptitiously, to reduce all human intellectual activity to logic and mathematics since these are more easily symbolized in computers. Walsche notes this:

> The suggestion that the mind or brain is a computing device which models by its symbols the external world, seems to be an attempt to describe the mind in terms of a very special and limited type of its own symbolism, that of logic and mathe- matics. The greater is subsumed in terms of the less, and the manipulations of strings of symbols according to the rules of a specific calculus is now being taken to be identical with thought itself.[46]

"Thinking" can be applied to machines only by a behavoristic definition in terms of *results*. An adding machine can produce the same sum as an intelligence. "In fact considering the *results* of them [the machines'] doings; they do *in a sense*, reason," 194, (emphasis added).

[46]Walsche, *Minds and Machines,* 173.

The loose and imprecise term "thinking" is often used for all intellectual activity, thus implying that all intellectual activity involves process. This homogenization is further achieved by reducing "thinking" to the meaningless barbarism "metalling."[47]

I have briefly shown that even at the level of logical and mathematical processes, the computer's activities are, of themselves, neither logical nor mathematical. Hence, even if all intellection could be reduced to logic and mathematics, the arguments of the reductionists would still fail.

It is clear that mathematical and logical reasoning can more easily be symbolized in machines than other intellectual activities. Mathematics and logical processes use univocal terms and necessary connections which, because of their uniformity, can easily be symbolically simulated by machines.

But, to have any plausibility at all, reductionists must ignore the rich diversity of human intellection. Mathematics, for all its intellectual complexity and practical value, is a very limited human activity. Logical reasoning is, perhaps, the least important of all intellectual activities. It is purely instrumental in the intellect's search for knowledge, understanding and truth and not the sole instrument, much less essence of intellection.

6. Further Characteristics of Human Knowledge

To do an adequate philosophical reflection on human intelligence would require a large volume. Here I will briefly discuss two unique characteristics of human knowledge.

I pointed out above that reductionists attempt to reduce intellection to "process." Computers always carry out processes; either they are performing sequential physical operations or they are not operating at all.

In human intelligence, "process" is a means toward achieving new knowledge, a new understanding, a new explanation. When the process is completed, the intellect now simply *possesses* the new knowledge and contemplates it *without further process*. Where the computer would have to quit—i.e., at the completion of process—the human intelligence achieves its full activity with regard to newly discovered truth. Of course, this contemplation is not just of subjective reality, but of objec-

---

[47]Wilson, *Mental as Physical,* 109–110.

tive reality itself through that knowledge. The computer cannot contemplate; it is intrinsically incapable—in principle and absolutely—of a non-processing activity.

This brings me to another more profound and more difficult aspect of human knowledge. When I think of the Cathedral of Chartres, and describe its windows, I am not thinking of an "internal" image of those windows (though I may indeed simultaneously have sensible images of them) or even of my knowledge of those windows. I am thinking about, talking about, describing the *real* windows, halfway around the world from me. *I project my awareness thousands of miles, though I am here and am using my subjective powers to do so.*

Thus, the human intelligence can, in knowledge, possess the other *qua other*.[48] I know the other, but I know it in *its own* reality. I submit that no piece of matter and no complexity of material entities can be *here*—and also *there*. No material process can be itself and yet consciously "become" the *other*. A computer may be able to match a picture of Chartres with previously gained patterns, but this is not to recognize Chartres *as other*. It may be able to print out a full and accurate account of the windows of Chartres, but this is no more knowing than is the corresponding article in an encyclopedia. In short, the most unique characteristic of human knowledge contradicts the essential characteristic of matter, and so, must be immaterial.

7. Summary

In summary, if the terms are used in their proper meaning and not metaphorically, computers know nothing and understand nothing; they do not perform mathematical nor logical operations; they cannot carry out anything resembling the highest activities of human intelligence. The dream of an artificial intelligence is what Wezenbaum called it: "a perverse grand fantasy." We conclude that the development of computer science provides no scintilla of proof for reductionism. On the contrary, when properly analyzed philosophically, it only emphasizes the enormous and radical difference between machines and the human intelligence.

---

[48]See Frederick D. Wilhelmsen, *Man's Knowledge of Reality* (Englewood Cliffs, 1956), 75–89; Joseph Owens, *An Elementary Christian Metaphysics* (Milwaukee, 1963), 213–247.

8. Postscript

The misleading statements of computer scientists have not only given false encouragement to the reductionists, they have created a computer mythology in our popular culture—which, by reverse influence, has belittled and degraded man himself. Consider the article in the *New York Times Magazine* (1/7/80, p. 40 f.) entitled, "Creating Computers That Think." The initial blurb reads: "Scientists believe they are now beginning to teach computers to think. . . ." The "perverse grand fantasy" of artificial intelligence is being popularized by the mass media.

However, worst of all, the pseudo-philosophy of computer science is creating the same mythology among scientists themselves.

E. General Conclusions

In this brief essay, I have tried to cut through the equivocations and endlessly repetitious arguments of the reductionists, in order to lay bare the basic presuppositions of their position. I have attempted to show that these presuppositions, however widely they may be accepted as valid and true in our culture, and even among educated people, are nothing but pure assumptions which have no evidential warrant.

In addition, I have tried to point out the essential weakness of their argument as it moves from scientific knowledge of the operation of the brain and the central nervous system, as well as from the operation of computers, to the activities of human intelligence. I have tried to indicate that the evidence itself, when represented without the equivocal reduction of "thinking" to either "mechanisms" or "brain events" tends rather to confirm the Thomistic position on the substantial unity of man, the integration of all his powers into human activity, and the respect for the radical diversity of some of his powers with the appropriate metaphysical consequences.

It would require an enormous volume to pick up each individual argument advanced, for example, by Edgar Wilson in his elaborate presentation of physicalism; but, in principle, almost all of these arguments reduce themselves to the same sort of illogical transition: one order of knowledge to another and from one level of reality to another.

Obviously, in so brief an essay, the task called for by Marjorie Grene, among others, of presenting an opposition to the reductionists' theses, a complete "adequate" epistemology and metaphysics could not be done. This is a task that must be pursued with the hope that we can reconstruct modern philosophy and divorce it from its partisanship and its narrowness.

XV

ST. THOMAS AND THE DEFINITION OF INTELLIGENCE

New Introduction: Father William Wade, S.J., was a brilliant teacher of Philosophy at Saint Louis University, who made a deep impression on all of his students. He was equally successful in developing the Department of Philosophy when he was its Chairman. After his death a group of former students and close friends set up a William Wade Lecture series providing for an annual lecture on Philosophy in his honor. I was happy and pleased to be invited to give the first lecture of this series and this is the lecture I gave.

Perhaps the most important point made in this article[1] is that there is no intrinsic limitation on the human intellect. This means: (1) that human intelligence can continuously grow in its knowledge of being and (2) that it is fundamentally capable of the Beatific Vision which alone can totally fulfill man's appetite for being and truth.

* * *

One of the tasks to which I addressed myself for many years was the philosophical examination of the diversity of disciplines which constitute modern culture. This examination led me to the conclusion that there is no way to formally define and evaluate a discipline totally from within. Each discipline displays its own mode of conceptualizing and defining, of gathering evidence and of explaining. A discipline is, therefore, both the creature and the captive of its own methodology. To

---

[1]First published for the William Wade Lecture of March 8, 1975; published in *The Modern Schoolman*, 53, no. 4 (May 1976): 335–346.

examine any methodology by its own methods, by the very same discipline, in almost all cases violates the formal nature of the discipline itself and, at best, results in a kind of pseudo-meta-discipline. One cannot, for example, determine the ultimate truth-value or the internal limits of chemical knowledge, but the use of test tubes and bunsen burners, or through the application of any chemical theory of the constitution of matter.

If all disciplines were intrinsically self-limiting not only in regard to subject matter or the empirical area of investigation (for example, geology does not deal with living plant forms) but also with regard to the formalities of disciplinary development (as, for example, through the application of mathematical models to physical events), the problems posed by this examination of the diversity of intellectual disciplines would be insoluble and human intellectual culture would have only an accidental unity, created by lateral relationships (e.g., the relationship of Physics to Mathematics, of Geology to Chemistry, of Linguistic Theory to Empirical Psychology).

The problem has been variously approached. As in so many cases, a reductionist procedure has seemed to be the simplest and the ultimately envisioned solution. If Biology could be reduced to Chemistry and Chemistry to Physics and, perhaps Physics to Mathematics, such a reduction could be a model for the ultimate simplification of human science. If Aesthetics could be explained in terms of Psychology and Psychology in terms of Biology, a similar bellows-like collapse could be achieved. The diversity of disciplines would thus be only a stage in the development of scientific knowledge, a stage preliminary to the final unification in a single science. In such a case, all science professors would at last achieve the title originally given *ex officio* to the President of the University of Michigan—"Professor of Universal Knowledge."

This approach is strengthened by the fact that such reductions have occurred—laterally—between parts of similar or cognate disciplines, as in the overlap areas between Physical Chemistry and Physics. One cannot deny that in the history of culture development continuously both diversifies methodologies and combines them. The pattern of the disciplines at any given moment is not static and eternally fixed.

Nor does it help to point out that the ideal unification has not been achieved and is not even in remote prospect. The reductionist hypothesis includes this fact as part of its doctrine, both explaining and exploiting it.

If this type of reductionism is in error, a dialectical criticism is inadequate. A self-establishing positive substitute must be presented.

Very attractive also is the notion of deriving, by analyses or induction, from a comparative study of the disciplines (often limited exclusively to the "scientific disciplines") a meta-methodology or a common denominator methodology which can then be used to define *the* "scientific" method and either explicitly or implicitly to define as well human intellection itself. This approach gives an appearance of success only if the study is limited to a group of disciplines determined to be "scientific" or rational. The obvious difficulty, however, is that all such studies result, if not in a reduction, at least in a restriction of human intelligence which, as Polany has pointed out, leaves out of account many things which, we all know we know. The approach does, however, have the positive value of high-lighting one of the most revealing characteristics of the human intelligence; namely, its ability to bring into the center of its conscious consideration its own acts—the pervasive, awe-inspiring, and unique ability of the human intellect to reflect on itself. Without the power of reflection, we would be unconsciously controlled in thought and action by even our methodologies as are any forms of material reality and any specializations of animal instinct—a theme brilliantly commented on by Bergson.

Clearly, self-reflection must be used in any effort to solve the problem. In fact, without it, we would be totally unaware of the problem. We would proceed about our various businesses as the hummingbird flies, drinks nectar, mates, and nests, as the wasp builds its home and lays its eggs.

The self-reflecting activity of intelligence is essentially subjective, not in a relativistic or romantic sense, but in the sense that what is reflected on is not (at least normally) open to public inspection. To obtain an agreed understanding, we must appeal to what "*omnis homo in se sentit.*" I believe, with Aristotle and Saint Thomas that, if one freely and fully exercises intense self-reflection, a common understanding can be reached and a consensus on human internal activity. No amount of blood tests, electrograms, X-rays, themal records, could make me understand what you mean when you speak of reasoning, thinking, willing, loving—only my own experience enables me to share a common understanding. We can communicate not through the magic of external symbols alone but from the basis of individual, separated, but common, conscious experience. Let this rest for the moment. I want now to start a different line of consideration.

It seems to me that, more and more, anthropology, psychology, and similar disciplines are coming to emphasize the *uniqueness* of the human species. We are the subjects and the authors of an evolution that is no longer regarded simply in animal or material terms; there is a stress on our "cultural" evolution. Man alone has a true "history"; the earth, the flora and fauna yield a record of development to man's inquisitive investigation—but they have no "history." Man develops a rich, free, creative, and cumulative culture; whatever his prehistoric or historical setbacks and disasters, man develops cultures and societies. He has diverse cultures—each as Robert Redfield has said constituting a "way" of being human; each indeed limiting his life and his understanding, but not confining him totally. He is able to transcend even his own culture, even the culture which, in a sense, gave him his humanity; he can learn a strange language, penetrate (to him) exotic societies and understand other value systems. Compared to human culture and society, the beautifully systematic, static, and self-perpetuating societies of the bee-hive and the ant-hill are indeed—as Bergson said—a "dead end" of creative evolution.

The reductionism of an earlier period of anthropology and biology found it necessary to subdue the uniqueness of man and identify him as totally as possible with a material world very materially conceived and understood. Man was not only linked with a natural animal lineage but was totally reduced to it. He was a biological species who at some point had turned right or left (depending on the standpoint of the viewer) in the evolutionary progression.

This very crude reductionism is still about, but each discipline that in any way deals with man—Biology, Anthropology, Psychology, Psychiatry, and others—seems to me to be, more and more, highlighting his uniqueness. The incredible wealth of human culture—taken in its broadest sense—is truly recognized. Man is uniquely different; this is a fact to be accepted, not to be washed away in the dissolving suds of a doctrinaire materialism.

Why is man unique? It seems to me that the particular disciplines reach an impasse at this point. This is a true test question for the universality and ultimate fundamental character of a discipline.

Man alone truly universalizes a tool-making capacity from the first shaped stone to the thousands of inventions recorded in the U.S. Patent Office. Said Chesterton: "The signature of man is art." One of the few things we know for sure about the "cave-men" is that some among them were consumate artists. Man has charms, jujus, and prayers. Man alone wonders about the meaning of the stars. Man alone argues about his own destiny and, to a large extent, consciously controls it.

Man came up out of the sea or down from the trees and, at some point, he began to think. To say as some scientists do that he "learned" to think is to beg the question. What we do know is that man thinks and that there is no evidence that, prior to the advent of man (however many millions of years ago we did that), there was any thinking on this planet and there is no reason to believe that, if man disappears, any thinking will go on after his termination.

The enormous diversity in every phase of human culture represents a deployment into all areas of the influence of human intelligence. For this reason, it is possible to give a variety of operational or special-aspect definitions of human intelligence. He thinks because he developed language; his thinking is an evolved tool for the survival of the species. It could even be argued that the achievement of thinking is bringing man himself to an evolutionary "dead end" since thinking has overflowed its biological purpose and has created fear, superstition, guilt, despair, and both a species death-wish and the deadly weapons to achieve it. Evolution would have overreached itself. A species has evolved which not only can now control its own evolution but will self-destruct in what—on the cosmic time clock—would be ten seconds.

Now to sum up what I have been trying to say, and to bring together my two lines of consideration. No essential definition or even true description of human intelligence can be derived from or built on top of any one or any group of the particular disciplines. Human intelligence is broader than any of its intellectual manifestations. No essential definition or true description of human intelligence can be derived from a study of any particular manifestations of human culture. Intelligence outreaches all of them.

Is there any way out of this impasse? We can solve the problem only if we can find a way to reach a fundamental view of human intelligence.

I must here introduce a philosophical distinction which is fundamental to my whole approach to questions of this sort.

Years ago, I began to develop a distinction between two radically different kinds of abstractive-intellectual[2] disciplines.

I have distinguished "ontological" disciplines from "constructural" disciplines. Briefly an ontological discipline works with basic insights into experience (what I call experiential data as opposed to empirical or experimental data) without re-forming or intrinsically manipulating them. No matter how sophisticated or complicated an ontological discipline becomes, its definitions, its analyses, its explanations, its reasoning are all controlled by intuition of, insight into, grasp of, or understanding of an intelligibility found in real things. A constructural discipline on the other hand derives in a variety of ways abstract concepts which do not simply embody the intelligibility of the real object. A crude example of this latter is the concept of an intelligence quotient. This is based on empirical evidence, but it is rather contrived than derived from reality. While Johnny does have an intelligence, he has not a real thing that is his intelligence quotient. Of an ontological concept, the Thomistic concept of final cause in human decision making would be an appropriate example.

What is needed then is an ontological epistemology. The only way epistemology can be kept ontological is to derive its first concepts from direct reflection on intelligence itself as *"omnis homo in se sentit."*

While we can all be immediately aware that we are conscious and reflecting, to develop the fullness of reflective insight is not simple or easy. We tend always to pass over the common evidence quickly and have recourse to something we have learned, or to clean-cut abstract non-ontological concepts.

When we do so reflect—after we have practiced it like yoga or artistic contemplation—what do we find? We find a pervasive, penetrating awareness that is both a self-awareness and an object-awareness; an awareness which embraces but is not limited to sight, objects, colors, textures, shapes, sound, internal feelings, and sensations—an awareness that embraces all and everything in a conscious grasp. We know what we are aware of; we know that we are aware of what we are aware of; we know the immediate differences in the whole vast set of things of which we are aware; in all this, depending on the direction of attention,

---

[2] I am using this term to differentiate from the humanistic disciplines in which intelligence creatively penetrates the area of sense, sensitivity, and sensation.

we are more or less simultaneously aware of ourselves. And, now a key—we find that, when we try to express any of this in our thought or through external signs, we do so in the form of existential assertions—the one common denominator of all our awareness is a recognition of, a grasp and expression of existential being.

The intellect in its activity has an object "being"; as an appetite, it hungers for being; as a developing life, it grows by intussusception of being. Being defines its object, its goal, its reach.

It should be noted that this character is discovered (neither imposed nor concluded to) prior to any elaboration of a particularized intellectual activity and prior to any theory. No matter how many divers modes of activity, of rationalization, of knowing the intellect may display as it lives and grows, the intellect-being relationship remains a pervasive given.

Thus, baldly stated, it appeared to present an impoverished and banal notion of intelligence. Indeed, this would be irretrievably so, if the "being" in this case were an abstract notion, the effete resultant of prolonged abstractions like the ultimate univocity of the Scotists or the Hegelian notion which at last comes to be indistinguishable from non-being. This would indeed ruin the whole enterprise. It is essential that we hold this understanding at an experiential, pre-constructuural level. To do so, we must concentrate on the primary experience of "being" as existential and as concrete. We find—through intellection—being in each being; it is there that we recognize it initially and assert it—not in some world of Ideas.

Even so, no matter how fixed our contemplation on the concrete realization of being and the recognition of it in these concrete manifestations, the discovery of the existential character of intellection seems to leave intelligence empty and in great poverty. Once again, if the initial discovery of being in the first reflection of intelligence were closed and fixed, the discovery might hardly be worth noticing. But, the relationship of intelligence to being is initially an openness to growth, a potentiality for growth. The initial discovery is but a premise and a promise of continuing enrichment and fulfillment.

This growth—an enrichment of knowledge and a deepening of understanding—takes place in at least two ways. First of all, the growth is achieved by continuing experience; concrete being is enlarged and expanded by the rich diversity of the concrete objects of our experience. Moreover, direct experience is supplemented and vastly extended by vicarious experience—as in novels, plays, displays—and by our own creativity—as in fantasy and in imaginative extension of actual experience. When all this richness is brought under the reflective recognition of the pervasiveness of being, all experience is seen as an enriching encounter with the myriad forms of being and all knowledge as a continuous conquest of reality.

The second way in which the insight into being deepens and develops is through the elaboration of an existential ontological metaphysics. (It seems silly to use such a concatenation of high sounding words, but we have so diversified and perhaps distorted the meaning of our fine classical terms that we are forced to such strained expressions of our meaning.)

Frankly, I have never been able to describe satisfactorily for myself the precise interrelationship of Thomistic metaphysics and the sort of epistemology that I am trying to present. I am convinced that epistemology cannot be deduced from metaphysics; it is not, as some Thomistic textbooks have seemed to say, an expansion of the doctrine of *ens est verum* of the transcendental character of *verum*. Epistemology has an independent origin in original experience. On the other hand, without a profound elaboration of a metaphysics, the corresponding epistemology seems to me to remain incomplete and impoverished.

The mind that does indeed encompass the understanding of being presented in Thomistic metaphysics is thereby, however you explain it, better able to sound the depths of an existential epistemology.

Thus, the growth in understanding of metaphysics goes in some correlated fashion with the growth in understanding of the nature of intelligence. Both disciplines are ontological and both relate to being; they have natural and essential relationships to each other somewhat as various mathematical disciplines have to each other. But, whatever this relationship may be, I am convinced that as epistemology is elaborated from its original and self-sustaining insights, it needs the continuing and increasing support of metaphysics.

Once we have related intelligence to being, we have not said that, in fact, human intelligence knows all being or will ever know all being. What we have said is that, even if human intelligence does not know all being, its failure to do so is not due to any intrinsic limitation of intelligence itself. To declare intelligence defined by being is to declare it intrinsically free of limitations. We can define sight in terms of what can be seen, hearing in terms of sound; in these and all similar cases our positive definition is itself negative; it sets limits and parameters. The definition of intelligence in terms of being dissolves limits; the parameters are non-parameters; the "formal category" is a non-category. Intelligence is intrinsically open to all reality.

Kant attempted to define pure reason in terms of various categories; yet he admitted that the mind could conceive the possibility of a *ding-an-sich*. This admission should have led him to revise his philosophy; it remains an inexplicable surd in Kantianism. However, it is a recognition that human intelligence is not limited by any confining categories; it transcends the relativities of particular experiences and in each experience reaches a non-relative objectivity.

If a faculty, a power, an appetite, an activity that is related to being as its constituent object, is thereby released from subjectivity and limitation, by the same token it is seen as open to an indefinite ingestation of reality. Some years ago, there was a group of theologians who argued that, although the Beatific Vision was a gratuitous and supernatural gift from God, man, because of the unlimited and indefinite perfectibility of his intelligence, had a *desiderium naturale,* an ontological hunger for God Himself, since only in infinite reality could the human intelligence reach complete and total fulfillment. Without the passage from finite reality to infinite reality, human intelligence would be forever reaching for a final term it could never in fact reach.

I introduce this consideration in order to emphasize the fact that a definition of intelligence in terms of being displays the total freedom of human intelligence from all intrinsic categorical limitations, thereby asserting its basic independence of relativism and subjectivism. The basic nature of intelligence includes a relationship to an absolute, both an absolute in understanding—Being—and an absolute in reality—*ipsum esse*—God.

I have asserted the fundamental independence of both epistemology and metaphysics from all categorical or particularized disciplines, especially from those which proceed by way of a constructural methodology. I have at least implied that God is reached by an intellectual elaboration from basic insights—not as a scholion to any physical theory—whether it be Aristotelian, Newtonian, or Einsteinian.

I have pointed out that human intelligence is a potentiality that slowly and laboriously actualizes itself. But, simply as intelligence, it has no inner resources except itself and its own mysterious and magnificent active power to take into itself reality insofar as it can find reality.

This last statement leads directly to a consideration of the utmost importance—that of the access of human intelligence to existing real things. I am not here interested in the problem, if it is one, of realism versus idealism; only in the question as to how the human intelligence actualizes its potentiality for being and so enriches its own reality. Here we face a fact which is a scandal to all Platonists and a convincing evidence to all materialists and reductionists. The human intelligence, bereft of inner riches, is immersed in a world of material experience; sense—sensation—imagination—all these words and many others—choose whichever you like—witness to an experiential fact of which we are all aware. The human intelligence does not have access to a bright and beautiful world of pure forms; it has no contemplative immediate vision of God. It has its being which is *intelligere* and its activity which is *intelligere* within the world of sense, of matter experienced by a material being.

I think I have briefly sketched the basis for what Maritain has called the "grandeur" of metaphysical epistemology and of metaphysics itself. Now must I speak of its shame? Of our souls exiled into the cave, of our grubbing among earthy clods instead of penetrating the immortal stars?

It is undeniable that our access to reality is limited by the fact that we move and live and have our being in a relativistic and limited world of matter. But, this world is not a world of non-being into which we have been plunged in some primordial punishment. I have no doubt that the human race in some way and in some phase fell from grace—but the fall from grace could not have been the imprisonment of pure spirits in a strait-jacket of matter. If we fell, nature—as St. Paul suggests—fell with us and together we groan for redemption—for a new earth and a new heaven and for a new humanity. But, our punishment—if there is one—is not our immersion in matter. The world of sense and matter is indeed like all finite being a limited reality, but it is real—not a shadow or a dream of reality—it limits our knowledge but at the same time magnificently enriches it.

Our life in the world of matter and sense is not split off as a separate life from that of our intelligence. Our souls are not Cartesian ghosts running a physical mechanism; we are not imprisoned angels. We are besouled organisms, organisms which are material yet are spiritualized by the permeating presence of intelligence. *Intelligere est esse intelligentibus*. Our reflective insight reveals this fact, that no matter how much reverberations of our physical states or our experience of sense fills our consciousness, that consciousness is totally penetrated and permeated by intelligence. When St. Thomas subsumes these facts under his metaphysics; he arrives at a metaphysical definition of man as a unified entity pulled together by a soul that is at once spiritual and the form of the body. This is his metaphysics of man which simultaneously rejects Platonism and materialism in all their derivative forms.

The human body taken in its fullest sense is part of the perfectibility and the perfection of man and, within the order of nature, is essential to the progressive actualization of the potentiality of the human intelligence.

If we take this positive and optimistic view of man's state, we can say that there is a unique "grandeur" in man's active experience of the world. Not only has each man and the race as a whole taken from the given of nature, in virtue of the active potentiality of human intelligence for all forms of reality, but the world in which we live has been enriched and ennobled by man's creations—vases and paintings, wheels and machines, theories and explanation—with a cumulative shared experience that is in continuity with the paintings of the cave dwellers and the fire sites of early man. Man through his intellect penetrated sense life and through his body has enriched the world, in fact increased its reality. To include here epistemological concerns, the vast and intricate deployment of constructural disciplines is a magnificent creative surrogate which constantly overcomes the limitations of our access to reality.

Well, one can sketch only a limited amount of one's philosophical positions in a short lecture. I believe I have asserted or, at least, implied (1) that human intelligence can be defined and described only in the terms of an existential ontological epistemology based on original experiential insights, (2) that this sort of epistemology can be maintained, developed and applied only through a similar ontological metaphysics, (3) that from these two disciplines there results a metaphysical definition of man that explains his uniqueness in nature, the rightness of his immersion in nature and yet leaves him open to a personal relation to infinite reality.

At this point, I will stop what I hope, at least, has been a series of philosophical reflections and now address myself to some more practical considerations.

I believe that most of what I have been saying I learned from St.

Thomas. You will recall Gibson's narration of how, in his effort to understand Descartes, he moved back in philosophical history and discovered to his amazement that the men who really knew how to do metaphysics were the great doctors of the Middle Ages, the exemplar par excellence being St. Thomas. I yield to no man in my love of Plato, my admiration for Aristotle, my enthusiasm for St. Augustine and for many others of later centuries, including our own, but I am more convinced than ever that, if you want to learn how to do metaphysics, you must put yourself to school under the tutelage of St. Thomas. In most fields we recognize certain achievements as being high points in human culture. It is not criticism of the poetic ability of other generations to say that Homer (whoever he was or however many he was) is still "grand against the morn." Thucydides, Vergil, Dante, and Shakespeare are classic giants despite their dates, their limitations and subsequent history.

And so, in metaphysics, St. Thomas is a great who has not yet been surpassed or even equalled.

It is currently out of fashion so to regard him. The lapidary phrases and succinct arguments he employed are unpalatable and unacceptable to this generation. But passing fads never finally eclipse classical achievers or achievements. Try as we may, we cannot escape them—and St. Thomas is still embodied, echoed, and used in our philosophy and our theology—even by those who are quite unaware of it. He will return to the schools!

As for education, if there is any sense to what I have been saying, an ontological epistemology and an ontological metaphysics ought to be intrinsic parts of any college education. They alone can maintain, in reflective understanding, the freedom and openness of human intelligence and safeguard a view of man that is neither materialistic nor reductionist. I know that, currently, required courses are in ill-repute and that a narrow relevance is often now the touchstone of curricula, but the hard-won fundamentals of our intellectual tradition ought to be part of the patrimony of every educated person, especially in Catholic and Jesuit education. We owe it to our students and to this generation to open the cumulative culture of our race before them. Otherwise, they will be forever rediscovering intellectual wheels—and often mighty inferior wheels to boot!

Finally, I cannot tell you how honored and happy I am to be a part of the William Wade lecture series and of tonight's celebration. It is both humbling and joyful to be able to honor two of my long-time colleagues in philosophy at this great university.

For many years, Father Wade and I both taught philosophy to the Jesuit scholastics. For a time, I taught epistemology to the first year scholastics who in the following year had Father Wade. As many of you know, Father Wade taught by a method of argument, challenge and almost impossible intellectual tour-de-force. He used to say, "Father Henle last year taught you such and such—but now just let us look at that." I can almost hear him saying, "Well, last Saturday Father Henle said such and such—but let's look at that."

XVI

A MEDITATION ABOUT KNOWING

N ew Introduction: One of the most surprising invitations to lecture that I ever received was the invitation to give the annual
Bode lecture[1] at the Ohio State University in 1964. The invitation was surprising because Professor Bode was one of the most militant
secularists in the profession of Philosophy of Education. He was profoundly opposed to having any religious influence in education.

I decided that when two people had developed each a sophisticated
philosophical position the only way to bring these people into reasonable discussion was to return to a fundamental common experience
hoping to find therein some common point of reference or agreement
that would permit a meaningful dialogue to occur. If I told Professor
Bode that I had a toothache he would understand what I meant and what
I was going through because I would be referring to a common shared
experience. It seems to me that we have many such common experiences in the area of knowledge and I thought that I might perhaps find
and explore some of these common experiences in this lecture.

Unfortunately the secularists and I are now so far apart that not
only the discovery but also the development of a common point of
agreement appears almost impossible. Yet, I think we must keep trying.

* * *

I would like to ask you to engage with me in a personal meditation
on knowledge. I have used the words *engage* and *personal* very deliber-

---

[1]First Published in *A Meditation About Knowing*, Bode Memorial Lectures 1964 (Ohio
State University), 3–24, 53–56.

ately. It is possible to listen to a lecture like this in a detached and abstract sort of way, understanding the ideas expressed and following the logical or rhetorical flow of presentation, without making the matter either "real" or "personal." But I want you to take a very active and personal part in this lecture by reflecting yourselves on the act of knowing about which I will be talking.

We shall try to carry on this reflective meditation at two levels, moving back and forth between them as we develop our theme.

This first level is that of direct and immediate reflection upon knowing as we actually find it. But where can we find knowledge existing, as it were, in its native habitat? Were knowledge an animal—like the platypus—we could outfit our expedition and study the platypus along the streams of Australia; were it a chemical, like sulfuric acid, we could smell it, taste it, weight it, and mix it. If knowledge were a thing like these, I could put it before you and point to it and say, "There it is. Look at it! Study it." But knowledge is not something that comes in chunks, or can be put in bottles, or passed around in samples. It truly exists only within the activity of a mind, or better, or at least more experientially, only within the activities discoverable within human conscious experience. I cannot point to it; in asking you to "look" at it in your own experience, I can guide and directly only by "talking," somewhat in the way the control tower "talks" the lost pilot down through the storm to a safe landing.

The first level of our meditation, then, is that of direct reflection on knowing as it goes on in our experiential consciousness. At this level, what we want to do is take a "fresh" look at knowledge, ideally without the encumbrance of theories, of habitual viewpoints, of sophisticated concepts. We want to look at knowing with the fresh and impartial curiosity of a child before a totally new experience. Let no one think this is an easy exercise. In the first place, it is extremely difficult to really look at things we are familiar with, the things that are always "there." The air around us our daily companions, our familiar rooms and offices, all these we take for granted, and we hardly ever really examine them. But if it is hard to "look" at what is familiar and common to the point of being commonplace, it is perhaps harder to come to "see" it with any genuine realization or understanding. We look without seeing, we see without understanding and we both look and see without the excitement of curiosity.

We are, in a sense, victims of our own compressed and highly formalized system of education. Our schooling has too often suppressed curiosity. I often tell graduate students that in a very strange way they have come full circle back to their childhood. When little children are growing up and beginning to talk, to look about, and to take note of things, they display one rather common characteristic—they are indefatigable question-askers. "Mama, what is that man doing?" "What for?" "Why is it Tuesday?" "Are there baby policemen?" And so on, over and over and over again, and mother says, "Go ask your father." Father says, "Don't bother me with foolish questions. Keep still. Go and play." We put our children in school; we tell them not to talk, we wait—in fact, we seem to do everything possible to stop the flow of questions from these bright little minds just beginning to come open before experience and to really notice the world. And so we make them like the rest of us, so glued to some little objective or limited interest that we do not even notice the world, let alone ask excited questions about it. Then at last they come to graduate school and we look at their passive faces and say, "For heaven's sake, be curious! Don't be satisfied with what you're told—explore, probe, ask questions. Ask questions!!"

If our effort to meditate on knowing results only in a heightened realization of what a marvelous and strange thing human knowing is, we shall have renewed ourselves as teachers. We want to open young minds to knowledge, to stimulate them to learn and to understand. To achieve this, we must bring to the task of teaching an excited enthusiasm about knowing itself. The contagion of genuine enthusiasm about the genuinely wonderful thing that is the life of learning and knowledge will readily be caught by bright, inquisitive young minds. God forgive us teachers for dealing dully with the most exciting things in the world.

I have said that at the first level of our meditation we are to reflect directly on knowing as we find it experientially in our own awareness, that we are to take a "fresh" look at it, like a wide-eyed child first encountering it.

But there is another way in which our education interferes with meditative reflection. In a few short years, we attempt to recapitulate for our young students the cultural development of Western civilization. We expose them to all the results of the reflection, the experimentation, the thinking, the experiencing that our race has done; we transmit the whole complex and sophisticated structure of our culture, its theories, its concepts, its viewpoints—all this to young people who have had a minimum of personal experience and, in many cases, almost no personal reflection. The period of personal experience, of that of savoring of reality, of that personal encounter with the given at a pre-systematic level, has been so syncopated and indeed so ignored that good bit of our schooling is almost sheer verbalism, and all of us are full of Whitehead has called "inert ideas." The very mass of our knowledge and the sophistication of our culture have choked us. It is difficult to give our students a genuine experience of "discovery," the exhilaration of being explorers in the world of knowledge. There was a time when one could quickly get beyond the known and charted terrain of science. The thrill of the discovery of simple mathematical truths still lives in the tales of the Pythagoreans. There was the excitement of the Greek astronomers when they finally established that the moon shines with reflected light, the passionate enthusiasm of Abelard and his followers in the rediscovery of ancient logic, and the vibrant joy of all our great explorers on land and sea, in laboratory and library, and in the mind itself. For example, let us recall the simple experiment of Torricelli's inverted tube. Père Mersenne,[2] learning of the experiment by letters from Italy, wrote posthaste to Pascal who arranged for a test experiment on the Puy-de-Dôme in France.[3] In the seventeenth century, this was *discovery*; it was news. Today Torricelli's tube is a routine commonplace in beginning physics, old had and dull. That was a time when Descartes was pushing forward in mathematics,

---

[2]This extraordinary priest (1588–1648) lived prior to the inauguration of scientific academies and learned journals and, in a sense, carried on the functions of both these agencies by letter. He was in correspondence with almost all the learned men of Europe. ("Gran trafficante fù il Mersenno, tenendo commercio con tutti i Litterati d'Europa." Carlo Dati, as quoted by Lenoble, *Mersenne ou la Naissance du Mecanisme,* Paris: Vrin, 1943, 1.) He kept the learned in communication by his continuous correspondence (five volumes of letters have been published!). And kept them constantly stimulated by his keen curiosity ("insatiable curiosité par des expériences de toutes manières." *Ibid.*) and by his special talent for posing questions. I dwell on Père Mersenne not only because he is interesting in his own right, but because he combined, it seems to me, those qualities which should distinguish a good teacher—curiosity, enthusiasm, and a desire to communicate and to stimulate. He was a catalyst, a teacher, an intellectual midwife for Pascal, Descartes, and dozens of others; he may be a model for us who wish to be the same for our students who, hopefully, will be greater than we, as Descartes and Pascal were greater than Père Mersenne.

[3]For a good historical and analytical account of this experiment with hints on how it might be taught as an "exciting" experiment, *see* James B. Conant, *Science and Common Sense* (New Haven: Yale University Press, 1951), 63–76.

Galileo in physics, Boyle in chemistry, Newton in celestial mechanics; today, however we have piled up so many discoveries and turned them into textbook summaries that our students rarely have the experience of even *re*-discovery.

This means not only that discoveries are encapsulated as facts and information and downed with a minimum of reaction, but that conceptual schemes, theories, hypotheses, abstract intellectual structures are transmitted with a minimum of reflection and all too little healthy skepticism. There are very few concepts or theoretical explanations that are more than provisional and partial; many are downright biased—not by prejudice, but by intellectual inadequacy—and incorrect. It is through this undifferentiated mass of face and theory, of verbalism and hard-won insight that we "look" at things and "see" what we have been led to expect we will see. The Rorschach testee does not "see" just ink blobs; neither does the trained scientist nor scholar nor even the graduate of our colleges "see" just the crude fact.

One can read an interesting illustration of this in Hans Driesch's account of his early independent experiments on sea urchins. Driesch had received his training in biology in the late nineteenth century German universities when a thoroughgoing mechanism was the philosophical structure of biological knowledge. When his experiments did not work out according to the mechanistic principles he had been taught, he could not comprehend and, at first, could not accept the facts to be seen in his laboratory. Driesch, however, did not brush them aside as contradicting established theory or the current "*We now know*" situation. The shock led to a higher reflection on the then current structure of biological theory and to the development of newer theories and concepts.

Thus, to acheive creative freedom coupled with responsibility to factual evidence, two intellectual attitudes are necessary. First is the loyal confrontation with experiential fact at a presystematic level. One must be prepared to look and reflect, to "sit down before" the fact, to bury oneself, alert and eager, in ongoing experience. But to do this one must achieve some kind of conscious control over his own "systematics" of knowledge. We cannot divest ourselves of the sophisticated culture which has become a part of us. We cannot be as intellectually nude as a child. We can control our "knowledge" only by rising above it; by a reflection which is postsystematic and meta-disciplinary. I would say that this is a condition not only of the "fresh" look at experience, but of any truly creative advance in any discipline. The graduate student masters his discipline only when he can stand outside of it. As long as his discipline is in him as a set of principles and habits according to which he acts, judges, and thinks, he is captured by it and is its victim. A great biochemist is said to have urged each graduate student in biochemistry to take courses in poetry—not that he, the biochemist, had any particular regard for poetry, but because he thought poetry might jar the students' imaginations and free them from conceptual captivity.

This digression makes it possible to elaborate further the two levels of reflection at which the meditation on knowledge must be carried on. The first level—that of the fresh experiential look—is a presystematic level; it is one logically prior to theory and formal conceptualization, the ultimate source of personal understanding, and one at which we must, at all costs, avoid *imposing* on experiences the conceptual framework and theories which we have learned elsewhere. The second level is the postsystematic reflection in which we stand above and outside of our particular concepts and theoretical constructions. Only by achieving this level of reflective knowledge can we free ourselves from the limitations of the great body of formal knowledge which we possess and make the first level possible at all.

But it should not be thought that all this factual and systematic knowledge is simply a handicap. On the contrary, to a large extent it *is* knowledge, and it has increased not only our understanding but our ability to understand. Without it we would be not only as fresh and innocent as a child, but we would also be equally ignorant and intellectually immature.

Hence, we want not only to be free of the trammels of our culture, but to be free also to use it to maximum effect. The level of metasystematic reflection enables us to achieve both of these goals while we turn back to the experiential consideration of knowledge as it goes on.[4]

---

[4]In an earlier (unpublished) paper, "Intelligence and Modern Philosophers," I dealt with reflection in a slightly different context. I quote a section which may help to clarify the text here:

I think there will be a large measure of agreement that there lies open only one avenue of escape. Man has escaped and can escape the automatization of life only through the use of reflective intelligence. Man is master of himself, of his own self-determination, only through reflective intelligence. He can be aware of and view as objects his own desires and passions, his

It will be noted that I have attempted no formal definition of *knowledge* or of *knowing*. It is not possible to define, in a technical sense, prior to the elaboration of systematic and abstract knowledge. A definition, if it comes at all, comes at the end of an experiential meditation, not at the beginning. Precisely what must be avoided is an *a priori* definition which then command our reflection and predetermine our vision. Most philosophers have attempted a definition of knowledge of its various levels and types, and in doing so have diverged so far from one another that common expressions like "knowing," "evidence," etc., become almost equivocal terms. John Dewey's definition, for example, has always seemed to me too *a priori* and too restrictive. By being so restrictive, it has allowed various ranges of noetic experience to drop out of philosophical consideration. Polany points up this general situation when he argues that, as a certain kind of scientific method takes over more and more areas of knowledge, certain things which we, as men, *know to be facts*, are excluded from the official area of "knowledge."[5] So, at the primitive level where we find the rich concrete reality of knowing activities, I can only "point," and this "pointing" must consist of my talking and your reflecting.

All languages of which I know anything at all have developed a whole series of words, overlapping and interlocking in meaning, which can be said to be variants on the basic theme of "knowing." *Cognitio, επιστημη, νοησις, sapientia* are some examples. These refer to the

---

own conceptions and motivations; he can, therefore, criticize them by an internal externality; he can evaluate them; and thereby he frees himself from their domination. Man does not, of course, at a stroke become free as a spirit; his glands and his nerves, his imagination and emotion, his ignorance and his past decisions are still trammels on his activity; external pressures solicit and force him; but a margin of self-determination appears which, by deliberate manipulation and self-training, can be extended to wider and wider areas of his life.

Man is the maker of machines and the creator of culture because he is intelligent; he is master of his machines and all else because he possess reflective intelligence. Through reflective intelligence he is master of himself and escapes thereby physical and physiological, psychological, and cultural determinism. Illusions, reflectively recognized as such, cease to influence; propaganda, unveiled by reflection, ceases to deceive; irrational urges, reflectively analyzed, can be allowed for and manipulated.

[5]Polany, Michael. "Scientific Outlook: Its Sickness and Cure," *Science* (15 March 1957): 125, 480–484.

basic common experiences to which I am pointing. There are levels here of simple awareness of fact, "I know that I feel a pain"; of insight, "I understand the nature of proof"; and of highly elaborated theories, such as those of modern physics. There are stages and degrees, "It is likely"; "I'm sure"; there are processes, "I'll try it"; "I'll test it out." In this whole complex experience there is a series of crisscrossing spectra or continua, showing wide variations but having, I would vigorously maintain, a primitive, common quality which justifies giving them a common name— "activities of knowing."

This may seem naive and oversimplified, but I am deeply convinced that part of our problem is that we move too quickly from what is primitive and simple to sophisticated, logical constructions. I would argue that we should let our meditative reflection move about through the sorts of experience I mentioned above, resting on them until we become immediately aware of both the fact, the nature of the common noetic quality, and the variants on the same theme. Chesterton said at one time that the first 99 times a man looks at grass he is perfectly safe, but the 100th time he is in danger of *seeing that it is green.*

The primitive noetic quality to which I am pointing and of which we may come fully aware at the 100th look is a *unique* thing. We can bring an understanding of it into our systematic philosophizing, but we cannot reduce it to a complex of logical categories without dropping out precisely its unique identity and nature. I am using the word *quality*, but to designate anything by this category is to throw it into a mass of heterogenous things. This unique quality must be found and experienced; it can then be named and used, but it cannot be reduced to any different set of logical notes.

A methodological digression might be in order here. It will be objected that I am proposing to rest a philosophy of knowing on introspection and on private evidence which bears a striking resemblance to a personal revelation. First of all, in the nature of the case, we cannot find knowing, actual concrete, ongoing knowing, anywhere except within a private, personal awareness. To reemphasize an earlier point, knowing is not something we can find in external nature; knowledge is not something we can "store" in books or on records or in computers. It is unfortunate that we have come to talk about knowledge in materialistic and industrial terms.[6] It is particularly important for us teachers to remember that education is not a matter of passing on pieces of knowledge or transmitting quanta of information. We are extrinsic agents who by indirection, by stimulation, and by example must bring young people to knowing activities in their own minds.[7] Long ago Aquinas pointed out that the *active principle* of learning is in the person being taught who first of all is able to learn by personal discovery but can also learn through being taught by a teacher whose main task is *to bring the learner to discovery.*[8]

There is then no escaping the reflective method if we want to see and grasp what knowledge is in its actuality. But to a very large extent the objection to so-called "private" evidence is a specious one. Those particularly who derive their criteria of evidence from the physical sciences insist that "real," "genuine," "valid" evidence must be as public as were the barometric experiments of Torricelli and Pascal.[9]

---

[6]Compare the *title* of Fritz Machlup's book: *The Production and Distribution of Knowledge in the United States* (Princeton: Princeton University Press, 1962).

[7]*Cf.:* "By production of knowledge we understand any human (or human-induced) activity effectively designed to create, alter, or confirm in a human mind, one's own or anyone else's, a meaningful apperception, awareness, cognizance, or consciousness of whatever it may be." (*Ibid.,* p. 30.) This definition has the merit of stressing: (1) *the activity of knowing,* (2) its proper locale, (3) the wide range of variant activities.

[8] In eo enim qui docetur, est principium activum ad scientiam: scilicet intellectus, et ea quae naturaliter intelliguntur, scilicet prima principia. Et ideo scientia acquiritur dupliciter: et sine doctrina, per inventionem; et per doctrinam. Docens igitur hoc modo incipit docere sicut inveniens incipit invenire: offerendo scilicet considerationi discipuli principia ab eo nota, quia omnis disciplina ex praeexistenti fit cognitione (I Poster. I. 1; 71a), et illa principia in conclusions deducendo; et proponendo exempla sensibilia, ex quibus in anima discipuli formentur phantasmata necessaria ad intelligendum. (*Summa contra Gentiles,* Bk. II, cap. 75 ad fin. Ed. Leonine manual, 181.)

See also the excellent exposition of this principle in Tad Guzie, *The Analogy of Learning* (New York: Sheed and Ward, 1960), 180–184.

[9]But *cf.* P. W. Bridgman, The Nature of Physical Theory (New York: Dover Publications, 1936), 13–14. "In the last analysis science is only my private science, art is my private art, religion my private religion, etc. The fact that in deciding what shall be my private science I find it profitable to consider only those aspects of my direct experience in which my fellow beings act in a particular way cannot obscure the essen-

Anyone can repeat for himself the experiments on the Puy-de-Dôme. But in a very sound sense, no evidence is external or public or independent of what is internal and private. The tube, the mercury, the bowl were not evidence; they meant nothing until they were "taken in," understood, and analyzed in someone's consciousness. Evidence need not be subjective or biased, but it is always evidence *for someone*. You can repeat experiments a thousand times, but to a mind unable to grasp their meaning, they will never be "evidence."

On the other hand, the private experience to which we are appealing is not something so individually conditioned (as might be the first lone astronaut's "feel" of the atmosphere of Mars or one's memory of a certain June night when she said "yes"), so idiosyncratic, peculiar, and personal that it lies outside anyone else's experience. On the contrary, we are pointing to common experiences which most men can discover in their own consciousness or awareness. The experiences of being aware of differences and of their qualities, of insightful moments, of drawing conclusions, of generalizing, etc., can be repeated by each man as surely as Torricelli's experiment can. And because they are common to all of us, though each man for his own is a privileged observer, we can share them just as much as we can share external events.[10]

There is another methodological consideration. It is common fashion to assume that at this point of direct contact with ongoing experience, with "concrete fact," we must turn to the scientist, to the controlled experiments, and to the precise descriptions of the scientific method strictly so-called. It is the psychologist who, in Huxley's phrase, sits down before the fact and describes it. The philosopher then must simply await the deliverance of the psychologist before he can proceed to his own proper work. This, I think, involves a very mistaken idea of the nature of scientific method and, above all, of that method as applied to the intellectual life of man.

The facts with which scientific method deals are not the brute facts

---

tial fact that it is mine and naught else. 'Public Science' is a particular kind of the science of private individuals."

[10]I still remember my first experience of the odor of burning sulfur. Our freshman laboratory manual directed us to smell the burning sulphur. I enthusiastically inhaled deeply directly from the test tube. The others in the laboratory enjoyed my naivete highly, but they shared not only my gasping, my choking, and my weeping; they shared the inner conscious experience because of cognate experience of their own.

of nature or the concrete integrity of any human experience. On the contrary, facts are facts for science only in virtue of an interpretation of experience, a reduction of experience to a schema imposed by the particular scientific method, and for the conceptual framework employed. Eddington's ichthyologist's net is a good illustration:

> Let us suppose that an ichthyologist is exploring the life of the ocean. He casts a net into the water and brings up a fishy assortment. Surveying his catch, he proceeds in the usual manner of a scientist to systematise what it reveals. He arrives at two generalisations:
> (1) No sea-creature is less than two inches long.
> (2) All sea-creatures have gills.

These are both true of his catch, and he assumes tentatively that they will remain true however often he repeats it.

> In applying this analogy, the catch stands for the body of knowledge which constitutes physical science, and the net for the sensory and intellectual equipment which we use in obtaining it. The casting of the net corresponds to observation; for knowledge which has not been or could not be obtained by observation is not admitted into physical science.

> An onlooker may object that the first generalization is wrong. "There are plenty of sea-creatures under two inches long, only your net is not adapted to catch them." The ichthyologist dismisses this objection contemptuously. "Anything uncatchable by my net is *ipso facto* outside the scope of ichthyological knowledge, and is not part of the kingdom of fishes which has been defined as the theme of ichthyological knowledge. In short, what my net can't catch isn't fish." Or—to translate the analogy—"If you are not simply guessing, you are claiming a knowledge of the physical universe discovered in some other way than by the methods of physical science, and admittedly unverifiable by such methods. You are a metaphysician. Bah!"[11]

---

[11]Arthur Eddington, *The Philosophy of Physical Science* (New York: Macmillan, 1939), 16.

The facts dealt with by the various scientific methods have already been removed from the matrix of concrete and integral experience.

The immediate reflection on knowing for which I am asking is prior both to formal philosophy and to formal science. It is indeed presupposed by scientific psychology; no matter how self-contained and self-defining scientific systems may become, they ultimately have no meaning if they do not refer to basic experience and cannot be rooted, however indirectly, in the personal experience of each man. Some will think this an effort to bring naive common sense to bear on science and philosophy, but I would argue that the whole mass of modern phenomenology and existentialism is so much evidence that a highly sophisticated, independent, and primary reflection can be conducted on immediate experience anterior to scientific construction or philosophical systematization.

However, there is another reason, specific to current psychology, why presystematic reflection and philosophical analysis must be carried on *in the first instance* (not totally) independently of empirical psychology. Current psychological schools and systems, above all in their first-level interpretations, assume and presuppose a philosophical viewpoint.[12] For example, in an excellent recent study of thinking, the introduction lays out as a sort of general frame of reference a nominalistic theory of knowledge.[13] If philosophers must pick up where scientific workers leave off, if it is from their conclusions that we as philosophers must work, the vicious circle seems closed. Facts and data already impregnated with a certain philosophy may well be expected to yield up, under analysis, this same philosophy and no other.

I would say, therefore, that it is doubly mistaken to elaborate a

---

[12]For a more elaborate discussion of this point, *see* Alden Fisher, "Freud and the Image of Man," Proceedings of the American Catholic University of Philosophical Association (Washington: The Catholic University of America, 1961), 48–56. David Rapaport recognizes this fact and neatly bypasses it: "I shall avoid here the philosophical question of whether psychology—*itself based on fundamental assumptions of the sort epistemology studies* (italics mine)—can claim competence ot answer epistemological questions. From the point of view of science, this is not a philosophical problem, but one of methodological theory and empirical findings," *The Organization and Pathology of Thought* (New York: Columbia University Press, 1951), p. 722.

[13]Jerome Bruner, Jacqueline Goodnow, George Austin, *A Study of Thinking* (London: John Wiley and Sons, 1956), 1–24.

philosophy of knowledge on the facts and data prepared by experimental psychology. The philosopher has a proper operation to perform on the original experience itself, a task which, as Hawkins has pointed out,[14] is prior philosophically to the work of science itself and, therefore, in its initial stages at least, independent of, though not finally indifferent to, the conclusions of science.

So what I am pleading for is a reflection on actual knowing which is prior to both science and philosophy and is *a prelude to philosophizing.*

I stress this stage of reflection also because it is only here, it seems to me, that we can achieve a genuine philosophical dialogue. You can bring together a group of logical positivists or a group of pragmatists and have a fine discussion. Two Thomists can talk to each other, argue fruitfully, and discuss with mutual understanding. But bring together a Thomist, a logical positivist, an Augustinian, a naturalistic atheist, and a Presbyterian minister, and try to have a dialogue—you get five monologues. How can we get philosophers to engage in genuine philosophical argument? How can we truly communicate *from within* fully formed, highly organized, but divergent systems of thought? This is a problem that has engaged my attention for many years. As my friends in the Philosophy of Education Society know, I have spent a great part of my life trying to talk to and, more importantly, *talk with* philosophers whose positions are radically different from my own.

For some eighteen years I taught an advanced basic course in the history of modern philosophy. I became convinced the oat one would never understand these philosophers unless one attempted as loyally as possible to play the same intellectual role as they did, to think as they did in the same context of the history of ideas. I felt that I had to divest myself of my own convictions and habitual philosophical principles and be, turn by turn, Descartes, Spinoza, Leibnitz, Kant, and the rest. I told my classes that our first task was to understand the men we were studying, from within, by identifying ourselves as far as possible with them as they developed their systems. It is not an easy task, rather an impossible one, but the effort is well worth it if the objective is only partially achieved. I assure you that the pseudo-Descartes that emerges

---

[14]D. J. B Hawkins,. *The Criticism of Experience* (New York: Sheed and Ward, 1945), 25–26.

from this effort can understand Cartesianism and discuss with Cartesians much better than the real Thomist. If I can empathize with Descartes as he sits brooding in Germany, if I can somehow feel the impact of Hume as Kant did, if I can follow out the "plain historical method" of Locke, I will be in an honest position to do some internal criticism of their final systems. In this way, one finds the historical conditioning, the cultural determinations, the semantic confusions, the overlooking of evidence, the illogical leaps which render systems vulnerable, but leave, at the same time, a great deal of permanent value.

Too often philosophers approach each other with the primary aim of criticizing and refuting, rather than of first understanding. A pragmatist reads an exposition of natural moral law. He checks it. There are no empirical or pragmatic arguments. Bah! Worthless. Into the basket with it! A Thomist looks at Dewey. What, no metaphysics of being? So what can he have? Why waste time reading him? And so, we unseat adversaries by the dozen in our studies, in our articles and footnotes, and they ride on untouched.

The sympathetic role-playing mentioned above may be an effective way to come to understand other systems of philosophy. It may also enable one to carry on a reasonable and somewhat effective internal criticism. But it does not bring about genuine human dialogue in which two minds really enmesh in discussion.

I have often been impressed by the fact that philosophers who disagree violently in the theory of knowledge and the philosophy of intelligence show a common understanding of teaching, of evidence, of science, etc., when they are not talking *as* philosophers. They will agree that certain individuals, books, articles, theories are intelligent and that a wide range of known facts are known! I think the factors which explain this are twofold: (1) the extent that they are withdrawn formally from their theoretical positions, and (2) the extent that they come under the control of common human experience and our common humanistic culture.

It is the first of these that is relevant here. I am convinced that the basic intelligibility of our knowing experiences and activities is one of the humanly common things. To the extent that we can articulate and share this basic experience prior to our theories and systems, to that extent we can philosophize together. Once an individual's highly integrated system is under way, it is too late. Grant the assumptions of the *Critique of Pure Reason* and you are, to a large extent, powerless to stop the flow of the system. Let Hume once crystalize his interpretation of consciousness, and you will never rejoin his thought. The options are made when one "takes off" from common immediate experience or even without looking at it at all. I would argue that most systems of epistemology have operated with a minimum of control from real human experience. I have argued elsewhere that what Thomism needs is a phenomenological inventory of, and insight into, experiential human knowing activities.[15] I am arguing here that we all need this, and that in the process of carrying out this phenomenological task by direct reflection on and into immediate experience, we can build a common ground and a body of agreements. We could thus set up a *phenomenological test* of philosophical theory.

I do not believe that John Dewey's internal experience of learning and knowing was very different from mine, If we, he and I, could have carried on a discussion at this level, mutually exploring our experiences and learning to communicate about them, we would have had a firm, common ground for further discussion of a meaningful sort and a matrix of reality to which to tie our theories.

Of course, no one really develops a philosophy (or any other body of knowledge) directly from experience by personal "discovery." We have all been taught; our knowledge comes to us from others, from books, pictures, maps, movies, lectures, conversations, and so forth. If human lives were longer by several centuries, we might let our students rediscover and reconstruct for themselves (as Pascal did geometry). As it is we must be taught. But even so, what we learn from teaching we learn only by virtue of personal experience. All taught knowledge is grasped as a function of experience. All taught knowledge is grasped as a function of experience. To the extent that new knowledge can be grounded in one's personal experience, to the extent it becomes *real* and is *really* possessed. Whitehead spoke of the mass of "inert ideas" resulting from formal education. Newman analyzed the "notional assent" one gives to matters held in an abstract, impersonal way.[16]

---

[15]R.J. Henle, "A Phenomenological Approach to Realism," *An Etienne Gilson Tribute,* Gerald Smith *et al.,* eds. (Milwaukee: Marquette University Press, 1959), 68–85 [Article VI].

[16]Thus, it is calling upon the learner's natural habit of real assent that the teacher is able to resolve the tension between formal organization of subject matter and natural discovery, the tension between words and things. In this light, the use of "sensible

Rapaport speaks of our knowledge becoming "our own" through personal use of it.[17]

From this standpoint, the personal and direct reflection on knowledge is only a specific instance of what must be done in every discipline. A constant return to concrete experience should be an intrinsic part of any process of education.

However, I would argue that this is particularly necessary for philosophers. Instead of perpetually becoming more abstract and more conceptual, they should repeatedly return to the contemplation of experience. They should strive to combine the sophisticated approach of a mature intelligence with the fresh approach of a child.

Philosophical thinking, therefore, should be carried on under the control of the two levels of reflection to which I am constantly referring. On the one hand, we should continually develop a heightened awareness of experience itself, using it as a down-to-earth check on theories and conceptual schemes. On the other hand, we should reflect on our theories and concepts themselves, on our "learned" knowledge, in order to be free of it all and yet be able to make free use of it all.

I know that there are those who think we can never reach a truly rock bottom element in human experience and that there are others who maintain we can never free ourselves from our language, our culture, and our subjective concepts. One might argue that if we were truly imprisoned to that extent, we would not be able even to conceive, as we

---

examples"—and here all the tools of primary and secondary perception offer themselves to the teacher—is not just a helpful supplement in pedagogical method. Rather, it is a *necessary* part of any learning process if, in Aquinas' words, learning is really a matter of discovery and teaching a matter of helping the student to discover; or if, in Newman's language, notional assent is ever to give way to real assent. The completeness of a learning process proportioned to the real nature of human understanding depends upon the personal experience of things in much the same way that the organism depends for its growth upon food. For concrete experience is in a sense the natural food of the intellect that *really* learns. (Guzie, *The Analogy of Learning* 183–184.)

[17]Knowledge, when first acquired, remains fragments from various textbooks. It is only later that the local memories of the text books and of their dividing-lines recede. This recession is accompanied by a progress in the applicability of knowledge to instances and relationships other than those given in the texts. The result of this process is that knowledge, originally learned as this or that teacher's or text's, becomes *our own*. When needed, it is spontaneously available and does not require the self-questioning: "What does Woodworth say about it?" Or "How does Koffka regard this?" (Rapaport, *Organization and Pathology of Thought*, 725–726.)

do, the possibility of surmounting our subjective limitations. I will only say here, however, that there is a vast amount of evidence that we can do so, but that the main proof lies, once again, in a personal trial of it. *Expertus potest credere.*

I propose now to make a brief and modest essay at this sort of reflective investigation of intellectual knowledge. When attempting to grasp specific characteristics of knowledge, it is customary to introduce certain standard considerations, such as the universality of knowledge, the grasp of abstract relationships, and so forth. I propose, rather, to begin with a very simple type of instance and to try to determine whether anything emerges that may be characteristic.

Suppose I tell a friend that there are groups of statues around the high altar in the Cathedral of Chartres in France. What sort of experience do I have? In doing this, I am not just communicating to my friend information about my own conscious life. The information I am giving him, and which he understands me to be giving him, is about the real stone images which are at Chartres. To these my attention and, through mine, his attention are directed; and I am consciously aware that my attention is so directed. In some sense, other than spatial or physical, these images come into, are in, or arise in my consciousness. This seems to be, and I would insist that it is, a simple, everyday, straightforward fact; but I would add that it needs the most insistent reflection to realize its full meaning and to maintain it as we move to the level of theoretical explication. Many philosophers have ignored this fact; of those who have theoretically dealt with it, many have quailed before it and have sought to escape it by substituting for it a simpler, more manageable situation which does not, in fact, exist.

For consider again this simple but troubling situation. The stones of Chartres are not here in this room; I have actually, at the moment, no physical contact with them; yet I am aware of them. On the other hand, I am not aware of them as I am of fictions. I know the difference between my saying, "There are statues at Chartres" and, "The gods of the Greeks dwell on Olympus." What I am aware of and what I assert are the real statues of Chartres, which were made by real craftsmen and have been seen by millions of people. And I do this with full awareness of my meaning—for my consciousness is not limited to the stones of Chartres as a ray of light may be focused on a single spot; I am aware that I am attending to the stones of Chartres. I am not thinking of an *idea* of stones and annexing to it an *idea* of existence.[18] This would remove precisely the remakable characteristic to which I am pointing and would simply misstate the fact. It cannot be reduced to meanings alone if these be taken in an abstract sense. For the man who knows nothing of this statuary understands the meaning, in this sense, of saying, "There are statues at Chartres," though he cannot assert it; he does not know the stones themselves. When I know and assert this knowledge, I grasp and assert not an idea of existence, but the existence of the stones, the existing stones. Nor can this knowledge be reduced to sense images or combinations of sense images. Let me have the most vivid imaginative re-enactment of the statues themselves. This is certainly not the same thing as the assertion of real statues.[19] The sense images may be present within consciousness; they may be necessary to this knowledge, but they are not identically the same thing as the knowing. Over and above the sense images is the conscious assertion of

---

[18]Having started with the bland assumption that knowledge deals with ideas in the mind an only these, Locke found it impossible to account for the fact of existential knowledge or existential judgments. He was forced to the expedient of the "idea-of-existence," by assumption, not by experience.

[19]One recalls the once famous and widely accepted explanation of meaning put forth by E. B. Titchener, "Meanings" consisted of sense images. "A cow is a longish rectangle with a certain facial expression, a sort of exaggerated pout," *Lectures on the Experimental Psychology of the Thought Processes* (New York: Macmillan, 1909), 18, and so on through an amazing inventory of bright fragmentary images. What is fantastic is that this theory of meaning was even seriously discussed. By the test of experience, it fails *prima facie.* Consider this simple criticism:

> The accidental image is in every way inadequate to explain naming behavior. It is unlikely, for instance, that any of us will say that we "see" Titchener's image of the triangle and yet we will call the same entities by this name as he would have done. Accidental images are different from one individual to another and yet these individuals may agree perfectly in their denoting behavior. Students in Titchener's seminars agreed with him in finding imagery to be the contents of consciousness but they did not agree on the specific images. Where Titchener saw a colored scoop for "meaning," one student saw a great scroll unrolling, and another saw a tangled skein being straightened out. These diverse images suggest no agreement at all on the meanings of words. Language is a cultural possession, shared by members of a society. The variable, accidental image will never explain how we are able to agree in labeling the objects about us, nor can it explain how we are able to communicate with one another. (Bruner et al., *A Study of Thinking,* 274.)

the particular real statues. If Hume's investigation establishes anything, it surely is that on the assumption that all knowledge must be reduced to sense images, there can be no knowledge of objective existence. And more than that, there can be no conception of the meaning of knowledge of objective existence. Even if one denies the objective existence of the statues of Chartres, he still allows, either implicitly or explicitly, for the meaning of the question. The power to grasp objective existence remains a fundamental ability, at least a possibility, within the nature of knowing.

The situation we are considering reveals, then, an activity, a process, and an experience which is not reducible to the psychological events within my consciousness. It evades every effort to confine it within a closed circle of subjective happenings. It is intrinsically related to something beyond and outside all these events, not only in the sense that the object of knowledge is not identical simply with the act of knowing, but that the object of knowledge, even as a possibility, lies outside the subjective data of conscious experience *and is known so to lie outside.* Intrinsic to the concrete act of knowing is a reference, a relation to the thing itself in its own existence, for it is this existence which the act asserts. But, once again, this reference is not like that between the picture in the paper and the President in the White House. It is a conscious self-aware relation.

Nor is this a matter to be explained by symbolization or by symbolic reference, for the reference is such by an awareness of meaning and is the grasp of the reality itself. Symbols undoubtedly appear within intellectual processes, but their very use implies a previous understanding that is not symbolic in character.

We are brought thus to find within this simple act of knowledge a consciousness and indeed a self-awareness, which, while remaining itself, goes beyond itself, transcends its own limit while, in the same act, maintaining those limits. For this characteristic or property of knowledge I will use a traditional term, "intentionality," together with a qualifying adjective, "objective." To call knowledge "intentional" is to say that it cannot be reduced simply to the act of knowing, for it lies in the very nature of knowledge[20] that it have an object other than the act itself. "Intentionality," that it have an object other than the act itself.

---

[20]As discovered in concrete experience, not as derived from an abstract definition.

"Intentionality," in this sense, was restored to full theoretical status in modern philosophy by Brentano and Husserl. I have added "objective" to indicate that intentionality as we find it in knowledge, at least in its fullest exercise, is more than that—it breaks out of the subjective limits of consciousness and brings into consciousness the real existence of objects precisely as not belonging to consciousness.

There is a simple escape from this conclusion; one may withdraw into some form of epistemological idealism. The price of this escape, it seems to me, is the surrender of fact. It is an escape from the control of empirical data. But this discussion I must leave to another occasion.

Many a modern Naturalist rejects the reductionist materialism of an older tradition. I think the obvious facts of experience force this rejection. These Naturalists see in knowledge a high-level category not reducible, functionally, to the categories of chemistry, of physics, or even of biology. Again I would agree that the fact of objective intentionality, as well as other facts which I have not introduced into this discussion, forces this conclusion. Thus, it seems to me that Naturalism, in general, has made progress by freeing itself from earlier assumptions and has come towards a more just view of knowledge.

Yet, it seems to me, the Naturalists still slight the evidence, for finally they do reduce this high-level category to a function of matter. Thus the irreducibility discovered in the facts of experience ends in a reduction at the level of philosophical theory.

Now I would argue that the objective intentionality to which I have pointed[21] makes such a reduction impossible, not because it involves new properties (in a sense a machine has new properties which are not possessed by its component parts taken separately), but because it displays properties which are contradictory to the properties of matter; objective intentionality displays in the act of knowledge precisely as an act of knowledge an independence of spatiality which is the condition of all functions, primitive or emergent, of matter. Moreover, the functioning of matter follows categories of causality which involve physical interactions within the very functioning, while here we have a function which can realize itself only to the extent that it is beyond the physical interactions. Between myself and Chartres there is no physical interaction in the act of knowledge itself. To explain the knowledge as a

---

[21]In reflective experience, not in theory.

physical interaction is precisely to destroy what it is. There are, of course, physical interactions required for the genesis of our human knowledge. But, as Roy Wood Sellars has said, that is just an "initiation";[22] it is not knowledge.

I can here only indicate directions of argumentation, not develop them fully. Yet, I believe that if Naturalists continue to examine the evidence as it is in itself, they will come to see that this "high-level category" of intellectual knowledge lies above matter and is not reducible to it through any pattern of organization or integral functioning. A new level of reality appears, which, since we discover it in contradistinction to matter, we must call immaterial. And yet, since we find it by examining the data of our experience, it is still a natural category. It is neither mystical nor supernatural.

This means that an epistemology developed in dependence upon the facts reveals a level of reality within man which is neither material nor a function of organized matter. But it does not mean that we find here a justification for the Cartesian theory of mind-body relationships. The evidence for the functional interrelationship of all levels in man is too strong to permit so simple an explanation. It is far more accurate to speak of a "minded organism" as does Roy Wood Sellars. Sellars asserts that the knower is the "I" and "The I is the self, the concrete human being."[23] Thomas Aquinas asserted, against the Cartesian-type theories of his day, that it is the man who knows and not the body or the intellect or the senses.

It seems to me that only these latter views fit the facts. But, on the other hand, what becomes of these positions at a higher theoretical level of Naturalism—where mind is to be "naturalized?"[24] At this point intellection is reduced to a functioning of the brain and so brought once more under the fundamental conditions of material functiuons; the minded organism becomes simply organism. Laland's penetrating

---

[22]Roy Wood Sellars, "Critical Realism and Modern Materialism," *Philosophic Thought in France and the United States,* Marvin Farber, ed. (Buffalo: University of Buffalo, 1950), 465.

[23]*Ibid.,* 467.

[24]*Ibid.,* 466.

analysis of this move seems simply right.[25] Materialism, in the face of massive evidence, has surrendered its fundamental starting point, the one alone which can justify this conclusion, and yet comes out at the same point as the old "reductionist" materialism which it now repudiates. Moreover, at this point also, Sellars, at least, turns the development of theory over to the scientists. The investigations which will clarify the unity of levels in man must, he says, "be left to the psychologist and neurologist."[26] This, as I have already pointed out, appears to be a serious methodological error. The evidence has been developed up to this point in a philosophical manner; to turn the argument over to the scientist, at this point, is to violate the continuity and formal nature of philosophical inquiry.

I have engaged in this brief exploration only as an indication of the possibilities of such discussion. For it seems to me that, in the efforts toward meaningful description (description by insight and not by extrinsic pointing), points of agreement begin to emerge. On the other hand, when we ask why Naturalism, as it moves beyond this point, having recognized the *sui generis* character of intellectual knowledge, undertakes to materialize the entire situation, we begin to clarify the precise point where alien considerations are introduced. For there is, so far, nothing in the epistemological data which demands the "naturalization," i.e., the materialization, of knowledge. This becomes a task to be accomplished only because of a general assumption of the universal material character of "nature."

Let this stand then as a brief example of a reflection at two levels, with an effort to control theory by the test of *integral,* concrete experience.

I have been arguing that we need a presystematic reflection on the activity of knowing, as we find it, going on in our conscious awareness, which is the only place it exists. I have asked for a fresh look, with the excitement of discovering, a prolonged look, so as to see not only that something is there but that the something is *what* it is. I have asked that we not impose, in the very looking, any prior scheme—a Kantian, an

---

[25]André Lalande, "Reflections of a French Philosopher on the Preceding American Essays," *Philosophic Thought in France and in the United States,* Marvin Farber, ed. (Buffalo: University of Buffalo, 1950), 758–760.

[26]Sellars, "Critical Realism," 466.

Aristotelian, or a pragmatic theory, or what you will—but rather, that we free ourselves by a third-level metareflection from the control of theory and assumption. Yet, we should come to our fresh look like wondering children indeed, but with a mature and trained intelligence, ready to use, in freedom and creativity, all its knowledge resources. Remember the first 99 looks are safe; the last look may finally reveal what knowledge really is.

XVII

A PHILOSOPHER'S INTERPRETATION OF ANTHROPOLOGY'S CONTRIBUTION TO THE UNDERSTANDING OF MAN

New Introduction: A long discussion with Dr. Spitzer and his wife Lillian had given me an interest in anthropology both as a discipline and as a study of human nature. Allen persuaded the Philosophy Department of Saint Louis University to plan a conference in which we would confront philosophy and anthropology, in which we would interface philosophy and anthropology. Robert Redfield for whom I had developed a high regard was asked to give the initial paper. Subsequent papers would comment and develop that initial paper. Robert Redfield agreed to do this, but unfortunately he was never able to read the paper himself since he died before the conference began. But someone else read the paper and I commented on it and that com-ment is developed in the present article.[1]

* * *

My prescribed task here is to reflect for you and with you upon Robert Redfield's reflection upon his own and other anthropologists' contribution to the understanding of man. We must note at one that Redfield has placed his presentation within a certain conception of anthropology; a large part of his paper is devoted to delimiting the scope and method of anthropology. Well we have seen during the days

---

[1]First published in the *Anthropological Quarterly*, 32, no. 1 (January 1959): 22–40.

of this institute that anthropology does not admit of being reduced to a neat, universally accepted formula, of being cabined, cribbed, and confined in a standard definition. It is, therefore, very proper for Redfield to set the limits of discussion within the reach of a certain kind of anthropology. Granted that other anthropologists may approach their subject in other ways, may repudiate, in whole or in part, Redfield's conception; it is upon his conception that our reflection here bears.

Now I, as a philosopher, am in somewhat the same position. There is wide difference of opinion as to the nature and function of philosophy; even within that ample and ancient tradition from which I draw my own inspiration, within Thomism itself, there are marked differences of opinion on these same points. Indeed, it is no secret that there are Thomists who maintain that Robert Henle is no Thomist at all. It will, however, have to be my philosophy and my Thomism (granting certainly that my Thomism may be a "free-wheeling" sort) which serve me as instruments in this reflection.

Well then, it is understood that this will be a confrontation between Robert Henle's philosophy and Robert Redfield's anthropology.[2]

And so, what sort of anthropology is Robert Redfield talking about? Can we find any clues to a formal specification of what he describes as his anthropological approach? He tells us that his conclusions will be drawn from what he takes to be "central" in anthropological approaches, namely: "the study of entire cultures or societies," of the "total, traditionally organized life-ways of many a human group." The approach is to the "totality"; the unit of consideration is a "whole way of life." Redfield himself clearly stresses the study of "whole" societies; but there is something else implied here, necessarily involved and clearly shown in the works of anthropologists, something just as important as the notion of totality. The anthropologists (of the type, at least, described here by Redfield) study this totality in its *concrete complexity*. Abstraction, indeed, is not necessarily opposed to "totality"; there is a sense in which the abstractions of the social philosopher express the totality of the social order; but the philosopher does not deal with the concrete unity and complexity of society as does the anthropologist. Anthropology is not simply an understanding of total social structure;

---

[2]The reader should consult, as a valuable supplement to Redfield's present paper, his article of 1957.

nor is it a theoretical X-ray of society, such as one may find in sociological theory. Indeed, anthropology may develop such theories, or at least move toward them; it may also borrow its theories, models, techniques, and so forth from other disciplines, but these theories and methods are always deliberately brought back to and related to the "whole." As Redfield says, they are used and understood by anthropologists "under the control of the entire life of the groups." One may stand back, analyze into separate patterns and functions, look at the economics, gather statistics, give psychological tests; yet to meet Redfield's description, he must replace all this within the concrete whole.

In this connection, we have been here discussing the difference between a clinical and a statistical interpretation of, say, tests. I should like to suggest that as the clinical use of techniques broadens out the interpretative framework of tests, which may be statistically interpreted more narrowly, so the anthropological use broadens the clinical in to an "entire life" background.

Speaking philosophically but without pretending to sharp accuracy—I would say that the intellectual control of or with the entire group, in its wholeness *and* in its concrete real complexity, may be considered one of the formal specifies of anthropological understanding.

If this is so, Redfield's brief description of the sort of data gathered and employed by the anthropologists is wholly consonant and consistent. Redfield speaks of looking "out" at people. The anthropologist goes into a community and "looks"; he watches behavior; he hears what is said; he observes children at play, families at meals, men at work, men and women at prayer and engaged in social and religious ritual. The data is objective; it is "other." When Redfield comes to draw conclusions at the end, they will not be brought forth out of self-contemplation but from the collected and collated data of human societies through the world. Yet there is a qualification on this objectivity.

For, true though it is that the conclusions do not come from self-knowledge, nonetheless they cannot be reached without introspective knowledge and without using one's self as an instrument for interpretation and understanding. The anthropologist uses his own humanity and his experience of his own humanity as instruments for the understanding of the concrete behavior which he observes. This I think is a precious and important observation. It would be well to pause and reflect upon it. Here is the anthropologist going into a community and observing what is going on. He watches a burial and sees a widow weeping and wailing beside the open grave. This overt behavior is, in itself, ambiguous. It may well be that she is happy to be rid of the old gentleman, but she can't precisely show this at the grave, before friends and relatives. She may, then, be simply observing the cultural rules of behavior rather than expressing "tragic emotions." Now, even the realization that the situation is ambiguous presupposes some knowledge of ourselves as human beings. If the anthropologist had no self-knowledge whatever, he would be unable to understand and interpret this situation. The anthropologists must use an imaginative projection, a sympathy, what is often called "empathy." This empathy is possible only where there is some community of internal experience. There is, to a very limited extent, however, some sympathy between us and our animals. The dog wags his tail; we have some idea that he is glad to see us—but just what his experience of gladness is like we hardly can imagine. The little boy can have a certain "empathy" for his dog when it has been frightened. But what of the feeling of the setting hen; she just "likes" to set on the egg—but what sort of inner experience does she have? Her inner life is pretty much a closed book to us. And so would the lives of other persons and peoples be, had we no community of inner experience, no common humanity such that, through our own humanity, we could make an imaginative projection and thereby interpret the behavior of others. We need common experience, disciplined imagination, and out-going feeling in order to "look" as Redfield's anthropologist "looks." This is the qualification Redfield places on the objectivity of the "data"—I do not however believe that this qualification necessarily destroys the objectivity or substitutes for it a vague and romantic subjectivism. I shall leave this point rest here for the moment; I shall return to it later.

Now I should like to say that in my view of the matter, the anthropological discipline described by Redfield is an empirical discipline, and I want to make quite clear what I understand by "empirical." In this whole area of epistemology, terminology has gotten so mixed up: words, originally perfectly sound and useful, have acquired so many historical connotations that it is extremely difficult to find words expressive enough to say what you want to say and neutral enough not to betray you or mislead your hearers.

"Empirical," is, philosophically, a perfectly fine word which simply relates to experience in a broad and indeterminate way. It has, however, come to have a more limited meaning and several different connotations; it becomes necessary, therefore, to find another word to convey the broader meaning. Experimental might have done very well—but it, in its time, has been narrowed down to the notion of "experiment" as found in the physical sciences. I have been forced to employ another word to express the fundamental and universal relationship of knowledge of the real to experience. The word I usually use is "experiential." By calling a piece of knowledge "experiential" I simply mean that it is derived from experience, ultimately from a cognitional contact between the knower and some reality. The term thus excludes theories of *a priori* knowledge. The little child when he comes to school or, at least, when he starts out as a baby, isn't really packed tight with ideas, definitions, insights. It isn't our job as teachers, somehow, simply to open him up and pull out the ideas as though he were a well-packed little valise. "Experiential," as I use it, therefore, means that knowledge depends upon a first-hand contact between the knower and some object of knowledge.

Now, then, I wish to maintain that sociology (by any of its definitions), anthropology, and philosophy (as I understand and profess it) are all experiential disciplines. But I wish to add, that anthropology, as described by Redfield, is empirical whereas philosophy is not. What then do I mean here by empirical? I am using the term to differentiate disciplines according to the evidential basis for their generalized judgments.

In dealing with any judgment there are at least two questions which we can ask. First—What does it mean? "Meaning" is today a high-disputed and rather confused matter, but let us here be content to use a very simple everyday sort of "meaning" for "meaning." If we say—"He is angry"—well, what does this mean? I surely have to understand what it means to be angry; ultimately, I have to reach some experience from which I derive an understanding of "anger." (We may be very peaceful sort of people, yet we have enough emotion and enough of the beginnings of anger, to know what it is.) It is this sort of experiential source that enables us to understand what is meant by Redfield's generalizations. When, for example, he talks of a dimension of morality in every society—not that some precisely defined moral act is everywhere to the same degree praised or blamed—but that there be some kind of "ought" recognized in every culture, we have to understand what is meant by this "oughtness." This we do, at least ultimately and in its basic meaning, from our own experience; were we ourselves moral imbeciles, with no notion, no experience, no inference even of what "ought" is, Redfield's statement would be gibberish to us. The aspect of meaning—as aspect of any judgment or proposition—is the first question we can ask about any judgment; this question, though presupposed, does not however determine whether or not the proposition is empirical.

For this, we turn to the second question—Is the proposition *right*? I may well know what it means to say "He is angry" or "The view of things of every people includes rightness and 'oughtness'" and still ask—*But is it so?* If it is so, then upon what sort of evidence does your knowledge of *its being so* rest? Well, what is the evidence Redfield gives for the generalizations he proposes? It is simply that every society examined by the anthropologist displays this dimension; he speaks of "every people," the "people of all such groups." The evidence is simply that every society, when examined, does, as a plain matter of fact, display a moral awareness. The generalization refers to such facts and logically is as good as the given range of facts. These propositions are, therefore, experiential and empirical. I am not saying this with the intention of either devaluating or inflating them. I am merely trying to identify the sort of knowledge we have here.

To resume and extend the specification of Redfield's anthropology as it is being revealed by our reflective analysis, we can now say that it is a discipline which studies human societies in their wholeness and in their concrete complexity, using objective data but employing as an instrument of interpretation and understanding the anthropologist's own humanity and knowledge of that humanity; a discipline, finally, which arrives at generalizations by an empirical collation of fact.

We can now turn to another qualifying remark. There is a paragraph in which Robert Redfield points to what he considers a limitation on the common practice of anthropologists. He explains that usually the anthropologist does not explore the sort of thing that Freudians and depth psychologists look to, that the darker inner impulses of human life are not plumbed. I am not prepared to agree without qualification that this makes the anthropologist's work more "superficial." Let this go, however, for I am more interested in Redfield's next remark. He says that some anthropologists have been concerned with these matters, "but, if so, their language and ideas have not been developed from their own comparative study of societies and cultures . . . they (the deeper depths) are reported *in terms borrowed from the depth psychologist himself.*"

As I understand this paragraph, Redfield is setting up a distinction between what I shall, hereafter, call a "pure" anthropology and a sort of hybrid discipline. The kind of anthropology Redfield describes and practices does indeed develop its ideas from a study of cultures and societies.

Now there are a number of ways in which borrowing can take place. It is possible to borrow from other disciplines things which may be used as clues or techniques or sheer fact-finding instruments. Thus the anthropologist can use psychological tests or sampling techniques; but if these are always kept in subservience to a consideration of the totality and the concreteness of a society, they need not dilute the discipline itself.[3]

There are no doubt problems and dangers in this sort of borrowing, but, in the large view, it leaves the integrity of the discipline untouched.

The situation is quite different when theories, concepts, principles are taken over from other disciplines and incorporated in the guiding hypotheses, theories or explanations of a discipline. The result here is not a mere juxtaposition or addition but a blending such that the discipline taken as a whole is formally different throughout. One cannot distinguish at any one point what is derived from the borrowed element and what has come up from the discipline itself. This I will call a hybrid sort of discipline.

Such a discipline presents a series of problems. The hybrid discipline becomes as viable as the borrowed theory; if the latter is erroneous and mistaken, unbalanced and partial or only incomplete and changing, the hybrid discipline runs the risk of having for *constitutive* principles errors and half-truths. It is difficult to keep reconstructing a discipline in the light of developments in other fields. Moreover, there is always the personal difficulty; an anthropologist will ordinarily not be trained in philosophy or psychiatry to the point of competent criticism; he is liable then to be the victim of the field from which he is borrowing. He may not have a satisfactory understanding of the borrowed theories or his knowledge of them may be outdated or drawn

---

[3]When the historian uses the disintegration of certain chemical elements to subserve his establishment of chronology, he does not thereby make his history a "physico-history."

from too partial a set of sources.[4] Such workers often are using an older, outmoded version of the discipline from which they are borrowing.

I am happy to find Redfield favoring the "pure" type of anthropology. If anthropology has any sound, independent sources of data and of generalization, it will build much more firmly and profitably by working up from its own *given,* even though it may never reach the neat, closed-in perfection of systematic synthesis.[5]

We are now ready to look at Redfield's attempt to determine the nature of anthropology by relating it to "science" on the one hand and to "humanistic learning" on the other. Here is his basic statement: "We are, then, scientists, as is the biologist (1) in our assumption that there is a real world out there accessible to our observation, (2) in our reliance upon observation and inferences guided by reason and observation for our conclusions, (3) in our attempts to be objective and critical of our formulations, (4) in our responsibility both to the facts and inferences we alone have made and stand witness for, and (5) also to the correcting judgment, over time, of the scientific community," Redfield concludes

---

[4]Zirkle's remarks (1955) on "sociological biology" are here pertinent: "Biology is found in the elementary textbooks on sociology . . . It is not the biology of the biologists, however . . . it can be described only as sociological biology . . . it is a law unto itself."

[5]Leonard Bloomfield (1933) cites his own earlier presentation of the science of language as an excellent example: "In 1914 I based this phase of the exposition on the psychologic system of Wilhelm Wundt, which was then widely accepted. Since that time there has been much upheaval in psychology; we have learned, at any rate, what one of our masters suspected thirty years ago, namely, that we can pursue the study of language without reference to any one psychological doctrine, and that to do so safeguards our results and makes them more significant to workers in related fields. In the present book I have tried to avoid such dependence; only by way of elucidation I have told, at a few points, how the two main present-day trends of psychology differ in their interpretation. The mentalists would supplement the facts of language by a version in terms of mind,—a version which will differ in the various schools of mentalistic psychology. The mechanists demand that the facts be presented without any assumption of such auxiliary factors. I have tried to meet this demand not merely because I believe that mechanism is the necessary form of scientific discourse, but also because an exposition which stands on its own feet is more solid and more easily surveyed than one which is propped at various points by another and changeable doctrine."

There is a partial analogy here to the Aristotelian and Medieval theory of the *scientia media,* a science which borrows its formal principles from another science and, in and through them, organizes its own matter.

For a modern explanation, see Maritain (1946:83–89).

that anthropology is, therefore, a "science"; yet, he at once qualifies his conclusion, ". . . a science *with close connections with humanistic learning.*"

First, I must remark on the confusion surrounding the word "science." There is a traditional sense for this word—*επιστημη, scientia,* science which was established for us in the *Posterior Analytics* of Aristotle and was there presented both as problem and as a theoretical description. The ideal description of science laid down by Aristotle was broader than the usual modern description.[6] The thirteenth century Scholastic thinkers saw a way to bring even theology—or, at least, a certain type of theology—under the Aristotelian definition. This widely diffused meaning (science$_1$) has been counterbalanced by the emergence of a new type of knowledge, originally called "philosophia" (as in Newton's *Principia mathematica philosophiae naturalis*) but now known as science. The situation, however, is still more complex. "Science" and "scientific method" may be used in a very restricted sense to apply typically to the physical and biological sciences (science$_2$), extension of these terms to sociology, etc., being allowable only through assimilation to the former disciplines. Or again—a broad general notion of science (science$_3$) as "objective," "based on fact," etc., is current where an *ideal* of knowledge rather than a formal description of a *kind* of knowledge is in the forefront of consideration. Now, these last two uses of the term "science" are frequently identified, either consciously and deliberately, by the adoption of an epistemological theory which allows no other respectable intellectual method except that of the physical sciences; or unconsciously, through the influence of our ambient culture, a culture in which "science" has achieved such overwhelming prestige.

Now Redfield is here attempting to "place" anthropology as a discipline by using "science" and "humanistic learning" as the two coordinates. I submit that in so doing he falls into the confusion of identifying science$_2$ and science$_3$, though his description of "science?" is rather of "science$_3$" than of "science$_2$." Let us then return to his sentence.

The first characteristic he refers to is, I submit, not at all requisite for science$_2$ or science$_3$. Of course, I accept the reality—the "real"

---

[6]See Maurer (1953: vii–xxxvi).

reality if you will—of a world "out there," but a physicist, as such, need not do so in order to maintain and develop physics. A philosopher?—yes. A man, *as a man?*—yes!—but a chemist, a geologist—no. The point has been made dramatically. Consider two geologists—one who is also a Thomist and a philosophical realist, the other who is an idealist after the manner of Berkeley. They undertake, as geologists, to study the same mountain in Africa. They collect essentially the same sort of equipment, take the same boat, use the same sort of pick, study the same rocks, outcroppings, formations, and make the same sort of report to the Smithsonian Institution; in fact, simply confirm each other's findings. It doesn't make a particle of difference to them as geologists whether this mountain is, as the Thomist thinks, up there and stays there when he goes home or whether it is a complicated kind of picture-play which God puts on in our minds. Well then, science, I think, is self-contained enough and existentially abstract enough to proceed without even raising this sort of question.

With regard to the rest of Redfield's characteristics (2–5 in my numeration), I submit that these are descriptive of scienc$_3$ and are not restrictive. For these are simply characteristics of honest and capable intellectual work and do not, for example, differentiate essentially the work of the medieval scholastic thinkers from that of Galileo and Newton. There is a sense, as I shall point out later, in which "humanistic learning" as well must display these same qualities.

If then "science" is taken to be "science$_3$," it is too broad to describe a given discipline. If now "science" be taken as "science$_2$," I would argue that the use of two coordinates is inaccurate and inadequate. We are here brought back to the discussion of Dr. Lang's paper. Modern culture, I would argue, displays three, not two, basic intellectual attitudes in the elaboration of natural rational knowledge, the scientific (science$_2$), the philosophical, the humanistic. Although Redfield does hedge about his assertion that anthropology is a "science," I think he has succumbed at least a bit to the "scientism" which is a cultural determinant in our modern Western tradition.

Let us for a moment consider the humanistic qualification advanced by Redfield. He says that anthropological reporting is not wholly unlike that of a novel or a biography. I agree that this is a characteristic of both anthropological reporting and interpretation, and, moreover, I would argue that, if anthropology is to be the sort of discipline we have found Redfield describing, this approach is formally essential to it. If the anthropological way of working is to lead to an understanding of human beings in concrete cultural contexts, the humanistic mode of understanding must be part of its approach. I suspect many people would feel that it derogates from the position of anthropology as a discipline, at least as a *respectable discipline,* to say that it is much more like a novel than like a theorem in Euclid's Geometry or in gross mechanics. Don't we thereby deliver anthropology over to romanticism and subjectivism?

The criticism must be met, though I think it arises from a very narrow conception of intellectual "disciplines" (from, in short, the "scientistic" conception) and from a consequently very narrow conception of testability and validation. One thing surely that the newer phenomenological approaches and existentialism are showing us is that there is a *subjectivism* which is not *subjectivistic.* Certainly, in the humanistic methodology one cannot achieve the cold, calculated "objectivity" of mechanics. Though there is talk of the observer's getting into the observations even in physics, we can nonetheless get a pretty objective kind of situation when we are clocking billiard balls down an inclined plane or measuring the rise of mercury in Torricelli's experiment. Obviously love in an Indian village and prayer among the Yamana of Tierra del Fuego could not be reported or understood in so impersonal and "objective" a fashion. Here once again the observer must use his own humanity as an instrument, a formal methodological instrument, his own inner, "subjective" experience as a guide to interpretation. But even so, this is subject to the check of other observations, inferences, and the criticism of scholars: it is not "romantic"; it is subject to criticism and control and has its own sort of validity, as do dramas, novels and poems. A great novel portrays, indeed, a fictional set of characters and situations; but these must be authentically human. As the anthropologist displays and interprets a particular form of human living, so the novelist, if he is sound, portrays a possible form of human activity. The novels that are authentic literature, that endure through the changing tastes and probing criticism of succeeding generations possess their own validity as insightful interpretations of human life. We cannot write a novel about the billiard ball that refused to take part in the experiment. "I won't go down," said he, at the top of the incline. We can't write a novel about animals without making humans of them; in all the folk tales the animals are more human, one might say, than the people.

There is, then, a disciplined and responsible way to work within the humanistic mode. I should like to suggest here that the anthropology which Robert Redfield is trying to describe is found to display a methodology that is not simply "scientific" with "leanings toward humanistic learning." I repeat, I think Redfield is here handicapped by using an inadequate, culturally determined epistemology. Anthropology may turn out to be a distinct disciplined type of humanistic knowledge with its own proper materials and methods, controls, and theories.[7] In any case, Redfield is describing a kind of anthropology which is "pure" in the sense that it is not structured and controlled by borrowed theory, which is not scientific in any narrow restrictive meaning of the term, and which is intrinsically humanistic in general character. Frankly, I am most sympathetic with this conception of anthropology.

At this point I must digress a bit and deal in a deceptively brief fashion with some very difficult topics drawn from epistemology.[8] I have asserted above that at least three basic models of knowing must be taken into account, the scientific, the philosophical and the humanistic. At this point I wish to draw a difference between the scientific and the philosophical modes by distinguishing their respective types of conceptualization. Let us take "concept" to mean the intellectual grasp and "mental" expression of some meaning or understanding. When I understand the word "angry" or "house" or "triangle," I am grasping the meaning of the word; yet this meaning is not something about the word itself or about my mental operations, it is about something else, something in reality or at least something different from the word and the act of understanding "anger" as it can be found in human beings, a "house" as a real dwelling place for man, a "triangle" as a certain precise object of mathematical thought.

All such conceptualizations are derived ultimately from experience! The child grasps things experienced, their manifest qualities and operations; he learns to ask for water, for milk, for candy, for play; and

---

[7]There is an interesting similarity here to the epistemological status of Freudian psychology and psychoanalysis. Scientific-minded people have brutally criticized these approaches as lacking "scientific" form. It may well be that both in psychoanalytic theory and in anthropology we have emerging forms of a new type of intellectual discipline which, in its turn, will correct, limit and complete the predominantly scientific$_2$ thinking of our recent past. For stimulating suggestions on these points see Stern (1954:149–177).

[8]For the general theory of the disciplines here presupposed see Klubertanz (1955:89–104); Henle (1956:4–6); Maritain (1946:266–484).

though he is interested in the things, he holds them in concepts. The store of concepts thus built up to make things manageable and ordinary life livable is not such as to constitute a "discipline." Somehow, concepts must be elaborated, refined, developed. Now we find, if we examine our conceptualizations reflectively, that our concepts move towards a pure intellectual state in two different ways. The concept may retain and express simply and only an intelligible grasp—however intricate or refined—of the *nature* of some real kind of thing or situation or operation and so forth. A simple, unrefined example would be the child's grasp of the kinds of "shapes" displayed by the blocks with which he plays.[9] When the child uses the word "round," he is expressing only the quality of the block itself, the very kind of shape which it actually has. There is a direct *nature* relationship between the quality understood and the quality existent.

This sort of concept I call "ontological."

Now as we elaborate concepts to deal with things or situations where we are unable, either at first inspection or after long investigation and reflection, to grasp the *objectively given nature* we come to use substitutes for that nature, short-hand symbols for the complexities of the real, ingeniously devised schemata, models, and so forth to hold the real under control. Thus the concept of an "index of living cost" is an intelligible concept which does not express an intelligibility that as such can be found or made outside of my knowledge. Many factual elements have contributed to it; but it is formally constituted by a selected and devised manipulation. (Thus the concept of "ether" in nineteenth century physics, of the "censor" in Freudian psychology, or the "field of force" in modern physics, etc.) Such concepts I call constructural.

Now an organized discipline requires not just a set of concepts but a system of concepts, and a given system must display a homogeneity of conceptual mode within its main organizing concepts. A discipline, therefore, must be constituted largely by one or the other type of

---

[9]These are not the "shapes" nor the concepts of shapes with which the geometer works. Euclidean geometry has become so diffused in our thinking that we find it hard to realize that there is any other way besides a geometrical way of thinking "shapes." I am talking in the text about a direct and primitive apprehension of shapes as qualitatively different qualifications of real objects. I use the example of the child because *he* has not yet either been (1) confused by geometry, or (2) turned into an unconsciously universal geometrizer.

concept. I am maintaining that philosophy proceeds by using onto-logical concepts while science₂ is characterized by using constructural concepts.

However, I will assert, too, that the humanistic mode also is very largely concerned with ontological conceptualization, but differs from philosophy in that the conceptualization of humanistic learning is viewed always in relation to the concrete, the individual, the complex given, the unanalyzed totality and includes accidental, partial, or simply "given" relationships; whereas philosophy moves away from the con-crete and the individual, shucks off the accidental, and retains only the intelligibly and necessarily interrelated.

Let me take an example which will also bring us back to our main theme. The traditional definition of man—rational animal—is a philo-sophical definition. It is experiential indeed because its basic intelligible elements as well as its basic validation have been drawn from experience. But the philosopher retains in his understanding only what displays itself as essential to man as an intelligible nature; as he develops his philosophy of man only those connections are retained as intrinsic to the discipline which are seen to be intrinsically or essentially involved with this nature. Thus the Thomist finds human freedom or self-determination intrinsically related—not by a mere logical involve-ment or implication but by an involvement in reality grasped intel-ligibly—to the nature of man as rational. There may be—indeed there are—many different concrete forms that freedom and self-determination may assume under different cultural conditions—but to these philos-ophy pays little heed; it goes to the essential *nature* relationship and accepts this relationship not as resting on an *exhaustive* canvass of fact but on the *intelligible natures discerned and discovered in these facts*. This further clarifies also what I meant when I called anthropology experiential and empirical but philosophy experiential and non-em-pirical. The generalizations about man offered by Redfield do depend for acceptance upon a more or less exhaustive canvass of facts.

This brief analysis of types of concepts gives a sharp distinction between science₂ on the one hand and both philosophy and humanistic learning on the other—while the analysis of typical context and typical content of philosophical concepts begins at least to draw a difference between philosophy and anthropology.

Now I wish to make one further distinction in our understanding through concepts. We can say that there are two different ways in which conceptual understanding can grow. The first is by simply adding factors or notes or intelligibilities to the concept. What is a purple people eater? It has one eye—yes—one horn—yes—and it eats purple people. Well, that's what it is—and my understanding of it is just the addition of these descriptive bits. It is in some fashion that the zoologists describe and classify animals. Does it have a backbone or not? Does it have three sets of legs or not?

Definitions here explain and expand themselves by *addition*.

But there is another way of developing understanding. This is by deepening our insight into any given intelligibility. If we take something like human love or anger or desire, we can lay out a definition which even a college student can understand and to which nothing really needs to be added or can be added except depth of insight. The difference between the insight into love of the fifth grade kid, of the teenager, of the mature man and woman, of the Saint illustrates the possible levels of such understanding. This sort of deepening is the experience of philosophers, of artists, and of humanists.

Now it seems to me that the kind of anthropology which Redfield proposes precisely involves this sort of deepening understanding of man and of the "common human." As a philosopher I am confident that I understand the essential traits of what is "human." When Redfield tells me that everywhere man finds some significant order in the universe, I can quite understand why this is so and why it attaches so universally to human cultures—and this, though Redfield proposes that proposition as empirical while I would defend my position on quite other grounds. And so too when he concludes empirically to a common moral dimension, in fact also—so it seems to me—to a common metaphysical bent (or, as the judge's wife said in *You Shall Know Them,* to a universal occurrence of a juju[10]), I find these but completions of philosophical

---

[10](Sir Arthur's wife is speaking.) "I am not pulling your leg," she said. "Everybody has the *ju-jus* suitable to his age, I think. . . ." "You do need *ju-jus*, don't you, once you believe in something? . . . Even those bright people, I mean, who pretend they don't believe in anything, we see them seeking for something, don't we? They study . . . physics or . . . astronomy, or else write books: these are their *ju-jus* of a sort. . . ." "But if people really don't believe in anything," she said, ". . . if they have no *ju-jus* at all . . . then they have never asked themselves any questions, have they? . . . ."

(And later in court the judge, Sir Arthur, is asking—)

"But they (the animals) do not have *ju-jus*?" asked the judge.

"No."

knowledge. But when we turn to the full content and insight which the anthropologist brings to these conclusions from his experience, personal and vicarious, of widely differing cultures scattered across the globe and up and down the centuries, we will find, I think, whole new dimension of understanding. In a sense, the philosophical definition of man lays down in principle the potentialities of human development; the philosopher cannot predict or deduce the historical forms and cultural actualizations of human potentialities and so forth; his understanding lacks content, for potentialities known only in general principles are not truly understood; it is the concrete, definite actualization that gives genuine insight into potentiality. I do not mean to say that the philosopher knows only a potential human nature; I do mean to say that he knows the *particularized* potentialities of man only in principle. He cannot, therefore, establish the development of historic man, the contractions and expansions (to use Redfield's phrase) of human nature through the varied circumstances of rain-forest and arctic waste, of nomadic and city life, of devolution and revolution and so forth.

Redfield expresses this well:

> In effect I am saying that man is one kind of being while also this one kind is modified, developed or emphasized in particular groups into many different kinds of being. I am also saying that the one kind of being he is while being also many kinds is a being composed of sentiments, desires and mental dispositions that animals do not have and that provide a basis, in some part of this nebulous whole, for any people to feel akin to any other.

If I may now try to sum up this point: The philosopher, indeed, grasps the essential nature of man (in the intelligibility of that "one kind of being he is") and deepens this, indeed, in principle and through insight into the essential ("per se") inter-relationships of man's various traits—self-determination, rationality, morality etc. The anthropologist, indeed, comes by an empirical road, by a way of humanistic insight to a rather more nebulous and ill-defined realization of the comm-

---

"... They haven't asked the same questions."

"That is true," said Sir Peter. "The metaphysical mind is peculiar to man. The animal doesn't have it." Vecors (1953:163–164, 171).

human—but brings to this the *deepening* of his understanding of the "human" by seeing its "forms," the "human examples characteristically studied by anthropologists." The philosopher may be able to say, for example, that "art is the signature of man," but he has no way of deducing the forms and fashions which have *been* human art in fact; nor has he any way of incorporating the resulting insight formally into his philosophy. But to understand human art thus richly and fully and so also the men who have created it—the cave dwellers of Lascaux and Font do Gaume, the Greek vase painters, the craftsmen of the African figurines, the classic painters of China, and today's abstractionists—this is to understand man as artist: man indeed, and yet, a myriad of men, human even in their very differences; and this is the understanding of man as artist to which the anthropologist comes.

It seems to me then that the sort of anthropology described by Redfield comes to two different sorts of understanding. There is the rather obvious procedure of looking for what recurs, of crossing off the differences until one arrives at a set of empirical generalizations that rest on a check list of known cultures. In this way one comes empirically to some traits of the "common human." There is the deepening of understanding of the "human." There is the deepening of understanding of the "human" that comes simply from the kind of experience which is characteristic of the anthropologist, a reflective penetration of the concrete, the particular, the different which finds humanity not as a mere common *residue* but as *present* in and understandable in all its varieties of contraction and expansion, of concrete actualization.

I would wish to stress this point. Perhaps anthropology's greatest contribution to the understanding of man is not its derivation of impersonal generalizations about man but its grasp of cultures as totally and concretely and particularly *human*. Man is revealed in his every act, his every creation; even his sins display both his grandeur and his misery, for the sinfulness of mankind is revelation of both man's goodness and man's degradation. Sin is possible only to man. Animals cannot sin; man alone is capable of tragic moral mistakes. These mistakes themselves reveal, therefore, the moral dimension of man, the depths and potentialities of man.[11]

Now I wish to return one last time to the nature of anthropology. I think that anthropology can make this sort of sound and independent contribution to the understanding of man to the extent that it remains at least in its basic structure the kind of intellectual discipline Redfield describes. It must, therefore, resist the constant pressure of our culture towards gaining respectability by becoming more and more scientific (i.e., "science₂"); it must also resist the temptation to *borrow*, as a structural principle or an organizing theory, a theory of man whether from Freud or theology or sociology or philosophy. Let anthropology, in its basic structure remain "pure," "humanistic," and therefore independent. It will then be able to *use* the instruments and theories of other disciplines and to cooperate with and contribute to them.

Moreover, as an educator—and since this is also an educational institute—I would like to suggest that anthropology may well be the most promising of the modern disciplines for general education. I regret the passing of the classics ass a central instrument of mature education. But perhaps some of what we got from a profound classical education, from the great classical culture and literature, can be given students in this sort of humanistic anthropology. This anthropology might, indeed, be center and focus of an education, within the framework of modern disciplines and modern life, which would at once achieve much of the results of classical education while pulling together and balancing the social sciences, the older humanities, philosophy, history, and even science₂ itself.

It is not therefore without significance that so many competent cultural anthropologists have come from classical backgrounds. Indeed, we come again to the basic point. The anthropologist, in his method, must use his own humanity as an instrument to understand the people and culture he studies; if *his* humanity is a poor and underdeveloped

---

[11]What have I said in these last few paragraphs may well be taken also as a comment on Redfield's remark (1957:151). "These two contradictory aspects of human nature— hat men in every tribe or nation are all very much alike and that the differences among peoples are great and perhaps limitless—come to men at different times, for different reasons, and with varying emphasis on the one or the other. The prevailing emphasis depends in part, I think, on one's philosophical position. The man of positivist inclinations is more likely to stress the differences; *the Thomist, among others, the resemblances, the common human*" [italics mine].

thing—a "contracted" sort of human nature—the anthropological method in his usage will be feeble and fallible indeed.

I regret, indeed, that Robert Redfield is not here with us. We, who have read and discussed his works here, have come to a deep respect for him and his work. For we do find in his works a full and rich humanity, a warm sympathy and understanding for man, a hunger—though humbly and without contempt—for goodness. These are the personal traits, I think, which have made Robert Redfield's humanistic anthropology so powerful an instrument for the understanding of man and his interpretations so authentically human and so continuous with the deepest and best traditions of Western culture.

REFERENCES CITED

Bloomfield, Leonard. *Language*. New York, 1933.
Henle, R.J., S.J. "A Thomistic Explanation of the Relations Between Science and Philosophy." *Bulletin of the Albertus Magnus Guild* 111 (1956): 4–6.
Klubertanz, George P., S.J. "The Doctrine of St. Thomas and Modern Science." In *Sapientia Aquinatis,* 89–104. Rome, 1955.
Maritain, J. *Les dégrés du savoir,* 5th ed. Paris, 1946.
Maurer, Armand, C.S.B. *The Division and Methods of the Sciences*. Toronto: Pontifical Institute of Mediaeval Studies, 1953.
Redfield, R. "The Universally Human and the Culturally Variable." *Journal of General Education* 10 (1957): 150–160.
Stern, Karl. *The Third Revolution*. New York, 1954.
Vecors. *You Shall Know Them*. New York, 1953.
Zirkel, Conway. "Our Splintered Learning and the Status of Scientists." *Science* 121 (1955): 517.

XVIII

LEVELS OF NATURAL LAW

N ew Introduction: Some years ago Elizabeth Black, then a member of the Department of Philosophy at Pace University, started a small bulletin devoted to the Natural Law which she called *Vera Lex*. From the very beginning I was interested in this initiative of hers and encouraged her to continue. When I decided that the exposition of the development of natural law with a recognition of the different plateaus in the development would be valuable for the understanding of Natural Law, I decided to submit it to *Vera Lex*.[1] I thought that an analysis of Natural Law development would clarify the natural law itself and would give us an outline for the development of natural law as well as a guide for analyzing different systems of natural law. I still think that that is true and I believe that some of the confusion in the discussion of natural law is due to a failure to recognize the different levels of development in the natural law.

* * *

1. Introduction

John Finnis points out an important distinction often overlooked in discussions of Natural Law. He says,

> My present purpose . . . is not to anticipate later chapters, but to make some preliminary clarifications. A first essential dis-

---

[1]First published in *Vera Lex*, 11, no. 2 (1991): 1–5.

tinction is that between a theory, doctrine, or account and the subject matter of that theory, doctrine, or account.[2]

The distinction is between Natural Law theory and Natural Law as a fact. Natural Law as a fact is the subject matter of Natural Law theory.

Any normal human being, come to the use of reason and having a minimum experience of life, knows implicitly, i.e., without abstract formulation, the basic principles of Natural Law. These principles can be discerned in the decision-making and the actions of the members of even the most primitive societies, no matter how much they may be distorted or misapplied or mixed with superstition and evil customs. Hence, St. Thomas Aquinas maintains that the abstract principles of Natural Law cannot be totally abolished from the human mind,[3] though the less general principles can be distorted in actual decision making by passion, vices, and evil customs.[4] St. Thomas cites the report of Julius Caesar that among the Germans theft was not considered wrong.

Finnis maintains that Natural Law as a fact has no history while Natural Law theories and doctrines do have a history. Theories arise and disappear, but Natural Law as a fact does not.[5] This seems not to be altogether true. We can trace in different societies varying degrees in which Natural Law as a fact is embodied in the actual positive morality of those societies. Nonetheless, the basic distinction holds. Natural Law is a pervasive fact of human culture.

Because Natural Law is a universal fact in human society, we indeed do find basic moral similarities in widely divergent cultures. Early anthropologists were struck by the wide diversity of customs in the (to us) exotic cultures of the world. They therefore tended to accept a simple moral relativism. More careful observation and understanding have led to a greater recognition of the distinctive humanness in each culture. Thus, the philosopher-anthropologist David Bidney noted,

> I suspect that on the whole, there are more concrete similari-
> ties and identities in the cultural values of different societies

---

[2]*Natural Law and Natural Rights* (Oxford: The Clarendon Press, 1989), 24.

[3]*Summa Theologiae,* I–II, q. 94, a. 6.

[4]*Ibid.*

[5]*Loc. cit.*

than the cultural relativist has so far explicitly recognized. Otherwise, even the degree of cooperation in world affairs which mankind has so far attained would not have been possible.[6]

Working out from the distinction advanced by Finnis, I now propose to examine Natural Law according to a new pattern of analysis. This pattern consists of examining Natural Law at Four Levels. Perhaps this mode of analysis will clarify or partially solve some of the problems usually raised in discussions of Natural Law. The Four Levels are:

    a. Natural Law as a universal fact;
    b. Initial foundations of Natural Law values and principles;
    c. The development of a Natural Law doctrine as an ethical system;
    d. The integration of Natural Law ethics into a comprehensive, philosophical, and/or theological synthesis.

We can use this pattern in various ways. We can judge the stages of development of various societies. Thus, we can say that the Pygmies of the African rainforest are at the First Level. Many other tribes might be classified as being at the Second Level.

We can also distinguish the Four Levels all present simultaneously in a fully developed culture. Progress towards the Fourth Level does not eliminate the previous levels. Natural Law remains a fact in all societies.

2. The First Level: The Fact of Natural Law

a. *The Universal Recognition of Moral Obligation*

Moral obligation means the obligation to do an act simply because it is good or to avoid doing something simply because it is evil. The morally good is that which a human being as such should desire or choose; moral evil is that which a human being should rightly reject.

Every language has words like "ought," "should," "must." In many cases these words express an instrumental necessity. Thus, "You have

---

[6]David Bidney, "The Concept of Value in Modern Anthropology," in *Anthropology Today*, ed. A. L. Kroeber (Chicago: University of Chicago Press, 1953), 694. See also Robert Redfield, "The Universality Human and the Culturally Variable," *Journal of General Education*, 10, 150–160.

a high temperature; you ought to see a doctor." "Don't swim there; it's full of alligators." "If you want to go to medical school you should do a pre-med program and get good grades." But people also use these words to express an obligation that is not instrumental, not merely expedient or pleasurable.

The point is that in every society this *type of obligation* is recognized as arising from the human rightness or wrongness of certain acts. A tribal council in pre-colonial Africa upbraids a man for treating his nephew in a way *an uncle should not treat a nephew*. An Indian Chief decides that it is *wrong* to sacrifice a *maiden* to the god of the harvest. An American mother tells her son that *he* should not hit his little *brother*. Example after example can be found.

At this point of the discussion it is only the type of obligation, not the act to which it is applied, that is relevant.

As a matter of fact, this type of obligation is sometimes applied to acts that do not rightly fall under such an obligation. But even this still bears witness to the existence of a universal acceptance of such an obligation. It is the task of the Third Level to eliminate such deviant cases.

The distinguished anthropologist Robert Redfield summarizes the situation thus:

> Everywhere there are recognized obligations commitments, sentiments and judgments of what is good and what is bad. . .
> If we let "morality" stand for all such judgments and commitments as to what it is felt right or wrong to do, not because it is merely prudential or expedient but because it is in itself right and obligatory, then morality is universal.[7]

Positivists attempt to explain this moral obligation as simply due to social pressure in the particular society.[8] Certainly social pressure does exist and does demand adherence to a code of morality. But to state this fact as though it were an explanation is simply a sophism. The social pressure arises from the conviction of a given society that certain acts or attitudes are simply wrong in relation to human beings. There is

---

[7]Robert Redfield, "Anthropology's Contribution to the Understanding of Man," *Anthropological Quarterly,* 32, no. 1 (January 1959): 16.

[8]*The Concept of Law* (Oxford: The Clarendon Press, 1961), 165–176.

social pressure against child abuse because people find it simply wrong to mistreat a child.

At this First Level moral obligation is not reflected on or formulated in abstract terms. It is implicit in prudential decisions touching human beings in everyday life.

In the Second Level proverbs and maxims express moral obligation concretely and in non-technical terms.

At the Third Level the principle is expressed as, "The good is to be done, evil avoided." St. Thomas thus formulates the first principle of the Natural Law.[9]

b. *Substantive Natural Law as a Universal Fact*

i   Introduction

In the previous section I argued that the recognition of moral obligation, in the sense there explained, is a universal fact of human life. I did this, however, without referring to substantive moral good or any specific moral precept. In fact, as I there point out, even where, through some mistake due to ignorance, passion or prejudice, an evil act is brought under moral obligation, this fact still bears witness to the universal recognition of moral obligation as such.

In this section I point out that substantive precepts of the Natural Law are also universally recognized in concrete cases at this First Level. As a matter of fact, whenever human beings make judgments about the morally good or the morally bad, Natural Law comes into play. Such moral judgments are both the product of and the guide for practical reason. It is not surprising then to find that the substantive Natural Law is, to some extent, universally recognized in all human societies.

ii   Justice and Injustice

One of the most universal manifestations of the Natural Law is the recognition of and concern for justice and the universal reaction, often violent, against injustice.

Every society has someone or some group that has a care of justice. People go to the tribal chief, the tribal council, the emir, the sultan, the feudal lord, and British court for justice.

---

[9]*Summa Theologiae,* I–II, q. 94, a. 2.

Everywhere there are acts or rules that achieve justice. In hunting societies there is a concern for the proper division of the spoils of the hunt or the catch. Shares are set aside for the aged and sick, while the hunters haggle over the right division of the rest.

In agricultural societies, for example, at planting time, the communal land is allocated to each woman of the village in accordance with the number of mouths she has to feed—a neat example of proportionate distributive justice. Even where unjust customs or institutions exist, they are often tempered by rules of a sort of justice. Thus, for example, though polygamy is unjust to women, the women generally have some recognized rights, as, for example, the women may have a right of inheritance for their sons.

Clear cases of injustice bring forth blame and condemnation. He who cheats in the hunt, the tax collector who practices extortion, the judge who takes a bribe, are condemned and despised.

In all societies there are injustices which have become accepted as customary or institutionalized. It is the business of the Third Level to identify and correct such customs and institutions.

iii   Family Obligation

In all societies there is a recognition of family obligation, especially with regard to the care of children. In this matter there are abuses and deviant customs, but these vary from culture to culture while the basic concern is everywhere present. And usually these abuses must be justified by some alleged reason. Thus, the sacrifice of babies to Moloch was judged necessary to save the people from the wrath of this terrible god.

iv   Human Appetites

In the matter of human appetites, appetites for food and drink and for sexual and sensual pleasure, rules and limits of some sort are everywhere acknowledged. These appetites are powerful forces which human beings find hard to control. Hence, in all societies, whether simple and primitive or highly cultured and religiously directed, there are not only individual abuses but also accepted vicious customs. In this regard the reflective critique of the Third Level is particularly important. Yet, at this First Level the need for controls is clearly acknowledged and forms the natural basis for further reflective elaboration.

v   Conclusion

The positive morality, that is, the *de facto* morality of every society, is a mixture of Natural Law with its reasonable determinations[10] and evil deviations, customs, and institutions. This is true of both the primitive and undeveloped society as well as the most sophisticated and developed societies. However, in the First Level the precepts and values of the Natural Law are not explicit, not formally recognized and formulated. But as soon as people begin to make decisions of morality, the Natural Law comes into play. These elements of Natural Law appear in all cultures and are basically similar throughout human cultures.

At the Second Level, the elements of the Natural Law are formulated in general sayings, proverbs, or moral maxims.

At the Third Level, through critical reflection, we are able to formulate the general principles of the Natural Law with accuracy, to purify them from historical or other extrinsic considerations, to organize and interrelate them, to justify them and work out their application to the great diversity of human problems and situations. It is one thing to determine justice in a simple act of barter, quite another thing to discover injustice in the business life of a capitalistic society.

3.   The Second Level

At this level, explicit formulations of Natural Law principles appear. These formulations take the form of sayings, proverbs, maxims, or even lists of general principles without, however, being organized into a system of ethics or moral theology.

One of the most common formulations is one that embodies, in a personal guide to actions, a fundamental Natural Law attitude, namely, the Golden Rule.[11] The Rule appears explicitly and independently in many, if not all, advanced societies. Its formulation varies; sometimes its context is religious, sometimes secular. Most generally it takes a negative form.

The famous Chinese sage Confucius (c. 551–479 B.C.E.), when

---

[10]*Summa Theologiae,* I–II, *q.* 95, a. 2, c.

[11]Examples are taken from *The Gospel of Matthew,* translated with an introduction and interpretation by William Barclay (Philadelphia: The Westminster Press, 1975), 272–277.

asked whether there was one word that expressed a rule for one's life, replied, "Is not 'reciprocity' such a word? What you do not want done to yourself, do not do to others."

The Greek King Nicocles is said to have told his officials, "Do not do to others the things that make you angry when you experience them at the hands of other people."

Epictetus (1st–2nd century C.E.) Said, "What you avoid suffering yourselves, do not seek to inflict on others."

A Stoic maxim runs, "What you do not wish to be done to you, do not to others."

In the Buddhist *Hymn of Faith* we read:

All men tremble at the rod,
All men fear death;
Putting oneself in the place of others,
Kill not nor cause to kill;

All men tremble at the rod,
To all men life is dear;
Doing as one would be done by,
Kill not nor cause to kill.

The oldest list of moral rules is that of Hammurabi (fl. 1792–1750 B.C.E.) Many of the laws contained in this list are basic Natural Law Principles, though others are what St. Thomas call "determinations" by the human lawgiver.[12]

The Ten Commandments constitute a code of Natural Law. There is one exception. The designation of the Sabbath as the weekly day of worship is a positive determination.

An example that is hard to classify may be noted here. It is a list of principles, yet not an ethical system. This is the Roman jurists' *Jus Gentium,* Law of Nations.

In Roman Law only Roman citizens were bound by Roman Law or had standing to bring an action in a Roman court. As Rome expanded, incorporating other peoples (the *gentes*) into its Empire, the legal status of non-Romans became a problem. The problem was eventually solved by creating a set of very general principles of justice which the jurists

---

[12]*Summa Theologiae,* I–II, *q.* 95, a. 2, c.

thought all people would accept. These general principles, rather than the specific provisions of Roman Law, were used throughout the Roman Empire for cases involving non-Romans. (The great Roman jurists such as Gaius and Ulpian were Natural Law philosophers.[13])

The general acceptance of the *Jus Gentium* throughout the Roman Empire, despite the great diversity of cultures in that Empire, confirms what was said in 2b. iii. above.

4. The Third Level

At this level, the Natural Law is made the object of reflective, formal study. Its principles are identified, purified, and refined. Their origin from human experience and reason is investigated. The application of the principles is explored both in absolute terms and in reference to changing circumstances.

This intellectual effort presupposes the sorting out of customs, conventions, and moral principles, the distinguishing of the relative and the absolute, and the identification of vicious deviations.

In Western culture, this sorting out was the work of Plato, Aristotle, and the Stoics. Their efforts were an answer to the relativists of their day, the Sophists and others.

The result of these critical and constructive reflections is an integrated and systematic ethics or moral philosophy. A magnificent example is the *Nicomachean Ethics* of Aristotle, especially the Fifth Book in which Aristotle analyzes justice.

A modern example may be found in John Finnis's work, *Natural Law and Natrual Rights*.

At this level, too, a variation in explaining and justifying theories develops. Some theorists tend to establish a rationalistic basis for Natural Law; others, like Aristotle, are more inductive and experiential. Yet, despite theoretical differences, Natural Law theorists display fundamental agreement.

5. The Fourth Level

At this level, Natural Law theory is integrated into a comprehensive, philosophical, and/or theological synthesis.

---

[13]Excerpts from this writing are preserved in the *Digest* of the *Corpus Juris Civilis*.

This incorporation has two primary effects. It provides a final explanation of the Natural Law itself, and secondly, it may modify both Natural Law theory and Natural Law practice.

The first effect is achieved by relating the Natural Law to, and grounding it in, the ultimate explanation of the whole of reality. St. Thomas does this by deriving it from the Eternal Law existing in the mind of God and making the Natural Law a "participation" in the same Eternal Law.[14]

The second effect is achieved not by changing anything within the Natural Law but by making it part of a supernatural orientation of human beings to an eternal unification with God.

An example of such an incorporation is found in Stoicism. Its identification of nature and reason and elevation of the result into the ultimate principle of reality greatly emphasizes the idea of "living in accordance with nature" and the subsequent patient acceptance of events.

The great Roman jurists Cicero, Gaius, Ulpian, and others made Natural Law theory an integral part of Roman law, thus giving that theory a juristic orientation.

Another outstanding example of the Fourth Level is the vast synthesis created by St. Thomas Aquinas. By placing the origin of law in the Eternal Law, which is the plan and program for God's creative providence in the universe, Aquinas gave it an absolute origin and a final justification. And human reason has an ultimate guarantee since it is a "participation" in the reason of God.

6. We may now draw some conclusions.

a. Is knowledge of the Natural Law dependent on a knowledge of God?

Some people believe that one cannot discover the Natural Law without a previous knowledge of God. Some (Sir William Blackstone and John Austin) have identified the Natural Law with the Divine Law, i.e., with God's law as revealed in the Bible (e.g., the Ten Commandments and the Sermon on the Mount).

While St. Thomas recognized a substantial congruence within the

---

[14]*Summa Theologiae,* I–II, *q.* 91, aa. 1 and 2.

Natural Law and the Divine Law (taken in the sense just mentioned), he sharply distinguished them because of their mode of origin. Natural Law was promulgated by creation and human reflection; the Divine Law was promulgated by Revelation.[15]

The analysis presented here shows that, in the first instance, the Natural Law arises as a result of practical reason being applied to human nature as concretely revealed in human experience. This knowledge does not depend upon and is not derivative from a knowledge of God. At the First Level the Natural Law is often mingled with religious ideas and even with superstitions and vicious customs. Even at the Third Level, a knowledge of God is not necessarily a formal part of Natural Law Ethics, as Aristotle's secular ethics demonstrates. However, in the Fourth Level a knowledge of God is needed for a full understanding and justification of Natural Law.

b. Does the Third Level develop an ideology?

This analysis shows that what happens at the Third Level is not the theoretical development of an ideology that is then imposed on people as was the Communist ideology. The intellectual analysis and development at the Third Level is based on the human values already recognized in the two previous Levels.

In a simple, small homogeneous society the Third Level is not necessary. Thus the African Pygmies are able to live in simple peace and justice. But when societies become more complex and cosmopolitan, the activity of the Third Level becomes necessary to eliminate vicious deviations and to apply the Natural Law in highly complex human situations.

c. What is the function of the Fourth Level?

The Fourth Level gives a final understanding and justification for the Natural Law and gives it a meaning in the transcendent destiny of the human race.

---

[15]*Summa Theologiae*, I–II, *q*. 91, *aa*. 2, 4, and 5.

XIX

PRUDENCE AND INSIGHT

New Introduction: For a long time I had thought that philosophers had underplayed the insightful ability of the human intellect. When I began to work in jurisprudence I discovered the same neglect of insight. So I thought it would be important to bring together the various roles of insight and prudence in legal thinking. The result was the present article.[1]

Several important questions arise from this discussion, namely, (1) How can we develop and improve our insight? and (2) How can we validate insightful certitudes?

* * *

I am not going to offer any new startling philosophical doctrine. My thesis simply is that what has been called "prudence" and what I am calling "insight" have not received adequate attention either in moral matters or in jurisprudence. I am looking at law and morals simultaneously from an epistemological viewpoint because something can be learned by treating them together.

The matter is important because neglecting prudence and insight results in a tendency to demand fully principled justification for decisions both in ethics and in judicial decisions. Anything else is regarded as the personal bias or subjective feeling of the decision maker. This makes for rigidity and the absolutizing of secondary general principles.

---

[1]Paper presented to the Plenary session of the American Catholic Philosophical Association, Houston, Texas (April 17, 1982), 26–30.

Perhaps, a fundamental difficulty here is that we forget the importance of the traditional presentation of the human intellect as both insight (*intellectus*) and reason (*ratio*).

Insight is the direct apprehension of an intelligible object qua intelligible. The term "direct" excludes any reasoning process or any process that determines a knowledge conclusion. Since there cannot be a more basic activity of intellect as such, insight is the primary activity of the intellect. Deductive and inferential reasoning is wholly dependent upon insight: intellect without *ratio* is still intellect, but intellect without insight would be nothing at all.

Deductive reasoning depends upon insight in at least two ways. First, insight supplies the principles of the syllogism, both formal and substantial: thus, the principle of non-contradiction is an insightful expansion of the first principle of being: "Being is" or "Being is what it is" which in turn is developed solely by insight. Secondly, insight supplies substantive principles which may be used as majors in argumentation. For example, the principles of efficient causality which arise through insightful induction.

This insight (*intellectus*) is not parallel to *ratio* as though there were two distinct operations of the intellectual power.

We must also recognize that insight is not simply a series of acts. To expand Aristotle's metaphor, insight constantly illumines and irradiates all human consciousness. It permeates all sense awareness and thereby is able to reach the intelligibility of the sensible real directly. It flows through all intellectual investigations, reasoning, and judgment. And when reasoning fails to deal with the concrete, insight again assumes full charge.

The insight that gives rise to induction of moral and legal principles, of the foundations of natural and legal justice, is not some special activity of the intellect. It is the basic activity. It is insight applied to special concrete areas. Insight is the intellectual component of prudence whether legal or ethical.

Insight is therefore all pervasive and, for that reason, is frequently overlooked. It appears clearly when other more superficial intellectual activities fail—as in applying general moral principles to complex moral cases.

Before proceeding I must distinguish two basic situations. First there is the situation in which the material for the insight is fully presented and seen to be so presented. Examples are the apprehension of the first principles of being; the grasp of self consciousness; the grasp of quiddities given in perception; in such cases there is certitude and certainty.

In the cases we are dealing with, materials necessary for the insight are complex and heterogenous. A trivial but illuminating instance is that flash in which we get the point of a cartoon. We don't reason to it. For example, we don't say, "incongruity is funny, but this cartoon presents incongruity, therefore it is funny, therefore ha-ha-ha." But the insight does presuppose understanding of the elements of the cartoon and knowledge of some background elements. Thus, unless we know something of American foreign policy and the international situation, a cartoon about Secretary Haig will be unintelligible. There will be no insight. This need for background (not as premises) is one reason why it's hard to understand cartoons and jokes from another culture or time.

I must bring in this discussion some points about definitions and general principles in both law and ethics. I transmit to a different investigation the way in which we develop definitions and general principles. Here I point out that many (if not most) such definitions and principles are open-ended. For example, we have the principle that self-defense is justified provided only appropriate force is used (*servato moderamine tutelae*). It is impossible to define "appropriate force" with the precision of a chemical test or a mathematical formula. It lies with the prudence of a judge to decide individual cases. The same can be said of "due care" or "natural justice." In such cases an effort to rest the decision on principles either distorts the principle or constricts the decision. This emphasizes the absolute need to leave such matters to the judgment of the court. It emphasizes the need for the virtue of prudence and for seriously taking it into account. I find this missing from most jurisprudential discussion of judicial reasoning. The practical value of a consideration of the need to use insight (prudence) to close the open-endedness is shown by the fact that many cases turn simply on the extension, refinement or interpretation of a definition. (I have a large collection of relevant cases discovered by my students.) The application of definitions to variable individual cases is only a special case of insight.

In moral decisions we do have available general principles, but these are themselves the result of insightful induction (not scientific induction) from individual cases. While they express some intrinsic moral value, they are not absolute and they are open-ended. In simple cases, a deduction may be used, but in complex cases one cannot deduce the decision. The principles are part of the material for the insight. But all sorts of other factors must be viewed, assessed by insight and placed in a pattern the intelligibility of which can be grasped by insight.

In such cases there is an intellectual process but not a deductive one. The intellect (assisted by the imagination) goes over the material by what is called *cogitare,* that is *co-agitare,* tossing around together, juxtaposing, adding and subtracting etc.

One of the best examples I have found is a legal one. One of the most famous murder cases in the history of Chicago was the Loeb-Leopold case of the 1920s. There was no question of the guilt of the accused, but the judge had to decide on the sentence. He had three choices: capital punishment, life imprisonment, or some shorter prison term.

He looked at the practice of the Illinois courts: He considered the age and intelligence of the accused; he studied the psychiatric recommendations; he examined the arguments of counsel—going thus through a great deal of *cogitare.* He finally decided on life imprisonment. There is no way this opinion can be reduced to a series of syllogisms. The decision was not "principled" in the way demanded by the rationalists. There is a leap from all the material to the decision. The evidence did not determine the decision, yet the decision is intelligible.

I emphasize here that my generalization from such cases is that in a complex concrete moral and legal case, general principles, though guiding, cannot determine the decision. In such cases we fall back on the fundamental activity of the intellect, which, in these cases, takes the form of prudence. Prudence is an acquired skill of making correct insightful decisions in individual concrete cases. We all have some prudence; we have varying aptitudes for developing prudential skills. Mature prudence requires not only skill but experience and learning.

St. Thomas points out that there are some things (e.g., "The whole is greater than any of its parts") known by insight to everyone but others are known only to the "wise and learned."

Prudence cannot be taught as can Geometry or Metaphysics. It can be developed by reflection on other prudential decisions and on human experience.

Here I would like to point out that in a given society insights of wise men and prudential decisions of wise men leave an accumulation of practical wisdom on which each subsequent generation can draw. I view the common law as such an accumulation, self-corrective and self-adaptive. (As a therapeutic footnote: I do not mean to say that such accumulations cannot degenerate. But that is another matter.)

To return to the Loeb-Leopold case, while we can easily see that the judge's decision is understandable and obviously just, we can also see that it was not absolutely determined. Another wise and learned judge might with good reason have chosen one of the alternatives. In complex individual cases, insight is limited and generally cannot claim absolute certitude.

Another point. Just as insight in individual cases can modify the application of principles, so the same cases can modify the principles themselves. Thus our understanding of due process has continuously developed under the influence of sensitive insightful decisions in individual cases.

I once had a professor of moral theology who always talked of applying cases to moral principles. At first I thought it was a slip of the tongue, then an idiosyncrasy—but finally decided that it expressed a view of moral decision making. He saw each decision not as a one-way process but as an interaction between case and principle in which the result may modify both.

Finally, does this theoretical position have any practical effect? I think it does—Suppose a very complicated moral case which perhaps involves new concrete elements. The a priori deductive approach would lay down the applicable general principle, set the facts along side it and let the principle select the relevant elements. What I am saying is, that in such a case an independent and fresh evaluation of all the facts must be made (and this must be done by insight, prudentially) and that then this evaluation should be confronted with the traditional principles.

A modern example of such a situation is the debate over nuclear war or even modern war in general. I am not taking sides in the debate. I merely want to point out that the traditional principles applied traditionally are inadequate to handle the new situation. Whichever way the argument goes, there will be new generalizations based on new insights. Those who merely repeat the standard conditions of a just war are making no contribution to a solution.

For a historical example we can go to fifteenth century Florence. Florence was then becoming the leading banking center of Europe and was thus in the forefront of the new economic order. The bankers of Florence had problems of conscience. They appealed to Archbishop

Antoninus for guidance. In addition to being a theologian, he was a canon lawyer of considerable experience. One might have expected a rigid assertion of traditional principles. But Antoninus examined the new situation and began historical changes in the moral theology of economics.

A contrary example lies in the long refusal of canon lawyers to recognize that the modern situation demanded a change in their attitude towards civil religious liberty.

A concrete legal example can be seen in the shift of American law with reference to booby-trapping against burglary. Up to a rather recent time the courts defended the practice, basing themselves on the right of property and the sanctity of the home. Today, the law condemns the spring gun situation. This is due to a change in the insight into the value of human life as opposed to the value of property.

In this short paper I have tried to highlight the importance and some of the functions of insight and prudence in moral and legal decisions. Perhaps, I have at least stimulated some discussion.

XX

TRANSCENDENTAL THOMISM, A CRITICAL ASSESSMENT

ew Introduction: I have long thought that the greatest threat to Neo-Thomism was Transcendental Thomism. When I was asked to contribute an article to a conference at the Center for Domestic Studies of St. Thomas University in Houston, I decided to make a critical analysis of a prominent transcendental Thomist. So I chose the Thomism of Emerich Coreth. Transcendental Thomism disfigures the Thomism of St. Thomas by introducing into it Kantian ideas.

I think the article[1] is both clear and correct as it stands and needs no additional development or explanation.

* * *

I do not intend in this paper to give a balanced or comprehensive assessment of the "School" or "Movement" known as Transcendental Thomism. Some of the most brilliant Catholic thinkers of the last fifty years have either practiced the transcendental method or been deeply influenced by the movement.[2] The writings of these men contain many

---

[1]First Published in Victor B. Brezik, C. S. B., ed., *One Hundred Years of Thomism: Aterni Patris and Afterwards,* A Symposium (Houston: Center for Thomistic Studies, University of St. Thomas, 1981), 90–116.

[2]C.f. Otto Muck, S.J., *The Transcendental Method,* trans. William D. Seidensticker (New York: Herder & Herder, 1968), 12–13 (Henceforth referred to as: Muck). Muck lists J. Maréchal, S.J., J. de Vries, S.J., A. Marc, S.J., G. Isaye, E. Coreth, K. Rahner, S.J.,

profound philosophical reflections and some enduring contributions to the cumulative goods of philosophy.[3] But as Paul Elmer More once remarked, genius is no guarantee against error. It is, therefore, with the utmost respect for these men that I present here a deliberately negative critique of Transcendental Thomism. Moreover, I do not pretend that this presentation is complete and final. It is a brief preliminary statement of my own position vis-à-vis Transcendental Thomism—a position which I hope subsequently to develop and, if necessary, correct.

The denial that Joseph Maréchal founded a "school" seems to be based on the fact that individual thinkers have tried to carry out his original projection in very personal and different ways.[4] This fact has persuaded me to deal with the movement selectively, both in the authors studied and in the points emphasized.

The historical and doctrinal starting point is obviously the work of Joseph Maréchal (1878–1944) and the Magna Carta of the movement is his brilliant *Le Point de départ de la métaphysique*.[5] Since he laid

---

B.J.F. Lonergan, S.J., A. Gregoire, J.B. Lotz. We may add Joseph Donceel, S.J., and Gerald McCool, S.J.

[3]Cf. Etienne Gilson, *The Unity of Philosophical Experience* (New York: Charles Scribner's Sons, 1947), 301:

> On the other side, all those subtle shades of thoughts which qualify the principles of a philosopher, soften their rigidity and allow them to do justice to the complexity of concrete facts, are not only part and parcel of his own doctrine, but are often the only part of it that will survive the death of the system. We may wholly disagree with Hegel, or with Comte, but nobody can read their encyclopedias without finding there an inexhaustible source of partial truths and of acute observations. Each particular philosophy is, therefore, a co-ordination of self and mutually limiting principles which defines an individual outlook on the fullness of reality.

What Gilson says here of all great philosophers applies to the Transcendental Thomists, especially since they retain many basic Thomistic insights.

[4]"As he [Coreth] points out (p. 12) what has come from Fr. Maréchal is not a school but a movement, not a set of ready-made opinions repeated in unison by members of a uniform group, but a basic line of thought that already has developed in various manners and still continues to do so." Bernard J. F. Lonergan, "Metaphysics as Horizon" in Emerich Coreth, *Metaphysics,* English edition by Joseph Donceel (New York: Herder & Herder, 1968), 200 (Henceforth this translation will be referred to as: Donceel).

[5]Joseph Maréchal, *Le Point de départ de la métaphysique,* 3rd ed. (Paris: Desclée de Brouwer, 5 vols., I, 1944; II, 1949; Henceforth referred to as: Maréchal, I or II). See Muck, 26.

down the guidelines for the Thomistic use of the Transcendental Method, an understanding of Maréchal is essential to the understanding of any further development thereof. I will therefore make considerable use of his work. But my approach is bipolar and at the other pole I have selected Emerich Coreth, the distinguished German exponent of the Transcendental Method. Several considerations have guided my selection. First of all, it seems to me that Emerich Coreth does indeed lie within the authentic development of the "movement" with, however, the reservations to be mentioned later. Secondly, he presents in his *Metaphysik* a total and systematic metaphysics—"Eine Methodisch-Systematische Grundlegung"—worked out, according to his express intention by the exclusive use of the Transcendental Method.[6] Though the work is long and profound, it is almost a basic textbook in metaphysics

---

The 1949 edition of Cahier V was published after Maréchal's death, having been edited by L. Malevez, S.J. Maréchal had resisted efforts to republish the 1926 edition because he wished to revise, not his doctrine, but his presentation. Malevez made very few changes in the 1926 text, but he added (599–608) some comments originally published by Maréchal himself in the *Revue Néo-Scolastique de Philosophie*, 41 (1938): 253–261, as "A Propos du Point de Départ de la Métaphysique." See also: Notes de Métaphysique, *Novelle Revue Théologique*, 53 (1926): 329–334, 447–451, 510–525; Au seuil de la métaphysique: abstraction ou intuition, *Revue Néo-Scolastique de Philosophie*, 31 (1929): 27–52, 121–147, 309–342. Reprinted in *Mélanges Joseph Maréchal*, I (Bruxelles-Paris, 1950): 288–98. Les premiers écrits philosophiques du P. Maréchal, *Melanges*, I: 23–46. Jugement 'scolastique' concernant la racine de l'agnosticisme kantien, first written in 1914 but first published in *Mélanges*, I: 273–287. Le dynamisme intellectuel dans la connaissance objective, *Revue Néo-Scolastique de Philosophie*, 28 (1927), 137–165 (Reprinted in *Mélanges*, I: 75–101); Phénoménologie pure ou philosophie de l'action, *Philosophie Perennis* (Regensburg, 1930), I: 377–400 (Reprinted in *Mélanges*, I: 181–206). Le problème de dieu' d'après M. Edouard L. Roy, *Nouvelle Revue Théologique*, 58 (1931): 193–216, 289–316 (Reprinted in *Mélanges*, I: 107–259). L'aspect dynamique de la méthode transcendantale chez Kant, "*Revue Néo-Scolastique de Philosophie*, 43 (1959): 341–384.

[6]"Das neue transzendental-metaphysische Denken hat sicher schon bedeutende Leistungen vollbracht, aber es hat seine Aufgabe noch lange nicht erfüllt. Diese Aufgabe heisst, die gesamte Metaphysik von Grund auf new zu durchdenken, d. h. von einem ersten Ansatz her methodisch zu begründen und systematisch zu entwickeln. Dies soll hier im Grundriss versucht werden. Dazu ist vor allem eine differenziertere Fortbestimmung der transzendentalen Methode als der Grundmethode der Metaphysik erfordert. So wird auch in der Durchführung besonderes Gewicht gelegt auf die kritisch-methodische Selbstbegründung der Metaphysik, die in den ersten Abschnitten vollzogen wird." Emerich Coreth, *Metaphysik* (Innsbruck: Tyrolia, 1961), 13 (Henceforth this work will be referred to as: Coreth).

according to a Transcendental Method. I know of no other Transcendental Thomist who has made an effort to present a total metaphysics in such a systematic form. Father Donceel has produced in English a condensed translation of this work intended obviously to be used as a college textbook in the United States. Maréchal proposed to use the Transcendental Method as an alternative method and a roundabout modern way to arrive at the already existing metaphysical realism of St. Thomas.[7] One might then expect to find in Coreth's *Metaphysik,* some fifty years later, a systematic fulfillment of Maréchal's purpose.

I am deliberately leaving Bernard Lonergan outside my discussion except insofar as he comments on Coreth.[8] Lonergan seems to me to have antecedents other than those in the transcendental tradition and to have distinctive philosophical views which cannot be reduced to that tradition, however much they may converge with it.[9] He is, of course,

---

[7]Maréchal, V: 66–71.

[8]Lonergan's only published comment that deals directly with Coreth is his review of the *Metaphysik,* originally published as a review article in the *Gregorianum,* 44 (1963): 307–318 and reprinted at the end of Donceel's English version of the *Metaphysik,* 197–219. This review adds little to the understanding of Coreth and it is, in fact, a rather superficial attack on the Thomistic realism of Gilson. In my opinion this is perhaps the weakest piece of philosophical writing ever produced by Fr. Lonergan. For example, the one thing Gilson has consistently rejected is that there is an epistemological problem of the "bridge." "Prof. Gilson acknowledges a problem of a bridge and so arrives at his need for an intellectual perception of being" (Donceel, 215). This is simply absurd. Professor Gilson finds that as a matter of fact we do grasp being in every perceptual judgment and, consequently, there is no problem of the "bridge." Moreover, Lonergan calles Coreth an "immediate realist" (Donceel, 210). This is so far from the truth that Coreth never reaches external reality. And why did Lonergan give no reference for this in an article full of page references?

[9]Cf. Muck, 276–277 and 284. Muck displays the uniqueness of Lonergan's position and his difference from Maréchal while claiming to find the transcendental method in Lonergan's work. "But we have been able to show that despite his *unique viewpoint and terminological peculiarities* (which are, of course, direct consequents of the *development of his viewpoint*), the *essential elements of transcendental analysis* can easily be discerned while the distinctness of his concrete expression demonstrates a new and extent of the development power of this method" (Muck, 284) (Emphasis added).

"By reason of its unrelenting insistence on the empirical, Lonergan's transcendental method should be carefully distinguished (despite other common themes) from various other transcendental analyses with which it is usually associated, e.g., those of J. Maréchal, K. Rahner, E. Coreth, and A. Marc in Otto Muck, *The Transcendental Method* (New York: Herder and Herder, 1968). Lonergan's attention to this

of great importance in modern Catholic thought, but he deserves an individual and distinctive critique. Indeed some of what I say of the Maréchal-Coreth axis will apply to him, but I will not make the application here.

To return to Coreth there is another more profound and philosophical reason for selecting his as the current representative of the movement. He seems to me to represent, if not the logical terminus, at least the penultimate stage in the logical working out of the use of the Transcendental Method in accordance with Maréchal's original program. Gilson has shown how philosophical systems and doctrines develop not merely through history but in accordance with philosophical principles.[10] From this standpoint I believe that Coreth represents almost the final separation of Transcendental Thomism from Thomism under the intrinsic pressure of principles alien to Thomism and to metaphysical realism. Coreth represents the historical devolution

---

topic dates from a series of historical articles originally published in the late 1940's and later republished together in one volume edited by David Burrell, *Verbum: Word and Idea in Aquinas* (Notre Dame: Univ. Of Notre Dame Press, 1967)." Walter E. Conn, Transcendental Analysis of Conscious Subjectivity, *The Modern Schoolman,* 3 (1977): 216.

[10]"The philosophical events which have been described in the previous chapters cannot be wholly understood in the sole light of biography, of literary history, or even of the history of the systems in which they can be observed. They point rather to the fact that, in each instance of philosophical thinking, both the philosopher and his particular doctrine are ruled from above by an impersonal necessity. In the first place, philosophers are free to lay down their own sets of principles, but once this is done, they no longer think as they wish—they think as they can. In the second place, it seems to result from the facts under discussion, that any attempt on the part of a philosopher to shun the consequences of his own position is doomed to failure. What he himself declines to say will be said by his disciples, if he has any; if he has none, it may remain eternally unsaid, but it is there, and anybody going back to the same principles, be it several centuries later, will have to face the same conclusions. It seems, therefore, that though philosophical ideas can never be found separate from philosophers and their philosophies, they are, to some extent, independent of philosophers as well as of their philosophies. Philosophy consists in the concepts of philosophers, taken in the naked, impersonal necessity of both their contents and their relations." E. Gilson, *The Unity of Philosophical Experience,* 301–302.

of the movement to its historical demise.[11] It can only survive now as a Christianized version of German idealism.

Obviously, from Maréchal and throughout the history of the movement, the crucial issue has been that of the methodology of metaphysics, the so-called "transcendental turn."[12] We can, indeed, measure the distance from Maréchal to Coreth by examining their conceptions of the role and function of the Transcendental Method.

Maréchal held that there was already in existence a perfectly sound metaphysical realism established by a methodology that was both natural and correct. He did not propose to modify the metaphysics of knowledge or the metaphysical realism of St. Thomas Aquinas. The existence of this metaphysics as valid was a given in his approach to the problem.[13] However, he thought that for purposes of revalidating the

---

[11]In this view, Coreth is fulfilling the predictions made by Gilson in his criticism of the effort to combine, in any serious fashion, critical philosophy with Thomistic metaphysics. See E. Gilson, *Réalisme Thomiste et critique de la connaissance* (Paris: Vrin, 1939), 130–212.

[12]This is emphasized by the very title of Muck's book, *The Transcendental Method*. "The question concerning methodology is an indication of a crisis" (Muck, 11). It is the method, the transcendental "stance" (Muck, 20), the transcendental "approach" (Muck, 21), the transcendental "turn" (Muck, 9). It is the use of this method that is the form of unity in the "movement" and the determining characteristic of Transcendental Thomism (Muck, 21).

[13]"Vers la fin du Cahier (Livre III), nous userons de la seconde tactique indiquée plus haut, c'est-à-dire que nous rechercherons si les postulats initiaux du Kantisme (*objet phénoménal et méthode transcendentale d'analyse*) ne recéleraient pas, quoi qu'en ait cru Kant, l'affirmation implicite d'un véritable *objet* métaphysique. Qu'il faille répondre à cette question par un oui ou par un non, la valeur du réalisme ancien n'en demeure pas moins établie à nos yeux; nous ne jugeons pas toutefois ce surplus d'enquête totalement oiseux; car il y aurait bien quelque intérêt à constater que le réalisme métaphysique compénètre à tel point la pensée humaine qu'il est enveloppé déjà, de nécessité logique, dans la simple représentation "objective" d'une donnée quelconque." Maréchal, V:15.

"La Critique ancienne se confond avec la systématisation métaphysique et ne s'achève qu'avec elle: c'est la *voie longue* de la critique; mais c'en est aussi, selon nous, le *procédé naturel.*" Maréchal V: 60.

"La place reste libre pour une philosophie qui posséderait les avantages de l'Idéalisme transcendantal, sans en partager les tares essentielles: pour un finalisme rationnel, non rationaliste; pour une épistémologie qui réduise les prétentions illusoires de la raison, mais maintienne effective la suprématie de cette dernière sur l'entendement abstractif. "L'aristotélisme, précisé et complété—corrigé, si l'on veut—par les Scolas-

Thomistic synthesis within modern philosophy and in the face of the so-called "modern" problematic the method first developed by Kant and called by him "transcendental" could be so modified that, starting with it, one could arrive at the already given metaphysics of St. Thomas.[14] In other words, Maréchal saw two methodologies by which the same metaphysics might be established.[15] He did not propose to modify the traditional methodology of Thomism at all or to substitute another methodology for it. But he was convinced that the Kantian Transcendental Method could be corrected and used in such a way as to overcome Kantianism and establish Thomism, thereby beating Kant at his own game.

If we turn now to Coreth we find no longer an acceptance of two methodologies. Coreth sees the transcendental method as the *only* legitimate method for establishing a metaphysics; there are no alternative ways.[16] The approval and defense of the natural approach of traditional Thomism is completely discarded. The adoption of the transcendental method is not seen as an intellectual strategy or as a means of bringing Thomism into modern thought but as establishing, for the first time, a thorough-going valid metaphysics.[17]

Coreth's general conception of methodology is such that there can be only *one* proper methodology for each discipline.[18] He sees methodology as intimately associated with whatever discipline it is related to.

---

tiques et plus particuliérement par S. Thomas, répond aux conditions ici posées." Maréchal V:39.

[14]Maréchal V: 66–71.

[15]"S'il est vrai—c'est notre thèse dans ce volume—que la *Critique ontologique et la Critique transcendantale*, quoique différentes par le point de vue sous lequel elles envisage d'abord l'objet connu, convergent de droit vers un même résultat final traite l'une comme une simple transposition de l'autre." Maréchal I:70.

"Ces deux méthodes critiques, abordant, sous des angles complémentaires, le même objet total, doivent, poussées à fond, livrer finalement des conclusions identiques; car la Critique ancienne pose d'emblée l'Objet ontologique, qui inclut le Sujet transcendantal; et la Critique moderne s'attache au Sujet transcendantal, qui *postule* l'Objet ontologique." Maréchal V:60.

[16]Donceel, 7–14; Donceel, 17–31; Coreth, 88; Coreth, 93.

[17]Coreth, 92–93.

[18]Coreth, 55; Coreth, 94.

The nature of the investigation determines the methodology to be used and the methodology that is used determines the nature of the discipline as it develops.[19] It seems to me that Coreth's view in this matter is absolutely right. The methodological principles as well as the starting points of any discipline determine its character and its conclusions, and its character and its conclusions must be understood and interpreted in terms of the argumentation, both with regard to the initial substantive position and with regard to the mode of argumentation, the methodology itself.

This view of methodology was expressly developed by St. Thomas, not only in his general epistemological doctrine on the division of the disciplines but especially in his clear and fundamental distinction between the *Via Platonica* and the *Via Aristotelis*.[20] He understood that a position derived its meaning from its premises or from the general mode—the *via*—of the argumentation. Two methodologies could lead to a common position only equivocally.

If then Coreth is correct in his theory of the relationship of any methodology to its corresponding discipline one would expect that whatever methodology he selected for metaphysics would, in his opinion at least, be the one and only proper methodology. This is exactly what Coreth says with regard to the Transcendental Method. There is only one metaphysical method, the Transcendental Method. Furthermore, if Coreth is correct then Maréchal's assumption that there could be two basically different methodologies by which the same metaphysical positions could be established has to be rejected. As a consequence of this it also follows that if one adopts the Transcendental Method as the one and only method to do metaphysics then one would expect that the resultant metaphysics would be different from metaphysics established by a prior and different methodology.

It is my contention that this is exactly the outcome of the movement. When new principles are introduced into a given tradition the first impact may not be pervasive or profound. The full implications of the new principles, the full influence of the new methodologies may not be originally worked out or even suspected. What we have seen so far in the development from Maréchal to Coreth is the working out of the

---

[19]Coreth, 94.

[20]R. J. Henle, S.J., *Saint Thomas and Platonism* (The Hague: Nijhoff, 1956), 294-308.

substitution of an alien methodology within the Thomistic tradition in the hope that the same body of metaphysical knowledge will be thereby established. On the contrary, this cannot be done and has not happened. What we have now in Coreth's metaphysics is not a Thomism but a kind of Christianized transcendentalism, or an idealism corrected by Christian realism.

While earlier Transcendental Thomists were very insistent that they were arriving at the authentic metaphysics of St. Thomas and that they were reestablishing his basic positions it has become clear to the more recent exponents of the position that this is not the case.

Thus, it is very significant that one of the most distinguished members of the movement, Karl Rahner, has expressly recognized this fact. In his introduction to Muck's work on Transcendental Method he writes, "The author discusses the Transcendental Method in contemporary '*scholastic* philosophy,' i.e., he sketches the history of the reception of a mode of thought which so alters the recepting 'system' that it becomes an entirely new and different one. The reception of the Transcendental Method means the end of 'new-scholasticism' in the historical sense of the word."[21] Further on, he adds, "Nor does the transcendental turn mean merely the adoption of a brand new doctrine in an otherwise stable and static 'system,' but an entirely new conception of the 'system' itself. This is what leads us to speak confidently of the end of neo-scholasticism as it had been understood since the second half of the nineteenth century."[22]

I do not believe that that the continued validity of neo-scholasticism or of Thomism, or their future redevelopment, stands or falls with Transcendental Thomism. But I think that it is quite clear that at this point Transcendental Thomism can no longer claim to be Thomism and that some of its major exponents are recognizing this fact. Moreover, the failure of the Transcendental Method to carry out the program of Maréchal is, in my opinion, being demonstrated by history and one of the major demonstrations is the *Metaphysik* of Coreth.

It is not surprising therefore to discover that Coreth himself puts the development of his metaphysics and especially of his methodology in the line of Kant–Fichte–Schelling–Hegel and a group of modern

---

[21]Muck, 9–10.

[22]*Ibid.*

philosophers that includes Husserl and Heidegger.[23] It is to this "Richtung" that Coreth attaches his development of the Transcendental Method. He mentions as antecedents, if not as sources, the neo-scholastics Maréchal, G. Isaye, J.B. Lotz, A. Marc, and K. Rahner, but it is not this group that dominates the numerous comments (*Zusätze*) which appear thoroughout the *Metaphysik*. Further, it is noteworthy that Coreth's own research has concentrated so heavily on Kant and Hegel.[24]

Consonant with and confirmative of all this is the marked difference between Maréchal's and Coreth's reading of the history of philosophy. Maréchal saw the metaphysics of knowledge of St. Thomas (especially as synthesized in the 84th and 86th Questions of the *Prima Pars* of the *Summa*) as the definitive solution to the metaphysical problems of the ancients as well as of the earlier medieval thinkers.[25] It is here that Maréchal locates the valid and final realistic metaphysics. The subsequent decline of metaphysics, as Maréchal saw it, was due to the disintegration of the Thomistic Synthesis.[26] It was gradually forgotten. For Coreth, however, the sound tradition begins with Plato, is developed by St. Augustine, and is further refined by St. Bonaventure.[27] This tradition was eclipsed precisely be the triumph, not the collapse, of the Aristotelianism advocated by St. Thomas.[28] In this view, Descartes is the beginning of a return to the Platonic-Augustinian tradition, a return which continues through Kant and the German

---

[23]Coreth, 12–13.

[24]Muck, 286.

[25]"Pour la première fois, l'antinomie de l'Un et du Multiple se trouve nettement et complètement résolue. Loin de sacrifier l'unité, comme Héraclite; ou la multiplicité, comme Parménide; loin de creuser un fossé, comme Platon, entre le sensible et l'intelligible; loin même de laisser, comme Aristote, la transcendance de l'unité absolue enveloppée encore d'incertitudes, Saint Thomas équilibre, d'une main sûre, ces éléments divers, dont il découvre, en tout acte de connaissance objective, le centre humain de perspective et d'ailleurs la synthèse vivante." Maréchal I:121.

[26]"Nous allons devoir montrer, au cours de longs chapitres, que la pensée philosophique, dès qu'elle abandonne ce point de vue central et privilégié, retombe dans des antinomies et rend enévitable l'essai d'une nouvelle critique de la connaissance." Maréchal I:121.

[27]Coreth, 70–71.

[28]Coreth, 70.

idealists into Rahner and Coreth.[29] Thus, in Coreth, Transcendental Thomism is becoming more aware of its inner nature as well as of its true natural ancestry. It is not a version of Thomism. It lines up rather with the *Via Platonica* which is incompatible with Thomistic metaphysical realism.[30]

According, then, to Coreth, not only is the Transcendental Method the only valid method for metaphysics, not only is it the culmination of a long tradition that goes back—not to Aristotle but to Plato—but it is also the great contribution of Kant who explicitly identified, analyzed, and used it. For Coreth, the Transcendental Method, viewed in its purity, is an ahistorical permanent position, though it has been only imperfectly understood and defectively carried out by its great practitioners Kant, Fichte, Schelling, Hegel and, in a way, by Husserl and Heidegger.[31] Coreth's researches dealing with these philosophers was a guide to his understanding of the Transcendental Method and made it possible for him to separate it from the defects of its various concrete realizations. Muck notes, "Even this brief glance at some of the results of Coreth's investigation into the historical problems shows how a reflection on the failures of the Transcendental Method can yield *invaluable hints with regard to its proper use*"[32] (emphasis added).

Thus, for Coreth, the corrected and purified Transcendental Method as he describes it in the *Metaphysik* (pages 55–94) is not a method tied to and conditioned by the history of modern philosophy but a permanently valuable method—*the* methodology of metaphysics. As such

---

[29]The Platonic affinities of Kantianism are not often recognized. Bergson detected them clearly: "Briefly, the whole *Critique of Pure Reason* ends in *establishing* that Platonism, illegitimate if Ideas are *things,* becomes *legitimate if Ideas are relations,* and that the ready-made idea, once brought down in this way from heaven to earth, is in fact, as Plato held, *the common basis alike of thought and of nature.* But the whole of the *Critique of Pure Reason* rests on this postulate, *that our intellect is incapable of anything but Platonizing*—that is, of pouring all possible experience *into pre-existing moulds.*" *Introduction to Metaphysics,* trans. T.E. Hulme (Indianapolis: Bobbs-Merrill, 1949), 58–59.

[30]See R. J. Henle, S.J., *Saint Thomas and Platonism,* 322–350.

[31]Coreth, 35–43.

[32]Muck, 288.

it should not be essentially tied to any dated presupposition or parochial problems.

In order to evaluate this apotheosis of the Transcendental Method into an idealized Platonic realm, we must review the origins of the Kantian *Critique*.

It is clear that at the end of the eighteenth century there came a critical moment in the history of philosophy. Empiricism had come almost to its full logical term in Hume. Kant thought that if Hume could not be answered there would be an end not only to metaphysics but also to all scientific and rational knowledge. On the other hand, the rationalism of Leibniz, Wolff, Baumgarten, and of Kant himself appeared, after confrontation with Hume, to have no firm foundation. This philosophical confrontation was taking place in the period in which *the* great intellectual success was the new physics and the developing mathematics. In the same period, metaphysics appeared to be finally discredited. Kant tried to find a way out of this confrontation that would save, at least, the scientific rational knowledge of physics and mathematics. I repeat these well known facts because of two points.

First, it was quite understandable that Kant would accept as his presupposition or incorporate into his starting point that in which both traditions, that is, both parties to the confrontation, the Empiricists and the Rationalists, agreed, namely, that it is impossible to derive necessary and universal knowledge from experience and that, *a fortiori;* no transcendental could be in any way extracted therefrom.

Now it requires no subtle reworking to confront St. Thomas with this position. In the 84th Question of the *Prima Pars* of the *Summa,* he clearly and explicitly identified this position as one of the basic errors of the *Via Platonica* and firmly rejected it. It will be recalled that it was precisely in the 84th Question that Maréchal found the definitive establishment of metaphysical realism.[33]

Secondly, as Kant sought a methodological solution to his problem he did not even consider the sort of metaphysical realism that Maréchal, for example, identifies both as definitive philosophy and authentic Thomism. Gilson remarked, "I am well aware of the objections that

---

[33]Maréchal I:101–121. In these pages Maréchal repeatedly states that St. Thomas' solution is definitive.

Kant might have made to the Aristotelian-Thomistic position, but, *as a matter of fact, he never gave it a thought*[34] (emphasis added).

There was good reason in eighteenth century Germany for Kant to become the Kant of the *Critique*. There is no reason today to adopt a method, even in a modified form, that was a dated solution to a false problem.

But Coreth and Donceel are not merely adopting and modifying the Kantian methodology. They accept his presuppositions. Kant is credited with *seeing* that since all experienced objects were singular and contingent, no universality and necessity in knowledge could be derived from them. This alone excludes the experiential beginnings of Thomistic metaphysics and the intellective induction of characteristic of Thomistic method.

But Coreth not only accepts Kant's presuppositions, when he inventories possible methods other than the Transcendental Method, he gives no more thought than did Kant to the type of method employed by St. Thomas.[35]

Now, we have seen that a methodology is intrinsically determined by its discipline and intrinsically determines the resulting discipline. To adopt a methodology that is not only different from but actually opposed to that of Thomism is to presuppose and to forecast—as Karl Rahner said—"an entirely new and different" system. There is no logical and consistent way in which the Transcendental Method can reconstruct the metaphysical realism of St. Thomas.

Let us examine this from another point of view. Maréchal, as we have seen, maintained that a sound Metaphysics of Being and of Knowledge exists—the Thomistic synthesis. He has also pointed out that the balanced solution to the philosophical antinomies developed by St. Thomas consists of a highly nuanced and unified body of theses.[36]

---

[34]Etienne Gilson, *Réalisme Thomiste et critique de la connaissance* (Paris: Vrin, 1939), 167–168.

[35]Coreth, 88–93.

[36]"Seuls les très grands systèmes philosophiques peuvent s'offrir á une épreuve éliminatoire aussi largement conçue: car elle s'étend á tous les plans de la réalité physique, psychologique, morale et religieuse. C'est précisément un des caractères les plus remarquables de la "synthèse thomiste" que d'avoir atteint cette universalité strictement enchaînée." Maréchal I:107.

Remove one of these theses and the whole collapses. There are no ad libitum positions in Thomism.[37] In fact, Maréchal develops his survey of post-Thomistic scholasticism in terms of the modification or rejection of the basic integrating theses.[38]

From what has already been said it is clear that Coreth alters theses basic to Thomism and, if Maréchal is right, thereby alters the whole synthesis. Throughout Coreth's *Metaphysik,* the repercussions are evident, though in this paper only a few instances can be examined.

At this point I think it is already clear, at least in a preliminary way, that one must choose between the Transcendental Method and the experiential realistic method of St. Thomas. One cannot have both. Transcendental Thomism is a contradiction in terms and in substance.

I will now examine a few illustrative instances from Coreth.

Coreth begins with questioning, the question which turns into the question of the question, and so turns on the conditions of the possibility of the question or of the *Vollzug,* the "performance," the "actuation" of the question.[39] The method does not ask about the "ontic" conditions—a condition whose *existence* is presupposed—or the logical conditions, which consist of the knowledge presupposed by the

---

[37]"Dans le vrai thomisme, il ne resterait de thèses 'ad libitum,' interchangeables, que celles qui impliqueraient des problèmes fictifs, ou mal posés, ou insuffisamment mûris." *Ibid.*

[38]Maréchal I:217–222.

[39]The problem of the "starting point" of metaphysics is of primary importance. As the old adage has it—a small error in the beginning becomes finally enormous—*parvus error in principio magnus fit in fine.* A distinction must be made. A personal approach to metaphysics may be made from almost any fact, a spark of a Roman candle, a love affair, a moral problem, a vague wonder about the meaning of things. But if one is thinking about the systematic starting point of a discipline already established, then there can be only one legitimate starting point. Since the starting point of metaphysics must be co-terminous with the human grasp of reality, it cannot possibly be the "question." I do not deal in this paper with this problem since I think that Professor Frederick Wilhelmsen has definitively shown that the "question" cannot possibly be the starting point of a metaphysics—certainly not of a realistic metaphysics. (See Frederick D. Wilhelmsen, "The Priority of Judgment over Question," *International Philosophical Quarterly,* 14, 4 (1974). While most of the other Transcendental Thomists started with an affirmation, a judgment, Karl Rahner defined the starting point of metaphysics as "questioning." *Spirit in the World,* trans. William Dych, S.J. (New York: Herder and Herder, 1968), 57–65.

"content" of the question, but about the conditions of the "act" of the *Vollzug* and which therefore are co-affirmed in the act of questioning.[40] These are "transcendental" conditions. Thus the method begins with a *Vollzug* that is first found in precision from either an "ontic" subject of inherence or an "ontic" object to which the question is related.

Both Maréchal and Coreth insist that this is a "precision" and not, as in Kant, an "exclusion." But, from the standpoint of drawing a realistic metaphysics out of such a methodologically isolated starting point, there is no difference between a "precision" and an "exclusion." All the evidence of natural realism and all the evidence of the "critique of the object" said by Maréchal to be an essential thesis of Thomism (and this rightly, I believe) must be excluded from consideration as metaphysics develops. The rich evidence which Thomism initially uses must be derived from the *Vollzug* of the question. Thus, at page 177 an *Objekt-an-sich,* is reached for the first time—up to that point everything proceeds as though the questioner were alone; only at page 519 is the material world established and in pages 521–528 man's "sensibility" is deduced. When "matter" is reached, it turns out to be *Materialität* and quite differently conceived than the Thomistic *materia*. But now I revert to the establishment of the "other" as an *Objekt-an-sich*.[41]

Kant's use of the Transcendental Method brought him to a metaphysical agnosticism. Maréchal and Coreth both admit that in the succeeding phases of German Transcendentalism the efforts to break through the Kantian limitation to a new metaphysics have always terminated in an idealism. However, Maréchal and Coreth both maintain that Transcendental Method can be corrected so as to overcome Kant and his followers and thereby avoid idealism.

This assertion is brought to the crucial test in pages 171–193 of the *Metaphysik*. Indeed, the transition from the subject to the object and the apodictic establishment of realism is said to be achieved at page 177: *"Hiermit entscheidet sich bereits—vom Ansatz im Fragen her—das im neuzeitlichen Denken so zentrale Problem zwischen Idealismus und*

---

[40]Coreth, 104–109.

[41]Coreth, 176–180.

Realismus,—*Hiermit entscheidet sich bereits*!" At this point the debate between Idealism and Realism is settled![42]

The basis for this assertion is reduced back to the question about the conditions of possibility of questioning. When I ask a question, in the identity of the *Vollzug* of my question I know myself as the questioner and the other as the questioned. Thus the opposition of subject and object is set up within the *Vollzug* itself. But—I quote—"Es ist noch nicht ein Gegensatz, der an sich gesetzt und im Vollzug des Fragens und Wissens vorausgesetzt ist: noch nicht der Gegensatz von 'Subjekt-an-sich' und 'Objekt-an-sich!'"[43] It is important to pause here and reflect on this moment of the Transcendental Method. For the sake of argument, I pass over the problem of the *Subjekt-an-sich*. At this point the *Objekt im Vollzug, das Gefragte, das Gewusste* is simply an object held in thought, in the act of questioning.[44]

Now, however, moving on, when I ask about "das" or "dieses," I already know something about the "das" or "dieses," otherwise I could not ask. But the "das" or "dieses" that I already know about is, from the standpoint of the Transcendental Method the *Objekt im Vollzug*.[45] It is simply the logical (or Transcendental) subject of the question. It does not carry with it the ontic implications of ordinary common sense. "Es ist im Wissen gesetzt." Now, if I ask, I don't know all about it. I am asking for something *noch nicht in Wissen gesetzt*. But now, the argument runs, if I ask about "it" (the object of *Vollzug*), I don't know all about it. I am asking for something *noch nicht in Wissen gesetzt*.[46] To keep this purely transcendental, I am asking what additional predicates can be added to the logical subject which I am holding in the *Vollzug*. These predicates are not yet contained in the *Vollzug*. But, says Coreth, it is a condition of the possibility of the *Vollzug* of the question that there be an Objekt-an-sich! Otherwise the question has no meaning." ... Wäre es nicht vorausgesetzt, so wäre die Möglichkeit des Fragens

---

[42]Coreth, 174.

[43]Coreth, 174.

[44]Coreth, 176.

[45]Coreth, 176.

[46]Coreth, 176–177.

grundsätzlich aufgehoben."[47] This transition from the *Gefragte*, as an object of thought, "Objectum im Vollzug," to an " Objekt-an-sich" that is not contained in the *Vollzug* nor presupposed as known in previous knowledge is, however much elaborated, the perennial illegitimate transition from thought to thing. If I, unthematically or however, know the specific *Objekt-an-sich* prior to the specific question, the question of realism would arise at that prior point and not within the subsequent questions. This would force a reductive consideration of initial natural realism which the Method has closed to Coreth.

The weight of the argument rests on the assumption that although the basis of the question is an object of thought which gives rise to the question, the question moves to an *Objekt-an-sich,* a reality independent of the subject and of the *Vollzug*. But it is far more consistent and logical to say that if I am asking a question about an object of thought, the answer should be in the same order—either another related object of thought (the *Gewusste* that is basic to the question) or an expansion of the given object of thought. After all, the development of Physics and Mathematics requires questioning and such development is quite consistent within the Kantian system. When I ask whether in a right triangle the square on the hypotenuse is equal to the sum of the squares on the other two sides I know something about a triangle; I don't know the answer to my question, but I don't have to postulate an *Objekt-an-sich*. I can work out the answer within the order of knowledge and so pass on to another *Vollzug*. The only way the argument will work is to assume a "das" which I already know to be an *Objekt-an-sich*. In reverting to a common sense analysis of asking a question, Coreth surreptitiously gives the argument a basis in natural realism which, theoretically, he should repudiate. The implicit realism must be washed out. Gilson, with profound insight, has noted that the idealistic systems can maintain themselves only by constantly, surreptitiously and, if you will, unthematically relying on natural realism.[48] We must conclude that both the Transcendental Method and the methodic use of The Question fail at this critical point. Coreth has not escaped the idealistic consequences of his method. From these ill-starred pages (171–193) to page 488 no additional argument is introduced to establish realism.

---

[47]Coreth, 177.

[48]*Ibid.* cf. Gilson, *Réalisme Thomiste et critique de la connaissance*, 173–174.

Another crucial test can be found in the argument given on pages 204–209.

First, I must call attention to the footnote on page 207. Three things are here asserted: (1) that the argument in the text is a proof for the existence of God (the first to be offered in the *Metaphysik*); (2) that no appeal is made to efficient causality; (3) that the basis of the argument is the "insight" ("*Einsicht*") that "every multiplicity presupposes a unity which makes that multiplicity possible." Now in the body of the text, the situation to which this insight (or "Principle") is applied is my knowledge of being as the identity in the difference of beings, that is, as a formal identity in real difference. If we pass over Coreth's previous failure to establish the existence of beings (*Seiende*) distinct—ontically—from the subject and from each other, the statement that there are really distinct individual beings may be assumed to be obvious. Now, however, we ask what is meant by a "formal identity" (*die formale Identität*)? It is distinguished from the real difference (*die reale Differenz*). If we take the word "form" to express that which makes a being to be what it is, there is no identity in the difference ("*in der Differenz*"), for the formal elements in the beings are as ontically or really different as the beings themselves.[49] In our knowledge of individuals we can see that they are similar (not "identical") in some respect or other and so express this similarity in an abstract (materially) universal concept. The unification is not in the difference, not in beings, but in the intellect. Coreth moves to specify that the identity of all beings is being (*das Sein*).[50] The movement of the argument goes then from the real difference through the formal identity to the existence of an absolute identity which must be absolute being (*absolutes Sein*). Once it is recognized that the formal identity is an identity (or unification) in knowledge, the ontological progression of the argument is broken and we are dealing with a modern sophisticated version of Platonism (or probably better, neo-Platonism). Coreth, in the attached *Zusatz,* expressly recognizes the Platonic background of the principle.[51] In Plato he says, "*Die Gemeinsamkeit in der Verschiedenheit der Dinge*

---

[49]Coreth, 204. Donceel also uses this argument in his own *Philosophical Psychology,* 2nd ed. (New York: Sheed and Ward, 1961), 260–261.

[50]Coreth, 204–205.

[51]Coreth, 209.

verlangt als Grund der Einheit die transzendente Idee." He properly
relates this to the Kantian search for a principle of unity, that is, for the
"*Einheit in der Mannigfaltigkeit.*" St. Thomas himself identified this
principle as Platonic.[52] However, in imbedding it in his own argument
he transfoms it into a principle of efficient causality instead of a
formality. This is in accord with his usual handling of "positiones" and
enables him to pair it with an Aristotelian text.[53] Coreth, however,
expressly repudiates the use of efficient causality and is thus involved
in the Platonic confusion of thought and thing, of formality and reality.

Now, I next select an illustrative case from Coreth's structuring of
limited beings.

At page 213 Coreth undertakes to mediate (in the sense of
"vermitteln") the metaphysical constitution of the individual beings.
Now, even if the argument terminating on page 177, truly established
an *Objekt-an-sich,* it told us nothing of the nature of that object, whether
it was one or many, directly or indirectly known, or anything else about
it. So now we must presuppose the existence of many, individual and
limited entities (*Seiende*) which are different from me (after all, at this
point even on Coreth's showing I know nothing of any other *Geist*
except God) and from each other. Again, the substitution of questions
about the individuals of our experience for the question about *das Sein
im Ganzen* surreptitiously puts back into the method a large dose of
natural realism. Knowledge of individuals is the condition for the possibility of questions about individuals. The questions about individuals
are directed to determining what separates beings from each other and
from *das Sein im Ganzen.*[54]

Essence (*Essentia; Wesen*) is discovered as the inner principle
which limits being (*Sein*). It is found to be a "relative-negation" or a

---

[52]"Respondeo dicendum, quod omnis cognitio est per assimilationem; similitudo autem
inter aliqua duo est secundum convenientiam in forma. Cum autem unitas effectus
unitatem causae demonstret, et sic in genere cujuslibet formae ad unum primum
principium illius formae redire oporteat, impossible est aliqua duo ad invicem esse
similia, nisi altero duorum modorum: vel ita quod unum sit causa alterius, vel ita quod
ambo ab una causa causentur, quae eamdem formam utrique imprimat; ..." St. Thomas
Aquinas, *De veritate,* I, 8, ad 8.

[53]*S.T.* I, q. 44, a. 1, c.

[54]Coreth, 215–216.

"negative-relation." This relationship to others is precisely what gives the limited beings their limitation and their determination. *Wesen* is neither being (*Sein*) nor an existent (*Seiendes*). In negative-relation to others, it denies the determination of others of its own existent, declares it "impossible." Thus it is seen as the potentiality of the determined limited being content of the existent. But its relative-negation and negative-relation to others underlies and is prior to its being itself a limited and determined possibility of being.[55] The difficulty here seems to be that Being (*Sein*) is not regarded as the act of existence and therefore the actuation of all acts but as a sort of Platonic universal—the *Sein alles Seienden*—which does not truly admit of an internal ontological (in Coreth's sense) analogy and is always in its full purity unlimited. The Platonic problem of non-being is thus resurrected and it is not surprising that a Platonizing solution is put forth—that essence should be seen as a relative-negation and a negative-relation which not only reproduces the Platonic principle of "otherness" but echoes the Spinozan establishment of the finite as a relative negation. One can say that what is positive in essence is here absorbed into Being as opposed to essence, and essence ceases to be a "real" component in the metaphysical order. Wilhelmsen, working along a somewhat different line of criticism, has uncovered this same fundamental weakness in Transcendental Thomism—the fundamental reduction of essence " to be *nothing more* (emphasis in the original) than a limit on existence. . . ."[56]

After studying the discussion of essence (*Wesen*) in pages 217–249, one would expect to find the metaphysical (Coreth's "ontological") function of form to be likewise reduced to a minimum. And this is exactly what we find. Although essence (*Wesen*) is ontologically analyzed and established by page 249, "Form" is not discussed until pages 500–509. Form turns out to be simply a principle (ontological to be sure) which determines the material principle. Its function as act in its own order, of constituting the reality of the existent (of the *id quod est*) is almost completely (or perhaps completely) lost in Coreth's metaphysical (ontological) constitution of beings. The important role of

---

[55]Coreth, 234–241.

[56]Wilhelmsen, "Priority of Judgment," 493. cf. St. Thomas: "Essentia dicitur secundum quod per eam et in ea res habet esse." *De ente et essentia*, c. 1.

form in the Thomistic metaphysical structure of finite beings almost totally disappears.

I have been able in this paper to give only a very preliminary and general assessment of Coreth's *Metaphysik* and of its relationship to the work of Maréchal. Much more extended analysis will be necessary to give a thoroughgoing critique. The project is rendered particularly difficult by a constant ambiguity of terminology. Thus we have seen that *Wesen,* though spoken of in Thomistic terminology, carries rather a Platonizing meaning.

This is particularly apparent in one absolutely basic theme which I shall only touch on here.

The Transcendental Thomists allege that the great fault in Kantianism is the total lack of or disregard for being. To turn the Transcendental Method into a Thomistic Transcendental Method and to turn the critical philosophy into a true metaphysics, "being" must be introduced as the central theme.

This is undoubtedly correct. But what understanding of being and what derivation of being?

Since the presuppositions of Kant have been accepted, neither the common nor the metaphysical understanding of being can be derived or extracted from the objects of our direct experience. Donceel, writing in his own name, explains, "That is why metaphysics is *a priori,* virtually inborn in us, not derived from sense experience, exactly as the soul is ontologically prior to the body and not derived from it. Yet we would never know any metaphysics if we had no sense knowledge, exactly as our soul cannot operate without our body. Hence, metaphysics is *virtually* inborn in us. We become aware of it only *in* and *through* sense knowledge, although it does not come *from* sense knowledge."[57] This is, of course, the Kantian view that *a priori* knowledge arises with experience, on its occasion, but not from it.

Thus we never truly "learn" about being; we simply become aware of what we have known all along. There need be no experiential check on metaphysics nor do we have to go through the laborious development of our understanding of being which is the substance and the vitality of Thomistic Metaphysics. This understanding is given in advance—since it cannot be derived from experience; it is already but

---

[57]Donceel, 8.

"unthematically" known; it and its laws are "virtually" inborn. "The Question" presupposes it in an "absolute" and "self-identical" way. It is seen as *das Sein alles Seienden*. What does this mean?

Donceel, in his "Preface," adverts to the problem of translation created by the German language and Coreth's use of "being" terminology.[58] There is certainly a translation problem here, but, beyond that, there is an intrinsic difficulty of philosophical meaning. On page 141, in *Zusatz* 3, Coreth gives at least three different meanings for *Sein*.

Many other words occur. In discussing the Suarezian position *Dasein*" is "*Existentia*" and "*Sosein*" is "*Quidditas*," whereas the Thomistic *esse et essentia* becomes *Sein und Wesen*.[59]

While Coreth recognizes the Thomistic use of *esse* as the *actus essendi* which is distinct from the essence, the metaphysical emphasis does not fall here. In fact, while admitting the distinction, Coreth maintains that he has gone beyond it. What goes beyond it is precisely the negative-relation and the relative-negation of the essence, discussed above.[60]

Now, in Coreth the truly metaphysical expression is *das Sein alles Seienden*. I can see no way of translating this into Thomistic Latin. *Ens omnis entis* means nothing. The *Sein* here cannot be translated as *esse*, i.e., *actus essendi*. Coreth precisely denies this meaning. Moreover, to say that the *esse omnis entis* is that which binds all existents together would be sheer pantheism. The *Sein alles Seienden* is that which makes all beings to be beings (not "to exist"); and it is that in which all beings are united and that which is intrinsically common to all beings. There is only one tradition in which this makes sense—the Platonic tradition. The *Sein alles Seienden* must be translated as the Beingness of all beings and treated like a Platonic idea. We saw above that in the constitution of an existent all its being, all its positiveness, comes from the beingness that makes it a being. Since this pure beingness is "absolute," that is, completely purified and separated, it cannot be limited of itself—but by something outside itself. This brings us back to Coreth's problem of the essence as being outside the beingness of the

---

[58]Donceel, 13–14.

[59]Coreth, 225–226.

[60]Coreth, 243.

existent. Analogous problems arise when Coreth deals with "*Materialität*" and "Forma." This Platonic turn explains also why Coreth believes his formalistic non-causal argument for the existence of God can work. Beingness is pure self-identity, pure unity; it is shared in by a diversity which violates its identity and yet without it would fall apart into pure multiplicity.

CONCLUSION

In this paper I have attempted to present, briefly and selectively, evidence in support of the following assertions which express my current view.

1. The realistic metaphysical methodology of St. Thomas is different from and incompatible with any reasonably authentic version of the Transcendental Method.

2. That the use of the Transcendental Method results in an idealistic-oriented Platonizing metaphysics which is radically different from Thomistic metaphysics.

3. That Transcendental Thomism has no philosophical right to be called "Thomism."

4. That Transcendental Thomism is internally inconsistent and metaphysically unsound.

As an independent and final observation I should like to add that Maréchal's grand strategy for bringing Thomism into the mainstream of modern thought has obviously failed. I suggest that in this regard Jacques Maritain has been far more successful—and precisely because his was an authentic Thomism.

XXI

REFLECTIONS ON THE ART OF HOSPITAL ADMINISTRATION

N ew Introduction: I am adding this article[1] to my collected works, although it is not philosophical, but it is I think a good example of what general philosophical reflection can do for a practical art like hospital administration. The background is this. St. Louis University has a program leading to a Master's Degree in Hospital Administration. It requires a year of class work at the University followed by a year of internship in a hospital. At the end of the internship the intern returns to the University for a summer of reflection and additional course work. One year I was asked to give the returning interns an address that would stimulate them to make the most of their summer, so I gave the talk. It was recorded, edited, and published in *Hospital Progress*. Subsequently the editors of *Hospital Progress* submitted the article to the National Academy of Hospital Administrators in competition for the award of best article on Hospital Administration for the year 1959. The article won the competition and was therefore reprinted in the Journal of the Academy itself.

I see nothing that I want to add or detract from this article. It still says what I think about hospital administration. In a letter to me dated May 1, 1997, an active Health Administrator wrote, "I noticed they were published in *Hospital Progress* in May 1959, yet I found the content very current and appropriate for today's health care facility. I

---

[1]First published as The Intellectual Development in *Hospital Progress* (May 1959): 86–91. Copyright by the Catholic Health Association Reproduced from *Health Progress* with permission.

have taken the liberty of making copies; I plan to share them with my administrative staff."

* * *

The rather pretentious title of this paper insinuates, at least, that we have to discuss the sort of person an "operationalist" ought to be. This topic was assigned, no doubt, on the assumption that the hospital administrator is indeed an "operationalist," that his main task is to run something, to do or practice or operate. His work does not lie in the construction of scientific systems of thought or in the reflective meditation and understanding of the philosopher and theorist. The proper task of the administrator is in the area of art and prudence, of practicality and application.

Yet, we are here asked to discuss precisely the growth of the administrator through the acquisition of intellectual attitudes and habits, of theoretical knowledge and understanding.

As an organizing diagram for the discussion, I should like to set up here a sort of "spectrum" or "continuum" of types of operations, running from A to Z thus: A————————Z.

Let us define the spectrum by locating opposite types at A and Z. At **A** let us put the completely routinized type of operation, the sort of operation that can be conducted according to clear-cut rules, can be described as a definite series of steps and so also can be easily taught. Let us think for example of the simple repetitive operations of machine operators in a factory, or of the business of taking temperatures or washing test tubes.

Now as we move from **A** to **Z** we move through operational types that are less and less subject to neat rules, to routine, to description as a series of steps until, at the extreme, we can place something like carving or painting. The artist is an "operationalist"; he paints. True, there are certain rules which, after a fashion, he follows; but, in general, his truly artistic work cannot be reduced to formulae or routine: there are individual decisions, freedom, creativity. In fact, every great work of art remains unique—the *Iliad,* the Parthenon, Michelangelo's *Pieta,* El Greco's *Toledo*—a creative achievement never quite to be repeated. To be sure, the work of art embodies universalities and realizes a pattern; after the fact we may derive classical rules from the work itself.

But great art does not come by rules, not even by these rules, and to the extent that artistic effort is reduced to the following of classical models and rules there result the stuffy and lifeless products of convention and "schools." In the work of the true artist there is always a degree of freedom and creativity, of new and unique decision.

Then in this spectrum we would have, ideally, at **A** an operation that is wholly routinized, at **Z** an operation that is pure creativity and freedom; thus we define the actual continuum of types of human operations.

In order to emphasize the characters of these operations let us, for a moment, move off the **A** end of the spectrum into non-human activity and examine routinized operations as we find them in the animal world. Let us use this as a sort of "control" case.

We find in the world of animals, among insects for example, certain remarkable and highly complex operations. The business of constructing a beehive involves the application of a very complicated mathematical formula. The structure of the cells within which the bee preserves its honey is a delight, I am told, to the theoretical mathematician. There is a certain kind of wasp that selects a type of caterpillar, paralyzes it by a single sting, then lays its eggs in the living but immobilized caterpillar. Thus when the eggs hatch, the young ones will have fresh meat of the right sort available immediately upon entering into their own form of life.

These operations, the laying out of cells and the surgical paralyzing of the caterpillar, would, if they were the result of study and training, require a high degree of skill. Yet the bee and the wasp carry them out with accuracy and precision—in a completely routine manner. They are not applying general principles. The bees have not devised mathematics from which they have worked out general formulae for the construction of the cells, nor has the wasp learned the anatomy of caterpillars and practiced in some surgical room for a long period of years to achieve this skill to strike—once and precisely—the right nerve center.

Here is an operation that is wholly crystallized and routinized, an operation that is complex, achieves a goal, requires an analogue to skill, which, if performed by a human being, would require a great deal of knowledge and understanding; and yet it is an operation that in its rigid, routinized condition is devoid of intelligence and understanding. The crystallization of these practices, these operations, in the animals not only enables the animal to do this thing with a great deal of skill and accuracy but at the same time makes it impossible for the animal to adapt to any large extent to any kind of a situation that would be different. The animal is caught within its routine.

In some cases there is a certain plasticity in the range of the adaptation of the animal, but by and large there is no freedom here. That's why Bergson considered instinct in the animals to be a kind of "frozen intelligence." In a sense the operation is intelligently carried out, but the understanding, the insight, the control, the freedom, the creativity of the human intelligent operation is gone.

Now let us return to our spectrum. At the **A** level we can find human operations which we can train a person to do almost wholly as a *routine*. We can lay out definite rules and steps. We can tell a person: "Now this is the way you do it—you do A, then you do B, then you do C, then repeat. Always do it this way." We teach many people—aides, technicians, assistants, factory workers—to do a great number of operations of this sort, to follow routines.

But now the less a person understands about the operations, the less that person understands about what the operation is intended to do, how it works, and why it works that way and the *more rigid the routine must be* (Hence Bergson's "frozen intelligence" in the animal). Plato pointed this out many years ago when he was discussing the limitations inherent in a written code of laws. He used the doctor as his example. When the doctor diagnoses the patient's illness and then has to go off to see other patients, he leaves behind a codified set of directions, a prescription of treatment and care. When the doctor leaves, Plato said, the people in the home who are taking care of the patient have to follow these rules rigidly while the doctor is gone. If the doctor himself were there, he might, after a while, notice a change in the patient and modify his treatment. But the others cannot be allowed to do this. They must stick to what the doctor has prescribed; they cannot have the freedom to change the rules. Why is this? Because the doctor *knows* and these people do not *know*. When knowledge is absent, when understanding is absent, the routine must be rigid.

On the other hand, to the extent that people understand operations and are masters of the knowledge involved they can be left to their own judgment, can be given control and freedom. To this extent also we can look for a certain creativity. For the person who has learned to do something routinely and does not understand what he is doing cannot devise a better way of doing it; improvement in such a case would be sheer luck. If you do not understand what you are doing, you cannot decide that step five is too long or that step seven can be left out or that a new step can be substituted for three old ones.

It is only when the routine is understood, only when its complete context is known that creativity and freedom, improvement, adaption and development can take place.

This is true not only for individual operations but also for whole cultures. In many simple cultures agriculture, for example, has been routinized for centuries. If you visit the remote Mayan villages of the Youcatan today, you will find the Indians, in cultivating maize, from the clearing of the ground to the eating of the bread, following a series of steps that was set in rigid routine at a time lost to record and human memory. Thus their fathers did it before them, and they know that if they do these things, they will have corn and bread. But there is no understanding of the scientific background of agriculture, nor of the laws of diet and nutrition; consequently, there is routine and stagnation. In America scientific knowledge has been applied to agriculture; there are changes, new methods, new kinds of crops, new species of grain, and so forth. Farming in the United States has almost become a learned profession.

Let us summarize once more: the less a person knows and understands about the operation in question, the more rigid and routinized it must be; and to this extent also there is less freedom of judgment, less possibility of creativity, and less actual improvement.

Now, please note. This is not a condemnation of routine. We cannot get rid of—indeed, we absolutely must have—set procedures and routinized operations. Indeed, it is only *because* we can routinize much of human activity that space can be cleared for important creative work.

Among human operations then there are some which can and, often enough, should be routinized. Thus, making beds, washing windows, running simple tests, and so forth.

But there are some operations which can be either simplified almost to a routine or carried out within a context of understanding. Here there is question of moving an operation slowly along our spectrum from **A** toward **Z**. Let us take, for example, the repairing of television sets. We can, in a very few months of training, turn out a television repair man. He will have learned certain tests, certain tricks of the trade; he will know the meaning of certain "symptoms" and what to do to get rid of them. But he will not understand "television." If we want to place these operations within context of technical understanding, we shall have to teach our man mathematics and physics; he will have to study magnetism, electricity and electronics. If we brought this knowledge to an ideally complete level, the man would *understand* television and so have an intellectual and creative control of all the repair operations.

Now there is another sort of operation that can't be routinized even to the extent that television repairing can be. This operation, by its nature, lies further over towards **Z** on our spectrum. Here let our example be a lung operation. The complexity of this operation and, above all, of the total context directly relative to it, makes simple routinization impossible. The surgeon must know what he is doing. He must understand anatomy and physiology; he must know the structure of bone and tissue, the effect of shock, the indicated post-operative treatment, *etc*.

Now in both of these cases—the types exemplified in television repairing and in surgery—the knowledge required is what I shall call, for purposes only of this discussion, technical knowledge. By this I mean knowledge that deals with its subject matter as things or objects rather than as persons, with the laws of things rather than with the values of personality. Let this point rest here for the moment.

Ideally then, we can, by putting an operation or a series of interlocking operations into the full relevant knowledge context, move the operations all the way over to **Z**, to a point where freedom and control, development and creativity are reached. Here there appears now—alongside our proper artist—the truly creative scientific research man, not the run-of-the-mill Ph.D. who is working with other men's ideas and testing other men's hypotheses but the truly imaginative scientist who so deeply understands his science that he is free of it, whose mind can leap beyond its current crystallized formulae and theories.

In a first-rate basic research institute the entire spectrum of operations—so far as I have described it for "technical" knowledge—can be discerned. From the simplest routines of the laboratory performed by assistants, the spectrum stretches through the work of technicians, junior scientists to the creative research designing of the director of the research team. Reflection upon this situation can reveal yet another important relationship within our spectrum. Let us say that for the research going on in this laboratory there is required absolutely clean, absolutely sterile, absolutely dry glassware. A routine is set up to prepare such glassware and to have it always at hand when needed. Instructions are given to some assistant hired to do just such jobs. But who determines that such glassware is needed, that it should be prepared thus and so, and when modifications are to be made in its preparation? Not the assistant but the man who *understands* the research operations, the man, finally, who *understands* the entire research project.

To the extent that a man's understanding of operations moves toward **Z** on the spectrum, to that extent he not only understands the operations he himself is performing but can and should *determine, dictate,* and *control* the routine operations which lie at the lower end of the spectrum.

THE SPECTRUM ADDS A NEW DIMENSION

Well then, what has this to do with hospital and administration? In the first place, the entire spectrum of operational types is to be found in every hospital within a wide diversity of technical areas: in the pathological laboratory, the surgery, the diet kitchen, the nursing service, the housekeeping and bookkeeping departments. There is a sense in which all of these operations come under the decisions of the administrator, but this relation of the administrator's decision to the whole spectrum of technical operations is different than that of the creative technical expert to the routinized operations in his own field.

The administrator does not have the technical competence to dictate and direct each operation; he cannot determine how pathological tests are to be run or the nature of post-operative nursing. Yet he must know, in a sort of extrinsic way to be sure, the results, actual and potential, of these operations and their proper contribution to the total work of the hospital. In a new sense this places the administrator over toward the **Z** of our spectrum; but this is inadequate to locate him precisely and properly. For if he does not determine and direct the individual operations in virtue of specialized knowledge and technical competence, in virtue of what does he do so?

To see this we must here step back from the spectrum and focus a new light upon the whole range and reach of technical operations. For while each operation is individually ordered to a technical goal, the whole system of operations is ordered, in a hospital, to the good of human beings. Thus all the operations are now inserted into a new context, no longer a context of technical knowledge merely—knowledge of "things" or "objects"—but a context of human concern, of human beings precisely as *persons*. A new dimension is thus added to the entire spectrum. And along this dimension run the operations of the administrator, from the formalized procedures of routine practice (**A**) to the insightful judgment and the creative decision which is the proper task of the administrator. For here is the proper meaning of those special kinds of decisions which determine and organize all the operations and direct them, beyond technical results, to the good of people.

The administrator's decision with regard to the technical problems of the diet kitchen, the administrator's decision with regard to medical care, the administrator's decision with regard to the organization of nursing service; these decisions must relate to the good of a human being, i.e., of the *patient*. Remove the patient; the organizing principle of the hospital is gone as well as the one reason for an "administrator."

UNDERSTANDING IS MORE THAN JUST KNOWLEDGE

But there is another fact besides the ordination of the hospital to the patient which subjects the administrator to the values of human personality. These values are found not only in the patient but in the operations of the hospital itself. The administrator orders not only the technical apparatus, machinery, space, drugs, and so forth to the good of the patient but also to the activities of other human beings. The people who maintain the operations of the hospital cannot be reduced to the status of pure means like X-rays or beds; the administrative decision must respect them as people.

The realm of the administrator's decision is thus, by a two-fold title, the realm of human concern. This decision must be made in the light of the good; consequently, in the light of an understanding of human beings, in the light of an understanding and appreciation of the values of personality. And this requires something other than just technical knowledge and something other than just knowledge.

It is true that within certain limits, there is a "technical" knowledge about people. There are elementary textbooks in which the salesman is told how to speak to the housewife, how to judge from her manner and her eyes which brushes should finally be pushed. But, taken alone this sort of knowledge enables us to manipulate people as though they were things and, taken strictly alone, leads to a sort of connivance of operationalists and scientists to twist human wills to selfish purpose, to make of human beings means and not ends. We have, in fact, developed a frightening amount of such technical knowledge. We can destroy sanity, overwhelm interior freedom, and reduce men to a kind of automatism. Let one report illustrate this.

The sales department of a large chewing gum company in checking geographical distribution of sales, discovered a certain county in which the sale of gum was deplorably low. So they called in a crack sales consultant with a staff of psychologists, sociometrists, *etc*. These experts reported that the county was a mining area in which illiterate and poor minors were struggling against the exhaustion and deterioration of the mines. They were frustrated and not interested in luxuries like gum. Well, did they have a solution? Oh, yes indeed! They had prepared a cartoon series repeating one single theme: frustration and defeat—suggestion of gum chewing (play up the wrapper)—chewing (with a hint of a smile)—solution (smiles, cheers, thanks to . . . gum). These cartoons were distributed; sales soared.

These gentlemen probably had degrees in psychology; they certainly had technical knowledge of human behavior. But this knowledge which permits itself to be used in exploitation and manipulation of human persons is worlds apart from the sort of appreciative understanding the administrator needs. Let us contrast this description of St. Francis of Assisi:

> I have said that St. Francis deliberately did not see the wood for the trees. It is even more true that he deliberately did not see the mob for the men. What distinguishes this very genuine democrat from any mere demagogue is that he never either deceived or was deceived by the illusion of mass-suggestion. Whatever his taste in monsters, he never saw before him a many-headed beast. He only saw the image of God multiplied but never monotonous. To him a man was always a man and did not disappear in a dense crowd any more than in a desert. He honoured all men; that is, he not only loved but respected them all. What gave him his extraordinary personal power was this; that from the Pope to the beggar, from the sultan of Syria in his pavilion to the ragged robbers crawling out of the wood, there was never a man who looked into those brown burning eyes without being certain that Francis Bernardone was really interested in him; in his own inner individual life from the cradle to the grave; that he himself was being valued and taken seriously, and not merely added to the spoils of some social policy or the names in some clerical document . . . We may say if we like that St. Francis, in the bare and barren simplicity

of his life, had clung to one rag of luxury; the manners of a court. But whereas in a court there is one king and a hundred courtiers, in this story there was one courtier moving among a hundred kings. For he treated the whole mob of men as a mob of kings. And this is really and truly the only attitude that will appeal to that part or man to which he wished to appeal. It cannot be done by giving gold or even bread; for it is a proverb that any reveller may fling largesse in mere scorn. It cannot even be done by giving time and attention; for any number of philanthropists and benevolent bureaucrats do such work with a scorn far more cold and horrible in their hearts. No plans or proposals or efficient rearrangements will give back to a broken man his self-respect and sense of speaking with an equal. One gesture will do it.[2]

To be this sort of person, St. Francis needed both an attitude and an understanding. But the understanding is not merely technical but rather broad and deep human insight into people which can adjust to the personal understanding of individuals. Here is understanding by intuition, by empathy, within the concrete fullness of human relationships. How do we achieve *this* understanding?

If you really want to understand human beings, there are plenty of people to go to besides psychologists. There are men, and women, who have a wonderful understanding of human beings, without having acquired it by any official scientific procedure. Most of these people are incapable of communicating their knowledge, but those who can communicate it are novelists. They are good novelists precisely because they are good psychologists. But they are not scientific psychologists: they are in a sense poets, and many of the poets (but not all) are first-rate psychologists. If one wishes to learn about psychology in a genuine, rather than a scientific, way, by far the best thing to do is to read masterpieces of literature.[3]

---

[2]Chesterton, Gilbert K., *St. Francis of Assisi* (New York: Doran, 1924), 141–143.

[3]Standen, Anthony, *Science is a Sacred Cow* (New York: Dutton, 1950), 128.

As Standen points out, we are here looking for that sort of humanistic psychology and anthropology which the tradition of art and literature, of history and philosophy brings to a man; for that sort of attitude which finds its highest and fullest form in the genuine love displayed by a man like St. Francis.

And so we come to a first formulation of an answer to our title. The operationalist who is a hospital administrator should have a broad and thorough humanistic education—an intellectual education, to be sure, but one which includes also the reach of human value—attitudes, and habits of appreciation and love. Nor are these strictly two separable things: for this sort of knowledge must be in function of appreciation, and this sort of love must arise out of sympathetic understanding.

And so we define the qualities of the true administrator. Here is his true field; here we finally run him to ground and locate him. For these reasons administration cannot become merely a procedural, operational know-how-to-do business. Nor is it simply a matter of putting a procedure or a routine into a context of increasing technical knowledge. To be sure, back of the administrative "act" there must be some technical knowledge, some understanding of the individual technical operations (whether routine or creative) and how they fit together in an over-all pattern for the good of human beings. But beyond this we must bring the "act" of the administrator to the level of a true "prudential" judgment.

We are, indeed, locating him here (at **Z**), rather with the artist than with the pure technical operationist (**A**). It depends upon the artist's judgment in this unique creation which is *this* painting with *these* colors; it depends upon his artistic judgment that he put these colors thus and so. There is no neat rule by which he can apply a meter or a color card to tell himself he has done it correctly. The true artist judges artistically.

So also in dealing with people as persons and in judging in the light of *their* good, the decisions of the administrator cannot be reduced to rules, charts or routines; they cannot be made matters of mere procedure. So the proper operation of the administrator isn't an operation that can be fully understood simply by technical knowledge, whether it be theory of administration or accounting or economics or patient care or anatomy or any other knowledge of this kind. It requires some technical knowledge, but above all it requires prudence which is born of an education, a deep education in understanding and valuing and appreciating human beings or human life and human death.

What we need is deep reflection upon these things—a reflection that moves into the area of decision and judgment and which we remember to apply as administrators not only to the goods which are the goals of our operations, but to the goods which are the people in the operations themselves. Then our decisions will remain creative and free. We will not become routinized. Our intelligence will not become frozen and our prudence rigid. We will have the flexibility to improve, the flexibility to dare to make improvements and move forward.

WHAT EDUCATION CAN AND CANNOT GIVE

How then do we get "administrators"? Well, first of all there must be intelligence. When we select prospective administrators, we must find young men and women with intelligence. There's no substitute for it and when it is missing, university programs are impotent. *Quod Deus non dedit, Salamanca non dat.* We must select a person who is basically —not without emotions but—emotionally mature and stable. Then there must be experience. We can't turn an administrator out of a program of education all ready to administer beautifully and perfectly. We can't do that. There's got to be experience. A long time ago Aristotle emphasized this. He was discussing the relative *operational* merits of theoretical knowledge and experience. He points out—very much as I did in setting up the operational spectrum—that animals by and large live by a kind of instinctive activity, learning very little from experience; but that man learns from experience and that out of many experiences he develops arts and sciences, and reasoning with these he arrives at understandings of activities and of things, and that this, in turn, feeds back into practice.

Theoretical knowledge was therefore, he said, very important; but if you were faced with choosing between a doctor who had theoretical training but no experience and a doctor who had experience but no theoretical training, Aristotle—one of the world's most confirmed theorists —said: "Call in the man of experience." The other man is all the more dangerous in that he has theoretical knowledge because he will think he knows a great deal more about what to do than a man who has no theoretical knowledge; whereas the man with experience has at least a practical understanding and some insight into the way things actually go in the world. However much we stress the need of education and training, without experience—without experience that is illumined by intelligence and without experience that is rendered fruitful by knowledge—we can't get a good administrator or operationalist.

But there should also be formal training. This must consist of at least two kinds of things. First there is that general understanding of the technical operations which constitute the actual operation of a hospital. But there must also be the other sort of broad intellectual, moral, humanistic, personal education which I have tried to describe. I would argue that the hospital administrator most certainly—but even nurses, doctors, and people in health fields generally—should have a very broad kind of culture, because the activities and decisions of these people are within the human dimension where understanding of human nature and of human good is decisive. For this understanding our culture has traditionally turned to literature and art, to history and philosophy and theology; we may add modern discipline like anthropology.

Administration is a high calling and a hard one. Even the most careful selection and the best-planned education do not guarantee perseverance. There is always a tendency to seek relief in routine and formalism; it is so much easier to judge cases by mechanical norms than to face the individual issues and push through the human complexities to an independent judgment. Of course, routines and procedures are necessary and useful; I am talking of the tendency to let the proper operation of administration—its creative judgment—slip to the lower end of the spectrum and become "frozen" in routine. I would plead for administrators to keep up their broad humanistic interests throughout life. It does not take a great deal. I would suggest that they then keep always at hand for regular reading one book that belongs to our great traditions and has nothing directly to do with immediate practicalities —a play, a novel, a biography, a book of poetry.

REAPPRAISAL CHANGES VALUES

In his later years, Charles Darwin wrote that his mind had seemed to become a sort of machine for turning out scientific generalizations; he found he could no longer enjoy music or poetry, Virgil or Shakespeare. This he regretted since he thought it not only adversely affected his higher intellectual operations but had also deadened his sensibilities. He added that if he had it to do over, he would, every week, listen to some music and read some literature. This is pretty much the regimen I am suggesting for administrators.

I suggest further that the administrator ought periodically, every day if at all possible, withdraw for a short period of time into a sort of meditative retreat and consider how his administration squares with the human dimension.

And so let us turn back once again to Plato, who first described the administrator as a philosopher king. This man wasn't a doctor and he wasn't an architect; he wasn't an anatomist or a pathologist, but he was a man who understood human nature, human life, human society, and human good. And therefore Plato said: "This is the man who should make the top administrative decisions. This is the man who should make the decisions at the level of statesmanship." Now all administration participates in statesmanship because it has to make decisions of this type. And this philosopher king of Plato can well be a model for all administrators because the kind of training he wanted to give this man was not any specific technical training but a broad liberal training. It was to be the "harmonia," the traditional humanistic culture of Greece plus the philosophical and theoretical education of Plato's Academy.

But to Plato's formula we must bring an additional qualification. Plato has been accused of describing in his "philosopher king" a fascist dictator, and there is ground for this charge in that knowledge alone is no guarantee that administration will not sink into exploitation and manipulation of human beings. We must think of a king who is "philosopher" *and "saint,"* for the administrative decision is in function of the total intellectual and moral personality of the administrator.

An evil man can efficiently repair a television set or even set a leg or carry out successful scientific research, but an evil man cannot be an efficient administrator. He may have the order of the drill field or the humming activity of the factory, but he will miss the human good which alone justifies the administrator's decision.

XXII

THE PRESENCE OF GOD

New Introduction: This article[1] really is a result of a period of time which I spent in the hospital during which I applied the thoughts of this article to my own situation and I also explained it to one of the members of the hospital spiritual ministry, who used it with patients and reported that they got a great deal out of it. This stimulated me to think of writing up these ideas since they might help other people. So as soon as I got home from the hospital, I formulated them in an article and it was published and received a very good reaction from many people.

I add it here to the other articles not because it is philosophical, which to a large extent it is, but because it's an example of how metaphysics can develop and strengthen the spiritual life. The main point of the article is of course that a true analysis of the reality of God's presence is much more powerful and important than any metaphor or simile that the spiritual writers can introduce.

* * *

The example of the saints and the teaching of spiritual writers both recommend to us the practice of the presence of God as an aid to our Christian living and our Christian sanctification. St. Ignatius, for example, advises his retreatants to place themselves in the presence of God before they begin to pray. Others speak of "putting" ourselves in the presence of God at the beginning of the day or at intervals throughout

---

[1]First Published in *Spiritual Life* 29, 4 (Winter 1983): 209–217.

the day or before making any important decision or prior to hearing Mass and so forth.

Many people use various devices to practice the presence of God. Metaphors are suggested such as imagining ourselves in a vast sea of being which is God. Again, God is presented extrinsically as watching us in the spirit of the old-fashioned sampler which displayed an eye and the admonition, "God sees you." I submit that these similes and other interpretations of the presence of God are inadequate to ground the full realization of what the presence of God means. I am here presenting a metaphysical approach to the presence of God dealing with the first component, namely the presence of God as our Creator in the very depth of our being. In this sort of consideration we need not introduce external metaphors or even external relationships with God such as, we are walking in His sight. I am therefore here presenting a metaphysical meditation which I believe would give a profound foundation to any practice of the presence of God and will open up the possibility of continuous growth in the depth of understanding of God's creative presence in us.

The understanding of God as Creator in an absolute sense is an essential part of the Jewish and Christian revelation and should there-fore be a fundamental part of any Christian revelation and should therefore be a fundamental part of any Christian spirituality.

Throughout the Old Testament, beginning with the first lines of Genesis,[2] God is presented and often defined as the Creator of heaven

---

[2]Eugene H. Maly, Genesis, *The Jerome Biblical Commentary,* eds. R.E. Brown, S.S., J.A. Fitzmyer, S.J., and R.E. Murphy, O. Carm., I (Englewood Cliffs, N.J.: Prentice-Hall, 1968). The important contribution of P in Genesis indicates this. The days of creation therefore are understood as normal 24-hour periods; as such they form the literary framework of the hymn and have no other significance. The primitive cos-mology of the author's time is used to teach the creation of all things by God. The abso-lute power of the transcendent God is emphasized. Whereas the pagan epics depict creation as a struggle between the gods and the forces of chaos, the biblical account stresses the effortless activity of the one God.

and earth,[3] the Master of all things,[4] Lord of the world,[5] in whose power all things stand and to whom all things belong.[6] God is not merely a tribal deity; He is not just the God of the Jewish people though the Jewish people are portrayed as His special people; He is not exclusively a Jewish deity. On the contrary, God is the God of the entire universe and of all peoples,[7] the Lord of history and the Master of nature who holds all things in the power of his hand.[8] The ancient Hebrews were not philosophically inclined nor did the Hebrew language provide a vehicle for the expression of metaphysical conceptions. But if one takes all the presentations of God as the Maker and Master of the universe as given in the Jewish scriptures and attempts to translate them into a metaphysics they can only be so translated in a metaphysics which sees God as the absolute source of being as such, which sees God as the Master of the very act of existence of every created thing, a continuing source of that active existence.

The doctrine of creation is so fundamental to Christianity that God as Creator stands at the beginning of all the great creeds. "We believe

---

[3]For thus says the Lord,/The creator of the heavens,/who is God,/The designer and maker of the earth/who established it,/Not creating it to be a waste,/but designing it to be lived in:/I am the Lord, and there is no other. (Isaiah 45:18)

[4]O Lord, God of hosts, who is like you?/Mighty are you, O Lord, and your faithfulness surrounds you./You rule over the surging of the sea;/you still the swelling of the waves./Yours are the heavens, and yours is the earth;/the world and its fullness you have founded. (Psalm 89:9,10,12)

[5]It is you, O Lord, you are the only one; you made the heavens, the highest heavens and all their host, the earth and all that is upon it, the seas and all that is in them. To all of them you give life, and the heavenly hosts bow down before you. (Nehemiah 9:6)

[6]Do you not know?/or have you not heard?/The Lord is the eternal God,/Creator of the ends of the earth./He does not faint nor grow weary,/and His knowledge is beyond scrutiny. (Isaiah 40:28)

[7]Sing to the Lord, all you lands,/Tell his glory among the nations;/among all peoples his wondrous deeds./Tremble before him, all the earth;/say among the nations: the Lord is king./He has made the world firm, not to be moved;/He governs the people with equity. (Psalm 96:1,3,9,10)

[8]He has sworn who made the earth by his power,/and established the world by his wisdom,/and stretched out the heavens by his skill./When he thunders, the waters in the heavens roar,/and he brings up clouds from the end of the earth;/He makes the lightning flash in the rain,/and releases storm winds from their chambers. (Jeremiah 51:15,16)

in one God, the Father, the Almighty, maker of heaven and earth, of all that is seen and unseen." Tresmontant[9] has shown that as the first paragraph of the credal tradition developed, it grew in the precise statement of the meaning of God's creative activity to such an extent that a metaphysics which can truly be called Christian can be derived from a study of the development of the first paragraph of the creeds.

We must not think that because man has been caught up into a supernatural order, that is, into a trinitarian relationship, that is to say, in a precise relationship to the Trinity as such and to the internal life of God as an adopted son, that the tremendous fact of his dependence upon God for his very being can be forgotten or ignored. On the contrary, of course, the fact of creation is presupposed by any supernatural elevation and remains within the total concept of man's relationship to God. A true understanding of the relationship of creature to Creator formally as such is a powerful part of our understanding both of God and of man and essential to a fully developed Christian spirituality.

It is therefore of great importance for a truly Christian spirituality and for the proper exercise of the presence of God to understand the creative activity of God properly. There are only two modes of human knowledge which are at all adequate to expressing the reality of God's activity. The first of these is the humanistic mode which presents the creative power of God after the manner of the prophets and psalmists of the Old Testament or of the Christian poets and large parts of the Christian liturgy. The second is the philosophical mode as we find it in the great scholastic theologians. While the humanistic presentation of a creative God may, in view of man's nature, be more calculated to inflame the heart and absorb man's devotion, the metaphysical under-standing of creation is the more profound and the more precise and, in the long run, the more effective.

To repeat, therefore, a profound understanding of the creative activ-ity of God in the natural order is an important component of the Christian understanding of God Himself and of man's relationship to God and a fundamental part of any Christian spirituality, but the crea-tive activity of God must be properly understood and not distorted by superficial explanations or inadequate metaphors.

At this point, therefore, we must eliminate one cause of confusion

---

[9]Claude Tresmontant, *Christian Metaphysics* (New York: Sheed & Ward, 1965).

in modern thinking about creation. The scientific mode of human thought such as we find it in the modern sciences, both physical and biological, cannot deal with the problem of creation; in fact, these sciences cannot even raise the question as to the absolute origin of the universe and its total dependence upon God. The natural sciences presuppose the existence of a material universe which they proceed to study precisely as material and to understand precisely in its material dimensions.[10] Sciences cannot, to repeat, even raise the question of the absolute origin of reality and certainly they can offer no solution to the question they cannot raise. The notion of a scientific creationism necessarily distorts either the understanding of modern science or the understanding of creation. Scientific creationism is an effort to bring the question of absolute origins under the control of the methodology that simply cannot deal with it or it is an effort to force a methodology calculated to study the material dimensions of reality, to yield more than such a study is capable of. The modern sciences simply have nothing to say, negatively or positively, concerning the absolute origin of all things and the nature of the creativity which gives rise to the existence of the universe in whole or in part.

There is another prevalent way of thinking of God's creative work which we should eliminate from our thinking. The argument from design was used so emphatically by British theists that many people think of God primarily as on the analogy of the watchmaker. The design of the universe, they have argued, indicates that a superintelligence has been at work in the universe and so God is conceived as a kind of super-watchmaker or an infinitely ingenious engineer or even as a great mathematician. This distorts the notion of creation. The important thing about the universe is not that it is ordered or neatly organized; the important thing about the universe is that *it is*, that it *exists*, and that everything in it *is* what it is. As Heidegger has said, the basic metaphysical question is, why is there anything rather than nothing? It is only by considering the existence of the world that we can come to a right

---

[10]It is therefore absurd for scientists to talk about creation being explained by any scientific theory such as, for example, that of the so-called big bang. Obviously, if there was a big bang there must have been something to go bang. Science does not deal with absolute beginnings but only with the transformation and development of a given material universe. There may have been a big bang, but it was simply an explosive and radical change of preexisting material reality.

understanding of the nature of creation. Creation is not an act of designing; it's an act of bringing into being what did not exist previously. Since the Creator is intelligent, the mark of intelligence will be on His creation but it is not simply a matter of design that is at stake, it is a matter of the very existence of things. This is why (Heidegger again) the question of the nature of existence may be the most important question in the whole of western thought.

Another misconception which must be avoided or eliminated is the deistic view that God once for all created things, then, as it were, stood aside and let them be. In the extreme version of this view, the universe goes off, as it were, on its own and God no longer pays any attention to it or displays any interest in it. In a less extreme version, God still runs and manages the universe but more or less from outside; He creates things and then His providence guides and rules them.

If, then, we must think of God present to us as the Creator, who constantly creates us, we must think of God as continuously active within us. This is already an important insight but here metaphysics itself raises a difficulty, the solution of which may deepen this insight. The metaphysics of being maintains that God is immutable and unchanging and it would seem therefore that to think of God as active would be to think of God as constantly changing through His activities in the created universe. What this doctrine means to say is that God being infinite reality cannot add to that reality or subtract from it, that God cannot pass from potency to actuation as we do when we act. There is nothing potential in God. This traditional doctrine however tends to lead us to think of God as rigidly and eternally immobilized in His absolute perfection. We must, however, balance this view by realizing that God is not only infinite being, He is also infinite activity. In God action (*agere*) and being (*esse*) are one and the same thing. God is already in act with regard to all possible activities. When He directs His activity to a given external effect, this act arises out of God's existing actuation and is not an activation of a potency. Technically, this is called an *actus perfecti*,[11] that is, an act of a being that is already fully actuated with regard to that act. This is a mystery but we can gain some understanding of it from an analogy drawn from human thought. When we learn some-

---

[11]Lonergan, Bernard J., S.J., *VERBUM: Word and Idea in Aquinas,* David B. Burrell, C.S.C., ed. (Notre Dame: University of Notre Dame Press, 1967), 101–107, 138, 147–148, 165–166.

thing, we pass from potency to act but after we have learned it we may consider it at will without a new passage from potency to act. Here a comparison that is extrinsic and inadequate may yet be helpful. A flashlight, once turned on, will illumine any object placed in front of it without itself undergoing any change. God thus can turn to an external effect of His activity without changing His own reality. Hence, it is eminently realistic to think of God in us not simply as an infinite being but also an infinite activity supporting us in our existence and our activities. It helps to see this within the context of the entire universe where God is everywhere active—in stones and stars but supremely so in human beings where He produces a creature made to His own image and likeness who, unlike stones and stars, can understand that God is thus active within him. A breathtaking realization indeed!

St. Ignatius presents this insight in a devout and humanistic manner in his "Contemplation to Gain Love":

Second Point. The second, to look how God dwells in creatures, in the elements, giving them being, in plants vegetating, in the animals feeding in them, in men giving them to understand: and so in me, giving me being, animating me, giving me sensation and making me to understand; . . .

Third Point. The third, to consider how God works and labors for me in all things created on the face of the earth—that is, behaves like one who labors—as in the heavens, elements, plants, fruits, cattle, etc., giving them being, preserving them, giving them vegetation and sensation, etc.[12]

At this point a brief excursus into Thomistic metaphysics is necessary. In Thomistic metaphysics everything other than God is regarded as consisting of two non-material, non-physical factors, namely its whatness, that which it is, and its act of existence, that by which it is. These two factors correspond to two basic questions one could ask about anything, namely, "what is it?" and the answer here yields a whatness, or, in technical terminology of philosophy, a quid-

---

[12]From "Contemplation to Gain Love" in *The Spiritual Exercises of St. Ignatius of Loyola,* translated from *The Autograph* by Father Elder Mullan, S.J. (New York: P.J. Kennedy & Sons, 1914), 120.

dity, and secondly, "does it exist?"; is it actuated in the real order by an act of existence.

The act of existence (*esse*) actuates its entire being, permeates, as it were, its entire reality. We can think of gold mountains, castles in the air or whatever but without an act of existence they are nothing at all. Thus the most important question about anything is whether it exists or not. If it exists, it exists with an act of existence that is not reducible to what it is.

Two points are of interest to us here. First, that the act of existence posits the reality of any being; secondly, that the act of existence is coterminous with that reality, permeates, as it were, its total essence.

Now, since God is being itself, *ipsum esse* and is the Author of all being, the per se object of His activity is the very act of existence. He therefore touches the creature in its act of existence and so is present actively in its most intimate reality. When we deal with other creatures we touch their act of existence only indirectly. First of all, we presuppose that they exist. God presupposes nothing. Secondly, we deal with accidents, properties, perhaps essences but never directly with the act of existence. Thus God, in His infinite being and His infinite activity is as close to us as our own reality.

Much of what I have said so far is summarized in a beautiful text of St. Thomas which I here translate.

> We must say that God is in all things, not indeed as part of their essence or as an accident but as an agent is present to that in which it acts. For every agent must be joined to that in which it immediately acts and touch it with its power. . . . Since, however, God is *esse* itself by His essence, created *esse* must be His proper effect. . . . However, this effect God causes in things, not only when things first begin to exist but as long as they are conserved in being. . . . As long then as a thing has existence (esse), so long must God be present to it, according to the mode in which it has *esse*. But *esse* (the act of existence) is that which is most inmost (*intimum*) to each thing and what is most profoundly in each thing, since it is formal with respect to everything that is in a thing. . . . Hence God must be in everything—*and intimately*.[13] (emphasis added)

---

[13]Saint Thomas Aquinas, *Summa Theologiae*, I. Qv. VIII, a., 1, c.

We now come to another metaphysical consideration of startling import.

Thomistic metaphysics shows us that God is a perfect one, not because He is impoverished but because the infinite richness of being is, in Him, brought to a perfect unity. He has no dimension and no parts. In this sense He is completely simple—God is therefore not spread out through the created universe. He is present everywhere by His activity but wherever He acts He is totally present. He cannot be divided among His creatures. To each one He is wholly present, though the effect of His activity is limited. He can be said to be present more powerfully where the effect is of a higher order. Hence, He is present to each one of us totally and is present to us as creatures that participate in His formal Divine perfections of knowing and loving. He is not only present to us in giving us being, but that very presence gives us the ability to understand and respond to His presence. As an important corollary, we must note that it is precisely the all-powerful God who is present to us. He is present as one who is able to respond to our needs, is ever ready to help us.

Now we will explore another consideration which, in a way, will confirm all that we have said. This flows from a clarification of the traditional statement that no real relation between God and His creatures is possible. Stated thus baldly, this position seems to make God so remote, so closed off from His creatures that the intimacy of which I have been speaking in this exposition would seem to be impossible. The creature is totally relevant to God, dependent and related by a real transcendental relation. But this metaphysical position intends to stress the fact that by creating, God in no way modifies His own reality, acquires any kind of accidental modification that can be compared to what happens in finite causality. In infinite causality, at least as a rule, the cause must change as it produces its effect and this change in the cause is the basis of a real relation of causality. Moreover, the cause is dependent on the effect to be a cause at all and the activity of the cause is completed in the effect according to the metaphysical axiom that the action is in the subject acted upon. But there's no doubt that God's relationship to the world is not of this sort and it is this that the traditional statement intends to emphasize. This, however, must be balanced by further metaphysical considerations. As we have pointed out above, God is totally present in His creative activity, in the inmost reality of the creature. Nothing stands between the creature and the

Creator. The whole of the divine being is in the most intimate contact possible with each creature in its totality because the creative activity directly touches the creature as having an act of existence. Therefore, in addition to asserting that there is no relation between God as the Creator of his creature which is truly parallel to the relationship between a finite cause and a finite effect, we ought to assert that there is a unique relationship, indeed, a transcendental relationship which involves the whole of God and brings Him into intimate contact with the creature which is a metaphysical interpretation of the presence of God in created reality.

Once we have eliminated the transference to God of the notion of causal relationships in finite being, we are forced to say that there is truly a real transcendental relationship between God and ourselves and that this should be borne in mind as we make ourselves aware of the reality of God's presence in our inmost being. All the conditions requisite for a real relation exist. God, the subject is real; the creature, the effect is real; God's activity is real. Consequently, we must understand that God is transcendentally related to each of His creatures through His creative activity in their inmost being. Thus, this metaphysical clarification provides more depth to our awareness of the inconceivable reality of and the intimacy of God's presence.

And now there is one remaining metaphysical consideration which brings us to the very heart of the mystery of the matter. Traditional metaphysics and theology say that the intrinsic finality of creation is the glory of God, the manifestation of His glory. To many this appears to make God self-seeking in His creative activity. It's as though He wanted to have myriads of intelligent creatures recognizing His great perfection or an enormous choir singing His praise forever or, in the Calvinist interpretation, intelligent beings manifesting all His perfections so that some are predestined for hell where, through their just punishment, they would manifest the justice of God; others predestined for heaven where, through their great joy, they would manifest the mercy of God. Actually, what this thesis states is that God cannot create anything except to project His own perfections, that is to say, any creature that God creates must, in its total reality, participate in divine perfections. Since He is infinite perfection, no perfections can exist which are not related to Him as manifestations. He is, therefore, the exemplar cause of all creation and of everything in it. The traditional doctrine also states that God as the supremely good and perfect entity must remain the supreme good of all things, that good towards which every created thing by its creaturely finality must tend as St. Thomas carefully expounds in the *Contra Gentiles*. Again, this must be balanced by other considerations. God gains absolutely nothing from creation. He has no need for the praise of creatures and no need for His own glorification. The act of creation is a completely free act. God acts neither from internal compulsion nor from external pressure. The Neoplatonic axiom that good is diffusive of itself has some merit in that it does indicate that God's creative activity is a manifestation of his great goodness, but in its interpretation as placing a necessity on the good to expand into a world of creatures, it is metaphysically false. This free act of God, in creating the universe, is therefore a completely gratuitous act. It is an act of pure benevolence as the Second Preface for weekdays says, very simply, "In love You created man."

The creation of man is thus the greatest act of self-giving that is possible for God in proportion to created nature. It is true that He immeasurably increased His self-giving through the elevation of man to the life of the Trinity; but His first great act of self-giving was in the act of creation which must therefore be seen as an act of unfathomable love.

We can and must then add to this awareness, the further awareness of the presence of God in our souls as Father, Son, and Holy Spirit dwelling there through the love with which the Holy Spirit floods our soul.

Finally, then, in summary, our practice of the presence of God receives a profound and primordial grounding in the understanding of these metaphysical insights. This understanding incorporates into our awareness of His presence the fact that He is most intimately present to our inmost reality, touching our very act of existence, almost closer to us than we are to ourselves and that this is a real intimacy that brings God in close relationship to us, not merely as an object of knowledge or love, but as a living and ever-present Lover and the fact that this God, who is so intimately present is constantly active on our behalf, that the God who is so present is also the God of infinite power and of unfathomable love who is always ready and able to help us, to console us, and to be our great Lover.

Frequent meditation on these truths will give us a habitual awareness of the presence of God, such that, at any moment, we can turn to Him almost without additional reflection and find Him in the depths of our own being. It is not suggested that anyone can keep the presence of God in the forefront of his consciousness continuously; it is suggested that we should meditate periodically, that we should turn to God, present within us, before prayer or hearing Mass, before every decision, in the midst of joys and sorrows. The ever present love of God will illumine our entire life.

INDEX